"Because I'm a notorious stickler for clear sourcing, I'm always skeptical of fly-on-the-wall accounts of dramatic events. Here Tony Silber has attempted exactly that—with an account, no less, of people and events that shaped, and saved, America more than 150 years ago. But he's done it! He's written a true drama of how Abraham Lincoln and his team somehow saved a Washington surrounded by enemy secessionists during the first twelve days of the Civil War—their fears, their mistakes, their scheming, their arguments, their triumphs. At every point where your reaction will be 'How does he know that?' you can turn to more than fifty pages of meticulous footnotes to find out. I'm in awe."

—STEVEN BRILL, author of *Tailspin* and *America's Bitter Pill*, creator of Court TV and *The American Lawyer*, and co-CEO of NewsGuard

"Written as only a reporter or war correspondent can write it, with vivid descriptions showing the art of audiovisual writing at its best. You can see the images without the need for pictures, and you can hear the sounds without the need for a radio or a television. Silber has combined his reporting skills and editing skills in one heck of a historical book that will be read for generations to come."

—SAMIR HUSNI, founder and former director of the Magazine Innovation Center at the University of Mississippi

"A well-researched and stirring account of the first twelve days of the Civil War. . . . Silber masterfully provides the historic background and creates a good read about the arrival of the New York Seventh and the Massachusetts Eighth regiments to secure the capital. The work fills a void in Civil War historic research."

—ALAN M. MECKLER, publisher, tech entrepreneur, and author of *The Internet's First Entrepreneur: Lessons and Wisdom for the Business Journey*

"Silber's fast-paced narrative captures the unnerving chaos and the uncertainty gripping a polarized republic in the early days of an increasingly deadly clash of cultures, politics, and armies. His ripped-from-the-headlines approach makes for a visceral plunge into a fraught and frightening past and serves as a thoughtful reminder of just how quickly a nation can unravel."
—JACK ALCOTT, former group managing editor for
Hearst Connecticut Media and author of
Grim Legion: Edgar Allan Poe at West Point

"Tony Silber draws in careful detail a complete picture of the frenetic effort to summon militias to defend Washington in the twelve days after the attack on Fort Sumter. Silber, who has a way with words, recaptures a sense of contingency in those twelve days, when both the capital and the state of Maryland were threatened by secessionists. Silber's prose is gripping and his sources (the memoirs of key figures in the events described) excellent. The book is difficult to put down. Silber places you in the middle of the fateful events with his skillful descriptions of the personalities and geographic settings that animated these events."
—WYNN GADKAR-WILCOX, professor and co-chair of the
Department of History at Western Connecticut State University

"Tony Silber brings the massive schism of America pulled asunder into bright detail by focusing his lens on the first twelve days of the Civil War. His narrative is engrossing and cinematic, weaving a vivid tapestry of strong emotions and passions. The stakes are captured in human terms as Silber combines the steady hand and clear eye of the observer with the empathy and sentiment of someone who cares deeply, a century and more later, for the men and women who risked their lives for their country."
—DAN MCCARTHY, media executive and writer

TWELVE DAYS

Twelve Days

*How the Union Nearly Lost Washington
in the First Days of the Civil War*

TONY SILBER

Potomac Books

AN IMPRINT OF THE UNIVERSITY OF NEBRASKA PRESS

CONTENTS

ILLUSTRATIONS

ACKNOWLEDGMENTS

It's proper to begin by acknowledging the people who produced a voluminous firsthand body of work about these first days of the Civil War.

There is an enormous trove of primary-source material written by actual participants, both at the time and in the decades following the war. Many of these authors, including those who served in the four-year war to come, viewed this two-week period as a highlight of their lives, the most exciting and dangerous moment they experienced. There are literally hundreds of sources: biographies, military archives, letters, speeches, pamphlets, diaries, unpublished documents, grand jury testimony, inquests, newspaper reports, magazine articles, military reports, and full-length regimental histories.

All these sources tell parts of the story, yet no published account has ever presented the full story from all its aspects, despite it being a time that Lincoln's secretaries, John Nicolay and John Hay, called "an epoch in American history."[1]

I've relied on this rich contemporary record as the basis of the book. In many instances, my research has produced not just one but several accounts of the same incidents. They're told from different perspectives but serve to confirm the accuracy.

It's appropriate to similarly acknowledge the unnamed professionals behind the revolution in research made possible by the internet. I've relied on the extraordinary HathiTrust Digital Library, the Internet Archive, Google Books, Project Muse, Newspapers.com, and dozens of other sources of digitized material, including from regional libraries and research sources. These include the Maryland State Archives, the Boston Public Library, the Acton (Massachusetts) Memorial Library, the Massachusetts Historical Society, the Missouri History Museum, and many others.

Because of these resources and the many people who toiled to digitize this material, page by page, I had access to hundreds of public-domain books, pamphlets, annual reports, military records, documents, and more. Many of them are exceedingly obscure. But virtually all of them were fully searchable and helped me discover anecdotes relating to the focus of my work. These digital volumes were all generally accessible through persistent web searching, though there was much trial and error.

To be sure, physical libraries remained the foundation of my research, and particular thanks are due to the New York Public Library, the District of Columbia Public Library, the Library of Congress, and my hometown system, the Trumbull Public Library, through which I had access to a book-sharing program with nearly every other library in Connecticut.

Thanks are due to my agent, Steve Harris of CSG Literary Partners, who masterfully steered my proposal through a series of potential publishers until he found Potomac Books. Steve recognized a great story and took a risk on an author with an unconventional background. I'm a journalist who specializes in media, not an academic with credentials as a Civil War historian.

My old friend from that aforementioned media career, Reed Phillips of Oaklins DeSilva + Phillips, connected me with Steve. A newer friend, Mark Holdreith, was instrumental in developing my ability to carve out an extended period of time in 2020 where I focused on finishing the book.

The authors Michael Capuzzo, Steven Brill, Charles Slack, Ellen Meacham, Michael Clinton, Alan Meckler, and John Alcott as well as U.S. representative Jim Himes of Connecticut, the distinguished professors Wynn Gadkar-Wilcox and Samir Husni, and the media executive Dan McCarthy all read the manuscript and offered encouragement and counsel. Each provided a testimonial blurb, and all have my sincere thanks.

Thanks also go to my editors, Tom Swanson and Taylor Rothgeb at Potomac Books, who guided me through the publishing process.

Finally, thanks go to my family—my wife, the author Debra Silber; my daughters, Jessica Silber-Byrne and Jennifer Silber; and my son, Matthew Silber. They're all skilled editors and writers in their own rights and knowledgeable and conversant in Civil War history. They all took the time to really dig into my work and help me sharpen it, focus it, cut a whole lot of tangential material, and offer tips, reality checks, ideas, and directions that I would not have otherwise uncovered.

PREFACE

In the popular literature and scholarship of the Civil War, the days immediately after the war's opening salvo—the Confederate assault on Fort Sumter—have received relatively little attention. They're overshadowed by the great battles and seismic changes in American life that came later and that ultimately would redefine the meaning of freedom and equality in the United States.

To the extent this period is studied at all, it's often done as a brief sketch, not as a determinative moment. It's seen merely as a preliminary interlude before the major fighting began at Bull Run three months later.

But the twelve days that began with the evacuation of Fort Sumter and ended with the arrival of the New York Seventh Militia Regiment in Washington were indeed consequential. The nation's capital never came so close to being captured by the Confederates as it did in this short span. Indeed, it has never been as vulnerable in the entire history of the country, with the possible exception of the British occupation in 1814.

It began on April 14 with President Lincoln's call for seventy-five thousand militia troops to suppress the insurrection. Released the following day, the proclamation electrified the nation, North and South. Washington, a Southern city, a slave-holding city, was the immediate focal point. It also was a city with strong secessionist leanings. It teemed with traitors. The federal government itself was compromised. The capital could barely be defended, only having about two thousand local militia troops of dubious training and loyalty. In Charleston, less than two days away by train, the Confederates had an organized army that was much larger and ready to fight. Both sides expected the first clash to occur near Washington.

To the south was Virginia. Within days it would follow South Carolina and six other states in seceding.

On the north bank of the Potomac River, Maryland surrounded Washington on three sides. That state's populous eastern sections were already reeling from violent, uncontrolled insurrection. It was in Baltimore that Northern troops on their way to Washington were attacked, and five of them were killed.

For half of these twelve days, Washington, the capital city of a great nation, would be utterly severed from the North. The telegraph lines were cut down, and the railroad bridges were sabotaged by secessionist police and militia members sanctioned by the Baltimore city government and at least tacitly by the state government—the city was cut off.

There was no cavalry coming. Not right away. The country had a tiny standing army in 1861, most of it scattered beyond the Mississippi. The federal government's only defense in this existential crisis would be state militias. But in state after state, the militia system was in tatters. With the country at peace for decades, militias had come to be seen as pointless nuisances. Active companies were regarded as social clubs for men, an extravagance not worth taxpayer dollars. In early April 1861, state militias were vastly undermanned, their weapons outdated and in short supply.

Each day brought calamitous new developments. Virginia's secession. The attack in Baltimore. The losses of the irreplaceable Norfolk Navy Yard and the strategic town of Harpers Ferry.

As the exposed capital's fate hung in the balance, Confederate political and military leaders advocated for an immediate assault on Washington. Strike the blow now, many urged. Push the theater of war north to the Susquehanna River. Link up with Maryland and add another state to the Confederacy. The Confederate flag would soon be flying over the U.S. Capitol's dome. Every day Southern newspapers clamored for an attack.

Everyone in the capital, from President Lincoln and Northern military leaders to Union state politicians and the humblest government clerks, believed a Confederate advance was imminent. Civilians began to stream out by the thousands, desperate to avoid the path of rampaging armies. The isolated federal government had only the barest idea of where its advancing troops might be.

If the Confederates had succeeded in capturing Washington, it would have changed the course of the Civil War before it even really started. It would have driven the president and the cabinet from the capital. It might have assured the secession of Maryland and placed Washington DC deep within the territory of a hostile nation. The Confederate States border would be just forty miles from Philadelphia.

It might have resulted in England's recognition of the Confederacy, clearing the way for other nations to do the same and opening vast new financial and material resources to the rebellion while threatening the United States with a second war—against Great Britain. It would have demoralized the North before it had even begun to fight.

In short, the outcome of the war that we're familiar with, the outcome that we assume a century and a half later, was not at all assured in April 1861. It was only due to a series of specific acts by many participants on both sides that the worst didn't occur that April. This book explores all of them.

What's more, the events of this brief period serve to foreshadow many of the themes and characteristics that would be revealed later in the war. Lincoln emerges as a master communicator. And even though he had virtually no executive management or military experience, he quickly masters those spheres as well. Meanwhile, we get our first glimpse of Jefferson Davis, a West Point graduate who fought in the Mexican War and later served as secretary of war. Despite every early advantage, he comes off as both distant and reactive, unwilling to fully commit.

We see in these first days a U.S. military that's mostly inept, with feeble leadership and commanders long past their prime. But we also see junior officers, including those in the militias,

proving themselves as brave, smart, and willing to take the initiative. After the twin shocks of Sumter and the call for seventy-five
thousand troops, Northern ambivalence about conflict with the
slave states was washed away by a powerful new resolve to uphold
the Union. We see the industrial and financial power of the North
begin to exert itself. And we see how actions taken by both sides
during these pivotal twelve days—their successful initiatives and
their mistakes—also foreshadowed and ultimately determined the
outcome of a cataclysmic four-year war. Yet this book isn't concerned with what-ifs. It's not an alternative history. Instead, it's
the story of one of the most critical periods of the Civil War—one
that's misunderstood and underexplored. It tells the story of what
might have happened and why it did not.

In recounting these first twelve days of the Civil War, I have chosen to tell the story from the ground level, from the perspective
of the participants themselves. We follow the president and cabinet, the senior military commanders, the mobilization and advance
of the Northern militias, the Maryland insurrection, and the
expanding Southern Confederacy.

We hear from day-to-day Washington residents as they walk
the city's sandy cobblestone streets, work in their government
offices, revel in the warm spring weather, trade gossip in packed
hotel salons, grab taxis for rushed rides across the city, and watch
barricades being erected around the public buildings as cavalry
clatters through the streets. The newspapers are here, with their
cacophony of voices, frequently wrong in smaller details but vital
and faithful to the broader progression of events. They're an extraordinary time capsule, a daily chronicle of life in 1861 by the Americans
who were present.

This is the story of Lincoln, his cabinet, and his military commanders all struggling to stay ahead of fast-moving events. It's the
story of secessionists and loyalists vying for control in the tinderbox that was Maryland. It's the story of how Northern state governors responded to a tidal wave of pro-Union public sentiment
and how they worked with the federal government as well as local

bankers, railroad executives, factories, and steamship operators to get their troops equipped and into the field.

This is a window into the vibrant world of 1861—the weather, the mood, the people, the conflicts—in the streets of Washington, in the White House, in the Northern state houses, and in the cities of Boston, New York, Philadelphia, Baltimore, Harrisburg, Annapolis, and Norfolk. It's also the story of Southern public opinion, Confederate decision-making, and troop movements— and their readiness in Northern Virginia, just across the river from Washington.

It follows the courageous Northern regiments and their commanders during their desperate advance to Washington. These citizen soldiers enjoyed triumphant sendoffs from their home cities but then endured days on jammed steam transports, hundreds of miles in brutally uncomfortable railroad cars, privations in food and rest, and forced marches under intense pressure to reach Washington.

I've told the story in real time, chronologically, alternating among the three main scenes of action—Washington, the advance of the Northern troops, and the Southern planning and military movements. I've purposefully minimized any abstract analysis and discussion of strategy. Instead, I wanted the reader to see events as much as possible from the perspectives of the participants. I wanted to emphasize anecdotes. You'll hear the same rumors they do, feel the same fog of war, regret their mistakes as they did, and get a sense of their capabilities at the same time they did. Most of these people—from Lincoln to the railroad executives, from the regimental commanders all the way down to the Northern privates— were in their first days of dramatically new roles.

In general, I've avoided direct quotes where the grammar and punctuation were antiquated or hard to understand. I preferred to blend my own narrative with selected short, crisp, more colorful passages to use in direct quotes. In some instances where the original text made extensive use of run-on sentences or semicolons, I stopped the sentence and added attribution, picking up with a new sentence where the writer had continued with his or her original sentence.

I likewise tried to avoid long quotes that included extended digressions. In those cases, I trimmed the digressions while sticking to the point the writer or speaker was making.

I standardized punctuation and style according to the norms of the period. For example, Washington was commonly referred to as Washington City—as New York City is today. For the purposes of consistency, I capitalized the word *City* even when a writer did not.

On rare occasions I substituted archaic nineteenth-century words like *thither* with the modern equivalent, *there*, or replaced the word *upon* when modern language accepts the word *on*. In other cases I updated spellings. For example, the word *defense* was sometimes spelled *defence* in 1861. I mostly updated it to the modern spelling, except in instances where the older spelling seemed necessary to the context.

Overall, my motivation was to make the work accessible to modern readers while preserving the intent of the original writers. In no cases did I change, alter, or shade the meaning of any quote or anecdote or eliminate any nuance that the original author had intended.

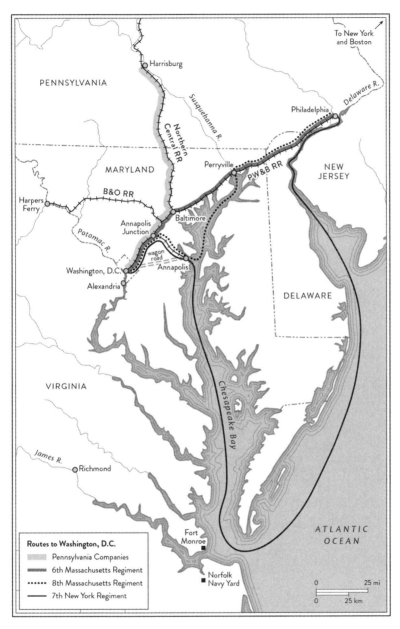

MAP 1. The strategic picture. Both sides believed Washington would be the site of the
first fight. In the days after Fort Sumter's surrender, Northern regiments rushed to
get to Washington, initially through Baltimore, a bottleneck for nearly all transport
from the North. When Baltimore was engulfed in a fiery insurrection, Washington
was plunged into darkness—cut off from the North and vulnerable to capture.
Northern troops had to find a new route, eventually going through Annapolis.
Created by Erin Greb Cartography.

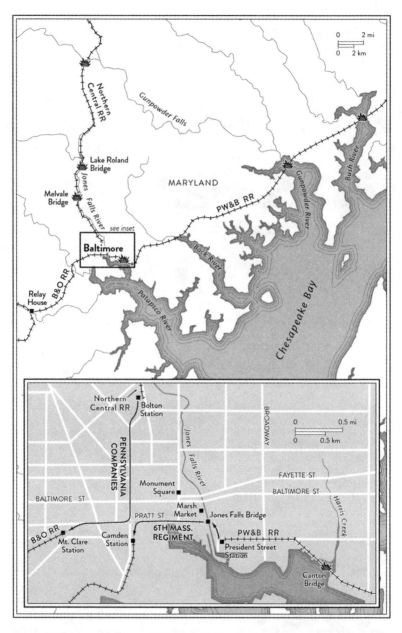

MAP 2. Chaos and killing in Baltimore. Baltimore was a secessionist flashpoint, and its top officials were Southern sympathizers. Five Pennsylvania companies made it through on April 18, but the next day the Sixth Massachusetts Regiment had to fight its way across the city. Following the riots, insurrectionists—with the approval of the government—destroyed six bridges on two crucial railroad lines. Created by Erin Greb Cartography.

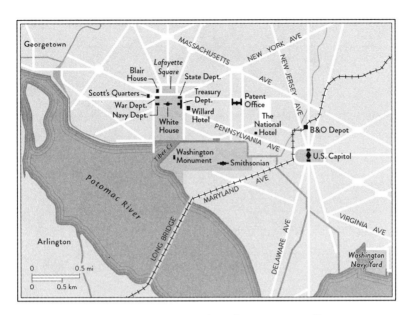

MAP 3. Washington in 1861. For seven days, the city was cut off—no trains, no telegraph, no newspapers, no information at all. With the capital extraordinarily vulnerable, deep in hostile territory, it fell to Lincoln and his national security team to hold things together as the government—and the nation—fell apart.
Created by Erin Greb Cartography.

1
--

Why Don't They Come?

The City

Abraham Lincoln, just seven weeks on the job as president of the United States, was alone in his second-floor office at the White House. The workday was over, with late afternoon now giving way to evening.[1]

Lincoln was pacing. He was naturally inclined to pace. He did it habitually in meetings. Now the president alternated pacing with quietly gazing out the two tall windows of his office.[2]

Even at this late hour, it was the warmest day of the year so far in Washington DC. The temperature had surpassed eighty degrees. The sun streamed in through the southern-facing windows, making the room stuffy. It was hard to see down the Potomac River—everything was silhouetted.[3]

Outside, the city was in bloom. The whole landscape had the vibrancy of spring. The air was warm. Insects buzzed. Birds flitted noisily from tree to bush. The grass, emerging from winter dormancy, was strikingly green, its blades shooting upward. The terrain still had some of the brown-green hue of April, but most of the trees had their first light-green leaves—small, still filling out, not yet infused with the dark-green color of summer.

As Lincoln gazed at a new season of life springing forth this April afternoon, perhaps his favorite poem—"Mortality," by the

Scottish poet William Knox—crossed his mind. It was a melancholic rumination on death as a great equalizer. Its final stanza is

> 'Tis the wink of an eye—'tis the draught of a breath,
> From the blossom of health to the paleness of death,
> From the gilded saloon to the bier and the shroud
> Oh, why should the spirit of mortal be proud?[4]

At this moment, Lincoln was presiding over a country whose mortal existence was hanging in the balance. And things looked exceedingly bad.

This Tuesday was the fourth day in a row in which Washington was cut off from the loyal states, surrounded by hostile territory where, Lincoln feared, a secessionist army was gathering. The only way to get to the capital by train from New York, Philadelphia, Harrisburg, and other points was via railroads that converged in Baltimore. And now the railroad lines to the north and northeast of Baltimore had been pulled up and the trestles burned. The telegraph wires were cut down. There was no mail, no newspapers. Travelers from the North could barely get through. The city was surrounded, isolated, and virtually defenseless against an attack.

For four consecutive days, some great calamity occurred. Virginia had seceded on the seventeenth. Harpers Ferry was abandoned and burned on the eighteenth. On the nineteenth, the Sixth Massachusetts Regiment and an unarmed Pennsylvania brigade were attacked in Baltimore. That same night, the railroad bridges connecting Washington to the North were burned. On the twentieth, the Norfolk Navy Yard was destroyed by federal forces in an effort to prevent anything of value from falling into Confederate hands. The attempt failed.

To make matters even worse, Jefferson Davis had repeatedly threatened an invasion of the North if war broke out. Now war was here.

Just two months earlier, Davis was en route from his home in Mississippi to the Confederate capital in Montgomery, Alabama, where he would assume the presidency. He made the threats in speeches along the way that were dutifully reported in the newspapers. "Gen. Davis arrived in [Jackson, Mississippi,] this evening on his way to Montgomery," the *Charleston Mercury* reported. "In a speech at the capitol he said if war must come, it must be upon Northern soil, and not Southern soil."

The next day, still in Jackson, he was even more warlike. "There will be no war in our territory," he vowed. "It will be carried into the enemy's territory."

A few days later, in Atlanta, he'd repeated the threat again. "War he regarded as an improbable contingency, but he held out the idea that if it had to come it would be more likely to be fought on Northern soil than on this side of the Potomac," reported the *New York Times*, citing the *Atlanta Constitution*. "No man ever succeeded with a single speech in so completely capturing the hearts of our people."[5]

Lincoln's secretaries John Nicolay and John Hay described the dread and pessimism in Washington. "This began to look like an irresistible current of fate," they wrote. An attack on the city seemed inevitable. "No popular sentiment could long stem such a tide of misfortune."[6]

At any hour, Lincoln knew, hostile forces could descend from Maryland, a slave-holding state to the north that was now in violent defiance. Or they could come from Virginia, a slave state across the Potomac that had seceded six days ago. Or an attack could come from both directions at the same time. Maryland was teetering, and Lincoln was powerless to stop it.

The stakes were enormous. If Maryland seceded, it could trigger an evacuation of the nation's capital. If some combination of Maryland, Virginia, and the Confederate forces attacked Washington and forced the government to abandon the city, it would trigger a Maryland secession. And if Washington was captured and held, it might trigger British recognition of the Confederate States. More than that, the British had privately warned the U.S. government that a blockade of Southern ports might force their recognition of the Confederacy. Lincoln nevertheless did that anyway, just a few days earlier. Now any of these things seemed possible, if not likely. And any of them would represent a monumental change in the dynamics of this new war, which would possibly end in defeat for the United States before it really started.

A Grim and Desolate Capital

The streets below Lincoln's window had a surreal, deserted look. The hordes of office seekers who'd thronged the White House and swarmed the city's hotels these last weeks had vanished. So had a quarter of the federal workforce, civilian and military, disloyal citizens heading south to join the Confederacy. The full-time residential population, too, fled from an assault they assumed was both certain and imminent. Washington was a Southern city, overwhelmingly secessionist. Treason, Lincoln knew, was all around.[7]

Those who ventured out were grim and hurried. Shops were locked. Row house windows were shuttered. Soldiers guarded the public buildings, which were barricaded with lumber and sandbags eight feet high in some places. Occasionally, a squad of cavalry would clatter through the cobblestone streets.[8]

It was just twenty-four hours earlier that the commander of the U.S. Army, Lt. Gen. Winfield Scott, intimated that an assault was coming. One of the many rumors circulating in the city was that two thousand troops were on the way from Harpers Ferry—fifty-five miles to the northwest—to join in an attack on the capital, Scott told Lincoln on the evening of the twenty-second. Scott was sure his men could defend Washington. Lincoln did not share Scott's confidence.[9]

Lincoln scanned as far as he could down the Potomac River, hoping to spot transport steamers carrying the Northern troops that he knew must be on their way. But he saw no transports. The tension and distress built. His government was alone, isolated, and virtually defenseless. It wasn't supposed to be this way. It was a mortifying situation for the president of a great nation, the successor of Washington and Jackson.[10]

Lincoln reflected on the events of the past eleven days since the attack on Fort Sumter on April 12. The gallant U.S. regulars in Charleston Harbor surrendered on the thirteenth and vacated the fort the next day. Lincoln then called for seventy-five thousand volunteer troops. The Northern governors responded with a deluge of support, promising more troops than Lincoln had called for. Men signed up by the thousands.

In Washington this all seemed like a mirage. The capital was marooned and had been since the early morning hours of the twentieth. And so it remained as Northern troops struggled to reach Washington in time to save it.

So where were they?

Lincoln was not often a demonstrative man. He held his cards tightly. Now he was close to his limit. Business hours had concluded. The office was deserted. Lincoln paced and gazed. Finally, after a half hour, thinking he was alone, he burst out in anguish, "Why don't they come? Why don't they come?"[11]

2
--

The Evacuation of Sumter

Most Americans now knew Fort Sumter had been attacked. But few knew the outcome. The tiny U.S. garrison had surrendered after a two-day artillery duel.

Five hundred miles south of Washington, the wind in Charleston Harbor was blowing hard from the ocean on this Sunday afternoon as U.S. Army major Robert Anderson, fifty-five, prepared to relinquish Fort Sumter to the Confederate States of America. The surrender had come the day before. The first fight of the Civil War was over. The United States lost, and the only thing left was to evacuate.

Dinghies, sailboats, steamers, and all kinds of vessels jammed the harbor and bobbed around the fort, which stood on a tiny, two-acre island three miles out from Charleston's waterfront. The sky was pale blue and clear. The water had the washed-out, gray-green hue that's common after storms. The scene had the soft pastel look of an impressionist painting. After three days of drama, local residents on the shore and in their boats watched as Anderson's garrison of just over eighty soldiers prepared to depart.

Even before the bombardment started two days earlier, Anderson had known he would have to give up Sumter. There was no choice. He was nearly out of food, outnumbered, and outgunned. The South Carolina forces had four thousand to six thousand men in about nineteen artillery batteries triangulating the fort, with nearly forty guns. Anderson had a total of 128 souls, including eight musicians and forty-three noncombatant laborers. Sumter had about as many guns as the rebels, but Anderson only had enough trained gunners to man nine of them. He knew that after more than thirty hours of dueling bombardment, his ammunition would soon be depleted.[1]

Already secessionists had seized U.S. forts and arsenals throughout the South without a fight. Sumter was the highest-profile holdout and became the flash point. Even so on April 11, Anderson had told the local Confederate commander, Brig. Gen. Pierre Gustav Toutant Beauregard, that he'd vacate by the fifteenth. This was not acceptable. For the Confederates it was a matter of sovereignty. They also knew Lincoln was attempting a mission to resupply the fort with nonmilitary support. If such a mission succeeded, it would extend Anderson's occupation for weeks.[2]

Beauregard informed Anderson early on the morning of the twelfth that he'd begin bombardment in an hour. A Louisianan acting in a provisional capacity on behalf of the newly created Confederate States of America, Beauregard commanded the South Carolina militia forces that Friday morning.[3]

What followed was thirty-four hours of artillery combat; two days of rain, wind, and heavy seas; and the ordeal of a three-thousand-round artillery bombardment. The fort was devastated. "The quarters and barracks were in ruins," surgeon Samuel Wylie Crawford wrote. "The main gates and the planking of the windows was gone. The magazines were closed and surrounded by smoldering flames and burning ashes. The provisions were exhausted, much of the engineering work destroyed, and the cartridges gone—with only four barrels of powder available. The command had yielded to the inevitable."[4]

The garrison fell silent that morning, spent, relieved, and disappointed as they waited for their departure from Charleston. "The enthusiasm that had so long inspired them seemed to have gone," Crawford wrote.[5]

The men assembled on the fort's parade grounds for a one-hundred-gun salute. The U.S. flag flew from a battered flagpole. Anderson ordered the gun salute to begin. The wind was blowing hard, directly into the muzzles of the guns. An ignited fragment of a cartridge bag blew back into a pile of cartridges behind the gun, causing an explosion that instantly killed Pvt. Daniel Hough and mortally wounded Pvt. Edward Galloway. Several other soldiers were severely wounded.[6]

Anderson finished his gun salute after delays from this horrific accident. Then the men marched out under the second-in-command, Capt. Abner Doubleday, with banners flying, drums rolling, and the band playing "Yankee Doodle."

South Carolina and Confederate forces occupied the fort at 4:00 p.m. The plan was to transfer Anderson's men to the small U.S. flotilla waiting just outside the harbor, part of the relief mission ordered by Lincoln on April 6. But the garrison had to wait overnight on a transfer vessel, the steamer *Isabel*, because the ocean transport *Baltic*—which was supposed to take them to New York—was too large to cross the sandbar into the harbor, and the *Isabel* had missed the tide and couldn't cross on the way out. The next morning as the federal troops passed out of the harbor, their Confederate adversaries lined the beaches in silent salute, hats off in a sign of respect.[7]

Three days later the *Baltic* and several accompanying U.S. warships arrived in New York, where Anderson and his men were hailed as heroes.[8]

The South relished its first victory. The well-connected Charleston socialite Mary Boykin Chesnut described the scene on Monday morning: "I did not know that one could live such days of excitement. Fort Sumter had surrendered! Our flag is flying there. Fire engines have been sent to put out the fire. Everybody tells you half of something and then rushes off to tell someone else—or to hear the latest news."[9]

None of the participants at Sumter nor the inhabitants of Charleston, New York, or anywhere else in the country could have comprehended on this April morning the catastrophic four years that were about to come. Nor could they have predicted the next twelve agonizing days—when the survival of the United States hung in the balance.

3

Washington, the Secessionist City

The Coming Storm

W ord of Sumter's surrender was circulating around the country. In Burlington, Vermont, "there was a whispered rumor," wrote the lawyer, banker, and Republican activist Lucius Eugene Chittenden, recently appointed register of the treasury by Secretary of the Treasury Salmon Chase. "Sumter had fallen. The effect of this information was stupefying, as when a deadly blow is struck across the temples. It was nearly two days before the reaction began. Then it swept everything before it. In a moment, the united voice of the loyal North denounced the treason and invoked judgment on the traitors."[1]

The City

In Washington President Lincoln met at the White House on this Sunday morning with his cabinet and national security team. The focus was on how to respond to the fall of Sumter, a response that needed to include calling out state militia troops and summoning Congress into session.

The meeting was in Lincoln's office, part of a business suite on the second floor. There was no West Wing in 1861. Visitors would walk up the White House's sandy circular driveway, pass through a vestibule, and enter a long east-west hall on the first floor extending from the East Room to the Grand Staircase at the western end of the building.

Upstairs on the opposite end were the business offices. The president's office faced south, offering broad vistas of the national mall and the Potomac River. It was sandwiched between the office of Chief Secretary John Nicolay, on the far southeastern end, and a reception room.

The president's "shop," as Lincoln referred to it, was the "nerve-centre of the Republic," remembered one of Lincoln's secretaries, twenty-five-year-old William O. Stoddard. It was a "wonderful historic cavern" and a "very well furnished room, hung around with maps, &c."[2]

The room was large, about twenty-nine feet by twenty-four feet. A long oak table dominated the middle. It was typically covered with papers, books, and maps. Cabinet members sat here during meetings. Beyond the table on the south wall were two large windows, offering unobstructed views of the unfinished Washington Monument, the Smithsonian Institution, and beyond. The sun streamed in all day.

The walls were covered in green-and-gold wallpaper. The carpet was dark green with brown and yellow accents.[3]

Along the west wall stood an upright mahogany desk with pigeonholes. Lincoln used this for work and filing papers. Stoddard called it "a second-hand desk from some old furniture auction—at least that's what it looked like."[4]

Closer to the main hallway was a fireplace with a large white-marble mantel. A painting of Andrew Jackson hung above the fireplace. Along the eastern wall was a couch and a series of large maps, some spring-loaded, like window shades. A glass-globe gas-light chandelier hung in the center of the room, and above the center table was a bell cord that Lincoln used to call his secretaries.

The room had a heavily used feel. "Folios of maps leaned against the walls or hid behind the sofas," Stoddard wrote.[5]

Lincoln liked to tell visitors that his "policy was to have no policy," an aphorism designed to preserve flexibility. It was untrue. His

policy, as outlined in his inaugural address and many times subsequently, was explicit and muscular. "I shall hold myself at liberty to repossess, if I can, places which have been seized before
the Government was devolved upon me," he told three Virginia
commissioners the day before. "And in every event I shall, to the
extent of my ability, repel force by force."[6]

Now on this Sunday, for the first time, Lincoln's policy of having no policy was cast aside. For the cabinet the policy was the
defense of the United States. The capital itself was vulnerable—a
weakly defended Southern city. Troops were urgently needed in
quantities that only the state militias could provide.

At this meeting there was no difference of opinion. The debate
had dramatically shifted. Now it was about defending the existence of the country. There was no hope among the cabinet members that a small force would suffice, wrote Frederick W. Seward,
reflecting the perspective of his father, Secretary of State William Seward.

"Each realized that the contest would be gigantic," Frederick
Seward wrote. The lowest number of troops suggested was fifty
thousand men. The highest was one hundred thousand. Secretary
of State Seward advocated for the largest number. In the end Lincoln went with seventy-five thousand.

Then came the question of calling Congress into session. The
executive branch had no power to establish armies or spend public money without congressional approval. The Lincoln administration had to balance its constitutional constraints with the likely
paralysis of "many men with many minds." The cabinet decided
to call Congress into session on the Fourth of July, and to "trust
their patriotism to sanction steps taken prior to that time," Frederick Seward recounted.

The cabinet worked up the proclamation calling for militia
troops and summoning Congress. Copies were given to the press
to appear in the Monday morning newspapers with the date of
April 15, 1861.[7]

The text read as follows:

April 15, 1861

By the President of the United States

A Proclamation.

Whereas the laws of the United States have been for some time past, and now are opposed, and the execution thereof obstructed, in the States of South Carolina, Georgia, Alabama, Florida, Mississippi, Louisiana and Texas, by combinations too powerful to be suppressed by the ordinary course of judicial proceedings, or by the powers vested in the Marshals by law.

Now therefore, I, Abraham Lincoln, President of the United States, in virtue of the power in me vested by the Constitution, and the laws, have thought fit to call forth, and hereby do call forth, the militia of the several States of the Union, to the aggregate number of seventy-five thousand, in order to suppress said combinations, and to cause the laws to be duly executed. The details, for this object, will be immediately communicated to the State authorities through the War Department.

I appeal to all loyal citizens to favor, facilitate and aid this effort to maintain the honor, the integrity, and the existence of our National Union, and the perpetuity of popular government; and to redress wrongs already long enough endured.

I deem it proper to say that the first service assigned to the forces hereby called forth will probably be to re-possess the forts, places, and property which have been seized from the Union; and in every event, the utmost care will be observed, consistently with the objects aforesaid, to avoid any devastation, any destruction of, or interference with, property, or any disturbance of peaceful citizens in any part of the country.

And I hereby command the persons composing the combinations aforesaid to disperse, and retire peaceably to their respective abodes within twenty days from this date.

Deeming that the present condition of public affairs presents an extraordinary occasion, I do hereby, in virtue of the power in me vested by the constitution, convene both Houses of Congress. Senators and Representatives are therefore summoned to assemble at their respective chambers, at 12 o'clock, noon, on Thursday, the fourth day of July, next, then and there to consider and determine, such measures, as, in their wisdom, the public safety, and interest may seem to demand.

ABRAHAM LINCOLN
By the President
WILLIAM H. SEWARD, Secretary of State.[8]

Lincoln's decision to delay in convening Congress until July 4, nearly three months later, gave him two advantages. He could act unilaterally for nearly nine weeks. And he could push to the legal limit the time he'd be able to keep troops in the field.

Several other passages were critical. The size of the call—seventy-five thousand troops—told the Confederates that this was no feint. Talking was over. Then Lincoln called on loyal citizens to aid in the effort to "redress wrongs already long enough endured." This notion that the North had done nothing but make concessions resonated powerfully. And finally when Lincoln said the first assignment for the troops would "probably be to repossess the forts, places, and property which have been seized from the Union," he forced the Confederates onto the defensive. The proclamation included no mention of defending Washington.

Now Lincoln needed a break. After his 2:00 p.m. meal, he rounded up his two younger sons and called for his chief secretary, John Nicolay, to get a carriage ready. The small group set out for an afternoon ride around Washington. It lasted several hours on that chilly Sunday.

Lincoln's secretaries, starting with Nicolay, were essential to his ability to perform his duties. They executed the typical functions of a secretary while also incorporating elements of the modern roles of White House communications director, press secretary, body man, and chief of staff.

John Nicolay was twenty-nine in April 1861, five feet ten, and a thin young man with sleek, dark-brown hair and a thick

Vandyke-style beard. He had emigrated to the United States from Bavaria in 1838. He became an editor of a newspaper in Pike County, Illinois, gaining a reputation as a forceful and politically influential writer. Nicolay subsequently became a clerk in the office of the Illinois secretary of state, Ozias Hatch, where he met a prominent, politically active lawyer—Abraham Lincoln.

In the White House Nicolay tightly controlled access to Lincoln. He was viewed as dour, brooding, and imperious. His assistant, William Stoddard, described him as having dyspeptic tendencies and as someone who could say "'no' about as disagreeably as any man I ever knew." The California journalist Noah Brooks called Nicolay a "grim Cerberus of Teutonic descent," a reference to the three-headed dog in Greek mythology that guards the gates of hell.[9]

Nicolay's assistant, John Hay, next in seniority, was much younger than Nicolay—just twenty-two in April 1861. Unlike his boss he was widely considered urbane and witty. The journalist William Howard Russell remembered meeting John Hay at a state dinner on March 28: "I was seated with Mr. Bates [Edward Bates, the attorney general], and the very agreeable and lively Secretary of the President, Mr. Hay."[10]

Born in Salem, Indiana, and raised in Warsaw, Illinois, Hay became friends with John Nicolay at a young age and through Nicolay got to know Lincoln. Hay had a master's degree from Brown University and studied law before the Civil War. He'd been admitted to the Illinois bar by the time he got to Washington in February 1861. The journalist John Russell Young remembered a young man who was "handsome as a peach, the countenance of extreme youth." Hay was, Young continued, "brilliant, shy," and "ever generous and helpful."[11] Lincoln was said to have loved John Hay like a son.

William Stoddard was brought in early on to assist Nicolay and Hay when the burden of presidential correspondence became too heavy. Officially he was a clerk in the Interior Department. But he was assigned to the White House, where he especially assisted Mary Lincoln. The first lady "liked 'Stod' better than she liked either my father or John Hay, and appears to have called on him for all kinds of services, which they were only too glad to delegate to him," wrote Helen Nicolay, John Nicolay's daughter.[12] Stoddard was handsome and usually diplomatic, but he could also be arrogant. He once admitted he had "not a drop of humility."[13]

In one of several books about his White House years, Stoddard tells a story describing Hay's manner but also the relationship that all three secretaries had with the president:

> Mr. Lincoln says that he must laugh sometimes, or he would surely die. He laughed right here, a few Sundays ago. The letters were about done, when in came John Hay, all one bubble. He is sober enough most of the time, but he had heard something funny, and he was good-natured about dividing it. Generally he [Hay] can tell a story better than most boys of his age, but he broke down on that one before he got well into it.
>
> The door was open and so was Nicolay's, and he heard the peal of laughter when the story proved too much for its narrator, and over he came, with a pen in one hand and a long paper in the other, and he sat right down to listen. Hay began at the beginning, and went on very well until the first good point was reached. It was nothing so wonderful for another time than this, but it was a first-class excuse for a laugh, and all three of us exploded as one.
>
> The whole floor had been as silent as a graveyard or a hospital, until this uproar broke up its Sunday stillness, and we did not know, or had forgotten, that anybody else was within hearing until:
>
> "Now, John, just tell that thing again."
>
> His feet had made no sound in coming over from his room, or our own racket had drowned any foot-fall, but here was the President, and down he sank into Andrew Jackson's chair, facing the table, with Nicolay seated by him and Hay still standing by the mantel.
>
> The story was as fresh, and was even better told that third time up to its first explosive place, but right there a quartette explosion went off. Down came the President's foot from across

his knee, with a heavy stamp on the floor, and out through the hall went an uproarious peal of fun.[14]

Rumors were flying wildly in Washington this Sunday on the streets and in the hotels. "We have had a large throng on [Pennsylvania] Avenue all day, with groups at every corner, discussing the war question," the *Philadelphia Press* reported. "The hotels are crowded, many of our citizens are congregating there, eagerly inquiring for intelligence from Charleston."[15]

The Patent Office examiner and Washington diarist Horatio Nelson Taft was struck by the excitement. Taft believed "the reports from Charleston [were] mostly 'bogus'" and that "Maj Anderson [had] probably not surrendered, but there [was] fighting there."

Taft, fifty-four, often spent his evenings roaming the city's hotel salons, seeking information and mingling with others who were doing the same. "I left Willards [the sprawling hotel just two blocks from the White House] about 1/2 past 10 this evening, never saw a more excited crowd," Taft wrote. "It is said that Martial law will be proclaimed tomorrow morning, and that the Prest has made requisition upon the States for 75,000 men or Volunteers to defend the Government. Think of sending my family out of the City immediately."[16]

It wasn't surprising that Taft wandered the city's hotels. Hotels were the social centers of the capital in 1861. This was especially true as the country entered an unprecedented civil war, with Washington at the epicenter.

Information was everything. Senators, congressmen, cabinet members, businessmen, and all varieties of private citizens, loyal and disloyal, went to the hotels to trade information, to network, and for many, to seek jobs in the first-ever Republican administration, which had many jobs to fill.

At the hotels you felt the vibrant pulse of a political city, a place that was both Northern and Southern and yet neither one completely. People would go to the hotels for dinner. They'd go after the theater, after government events, or after the twice-weekly public concerts on the White House grounds. They'd spend the hours before midnight chatting in the parlors or slowly walking around the public spaces.

There were several major hotels in Washington, mostly on or near Pennsylvania Avenue. Closest to the Capitol was the National Hotel. This was the largest hotel in the city—one of the largest in the country—with five stories. Its main entrance was on the north side of Pennsylvania Avenue, near the corner of Sixth Street.

A half-mile away the Capitol building, with its unfinished dome, rose on the small hill at the end of the broad sand-and-cobblestone boulevard. "The old National is the stamping ground of politicians and the grand center of political intrigue," declared the 1861 city guide *Philp's Washington Described*. "Its crowded halls and gay saloons and parlors are proverbial among old frequenters of the seat of government; while its proximity to the Capitol, and excellent management, render it the most favored hotel in Washington."

The National was a center of Southern sentiment. It was also the hotel from which Solomon Northup was kidnapped and sold into slavery in 1841, an experience he later recounted in his memoir, *Twelve Years a Slave*.[17]

But the city's most famous hotel was the Willard, or Willard's, a five-story structure at Pennsylvania Avenue and Fourteenth Street, just around the corner from the Executive Square, Washington's central government campus in 1861. The Executive Square included the White House along with the State and Treasury department buildings on the east and the War and Navy department buildings on the west—all in a park-like setting. The Willard was where the storied farewell dinner and ball was held in 1859 for Lord Francis Napier, the British minister to the United States—the last Washington social occasion where Northern and Southern white Americans fraternized happily with one another.[18]

Lincoln stayed at the Willard for ten days before his inauguration. The prominent building, extending a full block to F Street, was known for its elegant public spaces and modern amenities that included gas lighting and running water. The New England writer Nathaniel Hawthorne, in an 1862 article about the war, suggested that "Willard's Hotel could more justly be called the

center of Washington than either the Capitol, the White House, or
the State Department. You are mixed up with office seekers, wire
pullers, inventors, artists, poets, editors, Army correspondents,
attaches of foreign journals, long-winded talkers, clerks, diploma-
tists, mail contractors, railway directors—until your identity is
lost among them."[19]

The nation's capital in 1861 combined majestic federal buildings
and clusters of exclusive residential enclaves with a seedy appearance elsewhere. It had a population of about 75,000 people. There
were 60,764 white residents of the city, according to the 1860 census, plus 11,131 free Black people and 3,186 enslaved people. Slavery remained legal until April 16, 1862, when President Lincoln
signed a law abolishing slavery in the district.[20]

It was a Southern city, often a hostile place for Northerners. It
was conservative and aristocratic, its views largely secessionist,
especially among the permanent residents.

Southern-leaning Washington residents were appalled when
Lincoln was inaugurated, and not only because what they called
a "Black Republican,"[21] an abolitionist tool, had become president.
It also wasn't just because of the new threat to Southern "insti-
tutions" or the impending "subjugation" of the Southern states.

It was that an uncouth prairie lawyer from the far-western state
of Illinois was becoming the chief executive of the nation and his
wife the first lady. Washington had buzzed about it for weeks. "Elegant Washington ladies raised holy hands of horror at the thought
of such a rustic pair following the polished Buchanan," wrote Julia
Taft, daughter of Horatio Nelson Taft, the Patent Office examiner.
Julia, then sixteen years old, and her brothers were playmates of
the Lincoln boys during the first year of Lincoln's term.[22]

On Inauguration Day, March 4, Julia Taft had watched the procession from a storefront on Pennsylvania Avenue. She overheard
a woman say, "There goes that Illinois ape, the cursed Abolitionist.
But he will never come back alive."[23]

The incoming first family astonished Washington society, remembered a district historian, John B. Ellis: "Caste and privilege pro-
nounced the bold, independent newcomers barbarians, but the

horror thus affected accomplished nothing. Power had passed out of the hands of the privileged few, and reverted to the people."[24]

The Capitol's unfinished dome and wings looked like a Roman ruin, remembered the author William Augustus Crofutt. Few of the streets were paved, and even the cobblestone thoroughfares seemed unstable. On wet days, Pennsylvania Avenue was a river of mud.

"Along the north edge of the Mall crept a fetid bayou called 'The Canal,' floating dead cats and all kinds of putridity and reeking with pestilential odors," Crofutt wrote. "Cattle, swine, goats, sheep, and geese ran everywhere. There were only two short sewers in the entire city," he said, and those were choked and backlogged, sending their contents into cellars along Pennsylvania Avenue.

Even the Executive Square itself was underwhelming, Crofutt said. The secretary of state and his staff "were cooped in a small and dingy brick building," and the secretary of war, on the other side of the square, occupied an insignificant building on the front lawn of the White House.[25]

William Stoddard, as an outsider and a Northerner, noticed the prevailing antipathy. Washington had been Southern in sentiment for so long that disunion was spoken of loudly, openly, and freely. "There was actual personal danger in being as outspoken a Unionist as I was," Stoddard remembered.[26]

Southern women taunted passersby. "Going or coming, you are more and more convinced that all the young women of Washington know how to play the piano," Stoddard wrote. "There is a perpetual tinkle of secession airs pouring through the windows, which they leave open for the benefit of any Northern vandals who may happen to pass within hearing."

Their favorite song was "Dixie," followed by "Bonnie Blue Flag" and "Maryland, My Maryland." But "Dixie" most of all began to take on a "weird, spell-like influence."

"It makes one shudder to have that tune spring out upon him when he least expects it," Stoddard wrote.[27]

The Philadelphia journalist John Russell Young recalled a degraded Washington, a city of hate and distrust. "There was no love for the Union among Washington people," Young wrote. "'Oh,

you vile Yankee!' a comely maiden hissed at me one Sunday morning on her way to church. The maiden could not help it. She was
modest, fair and pious, but the animus was there! It pervaded
Washington. She could no more help it than the lark could help
its singing."[28]

This aversion was directed at Lincoln himself, and not just among
secessionists. The new president with a strikingly thin resume was
dismissed as unfit for the office or the moment by Democrats, by
leading members of Congress, and even by his own military and
cabinet. "Mr. Lincoln did not impress the capital as a welcome personal force," Young wrote. "He was not a popular man."

It was hard to point to Lincoln's actual friends or favorites. No
one ever really knew what he was thinking. That in itself generated
resentment, Young remembered. Lincoln made decisions alone.
He measured people around him for their value. "He knew their
worth, their fidelity, and in no sense distrusted them," Young wrote.
"But it was everyone to his duty." Writing decades later, Young
described a widespread skepticism: "What I confess was a distrust
of Lincoln. It comes back as evidence of the strength of the man."[29]

Abraham Lincoln had a powerful impact on the people he met.
Many details about Lincoln's appearance and personality were
consistent. Others reflected as much on the person making the
description as they did on the president. Lincoln had just turned
fifty-two in the spring of 1861. He had a head of thick black hair
and was vigorous and youthful, especially in comparison to his
predecessor, President James Buchanan, who was sixty-nine when
he left office. Lincoln had young children.

The president was uncommonly tall. He projected a kind
demeanor. He was attentive and genial, sometimes even jovial.
Still, he often gave the impression that his mind was elsewhere.
Henry Adams, the twenty-three-year-old grandson and great-
grandson of two presidents, met Lincoln at an inaugural ball in
1861. He noticed a distance in Lincoln's demeanor, and he dismissed the president as overwhelmed.

"Had young Adams been told that his life was to hang on the
correctness of his estimate of the new President, he would have

lost," Adams wrote, referring to himself in the third person. "He saw a long, awkward figure; a plain, ploughed face; a mind absent in part; features that expressed neither self-satisfaction nor any other familiar Americanism, but the painful sense of becoming educated and of needing education; above all a lack of apparent force."

No man alive needed so much education as the new president, the Harvard-educated Adams concluded, but even so, all the education he could get would not be enough.[30]

William Howard Russell, the forty-one-year-old reporter for the *Times* of London—already world-famous for his Crimean War dispatches—met Lincoln at the White House on the morning of March 27, three weeks after Lincoln took office. "There entered, with a shambling, loose, irregular gait, a tall, lank, lean man, considerably over six feet in height, with stooping shoulders, long pendulous arms, terminating in hands of extraordinary dimensions, which, however, were far exceeded in proportion by his feet," Russell wrote.

Lincoln was dressed in an ill-fitting, wrinkled black suit, reminding Russell of an undertaker. Still, whatever negative impression might have been created was offset by an appearance of kindliness. Russell concluded that Lincoln would never be seen as what European society would view as a gentleman.[31]

This helped explain the ridicule directed at the president. "The cold shoulder is given to Mr. Lincoln, and all kinds of stories and jokes are circulated at his expense," Russell wrote in his diary on March 28.[32]

David Homer Bates, seventeen, part of the new War Department telegraph office, saw the president as "homely," at least at first. "He seemed uncouth and awkward," Bates wrote many years later. "But afterward I saw Lincoln almost daily, often for hours at a time, and I soon forgot his awkward presence and came to think of him as a very attractive and, indeed, lovable person."[33]

Many observers noted Lincoln's unusual physicality. Russell described Lincoln's "sinewy muscular yellow neck." The Iowa senator James Harlan described the president as "lean, and his muscles as hard, as those of a prizefighter. He was obviously a very strong, powerful man."[34]

Virtually all Lincoln observers noted his skill with stories and anecdotes, which he often used strategically—to end debates, escape awkward situations, or charm people. William Howard Russell described one example during a state dinner on March 28. "In the conversation which occurred before dinner, I was amused to observe the manner in which Lincoln used the anecdotes for which he is famous," Russell wrote. "Where men bred in courts, accustomed to the world, or versed in diplomacy, would use some subterfuge, or would make a polite speech, or give a shrug of the shoulders as the means of getting out of an embarrassing position, Mr. Lincoln raises a laugh by some bold west-country anecdote, and moves off in the cloud of merriment produced by his joke."[35]

Almost everyone who wrote about Washington in these first days of the Lincoln administration was appalled by the mad scramble for jobs. For thirty years Washington's patronage had gone to the Democrats or the Whigs. Now Lincoln's supporters—the Republicans—expected payback. The clamor seemed like an absurdity as a war loomed, but it wasn't. The government couldn't function without employees, and now especially those employees had to be dependably loyal. Lincoln "was racing for his life with the wolves afoot and the wolves must be fed!" the journalist John Russell Young wrote. "For the very life of the Union they must be fed!"[36]

All through March the White House was one of the most anxious places on earth, William Stoddard remembered, and it wasn't because of the rebellion. The Lincoln administration had jobs to fill by the thousands, and Republicans from all corners wanted them. They came to Washington and thronged the hotels, the streets around the White House, and the building itself.

"Illinois is here in perfect hordes," John Nicolay reported to the Illinois secretary of state Ozias M. Hatch on March 7. "Even before the traitors had flown, the vultures descended in swarms and tore the carrion of political patronage into fragments," wrote Henry Adams.[37]

Job seekers would gather in groups outside the White House. It was even more dense inside. "For hours and hours, the anterooms and halls upstairs were so full that they could hold no more," Stoddard remembered. "This broad staircase itself was packed and jammed, stair by stair, from top to bottom, so that you could hardly squeeze your way up or down."[38]

The Willard was also crowded with job seekers. William Howard Russell wrote extensively, and comically, about the hotel and the persistent droves during March and April of 1861: "[The Willard] probably contains at this moment more scheming, plotting, planning heads, more aching and joyful hearts, than any building of the same size in the world. I was ushered into a bedroom which had just been vacated by some candidate—whether he succeeded or not I cannot tell, but if his testimonials spoke truth, he ought to have been selected at once for the highest office. The room was littered with printed copies of letters testifying that J. Smith, of Hartford, Conn., was about the ablest, honestest, cleverest, and best man the writers ever knew."[39]

Lincoln spent hours every day hearing the pleas of job seekers. Eventually Nicolay and Assistant Secretary Hay convinced the president to limit his business hours to 10:00 a.m. to 3:00 p.m.— and then from 10:00 a.m. to 1:00 p.m. This helped. Then Lincoln decided he would no longer weigh in on appointments his cabinet officers made. But the crush didn't really stop until a week after the fall of Sumter, when people started streaming out of Washington, fearing the advance of armies.[40]

When Lincoln got back from his Sunday ride through the city, he met that evening with his most famous political opponent, Stephen Douglas. Douglas had gone to the White House after 7:00 p.m. and spent two hours with the president.

Stephen Douglas was the Democratic candidate who ran against Lincoln in the 1860 election. He was also Lincoln's opponent in the famous 1858 Illinois senate race. He was a proponent of "popular sovereignty," the doctrine that held that the people who lived in a U.S. territory, and not the federal government, had the right to decide whether it would come into the Union as a slave or free state.[41]

Douglas remained Lincoln's opponent even now. He was already claiming that Lincoln was exceeding his legal authority. Both men, wrote John Nicolay and John Hay, were in the prime of their intellect. Both possessed undiminished vigor. Douglas had lost the 1860 election, but he wasn't defeated, and Lincoln knew it.

Until this time, though, Douglas had been consistent on one point: the Union must be preserved. And so the attack on Sumter was an egregious violation. He said, "That assault could no longer be disguised as lawful complaint—it was the spring of a wild beast at the throat of the nation." For Douglas, it changed the issue from coercion to anarchy.[42]

Douglas waived all party rivalry and assured Lincoln, without questions or conditions, of his support for the Union. In doing this, Douglas made himself the first, and the most important, of the many "War Democrats" who would be vital in the years to come.

But Lincoln knew Douglas well. He knew this needed to be on the record and widely publicized throughout the country. He knew that next to the support of the Republican Party, the most important thing was to get the unconditional support of his most prominent rival—it meant the support of the whole country, not just the Republican Party. Its value was immense.

And so the next morning, from Kansas to Cape Cod, people heard the news of the meeting between Lincoln and Douglas and read an authorized statement from Douglas. While he was "unalterably opposed to the Administration on all its political issues, he was prepared to sustain the President in the exercise of all his constitutional functions to preserve the Union, and maintain the Government, and defend the Federal Capital."

Douglas died just months later, on June 3, in Chicago.[43]

4
--

"If I Were Beauregard I Would Take Washington"

The City

This Monday morning brought rain. A storm was coming. News of the surrender at Sumter was circulating around the country, and soon President Lincoln's call for troops would hit like a second thunderclap.

In Washington Secretary of State William Seward wrote to his wife, Frances Adeline Seward, in Auburn, New York. "Treason is a painful fact, and at last we have the stern necessity of meeting and treating it as such," he declared.[1]

Elizabeth Lindsay Lomax, a pro-Southern Virginia aristocrat and Washington DC diarist, wrote with foreboding. Even for a Southerner, the disintegration of the country was devastating. "Sumter has surrendered—we are in great trouble," she said. Her son, Lunsford Lindsay Lomax, was serving in the U.S. Army, and she worried what these new developments would mean for him.[2]

Horatio Nelson Taft, the Patent Office examiner, vacillated between confidence and concern. "It seems pretty probable that 'Sumpter' is taken, but I think we cannot rely entirely upon the news," he wrote. "There seems to be a great war spirit up throughout the Country. Washington will soon be a great Military Camp."

Some things in Washington seemed constant. "I was down at Willards," Taft wrote. "The same crowd seems to be there still."[3]

William O. Stoddard was sworn in this Monday for three months in the Washington DC militia, one of a number of young men joining the National Rifles, the first company of city volunteers sworn in at the beginning of the Civil War. "None of the other boys, however, had to go and ask the President, and being young, I was proud of that," Stoddard wrote.[4]

Lincoln's call for troops was made under the Militia Act of 1795. The U.S. regular Army was tiny in those days, and the federal government relied on state militias in national emergencies. The law established rules for state militias in minute detail. In some ways it was similar to today's Selective Service system, which requires men eighteen to twenty-five to register. Under the 1795 act, all white male citizens between the ages of eighteen and forty-five, with a few exceptions, had to enroll. They'd be held liable for service if called.

The act defined three circumstances under which the federal government could activate state militias. The first was to execute the laws. The second was to suppress insurrections. The third was to repel invasions. Lincoln relied on the second criteria. The relevant passage stated,

> Whenever the laws of the United States shall be opposed, or the execution thereof obstructed, in any state, by combinations too powerful to be suppressed by the ordinary course of judicial proceedings, or by the powers invested in the marshals by this act, it shall be lawful for the President of the United States, to call forth the militia of such state, or of any other state or states, as may be necessary to suppress such combinations, or to cause the laws to be duly executed; and the use of militia so to be called forth may be continued, if necessary, until the expiration of thirty days after the commencement of the then next session of Congress.[5]

Immediately after Lincoln's call for seventy-five thousand troops was released, Secretary of War Simon Cameron sent details to the states. They included the requisitions in table 1.[6]

Table 1. Cameron's requisitions

State	Major general	Brigadier general	Regiments	Called
Maine			1	780
New Hampshire			1	780
Vermont			1	780
Massachusetts			2	1,560
Rhode Island			1	780
Connecticut			1	780
New York	2	4	17	13,280
Pennsylvania	2	4	16	12,500
New Jersey		1	4	3,123
Delaware			1	780
Maryland		1	4	3,123
Virginia			3	2,340
North Carolina			2	1,560
Tennessee			2	1,560
Arkansas			1	780
Kentucky		1	4	3,123
Missouri		1	4	3,123
Illinois		1	6	4,683
Indiana		1	6	4,683
Ohio	1	3	13	10,153
Michigan			1	780
Wisconsin			1	780
Iowa			1	780
Minnesota			1	780
Washington DC				
Kansas				
Total	5	17	94	73,391

Note: On April 16, Pennsylvania's forces were reduced to fourteen regiments; Massachusetts's forces were increased to a brigade, with a brigadier general, and provided five regiments; and Missouri's forces were raised on the basis of operating within the state only.

Lincoln met this morning with Lt. Gen. Winfield Scott, Pennsylvania governor Andrew Curtin, and the Pennsylvania legislator and newspaper editor Alexander McClure. They gathered at the White House for a 10:00 a.m. meeting in Lincoln's office.

The purpose was to strategize the role Pennsylvania would play in troop mobilization. Pennsylvania was the second-largest state. It had 2.9 million people and was the closest nonslave state to Washington. It conceivably could serve as a mobilization model for other Northern states.

McClure and Curtin arrived several minutes before the meeting. The cabinet was deliberating for the second day in a row in Lincoln's second-floor office, and the meeting was running late. Governor Curtin and McClure—who was also chairman of the Republican State Committee in Pennsylvania—waited in the reception room adjacent to the president's office. "We sat down by a window overlooking the Potomac, and in a few minutes the tall form of General Scott entered," McClure remembered. But now every chair in the room was occupied. Scott was a physically imposing man. At six feet, five inches, he was one of the few men taller than Lincoln. But he was also seventy-four years old, massively overweight, and suffering from a variety of debilitating physical ailments.

The commanding general of the U.S. Army, dressed in his blue uniform with gold trim, refused to sit because it would mean that either Curtin or McClure would have to stand. He was perhaps the only uniformed military man in the room. "We presented the ludicrous spectacle of three men standing for nearly half an hour, and one of them feeble in strength and greatly the senior of the others in years, simply because there were not enough chairs for the entire party," McClure wrote. "With all his suffering he was too dignified even to lean against the wall, although it was evident that he was in great pain."

Eventually the meeting with Lincoln started. McClure came to see how desperate conditions were in Washington and how helpless the U.S. government really was. McClure asked Scott if the capital was in danger. After all, the Confederates had a formidable force of well more than five thousand men in Charleston, and Charleston was only a few days away by train. Scott said no.

McClure asked how many men Scott had for the defense of Washington.

"Fifteen hundred, sir. Fifteen hundred and two batteries."

McClure asked how many men General Beauregard had at Charleston.

"General Beauregard commands more men at Charleston than I command on the continent east of the frontier," Scott replied.

"General, is not Washington in great danger?"

"No, sir, the capital can't be taken, the capital can't be taken, sir."

All the while, Lincoln sat listening, saying nothing, twirling his glasses between his fingers, gazing at Scott. Finally he spoke up: "It does seem to me, general, that if I were Beauregard I would take Washington."

This electrified the old soldier. He insisted the city was secure, but his words had a double meaning. The leaders of the government, including Lincoln and Scott himself, must not let it happen.

"Mr. President, the capital can't be taken, sir. It can't be taken."

McClure was unequivocal. "There was only one conclusion," he wrote. "The great Chieftain of two wars was in his dotage and utterly unequal to meeting the impending conflict. Governor Curtin and I left with the conviction that the incompetency of General Scott was one of the most serious of the multiplied perils that confronted the Republic."[7]

Indeed, there were only sixteen thousand troops in the entire army, scattered across the continent, and virtually none were in Washington. In these first weeks of Lincoln's term, Scott and others were working to activate local militia companies, but there were fewer than two thousand at this point, and many were disloyal to the Union.

Winfield Scott in 1861 was a series of contradictions. He was a veteran of the War of 1812 and a commanding general of the U.S. Army during the Mexican War, but he'd recently counseled Lincoln to abandon Fort Sumter and let the seceded states go. One U.S. policy option, he suggested to incoming secretary of state

William Seward the day before Lincoln's inauguration, could simply be "Wayward sisters, depart in peace!"[8]

On March 28, Scott had ventured even further into politics, writing in a memo to Secretary of War Simon Cameron that abandoning both Fort Sumter and Fort Pickens on the Florida gulf coast would bring the seceded states back to the Union and prevent the secession of more. "It would instantly soothe and give confidence to the eight remaining slave-holding states, and render their cordial adherence to this Union perpetual," Scott wrote.

Lincoln read the memo just before a state dinner that evening. His reaction was a "long pause of blank amazement," which was followed by a strong denunciation from Postmaster General Montgomery Blair and dissent from other cabinet members.

Lincoln was furious. Scott was furious and embarrassed. He stormed out of the White House just as the dinner was about to begin. Lincoln realized that he was on his own and couldn't rely even on his senior military advisor.[9]

Winfield Scott was an imposing man who enjoyed military finery and perks, but now he was in poor health. He was sometimes too infirm to come to Lincoln's second-floor White House office, but he could be found in his own office across Seventeenth Street, a block west of the White House, working past 11:00 p.m. He was a career military officer but also was mentioned as a presidential candidate several times. He won the Whig Party nomination in 1852 but lost the election to Franklin Pierce.[10]

Scott was a Southerner and a Virginian but also a staunch defender of the Union. He was the most revered soldier in the United States, the first person to hold the rank of lieutenant general since Washington. But in 1861 he was unable to lead troops in the field. He headed a decrepit officer corps in the top ranks of the military. In March of 1861, the U.S. Army's four generals were broken-down old men, long past their prime as warriors, three of them over seventy years old. In addition to Scott, then seventy-four, there was Maj. Gen. John Wool, seventy-seven; Maj. Gen. David Twiggs, seventy-one; and Brig. Gen. William Harney, sixty.[11]

It wasn't uncommon for President Lincoln or his cabinet secretaries to drop in at Scott's office or his personal quarters in a
rooming house on Pennsylvania Avenue between Seventeenth and
Eighteenth Streets, across from the War Department building.[12]

Edward Davis Townsend, the assistant adjutant general and a
close aide to Scott, described the general's idiosyncrasies. When Lincoln visited, Townsend said, Scott would always rise and insist that
Lincoln take the big armchair that Scott himself habitually occupied. Then Scott would recount the military activities of the day.

Scott could be prickly and eccentric. As a rule, he expected
one or more of his staff to have dinner with him. If there was no
pressing business, the general liked to tell stories. The staff did not
always enjoy these dinners, which took place in a room heated
by a six-burner gas chandelier, especially after a long, hot, mid-
summer day.

"The general had fallen into a way of speaking very slowly,
with sometimes long pauses between his words," Townsend wrote.
"These occasions were sometimes quite trying."

"One evening I had a dull headache, and sat with my hand
shading my eyes from the bright gas light," Townsend continued.
"Suddenly the general stopped in the midst of a sentence, and said
sharply, 'Colonel Townsend is now asleep!' I looked up in some
surprise, and said, 'Oh, no, general, I hear every word you say, but
I have a headache, and the gas hurts my eyes.' With a changed tone
he said, 'Oh, pardon me,' and went on with his story."

Another time, Townsend wrote, Scott was in a terrible mood.
His fellow diners thought the dinner was at fault. The old general
was snapping at everyone who spoke. The district commander,
Charles P. Stone, soon excused himself, saying he wanted to go
home and have a cup of tea.

When he left, Scott muttered, "I don't like tea sops."[13]

Reactions to Lincoln's Call

Cameron's telegraphic requisitions reached the states throughout
the day. On Monday afternoon the War Department's lines clacked
with responses that reflected a new patriotic fervor. "Great rejoicing

here over your proclamation," Ohio governor William Dennison
said. "We will furnish the largest number you will [accept]."

"Your requisition will have immediate attention," responded
Connecticut governor William A. Buckingham.

"On behalf of the State of Indiana I tender you 10,000 men,"
Governor Oliver P. Morton wrote.

The governors of the Southern states then still in the Union
reacted with scorn. "I can be no party to this wicked violation of
the laws of the country and to this war upon the liberties of a free
people," North Carolina governor John W. Ellis wrote to Cameron.
"You can get no troops from North Carolina."

"Kentucky will furnish no troops for the wicked purpose of sub-
duing her sister Southern States," Governor Beriah Macgoffin wrote.

All these replies—plus similar affirmative responses from the
governors of Vermont, Maine, and Wisconsin; an inquiry from
New York governor Edwin Morgan; and a longer exchange with
Massachusetts governor John Andrew about the preferred route
to Washington—came immediately, on the fifteenth.[14]

The emotional impact of a U.S. fort attacked by secessionists
shook the North out of its long prewar malaise. John Dix, a former
U.S. senator from New York who had also just concluded a brief
seven-week tenure as President James Buchanan's treasury secretary, believed the attack on Sumter sealed both slavery's and the
newborn Confederacy's fate—right there in the first hours of the war.
"The North rose as one man," Dix wrote in his memoirs.[15]

Even Lord Richard Lyons, the British minister to the United
States, sensed the changed mood. Lyons was an experienced diplomat, a favorite of Queen Victoria, and England's leading foreign-
service officer. Now he wrote to British Foreign Secretary Lord
John Russell in London and with great precision analyzed the
stakes in the impending Civil War, the strategies of the combat-
ants, and the essential variables: "Civil war is now imminent; or
rather, has already begun," Lyons wrote. "The loss of Fort Sumter
is not, of itself, of much importance, in a military point of view,
to this Government. As the beginning of civil war, it is a most
serious and a most unhappy event. It seems calculated to arouse

feelings of resentment and humiliation in the North, which will overwhelm the party of peace, and throw the people, with bitter eagerness, into the war."

The North, Lyons reported, had the superior position in numbers and wealth. It had the immense advantage of a strong navy. It had a well-organized, but small, regular army. This advantage would be neutralized by the resignations of secessionist Southern officers. "The South is, if the accounts which reach us are to be trusted, more unanimous," Lyons continued.

> It is more eager, and, as it has more at stake, is more ready to make sacrifices. The taint of slavery will render the cause of the South repugnant to the feelings of the civilized world. On the other hand, commercial intercourse with the cotton States is of vital importance to manufacturing nations. The conduct of Virginia and the other border States is now more than ever the critical question. If they remain true to the Union, the contest may be confined to small dimensions. Unless, however, they abandon their solemn declarations, they must now make common cause with the South.

The immediate focal point, Lyons believed, was Washington. "The apprehensions of the Government are for this city," he reported. "The chiefs of the Southern Confederacy loudly declare their intention of attacking it immediately if the border States join them. This Government, previously to the issue of the proclamation this morning, was already making arrangements with the Governors of the Northern States to obtain volunteers and militia to defend it."[16]

The South

As the call went out to the Northern states to get troops to Washington, many secessionists had the same objective: to get troops to Washington—not to protect it, but to seize it. Confederate troops, the insurrectionists believed, could assault Washington and perhaps capture Lincoln. Many Southerners believed a quick strike on the capital, located deep in Southern territory, might change the course of events, triggering the secession of Maryland and perhaps recognition from foreign governments. Washington's fate was nowhere near assured. It was entirely dependent on Northern state militias.

Benjamin F. Butler—the prominent Massachusetts lawyer, Democratic politician, and now a Massachusetts brigadier general—later wrote that if he'd been an advisor to Confederate president Jefferson Davis, he'd have urged Davis to attack Washington immediately in the days after Sumter. Butler had supported Davis at the 1860 Democratic convention. He knew and respected Davis from when Davis was the secretary of war and a U.S. senator.[17]

Butler reasoned that following the fall of Fort Sumter, the Confederates had four or five thousand trained troops at Charleston. They could have those troops on the railroad and at Washington in thirty-six hours. There was no force in the field then that could have stopped the Confederates or matched their numbers. "The temptation to do it must have been enormous and should have been controlling," Butler wrote. "The prize to be won was gloriously magnificent." The Confederate president could have been ruling over a captured Washington by the end of April 1861, Butler wrote.[18]

In fact the South did have a major head start in creating a war-ready military. By the time of the attack on Fort Sumter, troop callups by the Confederate government had produced 36,900 men. They were supplemented with 32,000 more in an additional call on April 16.

Unlike the brand-new Northern recruits, these Southern soldiers had weeks, even months, of training. By February 1, 1861, seven Southern states had seceded. South Carolina went out on December 20, 1860, followed by Mississippi, Florida, Alabama, Georgia, Louisiana, and Texas. As these states became "independent," they immediately began to call up and equip troops.

The result was that when the Confederate States government formed in Montgomery, Alabama, on February 8, 1861, it "found an army awaiting its call," the U.S. Army provost marshal general, James B. Fry, wrote in an 1866 analysis.[19]

South Carolina alone had organized four brigades by March 6, totaling 8,835 men, and on this same day, the Confederate Congress authorized President Jefferson Davis to raise as many as 100,000 men for military and naval service. By April 15, more than 7,000 soldiers were in Charleston, with 3,000 more gathering in Columbia.[20]

Edward Pollard, the secessionist editor of the *Richmond Examiner*, summed it up. "On the incoming of the administration of Abraham Lincoln, the rival government of the South had perfected its organization," he wrote. "The revolution had rapidly gathered, not only in moral power, but in the means of war."

Indeed, by the time Sumter surrendered on April 13, the Confederacy had already captured more than a dozen U.S. installations, among them Fort Moultrie and Castle Pinckney in Charleston; Fort Pulaski in Savannah; the arsenal in Mount Vernon, Alabama; Fort Morgan in Mobile Bay; Forts Jackson, St. Philip, and Pike, near New Orleans; the Baton Rouge Arsenal; the New Orleans Mint and Custom House; the Little Rock Arsenal; the Pensacola Navy Yard; and all U.S. property in Texas.[21]

Southern civilians were as ready for the fight as the military. "Men left their plows standing in the field, not to return under four years, many of them never," wrote D. Augustus Dickert, a captain in the Third South Carolina Regiment. "Carpenters came down from the unfinished roof. The student who had left his school on the Friday before never recited his Monday's lesson. The country doctor left his patients to the care of the good housewife. Never before in the history of the world was there ever such a spontaneous outburst of patriotic feeling."[22]

There was plenty of Southern bombast, even from top officials. Confederate secretary of war Leroy Walker—in a speech in Montgomery, Alabama, on April 12—made a telling proclamation. "I would prophesy that the flag which now flaunts the breeze here will float over the dome of the old Capitol at Washington before the first of May," he declared.[23]

For the next two weeks, newspapers across the South would beat the same drum relentlessly. And officials at the highest levels of the Southern government, military, and business would do the same, both privately and publicly. On April 13, Edward Pollard's *Richmond Examiner* was predicting a Southern assault on

Washington. "Attention Volunteers!" the *Examiner* proclaimed. "Nothing is more probable than that President Davis will soon march an army through North Carolina and Virginia to Washington. Those who desire to join the Southern army as it shall pass through our borders, had better organize at once for the purpose, and keep in constant readiness."[24]

Pollard's suggestion that Davis might move on Washington was more than idle chatter. The Northern state militia organizations were mostly a laughingstock. The race to reach Washington was on.

5

Northern Militia in Tatters

T he founders of the American republic never wanted a large standing army. This principle prevailed for most of American history, except during periods of wartime, and continued well into the twentieth century, through World War II. In December 1860 the U.S. Army had only 16,367 officers and men on its rolls. Most of the force was scattered west of the Mississippi.[1]

When conflict came, the nation would rely on the state militias. There was just one problem in April 1861. The militia system was broken. On paper, the United States had a massive potential army that spring. Under the eighteenth century federal militia laws, there were a total of 3.1 million militia members in all of the states, including the South. (Iowa, Oregon, and the territories kept no militia records.)

But this represented potential based on the population, not actual participants. Worse, the data from some of the states was from the 1840s or earlier.[2] The reality was that in state after state, militia organizations were in disarray. Indiana governor Oliver P. Morton managed to convey both bluster and panic in a single message to Secretary of War Simon Cameron on April 16. "The six regiments will be full in three days," he said. "I can send 500 men to Washington to-morrow, but they are not armed. I hope arms, tents, and stores will be sent immediately."[3]

Indiana had fewer than five hundred pieces of small arms in the entire state, in addition to eight pieces of "weather-worn and dismantled cannon," wrote state adjutant general William Henry Harrison Terrell. In short, Indiana had no arms, no equipment, and no ammunition at the start of the Civil War.[4]

Across the North, militias had become a pointless nuisance—"mere burlesques." The country had been at peace for decades, with the brief interruption of the Mexican War, which relied "in a gentle way" on the militia units and left no permanent change in attitude.[5] Units that remained active functioned mostly as social clubs for men. "Popular prejudice against doing military duty was insurmountable," wrote the journalist and politician Whitelaw Reid. In the North, military companies had gained a derisive nickname, "the Cornstalk Militia."[6]

In some large cities, the militia was used to put down the frequent riots of the mid-nineteenth century. But mostly, legislatures viewed them as an extravagance.

Minnesota, for example, should have had a relatively strong military organization. It had achieved statehood just three years earlier, and it was close to the frontier. An 1858 state law called for twelve brigades and twenty-eight regiments—twenty-four thousand men in all. But in the spring of 1861, Minnesota could only identify the remnants of eight volunteer companies, about 147 officers and about two hundred men.

In Illinois in February 1861, a bill to rebuild the state militia was working its way through the state legislature. It passed the state House of Representatives but then died in a state Senate committee. The chairman, R. J. Oglesby, a Republican, said it was frivolous. Illinois, with a population of about 1.7 million people in 1860, had very few uniformed militia members in the spring of 1861, according to its acting governor, John Wood. In a "State of the State" message on January 9, Wood urged a reorganization of an "inoperative" militia system—a "system of defects."[7]

New Jersey, meanwhile, had a pool of 81,984 potential militia soldiers. But when President Lincoln called for 75,000 troops to serve for three months in April 1861, the state's active militia was, according to one contemporary account, no more than a "system of shreds and patches, almost entirely worthless."[8]

Ohio, the third-largest state, with 2.3 million people, was in deplorable shape. "We can move two regiments this week, but they will not all be uniformed," Gov. William Dennison wrote to the War Department on April 16. "Send them on," came the reply.[9]

The truth on the ground in Ohio was stark. Jacob Cox, an Ohio state senator and a newly minted general in the state militia, described the situation. "A long period of profound peace had made every military organization seem almost farcical," Cox remembered. "A few independent military companies formed the merest shadow of an army; the state militia proper was only a nominal thing."

Cox, thirty-two, a lawyer, was close to Governor Dennison, who appointed him as a brigadier general in the militia in April 1861. Politically connected and a committed abolitionist, Cox's assignment was to help organize volunteers. Cox admitted he'd never even worn a military uniform.[10]

Around that time Ohio governor Dennison had asked the former U.S. Army captain George McClellan to come to Columbus for consultations. Cox understood that McClellan, now a railroad executive, was to be named major general of the Ohio troops. Cox met McClellan at the train station. By the end of the year McClellan, thirty-four, a civilian in April, would be the supreme commander of the U.S. Army, then one of the largest armies in the history of the world.

Today, he was dressed in a plain civilian suit, with a narrow-rimmed soft felt hat. He appeared to be what he was—a railway superintendent in business clothes.

During McClellan's meeting with Dennison, the governor laid out the challenges. The "destitution of the State of everything like military material and equipment was plainly put," Cox noted. "The governor spoke of the embarrassment he felt." Dennison offered McClellan the command of the militia. McClellan accepted.

The next morning Cox accompanied McClellan to the state arsenal. "We found a few boxes of smooth-bore muskets which had once been issued to militia companies and had been returned rusted and damaged," Cox wrote. "No belts, cartridge-boxes, or other accoutrements. In a heap in one corner lay a confused pile of mildewed harnesses, now not worth carrying away. The arsenal was simply an empty storehouse."[11]

The Mobilization

From this staggeringly weak starting point, the Northern states got to work.

In Lincoln's call Minnesota had been asked for a regiment of 780 men. Within two weeks it had nearly a thousand men, with double that number available for the asking.[12]

In Indiana by April 19, four days after the call, there were twenty-four hundred men in camp. Within a week, twelve thousand men had signed up.[13]

The New Jersey troop quota was filled by April 30. Four regiments were formed into a brigade by thirty-eight-year-old Brig. Gen. Theodore Runyon, a Newark attorney and Democratic politician.[14]

But only three states were able to mobilize men and fully provide arms and campaign equipment immediately after the call for troops. They were New York, Massachusetts, and Rhode Island. A fourth state, Pennsylvania, was disastrously unready but recovered quickly. Only these four were able to successfully deploy troops beyond their state lines in April 1861.

New York Organizes

New York, the Union's largest and most influential state, was unprepared. "The decadence of the military spirit had been gradual, but nearly absolute," wrote Frederick Phisterer, a German-born soldier who later served as New York State's adjutant general. "Public money expended to maintain a Militia establishment was regarded as wasted."[15]

But New York also did have something of a head start, thanks to the prewar work of its adjutant general, Frederick Townsend, and the more recent work of the governor, Edwin D. Morgan, during the winter months of 1860–61. Townsend took over the moribund state militia in 1857 and implemented a series of reforms. Among other things, he

inventoried the state's weapons, finding that the rifles and small arms were mostly worthless;

found that nonparticipation fines imposed on eligible men, as required by law, weren't being collected because militia companies and local tax collectors were too lax;

found that commutation fees—the money eligible men had to pay to be excused from service—weren't being collected for the same reasons;

pointed out that because of these poor enforcement efforts, the quota of weapons provided by the federal government was too small; and

created an instruction camp for officers only, where they learned regimental, battalion, and brigade maneuvers.[16]

Townsend lamented the militia's lack of readiness to fight in the months before Fort Sumter. "In view of the present imperiled condition of the Union, I urge upon your Excellency the importance of securing at least 50,000 rifled muskets, or weapons of similar range and precision, for the service of the State," he wrote to the governor in a January 1861 annual report. "For this purpose and the purchase of the proper accoutrements, at least one million dollars [about $29.5 million in 2020 dollars] is necessary."[17]

In late January Governor Morgan asked the legislature for more money for the militia. A bill was introduced to appropriate five hundred thousand dollars. It was tabled on February 15.

It took the fall of Sumter to shake New York awake. On the afternoon of April 14, the day Sumter was evacuated, Governor Morgan met with the attorney general, the legislative leaders, and the state's senior military officers. They drafted a bill that was submitted the following morning. It provided for the enrollment of thirty thousand volunteer militia to serve for two years and appropriated three million dollars—about eighty-seven million dollars in 2020 dollars—to cover the cost. It passed and was signed into law on the sixteenth.[18]

In the end New York would lead all of the states with an extraordinarily rapid deployment of troops, sending eleven regiments to the theater of war in less than two weeks.[19]

A New Generation of Minutemen Emerges

Massachusetts was the most prepared Northern state, thanks to the work of Gov. John Albion Andrew during the secession winter, assisted by John Murray Forbes, the railroad executive, merchant, and philanthropist. In these prewar weeks, Forbes was instrumental in lining up steam transports and working with railroad executives to carry troops to Washington.

Andrew had been elected in November 1860, the same election that put Lincoln in the White House. Before that, he was an abolition-activist lawyer based in Boston and a supporter of John Brown, the abolitionist zealot who was executed in 1859 for seeking to foment a rebellion of enslaved people. Andrew's view of an impending conflict was solidified during a preinauguration visit to Washington.

He met with U.S. senator James Mason of Virginia, who told Andrew that the South was through trying to coexist with antislavery Northerners. An "inevitable dissolution" of the Union was coming soon, Mason said. Any possible reconciliation would be contingent on the Northern states repealing all antislavery laws. "Here was the whole thing in a nutshell," Andrew's biographer, Henry Greenleaf Pearson, wrote. "The only reply was war."[20]

Among those who foresaw that ballots would soon give way to bullets, Andrew had a unique position: He commanded a state militia, and he used his power to get his state ready.[21]

Andrew's foresight was the foundation upon which Massachusetts was able to move five fully equipped regiments, more than three thousand troops, into the field with astonishing speed, less than one week after Lincoln's call.

Preparation began at the end of 1860, when William Schouler, the state's adjutant general, proposed to the outgoing governor that the active militia be placed on a war footing. "The present companies could be filled to their full complement of men, and the regiments to their full complement of companies," Schouler suggested, among a list of recommendations.[22]

On January 16, eleven days after taking office, Governor Andrew adopted the steps Schouler urged as General Order No. 4. Company commanders were ordered to poll their men, and those who were unable or indisposed to march immediately would be honorably discharged and their ranks filled with new recruits.

Massachusetts companies spent the winter months drilling and organizing on a nightly basis. In particular the Sixth Regiment, under Col. Edward F. Jones, stepped up. On January 19, three days after Andrew's order, the regiment offered its services to the governor.

On February 5, Jones offered an in-depth assessment of his regiment's condition. "The Sixth Regiment consists of eight companies, located as follows: Four in Lowell, two in Lawrence, one in Acton, and one in Boston," he wrote.

> Four companies of the regiment are insufficiently armed (as to quantity) with a serviceable rifle musket; the other four with the old musket, which is not a safe or serviceable arm, and requiring a different cartridge from the first, which would make confusion in the distribution of ammunition. Two companies are without uniforms, having worn them out. I would (after being properly armed and equipped) suggest our actual necessary wants: a cap, frock coat, pantaloons, boots, overcoat, knapsack, and blanket to each man. Such is our position, and I think it is a fair representation of the condition of most of the troops in the state.[23]

The Massachusetts legislature worked through the winter months drafting bills to codify the provisions of General Order No. 4, to address the arms and equipment issues Jones described, and to authorize the militia to respond to a call from the president. A series of laws passed in February, March, and early April, including one that created a $100,000 ($2.9 million in 2020 dollars) emergency fund for the governor to use as needed.[24]

Boston, Monday, April 15

It was late in the afternoon when the requisition for Northern troops reached Benjamin Butler of Lowell, the Massachusetts lawyer, nationally prominent Democrat, and brigadier general in the state militia. He was in the middle of a trial in a Boston court. "As I sat at the trial table," Butler remembered, "the order was placed in my hands that the Sixth Regiment of my brigade should report at Faneuil Hall on the morning of the 16th. I arose, and said to the presiding justice:—'I am called to prepare troops to be sent to Washington, and I must ask the court to postpone this case.' This was immediately done, and I left the court house at quarter before five, in time to reach my headquarters at Lowell by the five o'clock train. And that case, so continued, remains unfinished to this day."[25]

Before the war Butler was a decidedly pro-Southern Democrat. He'd supported Jefferson Davis for president the previous year, serving as a delegate to the Democratic National Convention in Charleston and voting for Davis fifty-seven times. The eventual nominee was Stephen Douglas. When the Democrats split along regional lines, Butler stayed with the Southern wing, supporting John C. Breckinridge of Kentucky—then the sitting vice president—for president. Butler ran for Massachusetts governor as a Breckinridge Democrat against John Andrew in 1860, coming in a distant fourth in a four-candidate race, with 6,000 votes compared to 104,000 for Andrew.[26]

Butler, forty-two, was bald and squat. But he was a force of nature. He had a brilliant intellect and a chip on his shoulder. He was relentlessly self-aggrandizing. His book, published in 1892, is dazzling in a lawyerly way but also replete with distortions that enhanced his own role and filled with extended arguments for why he was right in various disputes. He often was. Butler was a master of public relations, rarely missing an opportunity to spin an issue via the newspapers.

He was also by many accounts an effective prewar militia leader. Some of his men, in postwar memoirs, praised his efforts. Like Forbes, Andrew, and others, Butler was certain that war was coming.

He worked to get the Massachusetts troops prepared. "His success in the militia was beyond dispute," wrote Governor Andrew's biographer, Henry Greenleaf Pearson. "His fellow soldiers had elected him to higher and higher rank, and at last to the command of a brigade, which was one of the best in the state."

As a lawyer, Benjamin Butler was feared. This was both "for the things he was able to do and for the things he was willing to do," Pearson wrote. "In short, he gave the world to understand that he held strong cards; but as yet no man knew what his game was."

All these characteristics and more combined to create the first and most notorious of the Civil War's "political generals"—men who obtained their rank because of their civilian influence or because Lincoln, a Republican, desperately needed Democratic support for the war effort. For Governor Andrew personally, Butler would bring "numberless forms of personal and official annoyance."[27]

Throughout Boston and the surrounding towns, regiments were organizing on this Monday. The Sixth—Jones's regiment from the industrial cities of Lowell and Lawrence and surrounding towns—had offered its services in January. Now it had a head start and moved rapidly. Also in action were the Third and Fourth regiments, as well as the Eighth. Slightly behind them was the Fifth.

The Sixth's colonel, Edward Jones, got word of the president's troop call up on the afternoon of the fifteenth while in Boston. Jones, thirty-two, had a barrel chest and black hair and a thick beard and walrus mustache that drooped past the sides of his mouth. (Later in the war, the beard would be gone, and as an old man, the mustache would become much larger, like enormous white plumes extending off his face.) An air of authority and competence radiated through his youthful features. Like the rest of his men, he was not a soldier, having entered the militia full time in January 1861 as commander of the Sixth Regiment. Jones was a businessman from Pepperell, an entrepreneur, the inventor of a kerosene lamp, and the owner of a manufacturing company in Boston that made the lamps. He closed the business when war became certain.[28]

The men of the Sixth Massachusetts—more than seven hundred in all—were factory workers, farmers, mechanics, lawyers, professionals, tradesmen. They were almost all from the north-western suburbs of Boston—four counties and thirty towns in all—just miles from Lexington and Concord, where their great-grandfathers had helped forge a new nation on nearly this same date eighty-six years earlier. Now the regiment was called into service not by clanging church bells and galloping riders, like their ancestors, but through thoroughly modern technologies: the telegraph and the railroad.

"Not only did they leave the plough in the furrow, but business and professional men, without a moment's hesitation, abandoned every prospect and engagement," wrote John Wesley Hanson, the prominent nineteenth century minister and theologian, and briefly a chaplain for the Massachusetts militia. "In the uniforms of privates stood many who had forsaken places of great emolument for a soldier's poor remuneration."[29]

The regiment's second in command, Maj. Benjamin F. Watson, a lawyer, got word late in the afternoon on the fifteenth. "The order reached me at Lawrence at four o'clock in the afternoon and found me professionally engaged in a law-suit," he recalled. "Within an hour's time I was in uniform and on my way to Lowell, reporting there for duty about six o'clock in the evening." Incredibly, over 480 men assembled in the seventeen-hour span since Jones had issued orders to activate.[30]

Other Boston-area regiments also raced to fill out their ranks. But recruiting was random and ad hoc. David K. Wardwell, thirty-seven, a local artisan and Mexican War veteran, received permission from the governor to raise a company. In less than two days, his objective was accomplished. The "Boston Volunteers" would soon become part of the Fifth Massachusetts Regiment.[31]

Rhode Island Raises a Regiment

Ambrose E. Burnside was in New York Monday morning, April 15, at his job as treasurer of the Illinois Central Railroad, a position he'd held since last June. He was anticipating a call from the federal government to all former army officers with West Point educations. Burnside had graduated from the military academy in

1847 and briefly served in Mexico after the war but left the army in 1853. Now thirty-six, Burnside was trim and tall in the spring of 1861, with a round face and friendly eyes, completely bald, with massive, flamboyant whiskers that extended out an inch from his face on each side.

Burnside had experienced ups and downs in his career. After he left the army, he invented a breech-loading rifle and was apparently awarded a ninety-thousand dollar federal contract to produce them, but he refused an attempted bribe, and the War Department changed its plans. Burnside lost control of his patents and was ruined financially.[32] In 1858 he ran for Congress and lost.

Now in New York, he had balanced his railroad's books and prepared for a speedy departure if summoned. The call came from Rhode Island governor William Sprague, who said, "A regiment of Rhode Island troops will go to Washington this week. How much time do you need to come on and take command?" Burnside promptly responded, "One minute!"[33]

Burnside left that night for Providence and reported for duty the next morning, receiving a commission as a colonel of the First Regiment of the Rhode Island Detached Militia. "Colonel Burnside's activity, energy, industry, and military training accomplished wonders," wrote his biographer, Benjamin Perley Poore. Burnside instructed the officers and drilled the enlisted men. His promptness energized not only the regiment but the entire state of Rhode Island. "Every morning, he visited the hospital tent, to see that the sick were properly attended to," Poore wrote. "Every evening he went on the rounds of the camp. The men loved him. They looked up to their commanding officer with a kind of filial affection and devotion." By the end of 1862, Ambrose Burnside would rise up to command of the entire Army of the Potomac.

So it went in tiny Rhode Island, with a population of just 174,000 people in 1860. The state organized a regiment and a battery of artillery within days. It deployed half of that regiment—544 fully equipped troops, including the artillery battery—on Saturday, April 20, with the governor, William Sprague, in overall command. A second detachment of 510 men would leave Providence on April 24.[34]

Pennsylvania's Unarmed Patriots

Like all the Northern states, Pennsylvania was willing to defend the Union, but like most, it was far from able. This was an especially glaring situation for the second-largest state, and one so close to Washington; Philadelphia and Harrisburg were just a few hours away from Washington by train. Help was urgently needed, and Pennsylvania should have delivered it faster than anyone else. But armed and equipped troops were more than Pennsylvania could deliver right now. The secretary of the commonwealth, Eli Slifer, candidly summed up Pennsylvania's situation in a dispatch to Secretary of War Cameron: "Troops will be in Harrisburg in considerable numbers in twenty four hours from now, many of them without uniforms or arms."[35]

When Pennsylvania recruits were issued arms, they got obsolete smoothbore muskets. They didn't get needed equipment and uniforms until May and June.[36]

Nevertheless, Gov. Andrew G. Curtin and his militia commanders recklessly insisted on moving newly formed and unprepared units forward. In the coming days, Pennsylvania would twice deploy unarmed and ununiformed troops out of state and on a separate occasion advance three partially armed but unready regiments from Harrisburg into Maryland—all with humiliating and disastrous consequences. Still, by the end of April, twenty-five regiments had been organized and consolidated at Camp Curtin in Harrisburg.[37]

Lincoln's call for troops reached Pottsville, Pennsylvania—a small city in the foothills of the Appalachians, about fifty-three miles northeast of Harrisburg—at noon on Monday. The town had two active militia companies—the Washington Artillery and the National Light Infantry. That afternoon, the captains in charge, James Wren and Edmund McDonald, telegraphed Governor Curtin to offer their services. They were ordered to deploy immediately, without guns or uniforms or equipment. A flood of men signed up as they prepared to move to Harrisburg.[38]

Three other Pennsylvania companies responded to the initial call. They were the Ringgold Light Artillery of Reading, the Allen

Infantry of Allentown, and the Logan Guards of Lewistown. The real challenge wasn't recruits; it was arms and equipment. The Logan Guards had thirty-four rifles, and only thirty-four of its men had uniforms.

Reading's Ringgold Light Artillery was the best-prepared company of the five. It had been training almost daily since early January and was fully armed and uniformed and mustered 102 men.[39]

Frederick Yeager, a member of the Ringgold company, recalled that the men were on the field, drilling just outside of Reading, when word arrived of Lincoln's call for troops. The company telegraphed Gov. Andrew Curtin: "The Ringgold Light Artillery are on parade. Every one of them expects to be ordered on duty for the U.S. service before they leave their guns."

The secretary of the commonwealth, Eli Slifer, wired back: "Bring your command to Harrisburg by first train. If any of the men need equipments they will be provided here by the general government. Lose no time."[40]

In Philadelphia, Gen. William F. Small of the Pennsylvania Militia was pulling together a newly formed battalion—seven companies from two regiments comprising about one thousand men total. Called the Washington Brigade, it had no uniforms and few arms, but Small had offered the unit's services to Washington repeatedly. Secretary of War Cameron on the fifteenth told Small to send his brigade down—that they'd be accepted if they arrived within a week and would get uniforms and equipment on arrival.

This was a poorly considered decision on both sides. But Washington was virtually undefended, facing the threat of attack from the insurgents, and the government was desperate for troops.[41]

A War Correspondent Heads South

As Northern troops prepared to move toward Washington, William Howard Russell, the correspondent for the *Times* of London, headed south, looking to explore and report from the region that was suddenly at war with the United States. His train left from Portsmouth, Virginia, and the first major stop was at Goldsboro, North Carolina, about 155 miles and six hours from Portsmouth.

Here, the secession tide hit Russell hard. "The station, the hotels, the street through which the rail ran was filled with an excited mob, all carrying arms, with signs here and there of a desire to get up some kind of uniform—flushed faces, wild eyes, screaming mouths, hurrahing for 'Jeff Davis' and 'the Southern Confederacy,' so that the yells overpowered the discordant bands which were busy with 'Dixie's Land,'" Russell wrote. "Here there was the true revolutionary furor in full sway. The men hectored, swore, cheered, and slapped each other on the backs; the women, in their best, waved handkerchiefs and flung down garlands from the windows. All was noise, dust, and patriotism."

Russell's train had happened on a muster of local men called into the service of the Confederacy. "The enthusiasm of the 'citizens' was unbounded, nor was it quite free from a taint of alcohol," Russell wrote. As the train started again, there was renewed yelling, but this time it was different, "a savage cry many notes higher than the most ringing cheer," according to Russell—perhaps describing a proto version of the soon-to-be-famous Rebel Yell.

Russell had dinner at a wayside inn, where the attendants were "comely, well-dressed, clean negresses who were slaves—'worth a thousand dollars each.' I am not favorably impressed by either the food, or the mode of living, or the manners of the company," he declared.[42]

DAY THREE: TUESDAY, APRIL 16

6
--

"Take Washington City Immediately"

The City

Asense of foreboding pervaded Washington. Everyone sensed the dread that hung over the capital. Rumors were rampant. A late-season nor'easter lingered. All locals could do was speculate.

"Rained all night," the diarist Elizabeth Lindsay Lomax wrote. "Reported again last evening that Virginia has seceded, but it is not believed. Events crowd so fast that I cannot relate them in my diary."[1]

"Another rainy day, a continuation of the Easterly Storm," wrote the diarist Horatio Nelson Taft. The public buildings were all guarded, Taft noted, with 150 to 300 men quartered in each. "I was at the 'National' and 'Willards,'" he wrote in his diary. "NY papers scarce, could get only the *Tribune*. Came home about 9, read till 11. Cold wet evening. Everything looks gloomy."[2]

Local militia companies continued to expand. Troops were placed at various points, with artillery posted on the heights and roads leading out of the city. Twenty-five cartloads of cartridges, grape shot (anti-personnel munitions), and other ordnance was taken up Pennsylvania Avenue to be placed near the cannoneers and other soldiers.[3]

Replies from the states to Secretary of War Cameron's troop requisitions continued to pour in. "Our people are willing and anxious to stand by and aid the Administration," wrote Iowa governor Samuel J. Kirkwood. "Nine-tenths of the people here are with you."[4]

But the message that came from Virginia was hostile. "sir: I received your telegram of the 15th, the genuineness of which I doubted," wrote Gov. John Letcher. "The militia of Virginia will not be furnished to the powers at Washington. Your object is to subjugate the Southern States. You have chosen to inaugurate civil war."[5]

Cameron also clarified for some of the states when he wanted their troops. In effect, he was bowing to the reality of unpreparedness. He pushed until late May the anticipated troop arrivals for Michigan, Maine, Wisconsin, Iowa, New Hampshire, and Vermont.[6]

The South

South Carolina governor Francis W. Pickens this Tuesday urged Confederate president Jefferson Davis to seize Washington.

The Confederates had troops ready to go in Charleston, he reasoned. Virginia and Maryland were likely to secede within days. "You see the news from Washington, Richmond and Baltimore," Pickens wrote to Davis. "I have it from Va. & from high authority from my old friends in Maryland that they will both be out of the Union certain. I really do think if Virginia moves as she certainly will, that the true course is to take Washington City immediately, because I think it will spare blood at a more dangerous point in Fortress Munroe."[7]

Pickens, probably in sync with Davis's own thinking, said he'd prefer if Virginia and Maryland took the lead. The Confederates should act if called on by those states, he said. In that case, "it would do our cause no harm."[8]

Pickens didn't address how troops would cross North Carolina or Virginia, which, although deeply hostile to the Union, were both still part of it. But the fact remained that the Confederacy had up to eight thousand men under the command of General Beauregard in Charleston. When would they move north? It was a question of brinksmanship.

If Abraham Lincoln was concerned that Beauregard would be coming for Washington, Beauregard and the Confederates were concerned about the opposite. "I should suggest the possibility, even the probability, that the first attempt of the U.S. authorities will be to retake possession of Charleston Harbor," Confederate adjutant general Samuel Cooper wrote to Beauregard.

And rather than putting five thousand troops on trains headed for Virginia, Beauregard was focused on the minute details of defending Charleston. "The Dahlgren gun of Sullivan's Island and the rifled gun must be put in position at the Vinegar Hill battery," Beauregard wrote in a long note about harbor defenses to his assistant inspector general, Maj. William Whiting.[9]

The Militia Advance

Massachusetts Militia brigadier general Benjamin Butler was on the train to Boston this Tuesday morning. The trip from Butler's home in Lowell was a bit over an hour. Lowell, a fast-growing mill city of thirty-six thousand in 1860, was a planned community at the confluence of the Merrimack and Concord rivers, the largest industrial complex in the United States. Its focus was textiles, and its raw material—cotton—came from the South, which perhaps helped explain Butler's sympathy for the South.

Butler had learned overnight that the War Department was asking for four regiments of militia—a brigade—from Massachusetts and with it, a brigadier general. Butler wanted to be that general, but so did other Massachusetts Militia brigadiers. During his commute, Butler recognized James G. Carney, a lawyer and the president of the Bank of Mutual Redemption, in the same car.[10]

As Butler told it, he took a seat next to Carney. It was a raw, stormy day—the same nor'easter had blown into New England and would sit there for the next few days, bringing gusts of rain and sleet.

The train rattled across northern Massachusetts. Butler was acquainted with the state's finances. He wrote that he knew a $100,000 contingency fund (about $2.9 million in 2020 dollars) to finance the militia had been repealed by the state legislature just the prior week. His contention now was that the state had no money to send troops south.

So he asked Carney if it was possible for the bank to extend credit to the state. And he asked Carney to recommend that he be appointed to lead the new brigade. Carney did write to Gov. John Andrew offering to extend credit, as did many banks and individuals during these first days after Sumter.[11]

After these basic facts it gets murky, as Butler's accounts often do. Butler claims he went to see Andrew, with Carney's letter in his pocket: "The governor received me very kindly and said:— 'General, there is a difficulty; we have two brigadiers in the militia who are your seniors, and one of them, General Peirce, is now outside, I suppose waiting to ask for the detail.' 'Well, Governor,' I said, 'you know Brigadier-General Peirce, and you know me. Isn't this a case where the officer should be appointed who is most instructed in affairs with which he is to deal?' 'I suppose I can detail any brigadier,' said the governor. 'So do I,' said I."

At that point, as happens in Butler's stories, someone bursts in at a most opportune moment, serving to ratchet up the drama. In this instance it's Massachusetts state treasurer Henry K. Oliver, proclaiming that the commonwealth has no money to transport the troops. Andrew will have to call a special session of the legislature to get the necessary funds.

Wait, says Butler, I rode down on the train with the president of the Bank of Mutual Redemption, and he authorized me to say that $50,000 ($1.4 million in 2020 dollars) is at the disposal of the commonwealth. Well then, Butler claims Andrew said, this changes things.[12] Later that day, Butler was assigned to command the brigade.

Butler's story is nonsense, says Andrew's biographer, Henry Greenleaf Pearson. For one thing many banks, as well as influential citizen committees, were offering funds to the government. Then Pearson said, of the six brigadiers in the Massachusetts Militia, Andrew had already narrowed his choice to Peirce or Butler. Peirce held his position mainly because of longevity, Pearson writes, although at thirty-nine, he was three years younger than Butler. "Andrew realized that in point of ability and militia service Butler had a good claim to the appointment," Pearson wrote.

A still better claim was Andrew's calculation that by putting a political opponent, a Democrat who ran for governor against

Andrew just six months earlier, at the head of the state's troops, Massachusetts could demonstrate that all of its citizens stood united. These were the real reasons Andrew assigned the brigade to Butler. "Thus, before the war was two days old, this 'political general' was launched, thanks to Andrew, on his career as a national figure," noted Pearson.

Pearson says Butler's "unashamed" version of this appointment, that he brought the aid of the Boston banks to Andrew and hinted that it would be withdrawn if he were not appointed to the brigade command, was characteristic of Butler, but absurd. "It is not worthwhile to undertake the Augean task [requiring heroic efforts] of disproving the 'facts' of *Butler's Book*," Pearson wrote.[13]

At any rate, on Tuesday morning, April 16, the War Department officially increased Massachusetts's troop allotment to four regiments and added a brigadier general. Two regiments would go to Washington and two to Fort Monroe, at the entrance to the Chesapeake Bay.

Unlike other states, Massachusetts was ready, thanks to Andrew's efforts. When the Massachusetts senator Henry Wilson telegraphed, "Send on 1,500 men at once," the men of the Third, Fourth, Sixth, and Eighth Massachusetts regiments poured into Boston. The Fifth was formed by merging it with the Seventh. "Each day marked a step forward toward the foe," wrote the Fifth's biographer, Alfred Roe. "April 16th saw the ranks complete. The 17th witnessed their departure. The 18th their continued advance. The 19th the shedding of the first blood in Baltimore."[14]

This morning, April 16, the Sixth Regiment mustered in Lowell at 7:00 a.m. It was raining and sleeting hard. Colonel Jones recounted the chaos in a fiftieth anniversary *Boston Globe* article in 1911: "The scene at Huntington Hall [a combined train station and a public meeting facility] that morning was impossible to describe," Jones recalled. "It was a motley assemblage of children, sisters, sweethearts and a general public. 'Fall in' was the order, and while a hasty inspection was being made, the band played 'The Girl I Left Behind Me.'"[15]

When the Sixth Regiment arrived in Boston, at about one o'clock in the afternoon, it was escorted by thousands of people in the pelting rainstorm to Faneuil Hall and then to the Boylston Hall armory, where it quartered for the night.

Boston was filled with Union fervor. The carriages, train cars, cabs, and omnibuses were all bedecked with flags. The Boston Theater became a drill room for incoming soldiers. The dry goods merchant Hogg, Brown & Taylor offered to outfit any clerks who enlisted, pay their salaries while away, and hold their positions for them. Thirteen clerks, unnaturalized Nova Scotians, accepted.

The clothier Leopold Morse offered the governor two hundred pairs of pantaloons for the men. When the Sixth Regiment departed from the Worcester station, the news dealer gave his entire stock of papers to the soldiers.[16]

New York City

One hundred and seventy miles southwest of Boston this Tuesday, the officers of the famous New York Seventh Regiment—the "National Guard" as they called themselves—met at their armory.

The Seventh Regiment's armory building occupied a full city block on Third Avenue between Sixth and Seventh Streets in what's now Manhattan's East Village, across the street from a small park and the Cooper Institute. The three-story, cast-iron-and-brick building had just been completed the prior year, constructed in a partnership between the regiment—which occupied the top two floors—and a consortium of local butchers, which operated the Tompkins Market on the first floor. It was considered the finest armory building in the world.

Forty officers were present for the meeting. Lincoln, they were told, had called for Governor Morgan to send eight hundred men immediately to Washington. General Scott had specifically asked for the Seventh Regiment, which in the spring of 1861 was the most celebrated military unit in the United States, perhaps the entire world.

Members of the Seventh came from New York City's most socially prominent families—the leading entrepreneurs, financiers, and industrialists—plus a sprinkling of bohemians, such as poets, writers, journalists, and painters. Its ranks through the decades were filled with famous New York City names like Vanderbilt, Tiffany, Van Buren, Fish, Gansevoort, Gracie, Schermerhorn, and Hamilton. The regiment had a legacy of excellence and innovation in drilling.

The Seventh was well funded and well equipped, with custom-made and distinctive gray uniforms. It was difficult to get into the regiment, a sign of stature to be a member. It was, essentially, an elite upper-class social club with an emphasis on military activity.

But unlike the vast majority of state militia units in the North in 1861, the New York Seventh was equipped and ready to fight. The assembled officers unanimously adopted a resolution, saying, "This Regiment responds to the call of the country made by the President, and the Regiment is ready to march forthwith."[17]

Marshall Lefferts, the colonel of the Seventh, knew the regiment would likely face combat in the weeks ahead. He was determined to prove this elite unit could do more than march in parades—it would fight.

Lefferts had been the colonel for just a year and a half. He was a trim, youthful man who had just turned forty. He wore his dark hair neatly combed to the side, sideburns extending below his earlobes, and had the kind of bushy walrus mustache that was common to men of the era. In civilian life he was a telegraph-industry executive, currently working as an electrical engineer for the American Telegraph Co. Notably, he was the first telegraph-industry executive to hire female workers. He was a citizen soldier, with a full life outside the military realm.[18]

The men of the Seventh Regiment saw the conflict looming and responded as well as anyone could. The regiment traced its origins back to 1812, but its ascent to fame began with the Astor Place riots of 1849, a multiday rampage in which the Seventh ultimately opened fire on the rioters, killing at least twenty and wounding fifty or sixty more.[19] Over 150 members of the regiment were wounded. None were killed.[20]

It was an age of riots in New York. Social, ethnic, and political tensions constantly bubbled to the surface in a city with widespread inequality and few governmental mechanisms for resolving them. So when riots erupted, the government called out the militia and crushed protests with lethal force.

The Seventh quashed the arsenal riots in 1834, the abolition riots in the same year, the stevedore riots of 1836 and 1852, the flour riots of 1837, the Sixth Ward—or "Dead Rabbits"—riots of 1857, the Quarantine riot of 1858, and the draft riot of 1863.[21]

In 1859, Col. Abram Duryee, forty-three, resigned his commission in the regiment, and the popular Lefferts, at thirty-eight years old, was elected colonel. In October 1860, during the Prince of Wales's visit to the United States, the eighteen-year-old prince told the New York militia commander, Maj. Gen. Charles W. Sandford, "It is the finest regiment I have ever seen in any country."[22]

The Seventh Regiment at the close of 1860 was riding a crest of prosperity. As of January 1, it had an active strength of 895 men, an increase of 97 men from the prior year.[23]

In New York City, the days after the fall of Sumter were memorable. Everyone understood the stakes. "We are living a month of common life every day," wrote the New York lawyer George Templeton Strong, forty-one, whose journal has been described by American Heritage Magazine as the "best diary—in both historic and literary terms—ever written by an American" and "the richest and most informative day-to-day account of American life in the nineteenth century."[24]

"My habit," Strong wrote, "is to despond and find fault, but the attitude of New York and the whole North at this time is magnificent. Perfect unanimity and readiness to make every sacrifice for the support of law and national life. Still, I expect to hear only of disaster for a long while yet."[25]

Throughout this Tuesday, the men of the Seventh passed the time drilling. The regiment ultimately pushed its departure date to Friday, the nineteenth, so its quartermaster could arrange transportation and its men had time to settle their affairs for the month or so they expected to be in the field. That way, too, it could deploy with many more men than if it were to leave on the eighteenth as initially scheduled.[26]

The Seventh wasn't the only New York State Militia regiment now stirring.

On this April 16, the first drill of the season had been ordered for New York's Seventy-First Regiment, a unit smaller in number than the Seventh and not as famous, but drawn from same strata of manor-born young men.

The Seventy-First Regiment met that evening at the state arsenal on Seventh Avenue and Thirty-Fifth Street. Everyone already knew the scheduled drill wasn't going to happen—too much had transpired. Instead, they anticipated some reaction to President Lincoln's call for troops. There were 380 officers and men present and crowds of friends and family. It was hard enough to form up the regiment in the clamor—an actual drill was out of the question.

"The band played patriotic airs, and the audience wildly cheered," wrote Seventy-First Regiment biographer George Edward Lowen. "Finally, when Colonel [Abraham] Vosburgh gave the command, 'Attention!' there was perfect silence. He said that if they were willing to offer their services, he 'would lead them to Washington, and now if you should be called upon to fight for your country and the Union, would you be ready to go?' 'We are ready, Colonel!' 'Aye, Ready now!'"

Vosburgh, thirty-five, regimental colonel for nine years and scion of an old Dutch New York family, thanked his men and told them to stand by for further orders. The regiment was dismissed amid wild enthusiasm, the band playing, and everyone cheering, including the crowds outside the building.[27]

The Seventy-First was deeply rooted in the nativism of the era. "Up to 1840 the American workman was as independent, manly, and well situated a citizen as there was at that time in any land," regimental historian George Lowen wrote. "He had work in plenty, and he did it well. He never dreamed of 'striking,' for he and his employer were friends and neighbors."

"But during the decade of 1840–1850, his good fortune came to an end," Lowen continued. "Hordes of foreign immigrants, fleeing from the distress and famine of their native country, came to this land of promise; and the consequent lowering of wages, causing strong competition for situations, as well as the entry of the 'foreign element' into politics, filled the native American with alarm and indignation."[28]

Like the Seventh, the Seventy-First deployed repeatedly in the 1850s to quell the many riots of that time. The Bowery Boys, the Dead Rabbits, the police, the fire companies were all brawling and killing one another on the Bowery, on Mulberry Street, White Street, Bayard Street, and Mott Street—all streets that still exist—each crying out at their adversaries, "Go at them, boys!"[29]

Also preparing was the Twelfth Regiment. Like the Seventy-First and Seventh, it was based in Manhattan, and like the Seventy-First, it had roots in American nativism. One speaker at the Old Guard Association's annual dinner on April 21, 1894, thirty-three years to the day after the Twelfth left New York for the war, was Col. Richard Henry Savage, a former military officer and an author of popular mystery and adventure books.

"The gates of the United States are in our day open to many undesirable foreigners who have come here to breed internal dissension," Savage said in a toast to the "citizen soldier." "Unrestricted immigration is the curse of our land. In the time when sudden trouble comes, it is to the loyal native-born citizen soldier that we look for protection."[30]

On April 19, New York State Militia major general Charles W. Sandford issued orders to the Twelfth Regiment for immediate service at Washington.[31]

For all the bigotry and nativism, a striking aspect of this moment in the North was how there were no differences in the intensity of the response. Yes, the nativists were ready to defend the Union. Yes, rich fortunate sons were ready. But so were the newest of the newcomers. So were the people at the bottom rung of mid-nineteenth-century urban society.

Free Black men clamored to sign up, only to be told their services weren't being accepted.[32] Irish and Germans, the frequently despised immigrants, surged into the ranks, their whiteness being enough to overcome ethnic and religious differences. One such unit was the New York Sixth Regiment, known as the Governor's Guard. Under the command of Col. Joseph C. Pinckney, the regiment was markedly German, drawn from the Manhattan streets of what was then known as Kleindeutschland, or Little Germany. Over the middle decades of the nineteenth century, Kleindeutschland had grown to cover a major chunk of today's East Village and Lower East Side. Tompkins Square Park, called der Weisse Garten, was the social center, and Avenue B was the main commercial strip.

From these streets came the men of the Sixth Regiment. Pinckney, thirty-nine years old in 1861, was the colonel, and a smattering of non-Germans were listed among the officers, but many of the troops were German. A list of the names of company officers tells the story.

Second Lieutenant, Company A: Sigmund Lowenthal

Captain, Company B: Casper Schneider

First Lieutenant, Company B: George Schaefer

Second Lieutenant, Company B: John Deikhardt

Second Lieutenant, Company C: Jacob Zeiter

Captain, Company D: Nicolaus Muller

First Lieutenant, Company D: John Bauer

Captain, Company E: George Mittnacht

Captain, Company F: Alexander Abelspacher

First Lieutenant, Company F: Edward Steiglitz

Second Lieutenant, Company F: Julius Frankenstein

Second Lieutenant, Company F: Moritz H. Heimerdinger

On this day, Tuesday, April 16, General Sandford ordered the Sixth Regiment forward. New York's Union Defense Committee contributed $4,000 (about $116,000 in 2020 dollars) toward purchasing blankets, clothing, and other necessities, and the officers and their friends also assisted. The state contributed to this fund too, and subsequent to departure the men received new uniforms.[33]

And so, as Civil War became a reality, these new German Americans put their civilian lives aside. Only partially equipped, they joined the men of the Seventh, the Twelfth, and the Seventy-First—and the Massachusetts men too—and boarded trains and steamers bound for Washington, marching without hesitation to the defense of their adopted country.[34]

7
--

Virginia's Decision

The South

V irginia had drifted slowly toward secession for months. The pace accelerated in April. Virginia's psychic and economic ties to the Union frayed all through the secession winter and into the spring. There was only one reason: the pro-slavery sentiment that prevailed in the nation's largest slave state.

After Lincoln's election in November 1860, Virginia governor John Letcher called the state legislature into session to consider public affairs. In particular, Letcher said, the result was "the election of sectional candidates as President and Vice President of the United States, whose principles and views are believed by the Southern States to be in direct hostility to their constitutional rights and interests."[1]

When the legislature convened in January 1861, it established a secession convention. The law called for 152 delegates to be elected on February 4 and for the convention to assemble in Richmond on February 13. The *Richmond Enquirer* was hired to record and publish the proceedings.

The balance of sentiment on secession was initially close to even. About a quarter of the delegates were from the more Unionist part of the state—the portion west of the Blue Ridge Mountains to the Ohio River, the area that is now West Virginia.[2]

Much was at stake. Virginia had a central place in U.S. history. America's sense of self was tied up in Virginia. The first permanent settlement in what became the United States was in Virginia. The British surrendered at Yorktown, ending the Revolutionary War. Seven of the sixteen presidents through 1861—including Washington, Jefferson, Madison, and Monroe—were born in Virginia. John Marshall, the longest-serving chief justice of the Supreme Court, was from Virginia. Virginia represented the original comity between North and South.

It wasn't just Virginia's emotional connection to the Union that was at stake. If the state seceded, it would deprive the North of enormous resources in population, agricultural production, industrial output, and geography. Virginia was a large, influential border state with a diverse economy. So far all the seceded states had been in the Deep South, with agrarian, cotton-based economies.

Virginia was different. It was officially the country's fifth-largest state, with nearly 1.6 million people. It had the most enslaved people of any state—about a third of Virginia's population was in bondage. If only free populations were counted, Virginia would drop to seventh-largest, after New York, Pennsylvania, Ohio, Illinois, Indiana, and Massachusetts.[3]

Virginia ranked first in the South in farm value and acres under cultivation.[4] But its economy was more industrialized than most of the Deep South Confederate states. By the 1840s, Richmond had become the world's largest tobacco manufacturing center, with more than fifty factories. Richmond was a major port city, especially for exports. Flour, tobacco, and wheat were the leading exports in 1860. Richmond's Gallego flour mill was the largest in the world in 1860. By the late 1850s, Virginia had more than 4,800 manufacturing facilities, placing it fifth among the states.

Virginia also had an arms industry large enough to become the foundation of the Confederate war effort. Its Tredegar Iron Works in Richmond was the largest facility of its kind in the South and the third largest in the country, employing about 2,500 men.[5]

At its peak during the war, Tredegar had two mills capable of producing as much as fourteen thousand long tons of iron per year.

It had two gun foundries, an ammunition foundry, boring and gun mills, a locomotive factory, a boiler shop, a brass foundry, and fully equipped machine shops.[6]

The loss of Virginia would increase the likelihood that the Norfolk Navy Yard and Harpers Ferry would need to be evacuated. It would threaten U.S. control of Fort Monroe. The secession of Virginia would add to the growing flood of military and civilian resignations.

Most immediately, it would put an enemy right across the river from Washington, an enemy with the ability to block navigation on the Potomac and bombard the national capital from batteries at Arlington. And then, if Maryland left the Union, the capital of the United States would be surrounded by a hostile power. That alone would have changed the direction of the war.

The secession convention dragged on. White supremacy was persuasive. "What was the reason that induced Georgia to take the step of secession?" asked Henry Benning, a former Georgia Supreme Court justice, in a speech on February 18. Benning was serving as an out-of-state commissioner to the Virginia convention. Georgia's conviction, Benning said, was that separating from the North was the only way to prevent the abolition of slavery in the state. "By the time the north shall have attained the power, the black race will be in a large majority, and then we will have black governors, black legislatures, black juries, black everything," he roared. "Is it to be supposed that the white race will stand for that?"[7]

Lincoln's March 4 inaugural address had contributed to Virginia's drift. The president declared that the Union was perpetual, that secession was illegal, that he would enforce federal laws in all the states, and that he intended to hold and possess U.S. facilities. Lincoln knew Virginia was critical to the dispute. He worked to prevent Virginia's secession, even offering a radical plan in early April to evacuate Fort Sumter if Virginia would permanently adjourn its secession convention.[8]

That plan failed. It was too late.

Lincoln's call for troops on April 15 sealed the outcome. After that, the sentiment in Virginia shifted dramatically. For the next three days, debate focused on just one topic—impending war. "If the decision of the Administration at Washington be true, there is but one course left us to pursue," Robert E. Scott, a delegate from Fauquier County who had voted against secession on April 4, declared on the fifteenth. "This country is about to be plunged into one universal war."

Scott's perspective was widely reflected. "I ask any gentleman what Abraham Lincoln means by summoning 75,000 troops into the field," delegate James B. Dorman of Rockbridge County said on the fifteenth. Dorman had also voted against secession on April 4. "Is there a man in this Commonwealth who will hold himself up as such a fool as to say that he does not understand that it means war and subjugation?"[9]

On this Wednesday, the seventeenth, Dorman was even more direct: "We must fight. And the question is, which side will we take? That side is the South."[10]

And so Virginia voted in a secret session in Richmond on Wednesday, April 17, to secede from the United States. Or, as the language of the secession resolution put it, the vote was to "repeal the ratification of the Constitution of the United States."

The vote was eighty-eight in favor and fifty-five opposed, a surprisingly close tally.[11] An earlier vote on April 4 had rejected secession by eighty-eight to forty-five. The call for troops forced the issue. The decision was subject to a referendum in May.[12]

The text of the Virginia secession ordinance is clear on the motive. Virginia was interested in protecting slavery. It stated, in part,

AN ORDINANCE
To Repeal the ratification of the Constitution of the United States of America, by the State of Virginia, and to resume all the rights and powers granted under said Constitution:

The people of Virginia, in their ratification of the Constitution of the United States of America, adopted by them in Convention, on the 25th day of June, in the year of our Lord one thousand seven hundred and eight-eight, having declared that the powers granted them under the said Constitution were derived from the people of the United States, and might be resumed whensoever the same should be perverted to their injury and oppression, and the Federal Government having perverted said powers, not only to the injury of the people of Virginia, but to the oppression of the Southern slaveholding States.

The ordinance was ratified in referendum by the white men of Virginia on May 23, long after the state had been integrated into the Confederacy.

Losing Virginia was catastrophic for the United States. Virginia was the keystone of the secession movement. It ensured that the Civil War would be much longer than it would have been otherwise. Virginia was the eighth Confederate state to secede. Its exit triggered a second wave of secession, this time in the mid-South. After a two-and-a-half-month lull, Virginia left the Union, followed by Arkansas and North Carolina in May and Tennessee in June.

The vicious words of Henry Benning and the other white men in power in the South in 1861 served as a reminder of why Virginia and the other Confederate states betrayed the Union. They serve as a reminder even today, 162 years later, of the real cause of the Civil War and what was at stake.

More eloquent than Benning's, less hateful, and no less relevant were the words of the enslaved people themselves. These words underscored what was at stake. Hundreds of first-person accounts and memoirs by enslaved people from across the South during the antebellum period tell a grimly consistent story of capricious owners, forced family separations, children sold like livestock, whippings, beatings, rape, humiliation, and degradation.

But there were persistent escapes as well. There was an irrepressible will among the enslaved people to claim some semblance of independence—freedom of mobility, of religious practice, of family structure, and of community. Even then, white owners brutally enforced control. Enslaved people were generally restricted to their plantations unless their work required otherwise, and even then they needed specific permission, in writing, from their masters. In nearly all instances, they were required to be home by 9:00 or 10:00 p.m. Slave patrols—quasi-police organizations made up of white members of the community, often nonslave owners—enforced the rules and were empowered to apprehend and whip enslaved people for violating curfew.

James Lindsay Smith, an enslaved man in Heathville, Virginia (in Northumberland County, close to where the Potomac River meets the Chesapeake Bay), described life in slavery in Virginia. "We were treated like cattle, subject to the slave-holders' brutal treatment and law," he wrote in an autobiography published in 1881.[13]

If caught at slave meetings, religious or otherwise, they were as likely as not to be beaten, arrested, or even killed. Slave patrollers and allied law enforcement officials had wide latitude. "It was part of my business to arrest all slaves and free persons of color, who were collected in crowds at night, and lock them up," wrote a Norfolk, Virginia, constable, John Capheart. "It was also part of my business to take them before the Mayor. I did this without any warrant, and at my own discretion. Next day they were examined and punished. The punishment is flogging. I am one of the men who flog them. They get not exceeding thirty-nine lashes. I am paid fifty cents for every negro I arrest and fifty cents more if I flog him. The price used to be sixty-two and a half cents. I have flogged hundreds."[14]

The enslaved man George Teamoh described an encounter with Capheart. "I was arrested by Capheart—a noted night watch & cunstable [sic]," Teamoh wrote. "He asked for my 'pass.' I told him I lost it; 'then' said he, 'you must go to jail.'" Teamoh convinced Capheart he had smallpox and evaded arrest and flogging.[15] Teamoh escaped to the North before the Civil War and later moved back to Virginia, where he served in the Reconstruction government.[16]

In addition to the Virginia secession on this Wednesday, the Confederates struck the Union in another way. Confederate president Jefferson Davis issued a proclamation offering owners of private vessels the imprimatur of the Confederate States in attacking and capturing vessels of nations at war with the Confederacy. In effect, it sanctioned armed naval privateers.[17]

Elsewhere in the South, the North Carolina governor urged Jefferson Davis to attack Washington, just one day after the South Carolina governor had urged the same thing. "I am in possession of forts, arsenal, etc.," Gov. John W. Ellis wrote. "Come as soon as you choose. We are ready to join you to a man. Strike the blow quickly and Washington will be ours. Answer."[18] Unbelievably, as Ellis wrote this message, North Carolina was still in the Union.

The journalist William Howard Russell had reached Charleston a day earlier—Tuesday, the sixteenth—on his continuing tour of the South. One of the first things he noticed, at about 8:30 p.m., was the deep toll of a bell. "What is that?" he asked. "It's for all the colored people to clear out of the streets and go home. The guard will arrest any who are found out without passes in half an hour."[19]

The next day, near nightfall, Russell was walking to his hotel after an excursion to Fort Sumter. "The evening drove of negroes, male and female, shuffling through the streets in all haste, in order to escape the patrol and the last peal of the curfew bell, swept by me," Russell wrote. "And as I passed the guard-house of the police, one of my friends pointed out the armed sentries pacing up and down before the porch, and the gleam of arms in the room inside. Further on, a squad of mounted horsemen, heavily armed, turned up a by-street, and with jingling spurs and sabres disappeared in the dust and darkness. That is the horse patrol. They scour the country around the city, and meet at certain places during the night to see if the n_____s are all quiet."

"Ah, Fuscus! these are signs of trouble."[20]

"But Fuscus is going to his club," Russell continued. "A kindly, pleasant, chatty, card-playing, cocktail-consuming place. He nods proudly to an old white-wooled negro steward or head-waiter—a slave—as a proof which I cannot accept, with the curfew tolling in my ears, of the excellence of the domestic institution."[21]

The City

In Washington this Wednesday morning, Lucius Chittenden, the incoming register of the treasury, went to the Rugby House, a fashionable hotel on the corner of Fourteenth Street and K Street, to have breakfast with the new treasury secretary, Salmon Chase. Chase spent just a few minutes with Chittenden but then directed him to the office of the assistant secretary, George R. Harrington, to be sworn in. Harrington in turn directed Chittenden to a district judge, who, Chittenden observed, was peevish. Republican-office seekers annoyed him, the judge announced, and he transacted his business in court, not here, at his home. His court opened at eleven o'clock.

I am here, replied Chittenden, at the special request of the treasury secretary. The judge snatched Chittenden's commission, muttering. He scrawled his name on the paper and flung it back at Chittenden. It was, Chittenden said, this particular judge's last act: "He went South the next day. And I saw him no more. My first day of official life was neither cheerful nor satisfactory."[22]

The Advance

Four Pennsylvania militia companies from Lehigh and Schuylkill counties left for Harrisburg this Wednesday morning, the seventeenth. "The day was very cold, raw, and disagreeable; but notwithstanding this, the people flocked in by thousands from all parts of the County and it seemed as if its whole population had been poured forth to witness the departure of our gallant volunteers," the Pottsville *Miners' Journal* reported.[23]

They reached the state capital by the evening, joining the well-equipped Ringgold Light Artillery, which had arrived the night before. The Ringgold unit, led by Capt. James McKnight, had received orders to move to Harrisburg late in the morning of the Sixteenth and immediately embarked on a train for a fifty-five-mile journey.[24] All of these Pennsylvania volunteers were about to receive a glancing blow from a fast-growing hurricane.

Boston

Five militia regiments converged on the Massachusetts capital this Wednesday. It was pandemonium.[25] The men of the Sixth Regiment found their ranks expanded, with companies from Worcester, Boston, and Stoneham added, filling out the unit to over seven hundred men. They also exchanged old smoothbore muskets for modern rifles and were issued overcoats, knapsacks, blankets, and woolen drawers, undershirts, and socks.

At one point in front of the capitol, an enterprising food merchant took advantage of the throngs to sell popcorn. But then the vendor was suddenly seized with patriotic fervor—or guilt—and enlisted on the spot, departing with the regiment that evening for Washington.[26]

By the seventeenth, two short days after Lincoln's call for troops, Massachusetts had assembled and equipped four regiments and was ready to put them into the field. "One regiment starts at 6 by rail for Washington; another to-night, half by propeller [a reference to the ship's propulsion] *Spaulding*, half by steamer *State of Maine*, from Fall River, both direct for Fort Monroe," Governor Andrew wired Secretary of War Cameron on the seventeenth. "Another regiment starts tomorrow by rail for Washington, another within three days. Butler is brigadier. We work as fast as men can be properly equipped and moved."[27]

At noon this Wednesday, the Sixth Regiment had completed its outfitting. Soon after 3:00 p.m. the Fourth Regiment appeared at the capitol, and the scene was repeated. Then the regiment hurried off to take the train to Fall River and a steamer to Fort Monroe. At the end of the day, the Third Regiment was similarly dispatched, marching to the piers to board the *Spaulding*, which then anchored in the harbor for the night before heading south, also to Fort Monroe.[28]

After its break, the Sixth Regiment marched to the Worcester depot—a half mile away on the eastern edge of Boston—with full military honor guards, a fire department escort, and thousands of people lining the route. As bells rung, cannons fired, and the crowds cheered, a twenty-one-car train with two locomotives departed from the depot at about 7:45 p.m., bound for New York.[29]

All across the North, from Maine to Minnesota, every small hamlet and sprawling metropolis reacted the same way, with over-whelming support for the government and the troops.

8
--

The First Defenders

The Advance

I t was before dawn when the Sixth Massachusetts militia regiment arrived in New York City, barely seventy-two hours
after Lincoln's call for troops. The troops arrived at the old
New Haven depot on Twenty-Seventh Street following a 215-mile
overnight ride from Boston.

"The brave fellows left the cars, marched down to Fifth Avenue,
thence to Broadway, through Union Square," noted *Frank Leslie's
Illustrated Newspaper* on April 30. "The streets were lined with a
dense crowd, which cheered them vociferously."

Some companies went to the Astor House—at the corner of
Broadway and Vesey Street, at the south end of City Hall Park—for
breakfast and some sleep. It was the most luxurious hotel in New
York City, and probably the entire country. For a regiment of
mechanics, clerks, and factory workers, staying in a luxury hotel
surrounded by the adulation of tens of thousands of supporters
was a memorable experience.

By 11:30 a.m., after a meal and as much rest as they could get,
the Sixth filed out of their hotels and formed up on Broadway,
heading three blocks south for Cortlandt Street and the ferry to
New Jersey.[1]

New York was ablaze. John A. Dix—the former U.S. senator from
New York and future governor—who'd just finished up a seven-
week stint as President Buchanan's last secretary of the treasury,
remembered the Sixth Massachusetts' departure that morning.

Never to my dying day shall I forget the scene. A regiment
had arrived from Massachusetts. They came in at night. By
nine o'clock in the morning an immense crowd had assembled. Broadway, from Barclay to Fulton Street, and the lower
end of Park Row, were occupied by a dense mass of human
beings, all watching the front entrance, at which the regiment was to file out. It was a dead, deep hush. At last a low
murmur was heard; the soldiers appeared, their leading files
descending the steps. By the twinkle of their bayonets above
the heads of the crowd their course could be traced. Formed,
at last, in column, they stood, the band at the head; and the word
was given, "March!"

Still dead silence prevailed. Then the drums rolled out the
time—the regiment was in motion. And then the band, bursting
into full volume, struck up—what other tune could the Massachusetts men have chosen?—"Yankee Doodle."

I caught about two bars and a half of the old music. Instantly
there arose a sound such as many a man never heard in his life
and never will hear more than once in a lifetime. One terrific
roar burst from the multitude, leaving nothing audible. We saw
the heads of armed men, the gleam of their weapons, the regimental colors, all moving on, pageant-like; but naught could
we hear save that hoarse, heavy surge—one general acclaim,
one wild shout of joy and hope, one endless cheer, rolling up
and down, from side to side, above, below, to right, to left: the
voice of approval, of consent, of unity in act and will.

No one who saw and heard could doubt how New York was
going.[2]

After a brief ferry ride across the North River to the intermodal
depot in Jersey City, the Sixth Regiment boarded a train for Philadelphia, arriving in early evening. The enlisted men were barracked

in the Girard House on Chestnut Street, and the officers were at the Continental Hotel across the street.[3]

The welcome in Philadelphia was as overwhelming as it was in Jersey City, New York, and Boston the prior two days. But the mood was about to turn hostile.

Sixth Regiment major Benjamin F. Watson, in a speech twenty-five years later, described the difference between arriving and leaving Philadelphia.

> At sunset of the 18th, Philadelphia was reached, and amid the shouts of the people, the display of fireworks, and the booming of cannon, the Sixth made its way to the Girard House through streets [that were] thronged.
>
> Local residents rushed into the ranks, threw their arms around the men and emptied their pockets for the soldiers. It was late in the evening before the soldiers wrapped themselves in their blankets and lay down on the floors of the hotel. The rest didn't last long. At about one o'clock in the morning, the Regiment was roused and silently marched through what seemed miles of deserted streets to the train station, where the Philadelphia, Wilmington and Baltimore Railroad would take them south.
>
> The delusion that military service was a grand picnic was at an end. In place of enthusiastic crowds we saw empty streets. The occasional form of a night watchman afforded relief to the all-pervading loneliness.[4]

From Philadelphia, the Massachusetts troops would transit to Baltimore, one hundred miles to the southwest. The PWB railroad's president, Samuel Felton, was focused on assessing secessionist hostility south of the Susquehanna. Maryland was a slave state, likely to be unsympathetic to Northern troop movements. But it was difficult to know in advance how volatile things were on the ground.

Secession sympathizers viewed the administration's call for troops as unconstitutional subjugation. They saw the troops as a lawless invasion. Maryland's white population perceived the same aggression as the states to the South. The secessionists in Maryland had full sway.

On the eighteenth, the first direct evidence of this sentiment began to appear. Baltimore authorities pressured the railroad executives for information on Northern troops. One exchange was between the secessionist Baltimore police chief, Mar. George P. Kane, and Felton's Baltimore railroad agent. The chief probed for information—and made a subtle threat.

Baltimore, April 16, 1861.

Mr. Wm. Crawford:

Dear Sir: Is it true as stated that an attempt will be made to pass the volunteers from New York intended to war upon the South over your road to-day? It is important that we have an explicit understanding on the subject.

Your friend,

GEO P KANE.
April 16, 1861

Crawford passed the exchange on to his boss, PWB president Samuel Felton.

Dear Sir: The above is from our marshal of police. I have replied that I have no knowledge of anything of the kind. It is rumored that the marshal has issued orders to his force not to permit any [Northern troops] to pass through the city.

Yours truly,

WM. CRAWFORD.[5]

Felton, in turn, passed the exchange on to the secretary of war, Simon Cameron, who responded with a message to Maryland governor Thomas H. Hicks that came with a warning of its own: "The President is informed that threats are made and measures taken by unlawful combinations of misguided citizens of Maryland to prevent by force the transit of U.S. troops across Maryland,"

Cameron wrote. "The President thinks it is his duty to make it known to you so that all may be warned. It would be as agreeable to the President as it would be to yourself that it should be prevented or overcome by the loyal authorities and citizens of Maryland rather than averted by other means."[6] In Baltimore, it was becoming easy to find "unlawful combinations of misguided citizens." Since Lincoln's call for troops on Monday, the city had become a secessionist cauldron.

Crowds would flock daily to the rival newspaper offices—the Unionist *American* and the Southern-leaning *Sun*. The offices were located directly across from each other. The papers would publish extra editions throughout the day when big news was breaking and pin them to a post on the sidewalk. Fights between Unionists and secessionists broke out regularly in front of the newspaper offices.

By the eighteenth it was getting tougher for Baltimore's 398-man police force, each of whom was equipped with a sidearm, to maintain order as they raced from incident to incident all day.[7]

Around noon on the eighteenth, secessionists raised the Confederate flag on Federal Hill—the fifty-foot promontory just south of the inner harbor—in celebration of the secession of Virginia the day before.

Upward of two thousand persons had gathered. The police moved in and broke up the crowd. Elsewhere in the city "another large Confederate flag was hoisted about 4 p.m. at the intersection of Greenmount Avenue and Charles Street, and saluted with one hundred guns," wrote the Maryland historian J. Thomas Scharf.[8]

South from Harrisburg

At precisely the same time the Sixth Massachusetts Regiment was clattering across New Jersey this Thursday morning, five Pennsylvania militia companies were on another railroad rolling directly south toward Baltimore from Harrisburg.

These independent companies—476 men from Reading, Allentown, and the Appalachian towns of Lewistown and Pottsville—hadn't even had time to organize into a regiment. Reading's Ringgold Light

Artillery was equipped and in uniform. The other four companies
were mostly unarmed and without uniforms.

They'd converged at Harrisburg the night before and left that
city together at 9:00 a.m. this morning. They were joined for the
seventy-five-mile train ride by a detachment of more than fifty
U.S. troops coming from St. Paul, Minnesota, on their way to
Fort McHenry.[9]

When the Pennsylvania troops arrived in Baltimore at 2:00 p.m.,
they walked straight into a seething city. A crowd of about seven
hundred Southern sympathizers was already waiting. The Pennsylvanians disembarked at Baltimore's Bolton Street station, a sprawling multistory structure with six tracks, gabled windows, and a
large outdoor roundhouse.

A column formed as the troops left the train. The U.S. regulars
were first, followed by Lewistown's Logan Guards, only some of
whom were armed with Springfield muskets and in uniform. Then
came the Allentown company and the two companies from Pottsville. Finally, the fully armed Ringgold Light Artillery from Reading brought up the rear.[10] These troops came to be known as the
"First Defenders."

The column was escorted on both sides by files of Baltimore
police during the 1.8-mile march to the Mount Clare station.[11]
They were harassed the whole way—shoved, jostled, jeered,
pelted with rocks. Still, on this day the violence didn't spiral out
of control. Police marshal George Kane, who two days before had
sent the veiled threat to the railroad agent, fulfilled his municipal obligations.

The crowd directed its invective at the Pennsylvanians, leaving
the uniformed U.S. regulars alone. The two sides had mutually
hostile perspectives. The militia "presented as hard-looking spec-
imens of humanity as could be found anywhere," reported the
Baltimore Sun.[12]

"With the exception of the regulars and the company from Reading, they were a lean, ragged, filthy and hungry-looking crowd,
and their general appearance suggested that a major portion of

them volunteered for the purpose of procuring something to eat and a new suit of clothes," reported the *Daily Exchange*.[13]

On the other hand, the Pennsylvanians described the Baltimore mob as "roughs and toughs, longshoremen, gamblers, floaters, idlers, red-hot secessionists, as well as men ordinarily sober and steady."[14]

Things got especially hot as the troops marched passed the Howard House Hotel at the corner of Baltimore Street and Howard Street, a section of mostly three- and four-story brick buildings, still nearly a mile from the station. The mob had increased in size to several thousand.[15]

The crowd spat on the troops. They pulled the tails of the recruits' coats. Taunts flew: "Let the police go and we'll lick you." "Wait till you see Jeff Davis." "We'll see you before long." "You'll never go back to Pennsylvania."[16]

But the police were ready, and the troops got through without any major escalation. Several men were severely injured, incapable of duty for weeks. Pvt. David Jacobs of the Allen Infantry had his teeth knocked out when he was hit with a brick. He fell down from the blow and broke his left wrist. Pvt. Wilson Derr, of the same unit, was hit in the ear with a brick and permanently lost his hearing. But Derr "returned the compliment to his assailant by striking him with the butt end of his gun, which tore off the latter's ear."[17]

Another badly injured man was hit in the head by a brick, knocked to the ground, and cut so deeply that the bone was exposed. He was Nick Biddle, a sixty-five-year-old escaped slave who'd befriended the men of Pottsville's Washington Artillery years earlier. Officially, Biddle was an orderly serving the company captain, James Wren. But Biddle drilled with the Washington Artillery and wore its uniform. He was decades older than the other soldiers, and he was Black—an easy target for secessionists and racists. "N____r in uniform!" they screamed at Biddle, faces contorted with hate. "And poor old Nick had to take it," Wren remembered.[18]

Biddle survived the march through Baltimore. But the ugly memories never faded. He won recognition for the rest of his life as the person who shed the first blood in a hostile situation during the Civil War, but he was often heard to remark that he'd "go through the infernal regions with the artillery, but would never again go through Baltimore."[19]

At Mount Clare fifteen freight cars, modified to add seats, were ready to take the soldiers to Washington. The train departed late in the afternoon, arriving in the capital at 7:00 that evening.[20] No one had yet been killed.

The next day, President Lincoln and Secretary of State Seward visited the Pennsylvania companies at their temporary quarters in the Capitol. "I did not come here to make a speech," Lincoln told the men, including Biddle. "The time for speechmaking has gone by, the time for action is at hand. I have come here to give you a warm welcome to the city of Washington, and to shake hands with every officer and soldier in your company, providing you grant me the privilege."

Biddle, whose head was wrapped in bloody bandages, must have been of particular interest for Lincoln, given his age and the severity of his wound. Biddle declined Lincoln's suggestion that he seek additional medical attention, preferring to stay with his fellow soldiers.[21]

Nick Biddle's portrait was displayed in a place of honor at the company's headquarters for decades after the war, well into the twentieth century. "Negro slavery was the cause of the war, and the first blood shed in it was that of a negro in the streets of Baltimore," wrote John H. Bishop and James Archbald Jr. in a history of the company.[22]

The Baltimore Insurrection

Even after the Pennsylvania troops departed, this volatile day in Baltimore was far from over. Gov. Thomas Hicks had arrived in Baltimore the prior afternoon and today, sensing the undercurrent of rage, issued a proclamation attempting to calm the situation. It urged people to abstain from controversy, obey the laws, and keep the peace. It also, importantly, held open the possibility of secession and promised the power of the state would be used to "maintain the honor of Maryland."

"I assure the people that no troops will be sent from Maryland, unless it may be for the defense of the national capital," Hicks said. An upcoming special election for members of Congress would give people of the state the opportunity to express support for the Union or a desire to see it broken up, Hicks added.

Baltimore mayor George W. Brown seconded Hicks with a proclamation of his own, as both officials tried to balance the need to maintain order with the dangerous secessionist surge. In effect, they sided neither with the Northern states nor with their fellow Southern slaveholding states.[23]

Crowds of people roamed the city looking for trouble. Southern sympathizers converged that evening for a "monster" states-rights rally, the second of the day.[24]

Both rallies were held at Taylor Hall on Fayette Street, just off Monument Square in Baltimore's center city. The three-story structure, a social club for well-to-do, Southern-leaning city residents, had been a secessionist focal point for months. The powerful men of the city met inside, passing several resolutions, among them

opposition to Lincoln's stated objective—to use troops to recapture forts in the South;

opposition to garrisoning forts in the South with militia from the "free states";

opposition to massing federal troops in Washington—that, in the view of the convention, was "uncalled for by any public danger or exigency, is a menace to the State of Maryland, and an insult to her loyalty and good faith"; and

a call for "all good citizens to unite and present an unbroken front in the preservation and defense of our interests, to avert the horrors of civil war, and to repel, if need be, any invader who may come to establish a military despotism over us."

Of course, repelling "invaders" and averting civil war were opposing objectives, and the resolutions, once distributed, did what they were probably intended to do in the first place, which was to inflame the moment.[25]

Five Pennsylvania companies had just passed through Baltimore. Just now the Sixth Massachusetts was resting at its hotels in Philadelphia. And heading right into this tinderbox.

9

Washington Prepares for the Worst

The City

Washington was adjusting to a state of war. It was reeling from Virginia's secession. A hostile foreign power was now literally at its doorstep to the south. Maryland, teetering on secession, surrounded it to the north. No one could say for sure what might happen next. Everyone was certain an attack was coming.

Secessionist resignations from the military and federal civilian workforce were increasing. The government departments began to grapple with loyalty oaths. Military authorities in the city stepped up their activities, increasing patrols and building breastworks around the government buildings.

But Washington hadn't yet assumed the characteristics of a city in the dangerous path of armies. Five days after the surrender of Sumter and three days after President Lincoln's call for seventy-five thousand troops, the hotels were still packed.

April 18 was seasonably cool in Washington, but not cold. The temperature was in the high thirties during the night but climbed as high as seventy degrees by 6:00 p.m. "Cool pleasant day, fire comfortable," the diarist Horatio Nelson Taft wrote. "Business in the office goes on as usual and is increasing this month. It does not seem to be much affected by the excitement in the City."

As the Massachusetts and Pennsylvania troops advanced, the main rumor circulating in the capital this Thursday was that Virginia had seceded and seized Harpers Ferry and the Norfolk Navy Yard. "Soldiers are arriving from the North tonight and an attack is expected upon the City from Virginia," Taft said.[1]

Arriving to work at the Treasury Department the morning of the eighteenth, Department Register Lucius Chittenden found himself confronted by two clerks resigning to join the Confederate government in Montgomery. The clerks wanted Chittenden to sign off on their pay for the first two weeks of the month. Wait, Chittenden said. "Doesn't a deserter always forfeit any pay otherwise due him?"

Chittenden's clerk told him it was customary for resigning staff to get paid. This didn't sit right with Chittenden. Why should disloyal employees be asking for, much less get, a final payment? Chittenden told them he would not pay them without a direct order from the treasury secretary. "The injured clerks were filled with indignation," he wrote.

No sooner had the two secessionist clerks departed than the department's senior staff was called to Assistant Treasury Secretary George Harrington's office for a 2:00 p.m. meeting. Secretary Chase, Harrington told the team, wanted their views on the defense of the Treasury Department. Francis E. Spinner, the treasurer of the United States, spoke first.[2]

"I am for defending the Treasury," Spinner said. "But first I would put it into a condition to be defended." Disloyal workers needed to be cleaned out. "I don't wish to have men around me who require watching," Spinner continued.

Next, an all-hands meeting of clerks and messengers in each division was called for 4:00 p.m. The workforce was put to the test. Each employee was asked to sign a pledge: "I will defend the Treasury, under the orders of the officer in charge of it, against all its enemies, to the best of my ability."

"This was not received with enthusiasm," Chittenden wrote. Excuses flew. One clerk had a sick wife. Another was surrounded by secessionist neighbors. A third belonged to a family where heart palpitations were hereditary—brought on by any sudden shock.

In the end, Chittenden said, it fell to an old Southerner to put them all to shame. He was Francis Lowndes from Carolina, who had been at the department almost fifty years. "'I never fired a gun in my life,' the old Southern clerk said. 'I couldn't hit the side of a barn, and I have no doubt I am a coward. But as long as the star-spangled banner waves, I have something to live for.'" He grabbed the pen and became the first to sign. All but two or three of the others followed.[3]

At the War Department, just across from the White House, word was pouring in for the third straight day from Northern governors. From Ohio, Governor Dennison reported that his first two regiments would leave Dayton at 3:30 the next morning, bound for Pittsburgh and then Washington. In Providence, Governor Sprague reported that Rhode Island's troops were leaving in detachments that day, "one thousand men fully armed and equipped."[4]

Encouragement poured in, but not men. It increased the apprehension that a Southern assault was coming. "It is now leaked out that Virginia seceded on Tuesday, secretly," Cdr. John Dahlgren, second in command at the Washington Navy Yard, wrote in his journal.[5] "It is rumored that the Norfolk Yard and Harpers Ferry have been seized. Everyone believes, too, that a body of men are on the way to take Washington, and the alarm is intense. There are but 1,000 United States troops here, and 1,200 to 1,600 District volunteers. No troops have arrived from the North, though they have talked prodigiously. In the evening the railroad brought 600 or 700 men in poor order [the five Pennsylvania companies]. This was the critical night, and the chance for the South."[6]

As Lincoln and others went about their business this Thursday, Col. Charles P. Stone, inspector general of the Washington militia, was busy securing the city.

Stone, thirty-six, a West Point graduate, Mexican War veteran, and native of Massachusetts, had been appointed on January 1 to the rank of colonel. His job was to organize the local city militia into an effective force. "These people have no rallying-point," General Scott had told Stone. "Make yourself that rallying point." Since then, he'd been drilling the militia troops, recruiting more of them, and weeding out the pro-Southern disloyal elements.

On January 2, for example, Stone had met with the captain of the local National Rifles company, Frank B. Schaeffer, and complimented him on the unit's drill expertise. "'Yes, it is a good company,' Schaeffer said, 'and I suppose I shall soon have to lead it to the banks of the Susquehanna!' 'Why so?'" Stone asked. "'Why! To guard the frontier of Maryland and help keep the Yankees from coming down to coerce the South!'"

Schaeffer didn't know that Stone had just been appointed to command all the militia units in the capital. "I said to him quietly that I thought it very imprudent in him, an employee of the Department of the Interior and captain of a company of District of Columbia volunteers, to use such expressions," Stone wrote. "He replied that most of his men were Marylanders, and would have to defend Maryland."[7]

As part of his review of the district militias, Stone had learned that Schaeffer's company stood out not just for its openly secessionist views but also for its rich supply of equipment. Schaeffer was in the process of stockpiling small arms and artillery and was pushing to create an independent command for himself, with rifles, cannons, and handguns stored in his armory. He had also received a commission of major, by order of President Buchanan. Stone pressed Buchanan's secretary of war, Joseph Holt, to have all promotions and commissions to officers delivered through him.[8]

When Schaeffer came in to formally receive his promotion, Stone asked that he take the customary oath. "He hesitated," Stone wrote, "and said slowly: 'In ordinary times I would not mind taking it, but in these times . . .'

'Ah!' said I, 'you decline to accept your commission of major. Very well!' and I returned his commission to the drawer and locked it in. 'Oh, no, I want the commission.'

'But sir, you cannot have it. Do you suppose that, in these times, which are not, as you say, "ordinary times," I would think of delivering a commission of field-officer to a man who hesitates about taking the oath of office? More than that, I now inform you that you hold no office in the District of Columbia volunteers.'"

And so Captain Schaeffer left the National Rifles and with him, the secessionist members of his company.[9]

That was in January. Now, in April, Stone was a high-energy commander on the go. Trim with straight dark hair worn long over his ears and a Vandyke beard sprinkled with gray hair, he would catch snatches of sleep during all-night carriage inspections of the district.

Stone's militia companies had proliferated. A call was made to the Association of the Soldiers of the War of 1812 of the District of Columbia to convene at city hall the following Monday. War of 1812 veterans would have been in their early seventies in 1861.[10] By the last week of April, he had thirty companies—perhaps two thousand men—to guard the capital before the Northern troops began arriving.[11]

Stone was concerned about the security of the major avenues and the approaches to the city from the Potomac River. About five hundred men, consisting of infantry, artillery and cavalry, were stationed at the Long Bridge—which connected the city at the foot of Maryland Avenue to Alexandria, Virginia. All roads to the city were closely watched. Washington Mayor James G. Berrett issued a proclamation exhorting "all good citizens and sojourners to be careful to so conduct themselves as neither by word nor deed to give occasion for any breach of the peace."

Assessing the DC Volunteers

Not everyone was impressed with the DC militia. The journalist Henry Villard described a "motley" of small units and doubted much reliance could be placed in them. An underwhelmed William Howard Russell's observation was biting. "I had seen an assemblage of men doing a goose-step march dressed in blue tunics and gray trousers, who were, I am told, the District of Columbia volunteers and militia," he wrote. "They did not give any appearance of military efficiency. Starved, washed-out creatures most of them, interpolated with Irish and flat-footed, stumpy Germans."[12]

But Colonel Stone viewed the DC volunteer companies as excellent. "I have never found," he wrote, "among new troops, a finer spirit than was exhibited by those District of Columbia volunteers. They uncomplainingly performed arduous duty to which they were, of course, quite unaccustomed."[13]

Colonel Lee Resigns

On this same day, April 18, 1861, Col. Robert E. Lee—fifty-four years old this April, with a full head of still-black hair and clean-shaven except for a jet-black mustache—met in Washington with Francis P. Blair Sr. and separately with General Scott at Scott's headquarters on Pennsylvania Avenue, across Seventeenth street from the War Department.[14]

Both sides were suddenly interested in Lee. After thirty-two years in the U.S. Army, Lee had been relieved of command of the Second Calvary, based at Fort Mason, Texas, on February 4, and summoned back to Washington. General Scott had been waging a weeks-long campaign to keep his fellow Virginian in the U.S. Army—it was likely the reason he was called back to Washington.[15]

While in Washington, Lee had been promoted to colonel on March 28, barely three weeks before today's date, April 18, and assigned command of the First Cavalry, a duty he never assumed.[16]

The Confederates also wanted Lee. On March 15, he'd been offered a generalship in the Confederate Army by Confederate secretary of war Leroy Walker.[17]

The first of Lee's two meetings this Thursday was with Francis Blair at Blair's townhouse across the street from the War Department. Blair—an influential editor, political leader, and Lincoln advisor whose son, Montgomery, was Lincoln's postmaster general—informally offered Lee command of the U.S. Army.

A large army was going to be raised, and the president had authorized Blair to offer it to Lee, Blair said. Suddenly, command of an army of seventy-five thousand men—an unprecedented number—was Lee's for the taking. It was, as Lee's Pulitzer

Prize–winning biographer, Douglas Southall Freeman, noted, the supreme ambition of any soldier.

Lee turned Blair down. In an 1868 letter to Reverdy Johnson, a U.S. senator from Maryland and a former U.S. attorney general (who'd served an earlier term in the senate as well, in the 1840s), Lee explained his thinking: "I declined the offer, stating as candidly and as courteously as I could, that though opposed to secession and deprecating war, I could take no part in an invasion of the Southern States."[18]

Lee immediately crossed the street to see General Scott. He told Scott that Blair had offered him command of the army and that he had declined.[19]

Col. Edward Davis Townsend, an assistant to Scott in the adjutant general's office, described the meeting between Lee and Scott in close to word-for-word detail. Scott, Townsend wrote, had decided it was time for Lee to show his hand. Scott's office was the front room of the second story of the War Department building, overlooking Pennsylvania Avenue and the Blair house across the street, which Lee had just left. Scott had a round table in the center of the room, and Townsend had a desk in one corner. Other staff was in an adjoining room.

> When Lee came in I was alone in the room with the general, and the door to the aides' room was closed. I quietly arose, keeping my eye on the general, for it seemed probable he might wish to be alone with Lee. He, however, secretly motioned me to keep my seat, and I sat down without Lee having a chance to notice that I had risen.
>
> The following conversation, as nearly as I can remember, took place:
>
> General Scott. "You are at present on leave of absence, Colonel Lee?"
>
> Colonel Lee. "Yes, general, I am staying with my family at Arlington."
>
> General Scott: "These are times when every officer in the United States service should fully determine what course he

will pursue, and frankly declare it. No one should continue in government employ without being actively engaged." (No response from Lee.)

General Scott (after a pause). "Some of the Southern officers are resigning, possibly with the intention of taking part with their States. They make a fatal mistake. The contest may be long and severe, but eventually the issue must be in favor of the Union." (Another pause, and no reply from Lee.)

General Scott (seeing evidently that Lee showed no disposition to declare himself loyal, or even in doubt). "I suppose you will go with the rest. If you purpose to resign, it is proper you should do so at once; your present attitude is an equivocal one."

Colonel Lee. "General, the property belonging to my children, all they possess, lies in Virginia. They will be ruined if they do not go with their State. I can not raise my hand against my children."

The general then signified that he had nothing further to say, and Colonel Lee withdrew.[20]

Townsend's account is as close to a verbatim description of the meeting as there is, but Douglas Freeman, the Lee biographer mentioned previously, argues it's flawed. First it was written, apparently from memory, twenty-three years after the event. It gets the date wrong. Townsend says the meeting was on the nineteenth, but it occurred on the eighteenth. It quotes Scott and Lee saying Lee was on a leave of absence, which he was not.[21] It omits any reference to the meeting with Blair, which took place immediately prior to the one with Scott.

What's more, Freeman claims, Lee would never have said his children "will be ruined if I do not go with their state."[22] But Freeman gets the quote from Townsend wrong. And a 2021 biography of Lee by the historian Allen C. Guelzo argues that family stability was key to understanding what motivated Lee. Lee had a fraught relationship with his father, who squandered the family's wealth and abandoned his wife and children. This trauma, Guelzo argues, caused Robert to value stability and security.[23]

In any event, Lee took Scott's admonishment about equivocation to heart. After midnight in the early hours of Saturday, April 20, he wrote to Cameron:

Sir:

I have the honor to tender the resignation of my commission as Colonel of the 1st Regt. of Cavalry.

Very resp'y

Your Obedient Servant.
R. E. Lee
Col 1st Cav'y.[24]

Lee wrote a longer, seemingly heartfelt letter to Scott that same day. He wrote, in part, "Since my interview with you on the 18th inst. I have felt that I ought no longer to retain my commission in the Army. To no one, General, have I been as much indebted as to yourself for uniform kindness and consideration. Save in defense of my native State, I never desire again to draw my sword."[25]

Both contemporaneous and modern observers have pointed out the disingenuous nature of that last sentence. Lee became commander of the armies of a would-be nation, an aggressive entity that sought to maintain a system of human slavery across eleven states—not just his native Virginia. His army was responsible for the deaths of tens of thousands of loyal Americans well beyond Virginia's borders. The residents of southern Pennsylvania would point out that Lee's 1863 invasion of their state was not in defense of Virginia.

Before Lee's resignation had even been officially accepted or taken effect, he had gone to Richmond, was named by Gov. John Letcher to command the Virginia forces, and on April 23, was officially appointed to the post by the secession convention.[26] Lee did this, Nicolay and Hay note, "with all his military obligations to the United States intact and uncancelled; thus rendering himself guilty of desertion and treason. In the course of events, we find him not alone defending his native State, to which he owed

nothing, but seeking to destroy the Union, which had done everything for him."[27]

In contrast to Lee, Nicolay and Hay suggest, was the example
of Scott. When a committee led by the prominent Petersburg,
Virginia, politician and judge John Robertson visited with Scott
in Washington on April 20, probing whether he'd resign and join
the Confederates, Scott dismissed them with a wave of the hand:
"Friend Robertson, go no farther. It is best that we part here before
you compel me to resent a mortal insult."[28]

The South

The *New Orleans Picayune*, reporting this day on the Virginia
secession, predicted that "the first fruits will be the removal of
Lincoln and his Cabinet and whatever he can carry away, to the
safer neighborhood of Harrisburg or Cincinnati—perhaps to Buffalo or Cleveland."[29]

In the Shenandoah Valley–city of Winchester, Virginia, recruits
poured in. "All day long they continued to come until the population was more than doubled," wrote the author Virginia Mason.
"Some brought shot-guns, others had pocket pistols, the majority were without arms of any kind. Words fail to describe the tension when, soon after midday, a long and crowded train steamed
off carrying sons, brothers, and husbands and the people realized
that war had begun."[30]

In Charleston, General Beauregard was hard at work repairing Fort Sumter and repurposing the artillery batteries to defend
against an attack that the Confederates suspected was coming.
William Howard Russell—the war correspondent for the *Times*
of London, now in Charleston—visited Beauregard this Thursday
evening. "He was busy with papers, orderlies, and despatches, and
the outer room was crowded with officers," Russell wrote. "His present task, he told me, was to put Sumter in a state of defence, as 'the
North in its madness' might attempt a naval attack on Charleston."[31]

Beauregard's focus was absolute. There was no mention of taking his Charleston command north. "The General is a small, com-
pact man, about thirty-six years of age, with a quick, and intelligent

eye and action, and a good deal of the Frenchman in his manner and look," Russell wrote. Two vases filled with flowers rested on his desk, flanking his maps and plans. "A little hand bouquet of roses, geraniums, and scented flowers lay on a letter which he was writing as I came in, by way of paper weight."[32]

Russell was still haunted by the banal evil of slavery. "On my way home again, I saw the sentries on their march, the mounted patrols starting on their ride, and other evidences that though the slaves are 'the happiest and most contented race in the world, they require to be taken care of like less favored mortals,'" Russell wrote. "The city watch-house is filled every night with slaves, whenever they are found out after nine o'clock, p.m. without special passes or permits."[33]

10

Indecision at the Navy Yard
and Harpers Ferry Is Lost

I n the days leading up to the attack on Fort Sumter, the vulnerability of critical Union assets increasingly alarmed the federal
government. In addition to Washington, one was the Gosport
Navy Yard. Named after a village near the Virginia city of Norfolk
at the mouth of the Chesapeake Bay, it was also commonly referred
to as the Norfolk Navy Yard. The facility was about two hundred
miles southeast of Washington and twelve miles up the Elizabeth
River, which flowed north into the bay. Another was Harpers Ferry,
fifty-five miles northwest of Washington at the confluence of the
Potomac and Shenandoah rivers. Harpers Ferry was a critical rail
and river-transportation hub leading west to the Ohio River and
beyond, as well as south to the fertile Virginia breadbasket in the
Shenandoah Valley. For its part, the Chesapeake Bay was among
the most important geographic features in the country, providing direct access from the ocean to Norfolk, Richmond, Washington, Annapolis, and Baltimore—even into interior Pennsylvania.

Fifteen miles directly west of the bay's mouth was Fort Monroe,
an important army post guarding the approaches to the entire
Chesapeake and the tidewater rivers, including the James, York,
Rappahannock, and Potomac. Control of Fort Monroe meant control of the bay and access to the rivers.

The Navy Yard itself was on a wide, flat plain on the western
bank of the Elizabeth, south of the namesake village—a collection

of dingy wooden houses with narrow, crooked, and poorly paved streets. Large billboards advertised tobacco and oyster sellers, and the occasional church steeple rose above the rooflines. The navy yard shared the river with commercial businesses. A fleet of oyster boats plied the waters and anchored nearby. The smell of fish permeated the air.[1]

The Norfolk yard was a massive facility, the U.S. Navy's largest and most important shipyard. Its value wasn't just the ships or the strategic location. It was the facility itself. Gosport's shipbuilding capacity was unrivalled. Two massive triangular ship-construction houses dominated the riverfront. Workshops, paint stores, machine and boiler shops, and foundries served both sailing vessels and steam-powered ships during this transition from sail to steam. Gosport had sawmills, carpenter's shops, and rigging facilities. Most importantly, it had a massive granite dry dock that could accommodate any ship in the navy. It was one of just two such docks in the United States.

The dry dock, 319 feet long and 30 feet deep, first went into service in 1833. It remains in use today and was declared a national historic landmark in 1971.

This week in April 1861, the Norfolk yard had four active warships in port. The most important was the steam-powered, fifty-gun frigate USS *Merrimack*, undergoing a mechanical-equipment refit. Also, there were the sailing ships USS *Germantown*, USS *Plymouth*, and USS *Dolphin*. The USS *Pennsylvania* was there, a three-deck giant built in the 1830s that at the time was the largest warship ever built in the United States. The *Pennsylvania* was no longer a fighting ship but rather a "receiving ship"—a floating barracks for incoming recruits not yet assigned to other vessels. Several warships at Norfolk were "in ordinary." That is, to use modern naval terminology, they were in mothballs.[2]

The navy yard had a large civilian workforce of several hundred local Virginians, but fewer than twenty navy officers were posted there. Like virtually all U.S. military facilities in the country, it was woefully underdefended given the newly hostile circumstances.[2]

On April 10, Navy Secretary Gideon Welles had sent a confidential message to Capt. Charles S. McCauley, commander of the

Norfolk Navy Yard. Welles was alarmed. He and Lincoln had two conflicting goals for the navy yard. On the one hand, they wanted to protect the facility.

On the other, Welles had to be ready to abandon the yard and save the fleet—especially the *Merrimack*—should things come to that. Both objectives were vastly complicated by an imperative not to antagonize Virginia, which had been teetering on the brink of secession. Lincoln would do nothing that might be seen by Virginia as aggressive or duplicitous. Of course, acting on either objective—fortifying the yard or removing the ships—would be viewed by Virginia as aggressive and duplicitous. As a result, Welles vacillated.

Welles, fifty-eight, was a semicomic figure physically. He had a flowing white beard and an ill-fitting white wig that made him an easy target. He was mocked in the press as "Father Neptune" or "Grandmother Welles." His stodgy and humorless manner only added to the overall impression. From the start, many of his cabinet peers underestimated him.

The *Times* of London's William Howard Russell sized up all Lincoln's cabinet members. "Mr. Cameron, a slight man, above the middle height, with gray hair, deep-set keen gray eyes, and a thin mouth, gave me the idea of a person of ability and adroitness," Russell wrote. "His colleague, the Secretary of the Navy, a small man, did not look like one of much originality or ability. But people who know Mr. Welles declare that he is possessed of administrative power."[3]

In fact, Welles also was a keen observer of interpersonal dynamics and human nature. He had a knack for blunting repeated efforts by his peers to usurp him. Most important, he was indeed a strong administrator, with a rare sense of the strategic. During the Civil War, he modernized the fleet, rebuilt the navy's organization, oversaw the blockade of the Southern ports, and developed a critically important riverine-warfare capability.

That would come later. Now Welles was scrambling to keep up with events. He emphasized the importance of moving the *Merrimack*. Indeed, on April 10 he told the Norfolk commander,

Commodore McCauley, to either move or secure all shipping and all the yard's vast supplies—including three thousand pieces of ordnance. At the same time, Welles added in his message to McCauley, "It is desirable that there should be no steps taken to give needless alarm, but it may be best to order most of the shipping to sea or to other stations."[4]

It's easy to see how this message could be interpreted as passive and contradictory—especially by McCauley. At sixty-eight, he was an example of the decrepit state of the senior ranks of the U.S. military in early 1861. Their careers had gone on way too long. Many officers were too old for their posts—unable to rise to an unprecedented emergency. "Subsequent events proved him faithful but feeble and incompetent for the crisis," Welles wrote in a scathing narrative added to his diary after the war. "His energy and decision had left him, and whatever skill or ability he may have had in earlier years in regular routine duty, he proved unequal to the present occasion."

The *Merrimack* was a primary focus. Getting it in shape to depart seemed to be an insurmountable challenge. McCauley estimated it would take a month. But Welles wanted it to depart "with the utmost dispatch" and sent the navy's top steam engineer, Benjamin Franklin Isherwood, to Norfolk to expedite the order. Isherwood would oversee the work on the *Merrimack* and return it to operational status, and an accompanying officer, Washington-based commander James Alden, would take command.[5]

But on Tuesday, April 16, Welles backtracked disastrously. In a note to McCauley, Welles—after counseling urgent action for days—reverted back to his order of the tenth, which cautioned that "no steps should be taken to give needless alarm."[6]

These instructions likely guaranteed the loss of the yard. Stasis remained and critical hours were lost.[7]

Also on the sixteenth, Welles ordered the former commander of the Home Squadron, Hiram Paulding, to Norfolk to serve as the eyes and ears of the Navy Department and to communicate directly with McCauley regarding what the department wanted.[8]

The Situation Deteriorates

On April 17, engineer Benjamin Isherwood had finished his work. He had put machinists and boilermakers to work round-the-clock repairing the *Merrimack*'s engines in three days, not the month Commodore McCauley had predicted. Isherwood had the ship loaded with coal and engineer stores and rounded up forty-four firemen and coal heavers. By that afternoon, everything was ready—except for McCauley, who refused to let the *Merrimack* get underway.

"At 4 o'clock, I called on Commodore McCauley, and asked him if I should fire up at once," Isherwood reported. "He replied not that afternoon, adding that if I had steam on the next morning it would be time enough. Accordingly, a regular engine-room watch was kept during the night and the fires were started at daybreak."[9]

Virginia Makes Its Move

The news of Virginia's April 17 secession suddenly rendered Gideon Welles's and Lincoln's excessive caution about the navy yard entirely moot. Indeed, the Virginians were already plotting a move on both the navy yard and Harpers Ferry. Even before the secession vote, Virginia governor John Letcher had ordered state militia troops to proceed to Norfolk and seize the station. Specifically, the newly promoted Confederate navy captain Robert B. Pegram was instructed to work in cooperation with Maj. Gen. William B. Taliaferro, who was ordered to Norfolk to take command of Virginia's forces assembling in the region.[10]

"I know the fact that the harbor of Norfolk has been obstructed last night by the sinking of vessels" at the mouth of the Elizabeth River, former Virginia governor Henry Wise had said in the secret session of the Virginia Session Convention on April 17, confirming the fears of U.S. Navy observers from the previous day. "I know the fact that at this moment a force is on its way to Harpers Ferry to prevent the reinforcement of the Federal troops at that point."[11]

This Thursday, April 18, Welles unleashed a new flurry of orders. The restraint required to appease Virginia was gone. He was still intent on saving the vast naval facility, though the likelihood of success was fading. Welles now made Com. Hiram Paulding's assignment—which had been to serve as Welles's eyes and ears at Norfolk—broader and explicit. Paulding was directed to "take command of all naval forces there afloat. You will do all in your power to protect and place beyond danger the vessels and property belonging to the United States. On no account should the arms and munitions be permitted to fall into the hands of the insurrectionists. Should it finally become necessary, you will, in order to prevent that result, destroy the property."[12] In the end, it became necessary.

At 9:00 a.m. this morning, Benjamin Isherwood, the engineer who'd gotten the *Merrimack* ready to sail, again went to McCauley. Steam was up and the engines were working. This sleek, modern, heavily armed warship was tied to the wharf, engines humming, decks vibrating, pumps softly panting, heat radiating in translucent waves up from its single stack. "The only thing wanting was the order to cast loose and go," Isherwood wrote.

Again McCauley declined. He had not decided to move the *Merrimack*. But he said he'd tell Isherwood his decision in a few hours. The vessel was ready to go. Isherwood's work was complete. At 2:00 p.m. Isherwood again visited McCauley, who finally said he'd decided to keep the ship where it was. "Nothing then remained for me to do but to request he put his endorsement on my orders, which he did, and return to Washington and report the fact," Isherwood reported.[13]

Harpers Ferry

If the Chesapeake Bay—particularly Fort Monroe and the Norfolk Navy Yard—represented Washington's strategic left flank, then Harpers Ferry was the right. Harpers Ferry was located between the Allegheny Mountains on the west and the Blue Ridge Mountains on the east, the latter of which provided a natural screen for Confederate armies throughout the Civil War.

In addition to its vital location, Harpers Ferry was a significant U.S. arsenal and small arms–manufacturing center. An estimated fifteen thousand guns were at the armory.[14]

Like the Norfolk Navy Yard, part of Harpers Ferry's value was the stores, supplies, equipment, and materials present there. Also like the navy yard, Harpers Ferry was vulnerable. It was at the tip of a peninsula formed by the Potomac and Shenandoah Rivers and surrounded by steep bluffs from which a hostile force could dominate the town. It, too, was poorly protected. Capt. Henry Hunt of the Second U.S. Artillery was ordered to Harpers Ferry by the interim secretary of war, Joseph Holt, on January 3 to assume command. A company of eight noncommissioned officers and sixty privates under 1st Lt. Roger Jones was ordered to meet Hunt there. Hunt was relieved on April 2, and the command passed to Jones.

Just as with Welles's orders to McCauley at the navy yard in Norfolk, Hunt's and Jones's orders were to prepare for the defense of the armory—"without making a display" of such defensive preparations. Hunt had asked U.S. Army adjutant general Samuel Cooper for clarification on January 14 on how those two orders could be compatible. Holt, via Cooper, replied, "Major Hunt will conform strictly to the instructions originally given him. It is desirable to avoid all needless irritation of the public mind, and he will proceed quietly, so as to avoid all military display."[15]

That was where things stood when Jones took over. Jones had asked General Scott twice—first in February and again in March—for additional troops. Scott's response was, "I have no more troops, sir, that I can send you." Jones replied, "I don't expect to need any more, unless Virginia should pass an ordinance of secession. Then they will be needed."[16]

Virginia seceded on the seventeenth in a secret session to allow time for the state's militia to move on both Harpers Ferry and the navy yard.[17] Now it was too late to save Harpers Ferry. Jones's force, originally sixty-two men, had been reduced by deaths, desertions, and discharges to forty-nine. On the morning of the eighteenth, Jones received a telegram from General Scott. Three trains of Virginia troops were moving up the railroad heading for Harpers Ferry. "Be on your guard," Scott warned Jones.

As the day progressed, Jones, a West Point graduate who had just turned thirty, got confirmation of Scott's warning and became convinced an attack was coming. There was nothing left to do. Defending Harpers Ferry wasn't a viable option. Jones decided to burn the arsenal, abandon the facility, and retreat into Pennsylvania.[18]

At one or two o'clock that afternoon, Jones destroyed a bridge over a canal that supplied waterpower to the facilities. Later that afternoon Jones prepared to set fire to the armory workshops and arsenal buildings.[19]

"I detailed twelve men of my company, and ordered six of them to get their bed-sacks, which were filled with straw, and put a keg of powder in each one of them," Jones told Senate investigators later that year. "I proceeded in person with this party from the armory to the arsenal buildings. I distributed these sacks, with powder in them, in the two arsenal buildings, and with the aid of shavings and bituminous coal, and a quantity of lumber lying in the buildings, I prepared things so that a fire could be kindled in an instant." Preparations were completed by about 6:00 p.m.[20]

The rifle manufacturing works a half mile up the Shenandoah River were left untouched. "It would probably have led to the defeat of the plan, as I was surrounded by spies and persons in the interest of the rebel cause," Jones said. "I feared that by attempting too much I should fail in everything."[21]

Late that afternoon he telegraphed Scott that he'd gotten confirmation of Scott's morning message. What's more, a force of three hundred to four hundred men was said to be advancing from the southwest, along the road to Charlestown. Jones posted guards on the southwest line of the railroad.[22]

Everything stayed quiet until about 9:00 p.m. At that point while Jones was writing a report to Scott, he was repeatedly interrupted by people rushing in to say the assault force was advancing. One interruption was from a civilian riding in, who told Jones that three thousand men were heading toward Harpers Ferry by rail from Winchester, about thirty miles to the south.

"Under these circumstances, I decided that if anything was to be done it was to be done then," Jones testified. "I gave orders to fire the buildings. Having taken this step, there was but one course left to me and I immediately commenced a retreat to Hagerstown on the way to Carlisle, Pennsylvania. We started from the ferry at about half-past ten o'clock in the evening and marched all night on foot over the mountains, and reached Hagerstown shortly after seven the next morning."[23]

Four days later, writing from Carlisle Barracks in Pennsylvania, Jones reported that three of his missing men had rejoined him, having left Harpers Ferry the prior day. "They report that fifteen minutes after my command left the armory nine hundred troops marched into the town, and that they continued to arrive every hour during the night," Jones wrote. "They also report that the fire in the workshops was arrested, but that the arsenal buildings containing the arms, together with their contents, were completely demolished."[24]

Later that year during Senate Select Committee hearings, Lt. Col. William Maynadier wrote a message to Secretary of War Simon Cameron stating that the total value of the lost U.S. property was $1.2 million ($35.1 million in 2020 dollars) and that the number of arms stored at the arsenal wasn't the 15,000 that had been indicated but only 4,287, with a value of about $64,000 (about $1.8 million in 2020 dollars).[25]

In the end the damage wasn't enough. While the Confederates lost many of the rifles in the fires, they obtained a strategically vital geographic position that threatened Washington and prevented reinforcements from coming from Ohio, Indiana, and elsewhere along the line of the B&O Railroad. And they gained the critical rifle-manufacturing facility, which had not been harmed in the fires.

11
- - -

The New York Seventh Departs

The Advance

It rained overnight in New York City. But the morning of April 19 dawned with fair spring weather. The sun was shining, and the Tompkins Market Armory was bustling as the men of the New York Seventh Regiment prepared for departure. Company officers rushed from room to room. They gave instructions to the noncommissioned officers. They processed unexpected donations of funds.

Around noon, the men began to arrive in large numbers, accompanied by wives, parents, families, and well-wishers. Some had been given paid leave from their civilian jobs. Others had received advances on their pay. Others got donations of clothing, equipment, and handguns. "A feverish excitement throbbed through the city—the beating of that big Northern pulse, so slow, so sure and so steady," wrote Fitz James O'Brien, thirty-four, an Irish American science-fiction writer and a private in the Seventh.[1]

Col. Marshall Lefferts had issued these orders: "This Regiment will assemble at Head Quarters on Friday, 19th inst., at 3 o'clock p.m., in full fatigue, overcoat and knapsack, to embark for Washington. The men will each take one blanket, to be rolled on top of knapsack; suitable underclothing, one extra pair of boots (shoes are better), knife, fork, spoon, tin cup, plate, body belt, and cap pouch. The men will provide themselves with one day's ration."[2]

The Seventh wouldn't be the first Northern regiment to depart from New York this Friday. That distinction belonged to the Eighth Massachusetts, the commonwealth's second regiment to pass through New York in as many days. The Eighth had just arrived early this morning from Boston, led by the regimental commander, Col. Timothy Munroe of Lynn, and accompanied by Brig. Gen. Benjamin Butler. The regiment passed down Broadway around noon through a sea of New Yorkers.

But the main event in New York was the New York Seventh's departure. Excitement raced through the city. Commerce ground to a halt. A crowd began to gather at the armory in the street next to the Cooper Institute, where Third Avenue and Fourth Avenue diverged. Cheers went up as each new soldier arrived. On the street, dozens of young men begged to join the regiment. Soon the police had to clear the building.

You could overhear the conversations:

"Take care of yourself, old fellow, and I'll see to things at home."

"I'll come back promoted, father, or I won't come at all."

"Mother gave me this little flag. I'll never disgrace it."

"What do you think the governor said to me? 'Remember Sumter,' and he vowed he'd like to go too."

"God bless you, boys!"[3]

At 3:00 p.m. came the rapid roll of the drum—the call to assemble. The regiment formed on Lafayette Place. There were eight companies fully armed, equipped, and uniformed, fully ready. The regiment had 991 men in all facing their officers in the front, wearing gray uniforms with wide black trim on the pants and sky-blue overcoats. The regimental line extended in arrow-straight rows from Eighth Street to Fourth Street. Suddenly the command came to wheel to the right into a column—eighteen men to a row, rows clustered in groups of two.

The band struck up with a flourish, horns blaring, drums beating, cymbals crashing. The regiment moved out, first turning right onto Great Jones Street and then left onto Broadway. It was just past 4:00 p.m., and the New York Seventh was on its way.[4]

"New York was raving mad with excitement," Second Company captain Emmons Clark wrote. "Men cheered and shouted and rushed into the ranks to shake hands and stuff cigars, pipes, tobacco, wine, matches, knives, combs, soap, slippers, sandwiches and more into the hands and pockets of the troops."

Artillery company member Theodore Winthrop, thirty-two, of Connecticut, remembered that "one fellow got a new purse with ten bright quarter-eagles. I was not so fortunate." Winthrop was killed weeks later, on June 10 at the Battle of Big Bethel.[5]

Broadway was densely crowded. Through Greenwich Village past Houston Street and Canal Street, past city hall and past Newspaper Row the Seventh marched. Children shimmied up streetlight poles for a better view. Adults climbed onto upper-floor porticos to see the troops.

The lawyer George Templeton Strong watched from a loft at a carpet store near Spring Street and saw the Seventh coming in the distance—"a bluish steel-grey light on the blackness of the dense mob. As they came nearer, the roar of the crowd was grand and terrible. It drowned the brass of the band."[6]

From the balcony of a store on the corner of Spring Street and Broadway, Major Robert Anderson, the hero of Fort Sumter, reviewed the march. The week since the fall of Sumter had converted Broadway into a street of banners. The national flag floated from windows and housetops, and the air was filled with floating handkerchiefs.

Winthrop could barely hear the rattle of the regiment's gun carriages. "We knew now that our great city was with us as one man, utterly united in the great cause we were marching to sustain," he wrote. "It was worth a life, that march. Only one who passed, as we did, through that tempest of cheers, two miles long, can know the terrible enthusiasm of the occasion." "It will be remembered as long as any of those who witnessed it live to talk of it, and beyond that, it will pass into the recorded history of this fearful struggle," wrote the *New York Times*.[7]

The Seventh wheeled to the right onto Cortlandt Street for the final leg, which was three-tenths of a mile, to the ferry terminal.

Once on the ferry, the deafening noise died away. But the scene across the river at the Jersey City terminal was similar to Broadway. It was pandemonium.

On the train the men unslung their knapsacks, stowed their rifles and blankets, and sat down for a meal as they started an all-night trip to Philadelphia. All through New Jersey the scene was the same, with crowds along the route greeting the train as it slowly rumbled through the countryside well past dark. At the station stops, "rough hands came in through the windows, apparently unconnected with any one in particular until you shook them, and then the subtle, magnetic thrill told that there were bold hearts beating at the end," Pvt. Fitz James O'Brien remembered.

Winthrop wrote that the regiment "made a jolly night of it. The more a man sings, the better he is likely to fight. So we sang more than we slept."

O'Brien described a train full of troops flush with adrenaline, rolling through the New Jersey night, singing drinking songs and profane variations on college ditties. "A thousand young men were rushing along to conjectured hostilities with the same smiling faces that they would wear going to a party in Fifth Avenue," O'Brien wrote. "It was more like a festivity than a march."[8]

Philadelphia

Fourteen hours before the Seventh Regiment began its triumphant march down Broadway, the Sixth Massachusetts militia regiment, more than seven hundred men in all, was already in Philadelphia.

It was 1:00 a.m. on Friday morning, April 19, and the men were sleeping in two Center City hotels. The streets of America's second-largest city were deserted.

Then suddenly the call came signaling for the troops to fall in. The groggy young men staggered awake, got dressed, grabbed their gear, and ran to the street to form up. The Massachusetts troops were in their third day of full-time soldiering. After forty-eight hours of celebrating since leaving Boston, things were about to get rougher. Their commander, Col. Edward F. Jones, knew it. Right now, his main concern was whether his newly minted soldiers would be ready.

Jones had spent the night consulting with the civilian railroad authorities. His troops were to advance to Baltimore by rail, reaching that city by early morning, and then march through the city for about 1.4 miles—from the Philadelphia, Wilmington, and Baltimore (PWB) line's terminus to the southbound B&O terminal, where a separate train would take them to Washington.

But just now Baltimore was a hotbed of unrest, a cauldron ready to explode. Situated at the crossroads of the North and the South, it possessed characteristics of both sections. It was the southern-most Northern city and the northern-most Southern city. Unlike most of the agricultural South, Baltimore's economy was based on trade—shipping, shipbuilding, railroads, iron works, textiles, timber. It was the fourth largest city in the nation in 1860, after New York, Philadelphia, and Brooklyn, with a population of 212,418. It had one of the country's largest populations of free African American residents—25,000 people—and just 2,200 enslaved people. Like Northern cities, it had experienced large influxes of immigration in the mid-nineteenth century, overwhelmingly from Irish and Germans. A quarter of the city's population was foreign born.[9]

But it was also overwhelmingly pro-South and prosecession—the largest city in a slave state. Baltimore was known as "mob town" for its mid-nineteenth century gang violence and rioting, usually triggered by economic and social conflict expressed through political factions around elections.

Here in Philadelphia this early Friday morning, Samuel Felton, the president of the PWB Railroad, had considered all these things. He'd been meeting through the night with Pennsylvania Railroad president J. Edgar Thomson, PWB paymaster Nicholas Trist, and other railroad executives, seeking to process the latest information from Washington and Baltimore.[10] The level of alarm was high.

Colonel Jones had represented the Sixth Massachusetts in these meetings, along with Maj. Benjamin F. Watson, the second in command, and Brig. Gen. P. S. Davis of the First Brigade of the Massachusetts Militia, who'd been sent ahead to arrange transportation and housing. Also present was Gen. William F. Small, representing Philadelphia's Washington Brigade, a combination of two tentative Pennsylvania militia organizations—one a regiment of American-born volunteers, the other German, about one thousand men in all.[11]

Baltimore had the earmarks of a tinderbox. Officials knew that the Pennsylvania troops had been taunted and harassed as they passed through just yesterday. They couldn't rule out an attack in the city or sabotage along the tracks. The risk led Felton—in consultation with the Pennsylvania governor, the Philadelphia mayor, and the commander of the Pennsylvania militia—to activate a new plan, one that avoided Baltimore completely.

Rather than travel by rail to Baltimore, Felton suggested, the troops should take the train southbound only as far as Perryville, on the north bank of the Susquehanna River at the top of the Chesapeake Bay. There they'd board the steam ferry *Maryland*, which served as the link between the northern and southern sections of the PWB line in the years before a bridge was built over the Susquehanna. The ferry was massive, capable of carrying more than twenty train cars in one trip. But the troops wouldn't disembark in Havre de Grace, on the southern bank. Instead, they'd stay on the ferry and proceed down the bay roughly fifty-five miles to Annapolis.

Colonel Jones opposed this alternative. He was adamant. He didn't want to wait for federal sign-off on any new plans, nor did he want to deal with the uncertainties of a new and longer route. He'd take his chances getting through Baltimore in accordance with his orders.

Massachusetts Militia general Davis told Jones he would decline to take responsibility for sending the Sixth Massachusetts forward. Jones's reply was, "My orders are to reach Washington at the earliest possible moment. My orders are peremptory. Whatever may be the consequences, I must proceed." To which Davis shook his hand and said, "Colonel, if you go on, then I shall go with you."

That decided it. The Massachusetts troops would travel through Baltimore.

Jones's major concern was that an obstruction on the tracks, or a destroyed bridge, would cause casualties among his troops.

Felton agreed to send a pilot engine ahead of the troops to scope out the route.[12]

And so at around 3:00 a.m., ten companies of Pennsylvania volunteers and the Massachusetts Sixth troops converged on Philadelphia's Broad and Prime Streets depot, a mile south of the Center City neighborhood. They embarked on the same train, hauling thirty-five cars. "The train was a heavy one, having nearly 2,000 men on board, and moved very slowly," the *Philadelphia Public Ledger* reported.[13]

Jones boarded his men with precision, ensuring that once they disembarked, they'd be in the same regimental line they'd learned in drill. The Massachusetts combat troops occupied the first eleven cars. They'd take the lead. The unarmed, ununiformed Pennsylvanians were in the rear. The Massachusetts band, along with and the baggage and equipment, occupied freight cars between the troops.[14]

Once in Perryville, the cars were loaded onto the steam ferry and carried across the Susquehanna to Havre de Grace. Jones had intended for the railroad workers to put the train cars in the same order when they were reattached on the southern side of the river. That didn't happen, and the consequences of it would be seen later.

The rail journey toward Baltimore began again in the darkness. The soldiers' water-transport option was behind them now.

Railroad companies were mostly short-haul lines in the mid-nineteenth century. They built their own terminals. Unified—or union—stations had not yet become common. Passengers were often left to their own devices to get from one line to the next—grab a cab, take a bus, walk.[15]

Baltimore also had a city ordinance prohibiting locomotives from passing through the center of the city. These ordinances were common. Locomotives were a pollution source and a fire hazard. In addition, local merchants didn't want to lose business from transferring customers.

In Baltimore the PWB Railroad and the B&O Railroad cooperated to run shuttles between the stations. Teams of horses would haul the train cars, with the passengers in them, on tracks through the city from one station to the other, where they'd board a second train.

But Jones did not intend for his regiment to use the shuttle. He reconfirmed the plan with railroad officials in Havre de Grace. The men would disembark and march across Baltimore, moving from the PWB terminal on President Street to the B&O station at Camden Station. A march was more defensible than the shuttle, given the volatile conditions.

The route was fairly direct. Transferring passengers would head north on President Street—now the eastern side of Baltimore's Inner Harbor—and connect with Pratt Street, which ran along the wharfs, and proceed west about a mile to Howard Street, and then go a block south to the Camden Station. Should there be an incident, the men would have more agility and more firepower on the march than if they were trapped as individual companies in the horse-drawn shuttle cars.

The trip from Philadelphia to Baltimore was grueling even under the best of circumstances, and these predawn hours were especially tense and uncertain. Jones spent most of the ninety-five-mile journey checking his men's preparedness. He distributed ammunition to the soldiers and issued a very specific directive:

> The regiment will march through Baltimore in column of sections, arms at will. You will undoubtedly be insulted, abused, and, perhaps, assaulted, to which you must pay no attention whatever, but march with your faces to the front, and pay no attention to the mob, even if they throw stones, bricks or other missiles; but if you are fired upon and any one of you is hit, your officers will order you to fire. Do not fire into any promiscuous crowds, but select any man who you see might be aiming at you, and be sure you drop him.[16]

All through the night on this slow, thirteen-mile-per-hour trip south, the railroad company had been in touch with its employees on the ground in Baltimore. And at each stop along the way, it picked up telegraph messages: all calm, no disturbances reported.[17]

Because of these encouraging reports, railroad managers on the ground in Baltimore changed their minds about the plan to get the troops across the city. They decided to proceed with the customary transfer process—shuttling from the President Street depot to the Camden Station, where trains departed for Washington or westward points.[18]

But incredibly, no one told Jones. The regimental commander was fully expecting to disembark at the President Street Station with his whole regiment and march across Baltimore.[19]

There's an old military aphorism, variations of which are attributable to everyone from the nineteenth-century Prussian field marshal Helmuth von Moltke to the twentieth-century boxer Mike Tyson. "No plan survives first contact with the enemy," it says. Colonel Jones and the Sixth Massachusetts were about to find that out.[20]

12

The Baltimore Riots

T he long train slowed as it rolled through the east side neighborhoods of Canton and Fell's Point. It was shortly before 11:00 a.m., clear and cool in Baltimore this Friday morning. The temperature was about fifty-two degrees.[1]

The train passed an old racecourse. It moved along the harbor, past vacant lots, oyster-packing facilities, iron works, breweries, and lumber mills.[2]

Aboard were the men of the Massachusetts Sixth Regiment and Philadelphia's Washington Brigade. The soldiers were tense. They knew this was hostile territory. "Through the cross streets men could be seen, running and gesticulating toward the train," recalled the Sixth Regiment's second in command, thirty-four-year-old Maj. Benjamin F. Watson.[3]

The locomotive's chuffing softened as the engineer throttled back. The bell clanged; the cars strained in the turns. The whistle blared; the wheels squealed. Brakemen manually cranked handles outside each car. Just a block away, directly in front of the train, was the harbor, its briny smell wafting eastward.[4]

The train didn't enter the half-barrel shaped train shed at the President Street Station. Instead it moved up the freight track on the north side of the train shed. This track connected directly to rails that curved onto President Street and extended through the heart of Baltimore. Typically teams of horses would shuttle the passenger cars from this track.[5]

The train stopped. Colonel Jones and Major Watson were the first off. Jones ordered Watson to accompany the rear company—Company K—during the march. Jones would lead the regiment.

Watson moved toward the rear. "Much threatening and insulting language was addressed to me by policemen and others," he recalled. "I was assured in language neither gentle nor polite, that not a soldier would live to pass through the city, and that Baltimore would, to a man, repel the invasion of Maryland by 'Northern Abolitionists.'"[6]

Watson reached Company K's car and climbed aboard, joining company captain Walter Sampson. Neither man realized that their car was not the last on the train carrying the Sixth Regiment. There were at least four more. Railroad workers in Havre de Grace had not reattached the cars in the expected order. These cars, with about 220 soldiers, would be on their own today.

The Plan Falls Apart

In the front, Jones had barely stepped off before the train's first two cars were hitched to horses and began moving rapidly into the city. Jones's plan to march the regiment across the city fell apart. He watched in stunned disbelief. Railroad officials, acting on their own, had assessed the situation as safe. No one had told Jones.[7]

Two-tenths of a mile north of the station, a crowd began to gather on Pratt Street. The mob combined all the elements of Baltimore's population—dock workers, waterfront merchants, gang members, local roughs, prosecession police, politicians, curious onlookers, and a few Unionists.

The crowd watched sullenly as the first two cars rolled past. The soldiers were absolutely quiet, avoiding eye contact with the masses growing outside the windows.

Pratt Street was like a canyon, with multistory buildings hugging the street just off the sidewalks. There were commercial and residential buildings, hotels and retail shops with ground-level storefronts shaded by awnings.

On the left was the waterfront. Pratt Street had seven piers packed with three- and four-story brick warehouses, manufacturing facilities, workshops, and marine-services companies. Large ships, their rigging rising high above the streets, crowded the water beside the piers. It would have been hard to see any more than a brief glimpse of open water as the Sixth proceeded to the Camden depot.[8]

As the first car crossed the Jones Falls Bridge, just past the intersection of President Street and Pratt Street, the jeering started. "Shoot the God damned Sons of Bitches!" someone yelled. "Rally, boys, and attack the train—they have no business to go through this city!" shouted another. "The damned abolitionists ought to be killed!"[9]

Despite this, the leading cars and their horse teams continued up the gradual incline of Pratt Street westward in the direction of the Camden Station, a mile distant and not yet visible.

The First Attack

Back at the President Street Station, all seemed calm, so Colonel Jones boarded the third car leaving President Street.[10]

Seven cars back, Watson and Sampson—a twenty-six-year-old resident of Boston—waited for the order to disembark. It never came. Eventually, they looked out to find all the cars in front of them gone, and theirs being hooked up to a horse team.[11] Assuming the march had been called off, they remained on the car and proceeded up President Street.

The crowd swelled. A two-block section of Pratt Street was being repaved, with heavy cobblestones conveniently piled and available as weapons. At the same time, the bridge over Jones Falls was being repaired, and the workers had taken a break, leaving the bridge to the mob.[12] Jeers flew and the first attacks began, the crowd smashing clubs and iron bars against the train. "I saw [the notorious Baltimore gang leader] Bill Konigs [sic] pick up a paving stone and throw it into a car & strike a man," police officer Robert Meads testified later that year. "I called on officers to interfere, they told me it was none of my damned business."[13] Cobblestones, rocks, and shards of bricks started slamming into car's wooden sides. Splinters flew. Glass shattered.

All the exposed teamster could do was keep his terrified horses moving forward. They had a mile to go to reach the Camden Station.

Ernest Wardwell, an eighteen-year-old bystander whose classes had been dismissed as a result of the mayhem, remembered the stoic courage of the troops. "At first I was paralyzed with fear, but only momentarily, as I caught the frenzy and became as noisy as the others," he said. "Stones, bricks and missiles of all kinds were hurled into the car windows, through which could be plainly seen the uniformed occupants, who made no attempt at defense. . . . How the men were able to retain their places and drive the horses onward through that dense crowd seems little short of a miracle, but they did, the mob following like a vociferous army of howling wolves."[14]

Gunshots rang out. Watson ordered his men to the floor. When one soldier was shot in the thumb, Watson gave the order to fire back. "Boys, you may fire; shelter yourselves while loading, and then take good aim as you fire through the windows," Watson said.[15]

Now bullets flew from both sides. Three times Company K's car was derailed. Each time, Watson stepped out into the swirling maelstrom, in uniform and fully exposed, and helped the driver remove obstructions that blocked the rails.[16]

A third of the way to the Camden depot, the driver bolted. "The car was again stopped near large piles of paving stones," Watson remembered. "The driver and horses were making off through the crowd." Sampson suggested they abandon the car. Watson disagreed. The car offered the soldiers some protection. He took off in pursuit of the driver.

"Overtaking him, I ordered him to return to the car with his team," Watson recalled. "Hastily weighing the relative danger from the weapons of the crowd and from my revolver at his head, he decided to surrender to the latter, and preceded me with his horses through the mob. The horses were reattached and the car again moved on amid renewed volleys, the driver still requiring constant attendance."

The car itself was now a wreck. It moved slowly through the crowd. The driver was told that if he left the train again, "he was a dead man."[17]

When the car was a block from the Camden Station, Watson ordered the men to file off the train and march the remaining distance.

By this time the crowd had grown to at least a thousand people and probably many more. Local authorities, including Mayor George William Brown and Police Marshal George P. Kane, would later downplay the mob's size. But the Northerners perceived as many as twenty thousand people, a plausible estimate for the country's fourth largest city. Multiple eyewitnesses described impassible crowds as far as the eye could see.[18]

At the Camden depot, Colonel Jones and the executives of the Baltimore and Ohio Railroad were relieved that Watson's company got through but wondered what happened to the rest of the regiment. Four companies and the band were still missing.

The B&O's Baltimore superintendent, William Smith, whose people had been tracking the progress of the shuttles, told Jones that the track was blocked and the rest of the troops couldn't proceed. Word trickled in. B&O president John Garrett told Jones, "Your soldiers are firing upon the people in the streets." To which Jones replied, "Then they have been fired upon first."[19]

"No, they have not," Garrett said. "My men are disciplined: my orders were strict, and I believe they have been implicitly obeyed," Jones insisted.[20]

The March

A mile back, the car following Watson and Company K had been heading along Pratt Street when it had a problem with its brakes in the area where the road was being repaired. It stopped.

Someone hurled a cobblestone through a train window. Shattering glass sprayed all over the car. There was a moment's hesitation. Then the mob took this as a signal. Suddenly cobblestones, brick shards, coal, and iron scraps were flying at the train car fast and furious. The driver, exposed to the assault from the mob, managed to unhitch his horses from the front of the car, hook them to the rear, and haul the car back to the President Street Station, stones flying the whole time.[21]

Now the mob built a barricade across the tracks using cobblestones, loads of sand, and the wooden planks that crossed the gutters between the sidewalks and the street. Eight anchors dragged from a sidewalk at the wharf were piled on. The crowd was aided by a group of Black—presumably enslaved—sailors employed on ships from the South. These men "rendered every assistance in their power, hauling the immense anchors to the centre of the railroad track, with cheers for the 'Souf,' and 'Massa Jeff Davis,'" wrote the Maryland historian Thomas Scharf, using the same racist mimicry as the Baltimore newspapers.[22]

George Wilson Booth, a seventeen-year-old member of the Maryland militia, remembered the scene: "Just before noon I reached the corner of Gay and Pratt streets. The people had barricaded the tracks by emptying loads of sand from passing carts, and by dragging some old anchors from a ship chandlery on the corner. A car had reached the obstructed point, and, not being able to pass, the horses were attached to the rear and the car returned to the Philadelphia depot. The soldiers in the car were subjected to the most violent abuse."[23] Back at the President Street depot, the crowd swarmed. Regimental chaplain and historian John Wesley Hanson said the mob extended "as far as the eye could see."[24]

More than twenty train cars were still at the President Street Station, clustered in twos and threes around the sprawling grounds. Inside were the four remaining companies of the Sixth Massachusetts, the Sixth's band, and the one thousand unarmed recruits of the Philadelphia Washington Brigade. There were also about six cars of baggage and supplies.

In the shelter of the train, the officers of those remaining Massachusetts companies—C, D, I, and L—struggled for fifteen minutes deciding how to proceed. A large contingent of police arrived, drawn from local precincts. This timely show of official force likely stopped the mob from swarming the train entirely.[25]

The company captains knew they couldn't get through the city on the cars. They couldn't go back to Philadelphia. And they couldn't stay where they were. They had to march across Baltimore.

They chose Capt. Albert Follansbee, thirty-seven, of Company C to take command. They had to get 220 men safely through a huge, bloodthirsty mob. Outside the train, the crowd raged and surged, waved guns and knives, screamed and spit in the soldiers' faces, and smashed clubs against the cars and windows. The men filed off the train. Each company, each platoon, and each man was assigned a specific place in the line. The sergeants ordered the men to fall in. They did so, facing out from the train.

One of the soldiers, Sumner H. Needham, a thirty-three-year-old Company I corporal, was stepping off the car when he placed his hand on the shoulder of twenty-six-year-old Pvt. James Knights. "We shall have trouble to-day, and I shall never get out of it alive," Needham said. Knights smiled but assured Needham—a Lawrence man who operated a lathing business with his brothers—that whoever suffered would be well looked after. The soldiers took their places in line and never met again.[26]

The troops stood in single file, officers and noncommissioned officers facing them. The order of march was Company C in the lead, followed by companies I, L, and D.[27]

The mob pressed in, but the troops managed to get onto the sidewalk. Follansbee ordered the men to wheel into a column, two abreast. He had no idea how to get to the Camden Street station.[28] An obvious option was to follow the shuttle tracks. Follansbee gave the order to march, and the troops started toward President Street.

The crowd erupted. Before the soldiers had reached President Street, it surged in front of the armed soldiers, forcing them to stop. Follansbee ordered an about face. The mob rushed around to head them off. For several minutes, the regiment was surrounded, unable to move in any direction.

Finally, Follansbee maneuvered the troops into platoons four abreast and, aided by police, forced a passage through the seething mob.[29]

The regimental band, unarmed like the one thousand Pennsylvanians still in the cars, refused to join the march. That left the four companies marching forward with no sound to guide them. They had only the flag waving in front to focus on, along with the cadence calls of "left, right, left, right," barely discernible over the roaring mob.[30]

Seizing an opportunity, a few rioters lifted a secession flag at the head of the column and marched two blocks up President Street, mocking the Massachusetts troops. The crowd threw rocks and bricks. Several soldiers were knocked down. Baltimore police helped them back to their ranks, or to the local police station, or to the safety of local storefronts.[31]

Pvt. William Patch, twenty-three, described how he was cut off at the rear of the column. "I defended myself as I could with my musket," he wrote. "I ran, but was struck down. I found myself with half a dozen men on me. The police came up and took them off, and took me to a station-house." A doctor there told Patch he was too badly injured to rejoin the regiment. He was sent back to Philadelphia later that day, along with more than sixty other injured men.[32]

Back on President Street, Lt. Leander Lynde of Company L had had enough of the rebel flag. He hammered the flag carrier with the hilt of his sword, knocking the man down. He grabbed the flag, shoved it under his coat, and marched on.[33]

Baltimore teenager Ernest Wardwell and his friends pushed their way through the crowd, now wedged into a crushing mass, to the intersection of Pratt and President. "A body of city police made their appearance, ordering and pushing back the crowd," Wardwell wrote. "Closely following the police came a battalion of infantry soldiers with their guns at 'right shoulder,' and bayonets fixed."

The sight of anyone defending the Yankee interlopers only enraged the crowd more.

"You Yankee dogs, you'll never go back!"

"Kill them!"

"Cut throats!"

"Yankee scum!"

As the troops turned onto Pratt Street, the violence mounted. Rioters hurled themselves into the ranks, trying to wrest guns from soldiers. Huge lumps of coal, stone jars, bottles, pitchers, and dishes all hurled from upper windows and roofs found indiscriminate targets. "Many of the men in the ranks were injured by these flying missiles, as were a number of bystanders," Wardwell said.[34] Twenty-year-old Company E private Aaron Fletcher described irons and "queer missiles" (chamber pots) hurled by women at the soldiers. Writing in 1936 as the last surviving member of the Sixth Regiment, Fletcher made the only firsthand reference to women participating in the riot.[35]

Company C lieutenant John Jepson saw a man fatally hit with a rock and watched as his body was trampled under the mob. "It was one of the most horrible sights I ever saw," he wrote later. "I have been in many a battle, but I would rather face the enemy in the open field than go through such a scene as that in the streets of Baltimore."[36]

When a nineteen-year-old private was struck by a plank thrown from an upper-floor window, Jepson stooped down to assist, but "a gigantic rough" seized Jepson by his sword belt and yanked him into the crowd. "Jepson only got away by giving the fellow a blow, with his sword, in the face," John Wesley Hanson wrote. "The weapon was more for ornament than use, or the brute's head would have been cloven. The traitor's blood remains on the weapon to-day."[37]

Hoping to put some distance between his troops and the mob, Follansbee ordered a "double-quick"—essentially a run—shortly before the Jones Falls River bridge. This might have seemed like a smart move, but it backfired. First, the frenzied partisans thought running demonstrated cowardice, or that the troops had no ammunition, or that they had been ordered not to shoot.[38] Second, crossing the partially dismantled bridge was precarious. Joists, sawhorses, and materials blocked the way, likely placed there by the mob that had torn up Pratt Street.[39] The men were forced to jump from beam to beam, pushing obstructions out of the way as they went. "We had to play scotch hop across the torn-up planks," Follansbee wrote.[40]

Having crossed the bridge, the soldiers found themselves in the Center Market, also known as the Marsh Market or Market Place, a vast bazaar on a wide concourse running north to south on the right side of Pratt Street. It was, the author Letitia Stockett remembered, a place that was "full of color and raciness, filled with toughs, seafaring men, thugs, longshoremen, gamblers and rogues of every color."[41] On this day, the people pouring out of the market and onto Pratt Street were enraged secessionists.

Follansbee had had enough. "As soon as we crossed the bridge, they commenced to fire upon us from the street and houses," he recalled in a letter the next day. "I ordered the men to protect themselves; and then we returned their fire, and laid a great many of them away. I saw four fall on the sidewalk at one time."[42]

Hanson described soldiers loading their guns as they marched, dragging them between their feet and discharging them when opportunity presented a target. "There was no platoon firing whatever," he wrote.[43]

Casualties mounted on both sides. Addison O. Whitney, twenty-one, of Lowell, Company D, may have been the first member of the Sixth Regiment killed when he fell amid the shooting. "While marching through Pratt Street, near the bridge, he was seen to fall," Massachusetts governor John Andrew recounted in an 1865 memorial speech. "Some of his comrades tried to assist him, but finding he was dead, they left him where he fell. A bullet had pierced his right breast, passing down the body, causing instant death." The coat Whitney wore was later found stripped of every button. The place where the bullet entered was plainly visible, saturated with blood.[44]

The Mayor Marches with the Troops

As this was happening near the Marsh Market, Baltimore's Mayor Brown was rushing east along Pratt Street in the direction of the troops. The scene was stunning: soldiers in blue, in a ragged column, not marching but running, firing wildly over their shoulders, not bothering to aim, followed by a malevolent mass. To Brown's eye, the mob wasn't that large, but he noted it was hurling rocks and other objects and shooting pistols. The assaults came from the streets and from the buildings, including upper floors.[45]

The melee was furious when Brown finally reached Follansbee. People shouted, "Here comes the mayor!" Brown told the captain to stop the running, which the soldiers immediately did. "We have been attacked without provocation," Follansbee said. "You must defend yourselves," Brown said he responded.

Brown's presence initially subdued the mob. But as the battalion reached Commerce Street, not quite halfway to the Washington station, it was stopped by the mob. The Maltby House hotel seemed to be a type of headquarters for the mob, Ernest Wardwell remembered. "They poured a heavy fire of gun and pistol shots off its porches and windows, which did some damage—but was silenced when several guns of the soldiers were discharged in their direction."[46]

Mayor Brown, having assured Captain Follansbee that he could calm the crowd, walked with the besieged troops for about one hundred yards. But before long, Follansbee recalled, the stones and bullets whistling past his head changed his mind. He said, "'This is too hot a space for me' and left without saying by-your-leave," Follansbee wrote.[47]

Soldiers in the rear got the brunt of the attacks. "Paving stones were dashed with great force against their backs and heads and marching thus in close ranks they were unable to effectually defend themselves," wrote the *Baltimore American* the next day. "When they did turn and fire, it was without halt, and being thus massed together their shots took effect mostly on innocent lookers on."[48]

Those unfortunate civilians included several Black men employed in the area, described as "boys" by the newspapers and some historians in the racist parlance of the time. They included Patrick Griffith, who worked on one of the oyster sloops tied up near Pratt and Light streets, and William Reed, who was employed by a Pratt Street establishment known as the "Greenhouse" and who was "shot through the bowels while looking from a doorway on Pratt Street."[49]

Massachusetts soldiers were falling too. "At the intersection of Pratt and Charles streets, one of the soldiers, a Company L private named Andrew Robbins, 25, from Stoneham, Massachusetts, was shot in the neck by one of the citizens, and being picked up, was carried into the drug store of Mr. Jesse S. Hunt, where he was attended by Dr. Dunbar," the *Baltimore Sun* reported. Robbins survived.[50]

Luther C. Ladd, seventeen, of Lowell, Company D, was fatally shot on Pratt Street, hit multiple times.[51] Charles A. Taylor, estimated to be twenty-five years old, a resident of Lowell and a fellow member of Company D, was also killed. Taylor was a stranger to his own regiment, having joined the morning the troops left Boston. "He represented himself as a fancy painter by profession," Hanson wrote. "Such was the haste with which the companies were organized, and the lack of system with which the books were kept in those first days of the war, that his loss was not even known until his overcoat was received."

"The gentleman who sent it saw him fall, and testifies that the brutes crushed him with clubs and rocks, so that almost all trace of humanity was beaten out of him," Chaplain Hanson continued. "He did not wear a uniform, and so was taken for a civilian; and was therefore buried in Baltimore. No trace of his family or friends has ever been discovered."[52]

A mile into the march, the Baltimore police asserted themselves, according to the mayor's account. A squad of fewer than fifty officers, handguns drawn, formed a line between the soldiers and the mob, which had been trailing the troops. "'Keep back, men, or I shoot!' shouted Marshal Kane. The mob recoiled like water from a rock," Brown wrote. This account deserves a measure of skepticism. That fewer than fifty police officers with handguns—whose loyalty to the Union was dubious, led by an openly secessionist police chief—would strike fear in a mob of thousands, where 220 soldiers had not, strains credulity.[53]

Nonetheless, following this intervention the troops were able to march the four remaining blocks, turning left down Howard Street, to bring them to the station. Even then, the fighting flared. Seeing one of Follansbee's companies pressured by the mob, the troops on the train opened fire through the windows. Bullets smashed into the walls of surrounding buildings, sending chunks of brick and dust flying. "The faces of many of the soldiers, as seen through the car windows, were streaming with blood from cuts received from the shattering glass of the car windows and from the missiles hurled into them," the *Baltimore Sun* reported.[54]

The march through the city had taken close to two hours.[55] Nearly fifteen hundred rounds had been fired, including some after the men boarded the train. "Quite a number of the rascals were shot," Follansbee said.[56] Now nearly unified at the Camden Station, the regiment wanted to go back out and fight.

Jones wasn't having it. He had orders to get to Washington. The railroad officials were frantic. And the Baltimoreans had still not given up. They surrounded the Camden Station and moved down the line in an effort to obstruct the train's passage south. "The panting crowd, almost breathless with running, pressed up to the car windows, presenting knives and revolvers, and cursing up into the faces of the soldiers," the *Baltimore Sun* reported.[57] Marshal Kane sent men down as far as the Relay House, seven miles southwest of the city, to protect the tracks.[58]

The B&O's William Smith, knowing that the mob's fury was unabated and that the police couldn't hold them back forever, appealed to Jones: "For God's sake, Colonel, give the orders to start the train, or you will never get out of the city, they're already tearing up the track."[59] As rocks and bricks began crashing into the train, Jones ordered the men to shut the blinds. He knew his regiment wasn't fully unified yet—he had 138 men missing, including the entire band, and all their baggage and equipment was gone. He had three confirmed dead and close to forty wounded. He also had orders from General Scott to not delay in getting to Washington.[60]

Jones considered his options. "The surging crowd of thousands of maniacs, as far as the eye could reach, and so dense that their very bodies blocked the wheels of our cars, yelled defiance," Jones wrote in a letter to Watson years later. "Every impulse bade me accept the challenge, but I remembered that obedience to orders was a soldier's first duty."[61] He ordered the thirteen-car train to depart. It was around 1:00 p.m.

An eyewitness described the scene: "As the train left Camden Depot, the soldiers in the hindmost car had their muskets pointed out of cars. [Police deputy marshal Thomas] Gifford pointed a pistol at them, close to their heads, and cried, 'put in your muskets, you sons of bitches, or I will blow your brains out.' Another police officer did the same."[62]

The train moved a short distance and stopped. The tracks were obstructed. This happened several times. "Great logs and telegraph poles, requiring a dozen or more men to move them, were laid across the rails, and stones rolled from the embankment," the *Baltimore Sun* reported. "A body of police followed after the crowd, both in a full run, and removed the obstructions as fast as they were placed on the track. The police interfered on every occasion, but the crowd would dash off in a break-neck run for another position."[63]

The conductor reported to Jones that it was impossible to proceed—the regiment would have to march to Washington. "We are ticketed through, and we are going in these cars," Colonel Jones shot back. "If you or the engineer cannot run the train, we have plenty of men who can. If you need protection or assistance, you shall have it; but we go through."[64]

As they left the city, the Sixth Massachusetts would provoke one final incident to inflame the rioters. A dry goods merchant, Robert W. Davis, well known in the community, was among the people on the tracks southwest of the Camden Station who were watching the train pass. "The train carrying the troops at about this point was greeted by some boys with cheers for the Southern Confederacy," wrote Maryland historian J. Thomas Scharf. "Mr. Davis laughingly shook his fist at the train as it passed, all unconscious of any difficulty having occurred in the city."

"One of the soldiers ran his gun out of the window, and taking deliberate aim at Mr. Davis, shot him," Scharf added. A friend asked Davis if he was hurt. "His only reply was, 'I am killed.'"[65]

Jones also referred to this incident, but with a different spin. "After a volley of stones, some one of the soldiers fired and killed a Mr. Davis, who I have since ascertained by reliable witnesses threw a stone into the car; yet that did not justify the firing at him, but the men were infuriated beyond control," he wrote in his official report.[66]

The train continued out to the first stop on the Washington line, the Relay House, where the B&O's main line connected from the west. Eight miles from the Camden Station, it was also where the double-tracked urban line merged into a single track. Incredibly, the troops endured a tense two-hour delay as they waited for a northbound train that had the right of way. They finally got to Washington, thirty-five miles away, late in the afternoon.[67]

Attack on the Musicians and the Pennsylvania Volunteers

Davis's death further incited the rioters, who raced back to the President Street Station, fueled by rumors that more troops were about to arrive. In fact, only the unarmed Pennsylvania Washington Brigade remained there, along with the Sixth Massachusetts's band.

So far, the mob had spared the Pennsylvania recruits. But the Washington Brigade's commander, Gen. William Small, was increasingly worried. From his position on the train, a block or more east of the depot, he'd seen and heard the commotion around the depot as the four cutoff Massachusetts companies began their march.[68]

Now the Pennsylvania enlistees and Massachusetts musicians were sitting ducks. Their only protection, at least in the case of the Philadelphia soldiers, was that they were wearing civilian clothes and could easily blend into a crowd. Because the cars were detached and separated into groups of two or three, it was hard to communicate with other cars, or with the depot, located on the other side of the vast train yard.[69]

Small believed this day's conflagration should never have happened. He'd been in the overnight meetings with Colonel Jones and the railroad executives. He'd pushed for a much earlier departure from Philadelphia on a faster train, passing through Baltimore before daybreak, and by doing so, avoiding the mob entirely. The 3:00 a.m. departure, and the slowness of the heavy thirty-five-car train, resulted in a much later arrival in Baltimore.[70]

It was only a matter of time, Small knew, before the mob redirected its wrath to the President Street depot and his helpless men. He felt his only choice was to abandon the attempt to get to Washington. He sent two officers to the depot to find someone from the PWB Railroad who could secure a locomotive and get his men back to Philadelphia.

But Small's emissaries found no one who would acknowledge any responsibility. So Small himself went to the depot, even though it meant separating himself from his command. Lt. Col. Caspar M. Berry, who headed the First Regiment of the brigade, took it on himself to prepare. "I sent orders to the officers in command of each car to detail an officer or reliable man, with such a weapon as might be procured, to stand at each door of the car, and to have the windows closed," Berry wrote.

By 2:30 p.m., the mob descended, armed with pistols, knives, clubs, and paving stones. Stoked with rage over Davis's killing, as many as ten thousand people swarmed the cars, smashing them with rocks, clubs, lumber, fence posts, and whatever else they could find.[71] "The infuriated demons approached howling and yelling," the *Boston Saturday Evening Courier* said. "Kill the sons of bitches—hang them to the first lamp-post!" one rioter shouted. "That's right, boys, go in!" yelled another.[72]

Berry reported that his officers kept the car doors shut as best they could. His men behaved remarkably well, considering a large majority of them were raw recruits.[73]

A member of the Sixth's band was sent out to find General Small. On the musician's return, said band member Artemas S. Young, "he was set upon, driven into the car, followed by a number of the roughs. We fought them off as long as we could; but thicker and faster, some crawling from under the cars, others jumping from the tops, they forced their way in, in spite of our utmost exertions."

Band members called for help from the police, but in vain. "These fellows seemed to sympathize with the mob," Young said, repeating what many eyewitnesses said about the Baltimore police that day.

The rioters tore open the train car doors. Sensing their odds of surviving were as good outside as inside, both the Pennsylvanians and the Massachusetts band members leapt out and either fought with the mob or scattered. "We saw squads of police, who took no notice of us, evidently regarding the whole thing as a good joke," Young wrote. "I spoke to two of them, and was told to 'run—run like the devil.'"[74]

Young ran. A half-mile to the east, "we encountered a party of women, partly Irish, partly German, and some Americans, who took us into their houses, removed the stripes from our pants, and we were furnished with old clothes of every description for disguise."[75]

Young and his bandmates had been rescued by Ann Manley, a well-known boarding house and brothel operator who lived on Eastern Avenue and whose husband, James, was a political street brawler who favored the Whigs. The Manley's main opponents, going back more than a decade, were the same secession-sympathizing Democratic agitators leading the day's rioting.[76]

Back in the train yard, Pvt. George Leisenring, twenty-six, a Washington Brigade recruit serving in Company C of the Second Regiment, unarmed and with no uniform, was sitting in his car close to the roundhouse. He was in the last seat of the last car in the rear, as far from the swarm as possible. "Some of the miscreants jumped upon the roof of the car, and with a bar of iron beat a hole through it, while others were calling for powder to blow them all up in a heap," the *Courier* reported.[77]

Leisenring and his fellow recruits huddled on the train, peeking through shuttered windows. The word was to sit tight and wait for an official plan, presumably a return to Philadelphia.

Suddenly one of the rioters burst into the car and stabbed Leisenring, first in the back, and then, as the young soldier turned to face his attacker, in his side.[78] It was one of the day's last acts of deadly violence. The arrival of Maryland Militia general Charles C. Egerton, accompanied by a contingent of police, restored order just as the mob attempted to break into a nearby gun store.[79]

There are many conflicting accounts of the Baltimore Police Department's role that day. Kane, Brown, Scharf, and others, representing the secessionist position, claimed the police acted repeatedly to quell the riot. Ample eyewitness evidence supports that. But equally substantial evidence from Northern soldiers, local observers, and subsequent grand jury testimony indicates that at times the local police did nothing to stop the rioters and even egged them on.

There was a disinclination by the police to arrest violent offenders. "Saw nobody arrested except (a local butcher, Frederick) Cook for tearing up the secession flag," William P. Smith, of East Lombard Street, testified. Pvt. William Lynch, of the Second Maryland Regiment, saw the same incident and testified, "Did not see any man arrested except Fred Cook for trying to take away a Palmetto flag."

Lynch also described more violent encounters with the police:

Officer George Jones assaulted John Hoffman & broke his head with a spontoon [a type of ax used as a military weapon], crying 'You black son of a bitch, you came here to fight us white men.' Saw G. Konig [Konig was a notorious Fells Point/Causeway brawler and political street enforcer] at depot with Palmetto flag in his hand. Saw [Police Chief] Kane half a square from there, looking on and seeing troops assaulted . . . saw Konig & others go in the end of the train & driving out the unarmed men, and the police knocking them over the head as they came out.

Kane and Konig, it appeared, were on close terms. Police officer Robert Meads testified, "Saw Kane put his arm round Konig's neck & whisper something in his ear. Konig immediately then went on to hurrah for J.D. [Jefferson Davis] & riot generally in Kane's presence."

Witness Joseph Lee testified that "Konig came back leading the riot—the crowd then returned to Depot & beat all the soldiers as they came out & battered the cars. Kane came in and said, 'Boys you won't spoil my reputation will you?' Konig, who had a chain & iron ball in his hands, replied, 'No Marshal Kane, we are your boys we[']ll stand up for you.'"

"The police could have stopped the riot but did not try," said Edward Airey, a carter. "Stones came from right among the police."[80]

In the late afternoon, order was restored. A locomotive finally puffed to life. Slowly the scattered cars were reconnected. The Massachusetts musicians, with some of their injured comrades and the Pennsylvania recruits who had not been chased into the streets, were sent back to Philadelphia. Several members of the Sixth Regiment's band were severely wounded. Their instruments were destroyed.

Pennsylvania private George Leisenring was taken to Philadelphia, conscious enough to describe his stabbing to doctors, but he died three days later at the Pennsylvania Hospital. Leisenring, a German, had no relatives in the city.[81]

He was the fifth and last Northerner fatally attacked that day, joining four Massachusetts soldiers slain in the march to the Camden Station: Addison O. Whitney, killed instantly by a bullet in the chest; Luther Ladd, who praised the Union flag in his last words; Charles Taylor, the stranger from Lowell; and Sumner Needham, who had predicted his death earlier that day.

Needham, whose wife was then pregnant with their first child, was the last of the five soldiers to die but might have been the first to be fatally injured. Near the corner of President and Pratt, he was struck on the front left side of his head with a brick or cobblestone that fractured his skull. He also had a severe cut over his right eye. He was taken to the Lombard Street infirmary in Baltimore, where he lingered until April 27 and died after a botched brain surgery.[82]

The nature of the casualties indicate that the mob was mostly following the troops, which were marching in a four-abreast column, led by Company C. Companies I, L, and D followed. Company C escaped with just one man wounded. Company D had eleven wounded and three killed.[83]

Twelve civilians were known to have been killed, including at least three likely innocent bystanders. They were

James Clark (formerly connected with the No. 1 Hook and Ladder Company);

William R. Clark (twenty, who had recently enlisted in the Confederate Army and was expected to go South in a few days);

Robert W. Davis, the dry-goods merchant;

Sebastian Gill (forty, shot in the upper chest);

Patrick Griffin (employed at the Green House on Pratt Street);

John McCann;

John McMahon;

Francis Maloney;

William Maloney (twenty-five, shot in the left thigh, causing a hemorrhage);

Philip S. Miles (eighteen, shot in the abdomen and had his left leg shattered);

Michael Murphy; and

William Reed (a sailor from the oyster sloop *Wild Pidgeon* from York County, Virginia).[84]

Following the war, Colonel Jones tried for decades to locate Charles Taylor's remains. On June 20, 1910—forty-nine years after the attack—the *Baltimore Sun* reported that Taylor had been found in the Methodist cemetery at Lafayette Street and Loney's Lane in Baltimore. Jones, eighty-two years old and blind, now living in Binghamton, New York, had visited Baltimore in 1909 and advertised in the papers seeking information.

A local carpenter, Samuel T. Glenn, had seen the ad and found a grave marked "Killed in riot," the *Sun* reported. Jones returned to Baltimore on June 21, 1910. The grave diggers found nothing. "The search consumed two hours, but not a bone or any part of apparel was found," the *Sun* reported. "Not even a trace of the coffin was detected." Taylor's remains were never found.[85]

13

Insurrection in Maryland

In the early afternoon of Friday, April 19, Maryland governor Thomas Hicks finally acknowledged reality and concluded that Baltimore was out of control. He ordered out the militia. Nine companies mustered at the armories throughout the afternoon. They were assigned to work with the police keeping the peace.[1]

The Northern troops were leaving town—either advancing to Washington or retreating to Philadelphia—but the city still seemed likely to spin further into chaos. Hicks and Baltimore mayor George W. Brown had simultaneous and immediate objectives. They appealed to the national authorities in Washington to stop sending troops. And they set to work browbeating the railroad companies for the same reason.

Their most important endeavor was to calm the frenzied city. Written notices went up announcing that Mayor Brown had called a town meeting for 4:00 p.m. at Monument Square. The announcement neutralized the mood—but not before some rioters came to the telegraph office at the corner of Baltimore and South Streets and cut the line to the North.

"The leader, armed with a hatchet, demanded that the Northern wire be pointed out to him," the author William R. Plum wrote. "Without waiting, he hurried to a window and severed one of the lines. This was soon repaired, and a report was circulated, in order to mislead the public, that all the wires had been cut. But, in fact, one or two were crowded all day with government business." Even so, the overloaded lines worked poorly and sporadically.[2]

An hour before the mayor's town meeting, a throng had already formed on North Calvert Street at the square. By 4:00 p.m., ten thousand people had assembled, gathered around the thirty-nine-foot monument commemorating the Battle of Baltimore during the War of 1812.[3]

Crisis management may have been the meeting's objective, but it devolved to the edge of being treasonous. The defense of Maryland was paramount, the speakers said. The blood of their citizens was in the street, and it did all the talking that was needed. If the Union had been violated, creating a Northern military despotism, then it was better to stand with the South than live under the "fanatical tyranny" of the North.

Mayor Brown, in his own remarks, called for peace in the city and said it was his duty to protect strangers and citizens of the city alike. "Fellow citizens, be quiet that you may hear me," Brown said to the crowd. "I do not wish to be misunderstood."

No one disagreed with President Lincoln's call for seventy-five thousand troops more than he did, Brown said, but knowing that Maryland was part of the United States and that the troops were called to the national capital, it was his duty to protect them at the risk of his life. The authorities had done what they could to control the mob, but they'd also telegraphed the president to send no more troops through Baltimore. He'd sent the same message to the executives of the various railroads, Brown said.

Then Brown reached his central point. "We all feel and know," Brown said, "as we trust the people of the North will soon feel and know, that it is the height of madness or folly for one portion of this country to attempt to subjugate the other. The South could never be coerced—never! Never! Never! If neither section will yield, then in God's name, let them part in peace!"[4]

Governor Hicks wasn't in attendance for most of the rally. But he was finally asked to speak. The most important part of his brief remarks was the words Thomas H. Hicks is probably best known for a century and a half later. "I am a Marylander," he said, "and I love my state, and I love the Union, but I will suffer my right arm to be torn from my body before I will raise it to strike a sister state."[5]

Around midday, Hicks and Brown had telegraphed Lincoln, saying, "Sir: A collision between the citizens and the Northern troops has taken place in Baltimore, and the excitement is fearful. Send no troops here. The troops of the state and the city have been called out to preserve the peace. They will be enough."[6]

Then Hicks and Brown sought to block the troops by eliminating their means of transportation. In a joint telegram issued under police commission president Charles Howard's name, they advised B&O Railroad president John W. Garrett that troops should be sent back to "the borders of Maryland."

Garrett replied the same day, saying he was "most cordially approving of the advice" and would pass it on to PWB Railroad president Samuel Felton.[7] Felton said he'd comply—"at present"—and that he had asked Baltimore officials to confer with the appropriate authorities on the subject.[8]

Felton and Pennsylvania Railroad president J. Edgar Thompson immediately passed this information on to Secretary of War Cameron, saying, "We are informed by the Baltimore road that Governor Hicks states that no troops can pass through Baltimore City. In fact, the Baltimore and Ohio Railroad refuse to transfer. We will wait for instructions."

Lincoln and his advisors considered these messages, both from the Maryland officials and the railroad companies. The president and some cabinet members believed Hicks's and Brown's initial message—"Send no troops here. The troops of the state and the city have been called out to preserve the peace. They will be enough."—meant that no troops were needed to regain control of Baltimore. General Scott and Secretary of State Seward, however, read another meaning: that Maryland would not permit more troops to pass through the city. In the end, a sharp response went to Thompson and Felton from Cameron's adjutant general, Lorenzo Thomas: "Governor Hicks has neither right nor authority to stop troops coming to Washington. Send them on prepared to fight their way through, if necessary. By order of the Secretary of War."[9]

Later that evening, around 11:00 p.m., Hicks and Brown tried a new approach. This time, they sent three emissaries to Washington, carrying a message from Mayor Brown to Lincoln. The messengers were H. Lennox Bond, a criminal court judge in Baltimore; John C. Brune, president of the board of trade; and George W. Dobbin, a prominent lawyer. Their message said, in part, "The people are exasperated to the highest degree by the passage of troops, and the citizens are universally decided in the opinion that no more should be ordered to come. Under these circumstances it is my solemn duty to inform you that it is not possible for more troops to pass through Baltimore unless they fight their way at every step."

John Nicolay, writing in a contemporaneous memorandum, said the delegation from Baltimore arrived at 1:00 a.m. and that a messenger woke him. Instead of rousing Lincoln, Nicolay wrote, he went to the War Department, a short walk across the White House lawn, where Cameron was spending nights sleeping on the couch.

"The mission of the committee was to induce the govt. to send no more troops through Baltimore," Nicolay wrote. "I woke the Sec. War, who was not disposed to listen to such a proposition, and went to sleep again. I learned however from the Chief Clerk that there were no troops (to their knowledge) on the way which would reach Balt. before 8 next morning when they could see P with their proposal. This satisfied them for the time being and they went away."[10]

In Baltimore, rumors persisted for hours that more troops were on the way. All through the afternoon and into the evening of the nineteenth, spasms of violence continued. Throngs of armed men, in official militias and otherwise, roamed the streets.

They smashed into gun shops all over town, stealing weapons and ammunition. Several thousand rifles and associated ammunition were looted from shops across the city.[11]

Police Marshal Kane told the police commission in a report on May 3 that his office was "beset" that day by people trying to confirm whether more troops were on the way. He heard from a B&O

official that his Pennsylvania Railroad counterparts reported they were not going to be able to stop troops from advancing on the Northern Central Railway south to Baltimore.

Mayor Brown, meanwhile, said "there was also a report that troops were on their way from the northeast and might even then be at Perryville, heading to Baltimore."[12] Brown rashly concluded that city officials were on their own. The messengers to Washington had only departed at 11:00 p.m., leaving no time for a response before morning. But that didn't stop Brown. Something had to be done. "In this emergency," he wrote, "the board of police, including the mayor, came to the conclusion that it was necessary to burn or disable the bridges on both railroads so far as was required to prevent the ingress of troops."[13]

Troops from the North, Baltimore officials believed, would reignite the conflagration. Secessionist Marylanders believed soldiers passing through their state to supposedly invade the South was a grave affront. From the perspective of the city officials, burning the railroad bridges was justifiable.

Kane and Brown likely shared both perspectives—their sense of responsibility as city officials as well as a sense of outrage as secessionists. They went to see Hicks.

Hicks, sixty-two, had long been viewed with suspicion by Southern sympathizers in Maryland. He'd been elected governor in 1858 as a member of the American Party, or the Know-Nothings— a group considered to be generally anti-immigrant and anti-Catholic but pro-Union.[14] He'd followed a policy of inaction throughout the secession winter, ignoring or declining repeated calls to summon the state legislature into session to consider secession. Brown, on the other hand, was elected in 1860 as part of the Reform Party and had referred to the Know-Nothing rule of the city of the prior half-decade as a "reign of terror."[15]

The governor and the mayor were uneasy allies. This evening, Hicks had "taken refuge" at Mayor Brown's house. He'd been staying at the Fountain Hotel, but after the Monument Square rally, he'd been followed back to his quarters "by a large portion of the crowd," some calling out, "Hang him, hang him." Naturally as a perceived Unionist—even if a weak one—he felt threatened in the secessionist chaos.[16]

For most of the day on the nineteenth, the governor had been a nonfactor, leaving the response to the riot in the hands of the local authorities. Now the local authorities needed his approval for their bridge-burning plan.

Around midnight, Brown took his brother, John C. Brown, along with Kane and the former governor E. Louis Lowe, to Hicks's bed chamber, where they laid the matter before him. Hicks was feeling unwell.

The governor wavered. He pleaded lack of authority. He asked for time to consider the request. "The point was pressed that if troops were suddenly to come to Baltimore a terrible collision and bloodshed would take place and that the only way to avert the calamity was to destroy the bridges," Brown wrote. "To this the governor replied, 'It seems to be necessary' or words to that effect."[17] "The conversation resulted in the governor's distinctly and unequivocally consenting," stated Police Marshal Kane. Lowe, the ex-governor, similarly agreed.[18]

Whatever was said, the conspirators had obtained sufficient approval. But by adopting a plan to destroy the railroad bridges, the police, the mayor, and the governor of Maryland were preventing troops from coming to the defense of their nation's capital in a time of war. Whatever their motivation, it's difficult to characterize their action as anything other than treason.

Later Hicks denied that he had given any such approval. "I neither authorized or consented in the destruction of said bridges; but left the whole matter in the hands of the mayor with the declaration that I had no authority in the premises—that I was a lover of law and order and could not participate in such proceedings," he wrote in a May 4 statement to the Maryland Senate.[19]

The South

As Northern troops fought to get south, Confederate troops were starting to move north. Jefferson Davis on this Friday replied to Virginia governor John Letcher's request for troops: "Have ordered one regiment from Columbia, S.C., and one from Charleston, and two or three companies from Augusta, Ga., something more than your requisition, to proceed immediately to Norfolk.—JEFF'N DAVIS."[20]

William Howard Russell again spent time with Confederate general Pierre G. T. Beauregard in Charleston on this Friday. Beauregard was feeling expansive. Virginia was an immense part of the puzzle, Beauregard said, and as of yet, that state had not been as prompt as he'd hoped—Lincoln's call for troops was a declaration of war against the South, and all would ultimately be involved.[21]

Meanwhile, the Richmond diarist John Beauchamp Jones was speculating on the ease by which the Confederates might seize Washington. "From the ardor of the volunteers already beginning to pour into the city, I believe 25,000 men could be collected and armed in a week, and in another they might sweep the whole Abolition concern beyond the Susquehanna, and afterward easily keep them there," Jones wrote.

But Davis, Jones lamented, was a states' rights advocate who wouldn't make a move until after Virginia ratified its secession ordinance, scheduled for late May. "Thus a month's time will be lost; and the scene of conflict, instead of being in Pennsylvania, near Philadelphia, will be in Virginia."[22]

The City

The Sixth Massachusetts Regiment arrived in Washington around 6:00 p.m. Friday evening. The troops were greeted at the station by Maj. Irvin McDowell of Winfield Scott's staff, along with a crowd of five thousand cheering people.

Lucius Chittenden, the Treasury Department register, had broken away from work to see the arrival. He walked the mile and a half to the Washington railroad depot, located on New Jersey Avenue where it converged with North Capitol Street and C Street. It stood on what's now literally the Capitol grounds, just a block away from the modern Union Station.

"The crowd was large, and in no mood to listen to treasonable observations," Chittenden remembered. "I heard one man remark

that the regiment was one of those sent by that d____d abolitionist, Governor Andrew. The next moment he was sprawling in the
gutter. Not a word was spoken by his assailant."

The soldiers "left the cars and formed in two lines on the street,"
Chittenden said. "Then a procession of men with stretchers came
out of the station. On each lay a wounded man. I counted seventeen. Their dead they had left in Baltimore. The wounded were
placed in ambulances and sent to the Washington Infirmary."

An anxious and relieved President Lincoln came to see the regiment. Jones remembered, "President Lincoln grasped my hand,
and with tears in his eyes, said, 'Thank God you are here. If you
had not come, we should be in the hands of the rebels before morning. Your brave boys have saved the Capital. God bless them.'"[23]

The arrival of the troops added nothing to the dearth of information in Washington. The locals were as jumpy as the Maryland
secessionists. "We have rumors that 1500 men are gathering and
under arms at Alexandria (seven miles below here) supposed to have
hostile designs against this City," Lincoln's secretary, John Nicolay,
wrote at about 10:00 p.m., "and an additional report that a vessel was
seen landing men on the Maryland side of the river. All these things
indicate that if we are to be attacked soon it will happen to-night."[24]

Fear, intrigue, and uncertainty prevailed. "Many people are leaving the city," Elizabeth Lindsay Lomax wrote in her diary. "Great
excitement and unrest."[25]

"Another cool pleasant day but one of great excitement," Patent
Office Examiner Horatio Nelson Taft wrote in his diary.

> Reports from various quarters indicate that danger is iminent
> [*sic*] of an attack upon the City. Harpers Ferry Armory and arse-
> nal was destroyed this morning by Govt troops. The Steam Boats
> on the River have also been seized by Govt order. I went to the
> Depot to see the arrival of the Mass. Regiment. They came at
> last, after fighting their way through Baltimore loosing two men
> killed and firing upon the rioters, killing a number. A splendid
> looking set of men. They were marched directly to the Capitol
> and quartered there. I was at all the Hotels, home at 10 o'ck.[26]

The *New York Tribune* correspondent Albert Richardson remembered Washington in the grip of panic. "An attack from the Rebels was hourly expected," he said. Hundreds of families had fled in terror. The air was filled with startling rumors. For the three days he was there, Washington was virtually blockaded, receiving no mail, no telegrams, and no Northern reinforcements. "Martial law was sadly needed," Richardson said. "Most of the Secessionists had left, but enough remained to serve as spies for the Virginia Revolutionists. I left for New York by an evening train crowded with fleeing families."[27]

Much earlier this Friday, Lucius Chittenden was shocked when he arrived for work at the Treasury Department. Armed men guarded the entrances, where workers were busy placing huge beams for breastworks and piling sandbags. Stacks of rifles and boxes of ammunition filled the halls. Barricades closed the way to the vaults. All the while, Chittenden and his team were struggling with the upheaval in the workforce. Applications for leaves of absence were constant. "The epidemic of nervous diseases was on the increase," he wrote. "I granted them freely. I did not expect the applicants would return, and I was not disappointed."[28]

At the White House, Abraham Lincoln engaged in both small tasks and momentous acts. He inscribed the album of a visitor, Mary Rebecca Darby Smith, a friend of former president James Buchanan who'd attended Lincoln's inauguration, with the following:

White House, April 19, 1861.

Whoever in later-times shall see this, and look at the date, will readily excuse the writer for not having indulged in sentiment, or poetry. With all kind regards for Miss Smith. A. LINCOLN

Lincoln also issued a blockade of Southern ports. This would prove to be portentous. The proclamation read, in part,

Whereas an insurrection against the Government of the United States has broken out in the States of South Carolina, Georgia, Alabama, Florida, Mississippi, Louisiana, and Texas, and the laws of the United States for the collection of the revenue cannot be effectually executed, I, Abraham Lincoln, President of the United States, have deemed it advisable to set on foot a blockade of the ports within the States aforesaid. And I hereby proclaim and declare that if any person, under the pretended authority of the said States, or under any other pretense, shall molest a vessel of the United States, or the persons or cargo on board of her, such person will be held amenable to the laws of the United States for the prevention and punishment of piracy.[29]

The proclamation set the United States on a dangerous collision course with Great Britain. As early as March 20, the British minister to the United States, Lord Richard Lyons, had warned Secretary of State William Seward not to interfere with England's trade with the Confederacy.

"If a considerable rise were to take place in the price of cotton, and British ships were to be at the same time excluded from the Southern Ports, an immense pressure would be put upon Her Majesty's Government to open those ports," Lyons said. "It certainly appeared that the most simple, if not the only way, would be to recognize the Southern Confederacy." Lyons repeated this warning on April 12 in a message to Robert Bunch, the British counsel in Charleston, who was instructed to tell the journalist William Howard Russell that any interruption of trade probably would result in British recognition of the Confederacy.[30]

At this point in mid-April, British public opinion—and Lyons's own—was solid: the split in the American Union was permanent. This sentiment laid the crucial groundwork for official recognition of the Confederacy, a move that, if it came, would change the outcome of the Civil War. "If I had the least hope of their being able to reconstruct the Union, my feeling against slavery might lead me to desire to cooperate with them," Lyons wrote two weeks later, on May 6. "But I conceive all chance of this to be gone forever."[31]

Norfolk, Virginia

The situation was grave for the Norfolk Navy Yard, now in enemy territory. Navy Secretary Gideon Welles ordered Washington Navy

Yard commandant Franklin Buchanan and Buchanan's subordinate, John A. Dahlgren, to prepare to destroy the Norfolk yard.
They were ordered to get a ship underway as soon as possible,
led by Com. Hiram Paulding, who was sent to Norfolk on special
duty by Welles. Paulding asked for one of the Navy's best ships,
the uss *Pawnee*.[32] Dahlgren loaded it with forty barrels of gunpowder, eleven tanks of turpentine and 181 "portfires," or fuses.
One hundred marines were assigned to the mission. In addition,
General Scott had ordered U.S. Army engineer Capt. Horatio G.
Wright to join them, tasked with establishing a plan of defense.
So the *Pawnee* was coaled, supplied, and outfitted. By Friday evening, it was racing down the Potomac River. It reached Fort Monroe around 2:30 on Saturday afternoon.[33]

14

Washington Cut Off
and Insurrection Rages in Maryland

I t was well past dark on the most eventful day in Baltimore history—Friday, April 19, 1861. John H. Longnecker, publisher of the *Baltimore County American* and an acquaintance of Maryland governor Thomas Hicks, was passing through northern precincts of the city, heading home to Towsontown, about ten miles north. Longnecker was on horseback with a friend, close to the entrance to Green Mount Cemetery, well beyond the chaos still swirling in Baltimore. Cobblestone streets gave way to dusty country roads.

"I left Baltimore at precisely ten minutes past ten o'clock," Longnecker wrote in a May 29, 1861, letter to Governor Hicks that was intended to establish a timeline for when the bridge burnings began. "In about ten minutes, I reached a point about one hundred yards from the cemetery entrance, where I saw an omnibus [now known simply as a bus] with four horses, heads turned up the road. I had previously passed two groups of men, about fifteen each. And when we passed the omnibus I remarked to a friend who was with me, 'there is some devilment connected with that omnibus.'"

Longnecker was right. Several dozen heavily armed raiders, steely eyed and quiet—with axes, picks, crowbars, and a distilled form of turpentine called camphene—were headed out of town on buses that evening, bent on malevolent purposes.[1]

Longnecker's intent in his letter was to support Hicks. In the process, though, he also offered an eyewitness account of the early moments of an extraordinary act of state-sanctioned insurrection. Maryland, a state still in the Union, was moving to cut off the federal capital from loyal troops coming to its defense.

Baltimore in 1861 was a transportation and communications hub—or bottleneck. To get to Washington by railroad from the Northeast, the only way was through Baltimore.

If rail traffic through Baltimore was impeded, Washington would be cut off, leaving only much slower overland or seaborne routes. The water approach was inaccessible because Virginia controlled the southern side of the Potomac. Washington would be vulnerable to easy occupation by hostile forces. Three railroads served Baltimore. The PWB Railroad came in from the Northeast, rolling down the Eastern Seaboard. The Northern Central Railway ran straight south from Harrisburg. The B&O Railroad extended out of Baltimore to the southwest, and at a junction eight miles south of the city, it split, with a spur heading to Washington and the main line extending through Maryland into Virginia and through to Ohio.

As the nation was coming apart over slavery, its capital was surrounded by slave-holding states. The Mason-Dixon Line was sixty miles north of Washington, and the nearest large and friendly city, Philadelphia, was over one hundred miles away. Virginia had seceded. Secession loomed in Maryland. Washington was in a panic, and Baltimore, a strategic transportation center, was in full-blown revolution.

Late on the evening of the nineteenth, two squads numbering more than one hundred men each—police officers, militia troops, firefighters, and civilian vigilantes, many of whom had a hand in the mayhem that afternoon—left Baltimore, heading out to burn the bridges and cut the telegraph wires on two lines: the Northern Central Railway and the PWB Railroad.

Baltimore militia captain John G. Johannes led the demolition party on the Northern Central. Isaac R. Trimble, the lawyer, railroad executive, and Confederate sympathizer, had the same task on the PWB. Coincidentally, Trimble had been superintendent of that railroad between 1842 and 1853. He was fired in 1853 for a variety of graft-related allegations.[2] The B&O Railroad, south of Baltimore, wasn't targeted.

On the Northern Central, Johannes and his fast-moving band continued beyond the city line. The countryside became desolate in the two miles between Druid Hill Park and Melvale, evenly split between woods and open fields. The wagon road north paralleled the Jones Falls River, with the railroad on the opposite side. It was cold in the midnight hours of early spring. Leaves had just emerged, and many trees were still budding. Spent blossoms and seed pods littered the dusty country road as the men made their way through the night.

The railroad crossed to the eastern side of the river at Melvale, five miles from Pratt Street, the scene of the midday attacks. This bridge—with wooden-truss construction and perhaps one hundred feet across—was the first burned on the Northern Central Railway.[3]

Melvale bridge watchman Jackson McComas heard the rumble of hoofs and the clatter of the omnibuses before the demolition team finally rode into view. At this point, Mar. George P. Kane, the Baltimore police chief, was with the saboteurs.

"I was arrested by Dan'l Miller, a policeman, while I was on duty," McComas testified later that year during a grand jury inquiry. "After I was taken, Kane came up and said they were going to burn the bridge by the authority of the governor. They told me they were going to destroy the road for the purpose of keeping the northern soldiers back."[4]

Two days later, the newspapers started reporting the stories of the bridge burnings. The marauders demanded possession of the bridge, the *Baltimore Daily Exchange* reported. They tore up the watch house and parts of the bridge, piling wood on and under the bridge. "The turpentine was poured upon the mass and the torch applied, and in a few minutes the whole structure, which cost $6,000 to build, was one sheet of flame," the *Exchange* wrote.[5]

Four miles up the line from Melvale was Lake Roland, where the railroad crossed (and still crosses) a reservoir expanded in the late 1850s as part of the Baltimore municipal water supply. This bridge and a nearby relay house were at the junction of a branch line extending out to Westminster, Maryland.[6]

The *Daily Exchange* continued its first-person account: "Cheering and shouting, the citizens proceeded on their way, and as day broke citizens from the surrounding country joined them. Arriving at the bridge, they crossed, and after unscrewing the immense girders, the structure was turned over into the water, which is about 12 feet deep."[7]

After dismantling the Lake Roland Bridge, the saboteurs moved on to Cockeysville, another ten miles up the track, and destroyed a large bridge crossing the Big Gunpowder Falls River, close to the hamlet of Ashland, just eighteen miles from the Pennsylvania state line. Ashland was one of thirteen Northern Central Railway stops in the thirty-six miles to the border.[8]

A southbound overnight train had stopped at Ashland. "The passenger train from Harrisburg was within a half mile of the bridge, and it was burned in the face of the passengers, whoever they might have been," the *Daily Exchange* reported. "After daylight the parties dispersed, cutting telegraph wires and poles at several points upon the route."[9]

One thing was certain. The destruction was enough to stop Northern troops from advancing south from Harrisburg for several weeks.[10]

As Johannes was leading the destruction on the Northern Central Railway, another armed group of militiamen, police officers, and civilians, led by the militia leader and ex-PWB superintendent Isaac Trimble, proceeded with a similar demolition effort on the other main line into Baltimore—the Philadelphia, Wilmington, and Baltimore Railroad (the PWB).

The bridge closest to the center city was at Harris Creek in suburban Canton, barely a mile and a half and slightly southeast of the President Street Station. The Canton bridge, 104-feet long, had railroad tracks on one-half of it and a wagon road on the other. It was directly along the harbor.[11]

PWB president Samuel Felton had anticipated the vulnerability of his line and posted security guards along the tracks and at the bridges months earlier. "They were raw and undisciplined men, and not fit to cope with those brought against them by the redoubtable rebel, J. R. Trimble," Felton acknowledged, misidentifying Trimble's initials.[12]

Felton was right. As it happened, his men were either run off by Trimble's show of force or bought off with free beer.

Trimble, with 160 police and militia, converged at the Canton Bridge just before 3:00 a.m. His plan was audacious. He would destroy the first bridge, then go as far as the Susquehanna (thirty-five miles northeast), scuttle the steam ferry *Maryland* at Havre de Grace, and then move south back to Baltimore, burning the bridges after crossing them at the Bush, Gunpowder, and Back Rivers.[13]

Alex Wiley, the Canton Bridge watchman, was in his shed when the soldiers and police showed up. They seized Wiley, threatened to throw him into the harbor, and eventually took him to Trimble. "I asked what they were doing. They said it's none of my business," Wiley testified to the U.S. Circuit Court grand jury on September 17. "I begged them not to burn it."[14]

Trimble burned the bridge from the northbound side and then marched to the nearby engine house, where he waited for the overnight mail train. It arrived at 3:14 a.m. and was seized immediately. Trimble loaded his force onto three cars and started northward. Among the weary passengers ordered off the train and stranded in Canton was PWB paymaster Nicholas Trist, on his way to Washington to report to Secretary of War Cameron on the need to activate the Annapolis route for troops advancing to Washington. He'd left Philadelphia by the midnight train and now would be delayed for several hours in reaching Washington.[15]

Moving north from Canton, Trimble's train reached the Back River Bridge, about six miles from Canton, at about five o'clock in the morning. Here and farther north at Magnolia, Trimble seized telegraph operators—first William J. Dealy, who had been stationed here temporarily just a few days earlier, and then James A. Swift at Magnolia. The train made no other stops until after it crossed the farthest-north bridge at the Bush River.[16]

With Trimble's three-car train chuffing north at twenty-five miles per hour, he could feel the goal within his grasp. Not only would he destroy four bridges; he'd scuttle the railroad's ferry. He'd cut off the railroad route for Northern troops and return a hero.

But then sometime before 8:00 a.m., with the train barely eight miles from the Susquehanna, one of the train's enginemen along with the conductor, Charles Howard, gambled on a courageous bluff. They talked Trimble out of proceeding. Troops were concentrating at Perryville, they told Trimble. Felton recalled, "[They] told Trimble there were twenty-five hundred soldiers on board the ferry-boat, who would give him a very warm reception if he attempted to go to the river."[17]

Trimble decided his bid to scuttle the *Maryland* was too risky. The train crew had successfully deterred him. They lied about the position of the troops. They probably knew that Massachusetts troops had already arrived in Philadelphia. They knew the soldiers were likely heading south. But just as likely, they had no idea when the troops might get to Perryville. Nevertheless, the crew wasn't far off. The Eighth Massachusetts Regiment left Philadelphia around noon this day and arrived at Perryville at about 6:00 p.m., meaning that Trimble and General Butler would miss each other at the Susquehanna by about eight hours.

Trimble began the return to Baltimore, burning the bridges on the way, starting with the Bush River span.[18] He couldn't turn the train around, so with the locomotive still pointing north, Trimble moved in reverse, proceeding backward down the track in the direction of Baltimore.

The Bush River Bridge was the northern-most bridge of the three that were burned that day, twenty-four miles from Baltimore, and just over eleven miles south of Havre de Grace. The rail line traversed a wide estuary, over three thousand feet long. Here the bridge keeper's daughter, Jane Bowman, about twenty-three years old, decided she wasn't going to stand by and let Trimble and his raiders get away with it.

The train stopped directly in front of the Bowman house on the south side of the bridge. Jane bolted out. She walked directly up to Trimble and called him "a coward." She loudly urged Felton's security guards to do their jobs. "When she saw these men throw away their arms, some taking to the woods and others hiding in her father's house, she called on them again not to run, but to stand fast and be men," wrote Capt. James Green and 1st Lt. E. J. Smithers, Company D, of the First Delaware Volunteers, in a report to their colonel, Henry H. Lockwood, on July 11. (Green and Smithers were not present at the bridge burnings but were relaying anecdotes they heard from railroad employees.) Seeing a pistol lying on the porch, abandoned by one of the security guards, Jane Bowman grabbed it and ran to the master carpenter of the line, a Mr. Smith, and handed him the gun, saying, "Use it. If you will not, I will."

At the same time, one of her father's men was out on the bridge as it began to burn. Jane was the first to think of him. "She promptly called upon her father, or some one, to go for him in a boat, saying, 'If no one else will go, I will,'" Green and Smithers wrote.

Colonel Lockwood reported the Bowman anecdotes to Felton on July 13, saying, "The highly remarkable conduct of Miss Bowman calls, in my opinion, for some substantial reward from your honorable board. She is quite young, apparently not over 22 or 23, and really, for her station in life, quite an attractive young person. I have found her modest and retiring, and this character is given to her by the officers. I hope you will excuse me for troubling you with this matter, but I feel that I am only doing an act of justice to a worthy family."[19]

Jane Bowman's father, James M. Bowman, the Bush River bridge tender, offered his own perspective in grand jury testimony on October 7. "Trimble was lead man + ordered fire to be set to the bridge + the lumber [lying] about then. He forbade us to put it out," Bowman said. "This was just after the riot of 19th Apl—between 7 + 8 o'clock [in the morning]. The police officers had axes + did the work—all worked in burning the bridge."[20]

The party reembarked, crossed the longest of the four bridges—the 5,238-foot long span at the Gunpowder River—and then set that bridge's draw ablaze. Trimble's team made an attempt to destroy the Back River Bridge, but Felton's security guards had applied salt and alum whitewash earlier in the year, which rendered the effort futile.[21]

The raiders returned to Canton and celebrated, offering beer to anyone who happened by. Railroad employee John Seveline woke to the sound of the train returning and went to what was left of the Canton bridge. "Seven or eight officers were in the cars drinking beer; they called me to drink with them," he testified later.[22]

David H. Sullens, of 338 Eastern Avenue, testified that he saw a great crowd of police at the train. "They had two kegs open," he said. "They offered me a cap of beer out of the cars and drank themselves. These were govt stores—cars marked 'for Washington.' Militia Capt. Kenney was taking acct of the beer and other stores, including beef, as it was being taken away."[23] Fresh off their beer celebration at Canton, the arson teams "marched to City Hall, where they were received in triumph."[24]

Trimble, in his own account, downplayed the sabotage: "Two of the bridges on the Philadelphia Road had been rendered impassable for a week by burning the draw bridges, 18 and 20 miles from the city. I refrained from doing other damage to these costly structures, only burning the draws in the channel."[25]

This is untrue. Three bridges, including the one at Canton, were burned, and the fourth, at the Back River, was only saved because of the earlier efforts of Felton's men. It took several weeks to get the bridges operational again. Also, Trimble would have scuttled the *Maryland*. Numerous police officers confirmed the details of the torching of the PWB line—and their roles in it—later that year at the grand jury.

For example, Officer John McCleane testified on September 2, "I was under Lieut. Essender, who was under Boyd + we all regarded Maj Trimble as the leader. We burnt three bridges—I heard Maj Trimble give the orders—telegraph poles were cut down—we all took part—all participated—a military guard accompanied us."[26]

The end result, on this chilly midspring Saturday morning, was precisely what the Maryland secessionists wanted—Washington DC was plunged into darkness. The telegraph wires of both major rail lines were also cut, resulting in no communication from the North or the West, the *Washington Star* wrote.[27] The capital's local militia, plus the five unarmed Pennsylvania companies and the battered Sixth Massachusetts, were all that stood against a sudden Confederate strike.

In the aftermath of the destruction of the bridges and telegraph lines, recriminations began immediately. The participants, facing charges of treason once the U.S. government regained control of Maryland, scrambled to fudge the timelines and downplay their own involvement.

Baltimore's Mayor Brown and Police Marshal Kane claimed they acted on the authority of the city's board of police commissioners and the governor—who apparently gave verbal approval to destroy the bridges shortly after midnight on the twentieth. The police board had convened at 1:00 a.m. on the twentieth and voted unanimously to authorize Kane to destroy the bridges. That meeting adjourned at 2:30 a.m.[28]

Of course, by then the work was well underway, so the police board's approval was irrelevant. Longnecker's account suggests the plan was activated at least three hours earlier, ordered by Kane and Brown, who then used Hicks's verbal assent and the vote of the Police Commission to add official approval to an operation they'd already initiated. Indeed, a former police officer, Charles W. Bates, testified at the grand jury hearing on October 3 that the order to deploy came much earlier. "I took the order between 9 + 10 o'clock from Kane to destroy the bridges," he testified. "Brown was present in Kane's office at the time the order was given—police + military started for the purpose between 10 + 11 o'clock."[29]

Then Trimble made the improbable claim that he was home in bed at midnight when he was summoned by the mayor. "At 12am the 19th and 20th while at home in bed, I was sent for by the Mayor to repair to his office," Trimble recalled weeks later. "On my arrival he said that it had been decided to destroy the bridges on the two roads as the means of preserving peace and the lives of the Citizenry and concluded by saying he wanted me to break down those on the Philadelphia Road. I replied if the thing was to be done and he would give me a written order with the approval of the Governor, I would do it."[30] It's implausible that Trimble, a colonel in the Baltimore militia who would be named to command all city troops just two days later, was home in bed at midnight on the most eventful day in Baltimore history.[31]

Governor Hicks denied complicity. In a series of open letters to the people of Maryland, first on May 4 and then again in a comprehensive letter in June, he claimed that he had no authority to order the burnings and also no power to interfere with the mayor of Baltimore. "I unhesitatingly assert that I refused consent," Hicks claimed. "I do not deny that the proposed act, unlawful though it was, seemed to be the only means of averting threatened bloodshed."

Hicks also claimed the timeline didn't work. "The bridges destroyed on the Northern Central Railroad [sic] were 16 and 18 miles from Baltimore," Hicks wrote. "The bridges were fired a little after one o'clock. It being impossible for the men to have left Baltimore after it was alleged my consent was given, they must have started before my consent was asked."[32]

At least the Baltimore Police Commission, which had voted unanimously to approve the demolition, took unambiguous ownership in a report to the state legislature on May 3. The report was strikingly hostile. "The absolute necessity of the measures is fully illustrated by the fact that on Sunday morning a large body of Pennsylvania troops were stopped in their progress toward Baltimore by the partial destruction of the Ashland Bridge," the report stated. "The tone of the whole Northern press and of the mass of the population was violent in the extreme. Incursions upon our city were daily threatened."[33]

15

A New Route to Washington

The Advance

Close behind the Sixth Massachusetts, more Northern troops were pushing south. The Eighth Massachusetts arrived at the Prime Street Depot in Philadelphia shortly before 5:00 p.m. on Friday evening.[1]

The Seventh New York arrived nine hours later. The time between arrivals roughly corresponded with when the bridge destruction was planned and carried out—though the bridge wrecking continued into the daylight hours.

Massachusetts general Butler hesitated in Philadelphia. Just a day earlier, the Sixth Massachusetts had arrived in Philadelphia just before 8:00 p.m. and was on a southbound train at 3:00 a.m. Now Butler was nowhere near as decisive. The Eighth Massachusetts ended up becalmed in Philadelphia for nineteen hours.

PWB president Samuel Felton urged General Butler to forego the plan to go through Baltimore. Felton was reasonably sure it was impossible now to get through. He asked Pennsylvania Militia major general David Patterson to persuade Butler to take the same Annapolis route he'd urged on Colonel Jones the night before. (Patterson had been named commander of the federal Department of Pennsylvania the prior day.)[2]

If the train route through Baltimore was no longer possible, anyone with a map and a rudimentary sense of geography could plot out the alternatives. The rail line was clear through Perryville, on the north side of the Susquehanna, sixty miles from Philadelphia. The south side was the problem. Havre de Grace was thirty-five miles from Baltimore and seventy-three miles from Washington. Northern troops faced a march on foot of more than seventy miles. This would take days. And a march would almost certainly be opposed.

The more obvious routes were by water. One option was to steam from Philadelphia down the Delaware River to the ocean, then to the mouth of the Chesapeake Bay, and then either up the Potomac to Washington or up the bay to Annapolis. Another was to take the train from Philadelphia to Perryville, embark the ferry there, and sail down the bay to Annapolis.

Either way at Annapolis, troops could board a branch railroad line and connect with the B&O's own spur to Washington, forty miles from Annapolis. This was Felton's plan. Butler at first resisted the Perryville route. He wanted to go through Baltimore even if it meant marching overland. It wasn't until perhaps 3:00 a.m. on the twentieth that he finally agreed.

At 11:00 p.m., Butler telegraphed Massachusetts governor Andrew, "I have reason to believe that Col. Jones has gone through to Washington. Two killed only of the Massachusetts men. We shall go through at once." At midnight, Butler sent Andrew another dispatch. "I will telegraph again, but shall not be able to get ready as soon as I hoped."[3]

When Butler did make up his mind, it was to wait some more. He proposed combining the Massachusetts Eighth with the New York Seventh when that regiment arrived in Philadelphia, then advancing to Perryville by train and then by water to Annapolis. If Seventh Regiment colonel Marshall Lefferts wouldn't cooperate, Butler would take the Eighth forward alone.[4]

Butler called the Eighth's twelve officers together late that evening, explained his plans, and theatrically placed thirteen pistols on the table. He picked up the one in front of him and invited the officers to each pick up the gun to indicate they supported his plan and were ready to proceed. Each man took up a revolver.[5]

"My proposition is to join with Colonel Lefferts of the Seventh regiment of New York," Butler wrote in a dispatch to Governor Andrew. "I propose to take the fifteen hundred troops to Annapolis, arriving there to-morrow about four o'clock, and occupy the capital of Maryland, and thus call the state to account for the death of Massachusetts men, my friends and neighbors."[6]

"If Colonel Lefferts thinks it more in accordance with the tenor of his instructions to wait rather than go through Baltimore," Butler continued, "I still propose to march with this regiment. I propose to occupy the town, and hold it open as a means of communication. I have but then to advance by a forced march of thirty miles to reach the capital, in accordance with the orders I first received, but which subsequent events in my judgment vary in their execution. I have detailed Captains Devereux and Briggs with their commands to hold the boat at Havre de Grace."[7]

Butler might have mistakenly mentioned Baltimore in this message. Or perhaps he really intended to march from Annapolis to Baltimore before going to Washington, a notion astonishingly divergent from his orders to proceed to the capital. Maybe he really wanted to redirect his troops and pursue a fight in Baltimore; maybe he didn't. But Annapolis was forty miles from Washington—Butler mentioned a march of thirty miles, or about Baltimore's distance from Washington. He never explained this disparity.

Also, Butler's last sentence, implying that two companies were already on the way to secure the ferryboat *Maryland*, wasn't true. These companies never left the rest of the regiment.

In any event, he still had to convince Lefferts to acquiesce. They hadn't even met.

The Seventh New York arrived in Philadelphia at about 2:00 a.m. on the twentieth. Colonel Lefferts and the company officers met immediately with PWB president Felton. They expected to spend just two hours in Philadelphia and board a 3:00 a.m. or 4:00 a.m. train to Baltimore.[8] Their sense of urgency contrasted markedly with Butler's.

But Felton told the Seventh's officers that the bridges between Havre de Grace and Baltimore had likely been destroyed. They worked through the early morning hours to develop options. Butler never joined Felton and the officers of the New York Seventh for these consultations.

Several facts were clear from Lefferts's perspective. Everyone knew that the Sixth Massachusetts had been cut up passing through Baltimore. Everyone suspected that the Maryland insurrectionists were even now burning the railroad bridges below the Susquehanna. Everyone feared that the steam ferry between Perryville and Havre de Grace might no longer be available. If the bridge-demolition party had reached the river, Felton counseled, then the ferry, the *Maryland*, was likely disabled, destroyed, or commandeered. At 5:00 a.m. Lefferts sent a telegram to Secretary of War Cameron: "Sir,—Having arrived at Philadelphia, we are informed by the President of the Philadelphia and Baltimore Railroad that Governor Hicks states no more troops can pass. In fact, the Baltimore and Ohio Road refuses to transport. We will wait for instructions."[9]

But instructions wouldn't be coming. The telegraph wires were cut. Some messages were getting through, but only sporadically. Lefferts was on his own. Felton urged the Annapolis route in cooperation with Butler. But neither Felton nor Lefferts had any way to know for certain whether the *Maryland* was still available. Lefferts decided Annapolis was his objective and that he'd opt for the longer route—an ocean steamer from Philadelphia—rather than risk the journey to Perryville only to find the *Maryland* scuttled.

Early that Saturday morning, an aide came to Lefferts at the train station and said that "General Butler would like to see him at the Lapierre House." To which Lefferts replied, "Who is Butler?" Told he was the brigadier general commanding the Eighth Massachusetts plus three other regiments, including the Sixth, Lefferts added that he'd be happy to meet with Butler later.

Butler, according to the Seventh's biographers, showed up at the railroad depot at 7:00 a.m. and asked Lefferts "what he proposed to do." Lefferts said he was waiting for the War Department to respond.[10]

For the second time, Lefferts telegraphed Secretary of War Cameron asking for orders, this time with more urgency: "Will you give order to dispatch troops via Annapolis to-day from Havre de Grace by large iron ferry-boat? The Baltimore and Ohio Road decline to transport any more troops from the North. We think this is decidedly best, and are joined in this opinion by General Patterson, General Cadwalader, and Governor Curtin."[11]

The War Department finally responded, but the reply never got through to Philadelphia. "Send the troops now en route to this city by rail to Havre de Grace; thence by iron ferry boat to Annapolis, as suggested by Colonel Lefferts," Adj. Gen. Lorenzo Thomas wrote to Major General Patterson.[12]

But without knowing the federal government approved of his recommendation, Lefferts had made his own plans. He'd take the ocean route from Philadelphia to the mouth of the Chesapeake Bay and head either to the Potomac and Washington or to Annapolis, depending on circumstances.

Lefferts chartered the civilian steamer *Boston*. He fitted it out and loaded it with coal and three days' rations of beef and bread for the men, plus extra ammunition. He did this on his own authority and his own financial risk, drawing money from his own firm in New York.

Butler returned to the train station at 10:00 a.m., still hoping to convince Lefferts to join him in the Perryville-to-Annapolis plan. Butler had an aggressive, take-charge manner, becoming—in the words of the Seventh's biographer, William Swinton—a "doughty dare-all."[13]

Lefferts told Butler his own plan seemed better under the circumstances. It was unclear if the *Maryland* could accommodate nearly two thousand men. It might not even be at the Susquehanna. It might not be afloat. Butler proposed to retake the boat by force. In the end, Lefferts couldn't come around to it. He declined to advance with Butler.[14]

On the Move from Philadelphia

Most of the Seventh's men slept in the train cars till daylight, oblivious to the high-stakes scramble between the two commanders. Shortly after dawn, they were dismissed for an hour. They fanned out to find breakfast, mostly heading north from the barren streets around the depot. Seventh Regiment private Fitz James O'Brien and his comrades eventually found that the superintendent of the Pennsylvania Institution for the Education of the Deaf and Dumb, at Broad Street and Pine, half a mile directly north from the station, was willing to serve breakfast to anyone who asked.

Other soldiers of the Seventh, O'Brien wrote, "being luxurious dogs, went down to the Continental and Girard hotels [about 1.4 miles from the station], where they campaigned on marble floors and bivouacked on velvet couches. They are such delicate fellows, the Seventh regiment!"

Theodore Winthrop was part of another group that headed to the Lapierre House hotel for breakfast, near the intersection of Broad and Chestnut, just less than a mile from the station. When Winthrop got there, the restaurant was already filled with soldiers. "So being an old campaigner," Winthrop wrote, "I followed up the stream of provender to the fountain—the kitchen. Half a dozen other old campaigners were already there. They served us with the best of their best."

Back at the depot, the men found "a mountain of bread was already piled up," wrote Winthrop. "I stuck my bayonet through a stout loaf, and, with a dozen comrades armed in the same way, went foraging about" for still more food for the uncertain days ahead.[15] The depot was the center of attraction this morning for an immense crowd that came to see the famous regiment, the *New York Tribune*'s Philadelphia correspondent reported.[16]

In Philadelphia, the men of the Seventh New York met the soldiers of the Eighth Massachusetts for the first time. They took a liking to one another, though the initial reaction of the Seventh's men was tinged with condescension. "They [the Eighth Massachusetts] are in all sorts of uniforms, and drill in the funniest way," Robert Gould Shaw, a private in the Seventh, wrote to his parents on April 23. "All fishermen from Marblehead and shoemakers from Lynn, they seem itching for a fight."[17]

"The Massachusetts men presented a contrast to the members of the Seventh," wrote O'Brien. "They were earnest, grim, determined.

Badly equipped, haggard, unshorn, they yet had a manhood in their look. With us it was different. Our men were gay and careless, they looked battle in the face with a smile."[18]

The soldiers of the Seventh also met General Butler for the first time. They were not impressed. Second Company captain Emmons Clark said Butler was a man of "unsoldierly dress, dumpy figure, unprepossessing face." The regimental biographer William Swinton called Butler a "splenetic brigadier." Robert Gould Shaw described Butler as an "energetic, cursing and swearing old fellow."[19]

All this and more was true. Butler was always certain of his own judgment and was not shy about claiming credit for things he deserved—and things he didn't.

Sometime before 11:00 a.m. Butler vented in a telegram to Governor Andrew, "Colonel Lefferts has refused to march with me. I go at three o'clock to execute this imperfectly written plan. If I fail, purity of intention will excuse want of judgment or rashness."[20]

In the end, both Butler's and Lefferts's plans had advantages and disadvantages. Lefferts's route was more assured and provided more options. Sail around the Delmarva Peninsula along the eastern coast of Maryland and from there either directly up the Potomac to Washington or, if the Potomac was not passable, to Annapolis. But it was three times the distance. Butler's route was shorter and more direct but more uncertain. If the *Maryland* had been seized or wrecked, the Eighth Massachusetts might lose days seeking another way to cross the wide Susquehanna. Also, the Eighth had 724 men, and the Seventh had 991. The *Maryland* didn't have the capacity to carry 1,700 men and their supplies. It would have taken at least three trips down the Chesapeake Bay and at least another day to transport both regiments to Annapolis.[21]

Lefferts believed the longer route was more certain and improved the probabilities of getting to Washington faster. Also, he was part of the New York State Militia command structure. Even if he supported Butler's reasoning, there was no mechanism for putting his New York troops under a Massachusetts Militia general. Nor did he want to. Writing years later, men from both sides debated the decisions made in Philadelphia. The Seventh was bitter about

Butler's misrepresentations and that he had successfully wrested control of the historical narrative. "To go by rail to Havre de Grace was a mere experiment," Swinton wrote. "The route of the Seventh, and not that of General Butler, was adopted by all succeeding regiments from the North for many and many a day."[22]

The Seventh Regiment's Emmons Clark even jibed that Butler lacked the money to do what they did. "It is more than probable that General Butler would not have adopted so uncertain and unreliable a route, if he had had the same unlimited credit the Seventh Regiment possessed in Philadelphia," Clark wrote.[23]

"The men were not prepossessed in [Butler's] favor, and his manners and appearance failed to remove the unfavorable impression," Clark added. "He was captious and conceited, almost to rudeness; and his well-known political antecedents, as a Southern sympathizer, as a supporter of slavery, the cause of the rebellion, were not calculated to secure the confidence of the intensely loyal young men of the Seventh Regiment."[24]

On the contrary, claimed the Butler contingent, Colonel Lefferts had gotten squishy. "That officer, suddenly intrusted [sic] with the lives (but the honor also) of nearly a thousand young men of New York, was overburdened with a sense of responsibility," wrote James Parton in a biography of Butler. "It is impossible for a New Yorker, looking at it in the light of subsequent events, not to regret the refusal to join General Butler in his bold and wise movement," Parton added.[25]

At five minutes before 11:00 a.m., the Eighth Massachusetts, with 13 officers and 711 enlisted men, left the depot on a southbound train. The train was heading for Havre de Grace and an uncertain rendezvous with a ferry boat.[26]

At 3:00 p.m. on this uncommonly beautiful April afternoon, the Seventh formed up at the depot and marched down to the Delaware River wharf. The *Boston* was a tight fit—991 men plus the crew on a small steamer. Longshoremen cast away the hawsers at 4:20 p.m., and the Seventh Regiment was on its way, just over fourteen hours since arriving that morning.

The Eighth had a three-hour ride to Perryville, where Butler's plan was to halt the train a mile before town and advance

skirmishers. They'd rush the ferry if needed. Along the way, Butler went through the cars, inspecting the men and their rifles.[27] "I
said that we should probably lose a considerable number of men,
and that they had nothing to do but each in his own way to prepare himself for the event in the three or four hours that were left
us," Butler wrote later.

When the train reached Perryville, it was still daylight. The men
formed up for the advance.

But it was a false alarm. All was well on the *Maryland*, tied up
quietly on the northern bank of the river, waves lapping against
the boat. But now Butler had to get the *Maryland* to Annapolis,
fifty-five miles down the bay. A few of the ferry's officers and crew
remained; others had deserted. There was no coal on board, steam
wasn't up, and there were no provisions.

The *Maryland* was a three-level sidewheel vessel with an iron-
plated hull and twin steam engines. It was 238 feet in length, with
pilot houses on both ends, a beam of 36 feet, and an extreme breadth
of 66 feet. It had three railroad tracks on its main deck, allowing
as many as twenty cars to be rolled onto the boat—passengers
on the trains never had to leave their cars. It had large halls with
salons interspersed on both sides, and its water wheels were ten
feet high.[28]

Butler rolled four cars loaded with coal onto the boat. He had the
men fill empty whiskey barrels with water and load them aboard
too. The men's rations were mostly gone. Despite suspicions about
the loyalties of the crew, Butler and his men, packed tightly on the
ferry, cast off about 6:00 p.m.[29]

While Butler was taking control of the *Maryland*, the Seventh
was sailing through Delaware Bay into the Atlantic. The soldiers
wrote rich accounts of their voyage, framing it as a grand excursion. It was a picture for posterity of affluent, privileged, patriotic
young men "roughing it" on the most important mission of their
lives. "We floundered about the crowded vessel like boiling vic-
tims in a pot," Winthrop wrote. "At last we found our places, and
laid ourselves about the decks to tan or bronze or burn scarlet, according to complexion."[30]

The men gazed out over the rails at the passing sea. They slept on the decks. They climbed on top of the giant sidewheel housings and sat on superstructure decks, legs dangling off the sides. They played cards in small clusters. Fitz James O'Brien offered an extended, colorful account.

> The first evening, April 20, on board the *Boston*, passed delightfully. We were all in first-rate spirits and the calm, sweet evenings that stole on us as we approached the South, diffused a soft and gentle influence over us.
>
> The scene was exceedingly picturesque. Fellows fumbling in haversacks for rations, or extracting sandwiches; guards pacing up and down with drawn bayonets; knapsacks piled in corners, bristling heaps of muskets, with sharp shining teeth, crowded into every available nook; picturesque groups of men lolling on deck, pipe or cigar in mouth, indulging in dolce far niente [pleasant idleness]. I regret to say that all was not rose-colored. The steamer was imperfectly provisioned. In the first place, she was far too small to accommodate a thousand men, and we were obliged to sleep in all sorts of impossible attitudes. The men were jolly. I never saw a more good-humored set of men in my life.
>
> Fellows who would at Delmonicos have sent back a turban de volaille aux truffes [poultry with truffles], because the truffles were tough, here cheerfully took their places in file between decks, tin plates and tin cups in hand, in order to get an insufficient piece of beef and a vision of coffee. But it was all merrily done. Here I say to those people in New York who have sneered at the Seventh regiment as being dandies, and guilty of the unpardonable crimes of cleanliness and kid gloves, that they would cease to scoff had they beheld the honest, genial way in which these military Brummells roughed it.[31]

More Northeastern Troops Deploy

A wave of troop departures was accelerating in the northeastern states. In Providence, the first troops of the First Rhode Island

Regiment were ready. On Saturday morning, as Lefferts and Butler were sparring in Philadelphia, a detail from ten companies, totaling 544 officers and men, accompanied by Gov. William Sprague, left Narragansett Bay on the steamer *Empire State*. "It seemed as though almost the entire population of the State of Rhode Island crowded the streets, to witness the departure and to bid them Godspeed upon their dangerous enterprise," wrote thirty-five-year-old Augustus Woodbury, pastor of the city's Westminster Unitarian Church and the regimental chaplain, who authored an extended narrative of the campaign.[32]

In Boston, the same day the Sixth Regiment was battling the mob in Baltimore, orders came through for the Massachusetts Fifth Regiment to report. The troops, under Col. Samuel C. Lawrence, twenty-eight, of Medford, were ready by the next day, the twentieth. But as with nearly all these initial regiments, clothing and equipment was lacking. So the Fifth's deployment was delayed one day.[33]

Charles Bowers, third lieutenant in Company G, wrote a series of colorful letters home about the Fifth Regiment's journey. Bowers was forty-eight years old and the father of six children when he volunteered to serve as the third lieutenant in Company G of the Fifth Massachusetts, also referred to as the Concord Artillery.

He remembered this Saturday as a blur. In a letter home on April 28, he described the scene: "Men were coming in to enlist, friends calling to bring the few little things that had been forgotten. Loads of military equipment of all kinds landing on the hall; the unpacking and distribution of them to a thousand soldiers, now all ready to march."[34]

Meanwhile, three New York State Militia regiments—the Sixth, the Twelfth, and the Seventy-First, were scheduled to depart on Sunday morning, the twenty-first. A one-day delay served to allow more time for organization. "It was necessary to take 500 more men to bring the regiment up to full strength," wrote Seventy-First Regiment biographer George Lowen. "The difficulty was not to get men, but to refuse."[35]

The South

Confederate military preparations were heating up too. Volunteers were pouring into Richmond. Other Confederate state capitals were inundated. In Baltimore, Mayor George W. Brown's call for militia volunteers had produced fifteen thousand men—three quarters of them armed, most of them presumably secession supporters. The Baltimore volunteers were placed under the command of Col. Isaac R. Trimble, leader of the bridge raiders.[36]

Calls to attack Washington were becoming more strident. Henry D. Bird, superintendent of the strategically vital Southside Railroad, which linked both Lynchburg and North Carolina directly to Richmond, urged an assault on Baltimore and/or Washington in two telegrams to Confederate secretary of war Leroy P. Walker.

In one, Bird told Walker that Virginia governor Letcher had seized several Potomac steamers. These vessels provided part of a transportation network that could put seven thousand men across the river and into Baltimore within twenty-four hours, Bird said. They would connect to the South using his railroad's connections from Dalton, Georgia, and Lynchburg. "The Southside Railroad is at the service of the Confederate States," Bird told Walker.[37]

In another message to Walker, Bird elaborated. "Colonel Owen, president of the Virginia and Tennessee Railroad, has just reached here from Baltimore by way of Norfolk," he said. "He witnessed the butchery of Baltimore citizens by the Massachusetts regiment yesterday."

Baltimore was a city up in arms, Bird relayed to Walker. The bridges north of Baltimore were burned. Northern troops couldn't get through unless they marched in large bodies. Maryland was rising. "Lincoln is in a trap," Bird wrote. "He has not more than twelve hundred regulars in Washington and not more than three thousand volunteers. We have three thousand in Harpers Ferry. An hour now is worth years of common fighting. One dash and Lincoln is taken, the country saved, and the leader who does it will be immortalized."[38]

Virginia governor Letcher, looking to impede the advance of Northern troops, issued the following order—really a threat—to John W. Garrett, the president of the B&O Railroad: "In the event that you allow Federal troops to be passed over your road, I will take possession of so much of said road as lies within the limits of this State."[39]

But from the Confederate capital in Montgomery came silence.

16

The Fortified Capital

The City

On the morning of Saturday, April 20, Abraham Lincoln found himself presiding in an isolated city that feared the worst. "No troops today, all stopped beyond Balt.," Horatio Nelson Taft, the examiner at the U.S. Patent Office, wrote in his diary. "Bridges destroyed, track torn up and the Steam Ferry Boat over the Susquehanna scuttled and sunk. Balt in the hands of the mob."

A large body of rebel troops was said to be at Alexandria, just across the Potomac from Washington, with an attack expected any hour. As Taft made his rounds, he saw the damaged Sixth Massachusetts drilling: "They marched out and through Pa Ave to 15 St, making a fine appearance and being cheered frequently by the people. The Hotels are full and all seem agreed that Balt is a doomed City. 12 o'c."[1]

"Crowds everywhere, and soldiers on guard, and everything in a disturbed state," Elizabeth Lindsay Lomax wrote in her diary, noting that acquaintances were having difficulty visiting Alexandria and getting back to Washington. It wasn't surprising—Virginia was now hostile territory.[2]

"The streets were full of talk of Baltimore," John Hay, Lincoln's secretary, wrote. "The town is full of feverish rumours about the meditated assault upon this town. Gen. Scott seems to think that four or five thousand men will be a sufficient garrison to hold this town against any force that may be brought from the Maryland or Virginia woods."

Hay also noticed the Sixth Massachusetts marching on Pennsylvania Avenue. "They step together well and look as if they meant business," Hay said, offering an unflattering comparison to the other early arrivals from the North. "They afford a happy contrast to the unlicked patriotism that has poured ragged and unarmed out of Pennsylvania."[3]

A correspondent for the *New York Times* described Saturday as a "warm, sunny day. The air is redolent of bursting buds, and the Capitol Park is jubilant with the gushing songs of the birds and the humming of the honey bees," the correspondent wrote. The Capitol was no longer the seat of legislation, the *Times* continued. A password and countersign were needed to enter the building. Armed soldiers patrolled the grounds.

The sound of steel-ended rifle butts resounded through the halls. In the Senate chamber, where the men of the Sixth Massachusetts resided, Colonel Jones sat in the vice president's chair—"a frank, free-hearted, soldierly looking man," the *Times* said.

Statuary had been boxed for safekeeping. The artwork was covered with heavy planking. Commissaries were established in the basement. Outside, the porticos were barricaded to eight feet. Iron plates for the dome, which was still under construction, were used as breastworks between marble columns. Behind the plates were barrels of cement and piles of stone and timber, forming a defensive line.

"It seemed a strange contradiction to see the workmen engaged in the construction of the portico," the *Times* continued, "going on with their labor amid thousands of armed men; the click of the chisel, the stroke of the hammer and the ring of the trowel blending with the word of command, the challenge of the guard and the tramp of the battalions in the corridors."[4]

For Treasury Register Lucius Chittenden, it wasn't the weather or the troops at the Capitol that was most striking. It was the isolation. "On Saturday, April 20th, Washington was detached from the loyal states," he said. "We had no mails from the North, no communication by railroad or telegraph with Philadelphia, Harrisburg, or places north or west of either city."

There were only rumors. The bridges had been burned on all the railroads running into Baltimore. The ferry boat at Havre de Grace had been sunk. No Northern regiments could reach the capital. "For outside information we were served with the [states-rights leaning] *Baltimore Sun*," Chittenden wrote. The Treasury Department closed at noon that day, with the keys left in the doors (except the vaults) for the engineers and two hundred regulars under orders to defend the building.[5]

This Saturday was the fifth day since Lincoln's call for troops. Inquiries and updates from the Northern governors were coming in stronger than ever. Everywhere, people wanted to do more. From Maine's governor came a telegram that illustrated the moment.

Augusta, April 20, 1861,

Hon. Simon Cameron,
Secretary of War:

Our people are anxious to do something. Shall we commence in raising five regiments, and shall we prepare to send our troops by steamboat?

I. Washburn, Jr.[6]

At the White House, Lincoln had just finished breakfast when General Scott arrived, pulling up under the North Portico in a carriage. Lincoln's custom in these days was to spare Scott, beset with afflictions, the ordeal of climbing the stairs to the second-floor executive office. Instead he'd come to the door to chat with Scott.

At the foot of the stairs, Lincoln ran into the emissaries sent the night before by Maryland governor Hicks and Baltimore mayor Brown. Lincoln took the three—the Baltimore circuit court judge H. Lennox Bond, the lawyer George W. Dobbin, and John C. Brune, president of the Baltimore Board of Trade—to see Scott in his carriage at the door, where they made their case about the impossibility of marching troops through Baltimore. "March them around," Scott immediately said.[7]

The committee accompanied Lincoln back upstairs, where he wrote out a response to Hicks and Brown. Lincoln concurred with Scott: "For the future, troops *must* be brought here, but I make no point of bringing them through Baltimore. Without any military knowledge myself, of course I must leave details to Gen. Scott. He hastily said, this morning, in presence of these gentlemen, 'March them around Baltimore, and not through it.' By this, a collision of the people of Baltimore with the troops will be avoided, unless they go out of their way to seek it."[8]

Lincoln also left the Maryland officials with an oblique warning: "Now, and ever, I shall do all in my power for peace, consistently with the maintenance of government."[9]

Baltimore's Mayor Brown and Governor Hicks initially accepted Lincoln's and Scott's proposal. "No troops to pass through Baltimore if, as a military force, they can march around," Brown wrote to Hicks. "I will answer that every effort will be made to prevent parties leaving the city to molest them. Do you agree?"

"I hoped they would send no more troops through Maryland, but as we have no right to demand that, I am glad no more are to be sent through Baltimore," Hicks replied. "I know you will do all in your power to preserve the peace."[10]

Lincoln remained skeptical. As he wrote out the telegram, he told the Baltimore committee, partly in jest, "If I grant you this concession, that no troops pass through the city, you will be back here to-morrow demanding that none shall be marched around it." Lincoln was right.[11]

Having sent that message back to Baltimore, Lincoln now learned that Hicks had backed off his offer to provide four regiments to the federal government. The Baltimore secessionists had control of the city, Hicks told Secretary of War Cameron. They had control of most of the state's organized military forces and possession of the armories. Hicks couldn't deliver. "I therefore think it is prudent to decline (for the present) responding affirmatively to the requisition made by President Lincoln," he wrote.[12]

Meanwhile another Maryland delegation—the second of the day, this time the U.S. senator Anthony Kennedy and the former Baltimore congressman J. Morrison Harris—called on Lincoln. Like the other officials, they said their aim was to "prevent further bloodshed" and secure a recall of the orders to move troops through the state.

Lincoln was fed up. "My God, Mr. Harris, I don't know what to make of your people," he said. "You have sent me one committee already, and they seemed to be perfectly satisfied with what I said to them." Harris responded that he didn't know anything about that meeting and merely wanted to state the facts as they existed—more troops coming through Maryland would lead to a bloody battle.

"What am I to do?" Lincoln replied. "I had better go out and hang myself on the first tree I come to, than give up the power of the Federal Government in this way. I don't want to come through your town, or near it, but we must have troops here, or we shall die like rats in a trap." An account of this meeting was published in the prosecession *Baltimore Daily Exchange* under the headline "'Old Abe' Frightened."[13]

Now Lincoln decided it was time to deal directly with Hicks and Brown. He fired off a telegram that evening. "Gov. Hicks, I desire to consult with you and the Mayor of Baltimore relative to preserving the peace of Maryland," Lincoln wrote. "Please come immediately by special train, which you can take at Baltimore, or if necessary one can be sent from hence. Answer forthwith."[14]

Brown replied around 1:00 a.m. Hicks had already left Baltimore for Annapolis, he said, but he was willing to come without the governor immediately. Nicolay woke Lincoln and asked for instructions. The reply to Brown was a single word: "Come."[15]

Elsewhere in Washington, Assistant Secretary of the Treasury George R. Harrington was responsible for distributing all official telegrams delivered after hours. One from Baltimore read, "The rebels are about attacking this building." Just minutes later came another telegram from Baltimore. "They are in the build—."

The unfinished sentence, Harrington wrote, made it clear that the Baltimore telegraph office was now in the hands of the insurrectionist mob. Communication between the federal government and the friendly North had been severed. "Washington and its national treasures was at the mercy of its foes."[16]

Other incoming telegrams described ominous news from Missouri. The word from St. Louis was that Brig. Gen. William Harney, the Tennessee-born commander of the Department of the West, was refusing to arm the loyal militia and that Missouri insurrectionists were threatening to seize the arsenal and the state treasury.

Harrington needed to connect with his boss, Treasury Secretary Salmon Chase. "As I came to the Treasury, I caught sight of a vehicle moving in the darkness, which I hailed at random, shouting— 'Thomas, is that you?' 'It is, sir,' replied the driver. 'Have you the secretary inside?' 'I have, sir.' 'Then stop.' Entering the vehicle, I directed him to drive to Secretary of War Simon Cameron's house."

Harrington and Chase found Cameron in bed, under the weather. They described the situation, particularly the news from Missouri. They suggested that they could draft replies and come back for Cameron's signature.[17] "Well, then, since the wires have been cut, how do you propose to get these orders off?" Cameron asked.

"I propose to see to that matter in person," replied Harrington. He tried all night to secure a horse for a dash from Washington to York, Pennsylvania, or some other point. He couldn't find a horse. As daylight returned, Harrington gave up and went home to get a few hours of sleep, his urgent orders to St. Louis undelivered.[18]

Norfolk, Virginia

Time was running out for the Norfolk Navy Yard. Its commander, Com. Charles McCauley, was paralyzed with indecision. Confederate militia units were massing around the facility. The civilian workforce had mostly melted away.

The uss *Pawnee* reached Fort Monroe after steaming down the Potomac River through the night. On board was Com. Hiram Paulding, sent by Welles to restore control of the yard, plus one hundred U.S. Marines and other senior naval officers. An army captain, Horatio G. Wright, joined with orders to create a plan for the defense of the navy yard.

The group arrived at Fort Monroe around 2:00 p.m. It turned out that two Massachusetts regiments—the Third and the Fourth—had just arrived via ocean steamer from Boston and Fall River that morning.

The commander at Fort Monroe, Lt. Col. Justin Dimick, ordered six companies from the Third Massachusetts, 349 men under Col. David W. Wardrop, to accompany Paulding and Wright to the navy yard on the *Pawnee*. At 5:15 p.m., the regiment went onboard. The "undisciplined" troops "took up all the spare space on the *Pawnee* and delayed us for some hours," wrote the churlish captain Charles Wilkes, who was part of Paulding's contingent and designated to take command of the *Merrimack* and lead that ship out of the yard with a skeleton crew.[19]

At 6:45 p.m., the *Pawnee* got underway, heading west across Hampton Roads. It steamed slowly up the Elizabeth River into the heart of darkness. Passing Sewell's Point at the river's entrance, the men noticed several vessels that were sunk as obstructions by the Virginians, their masts rising malevolently from the water.

The *Pawnee* glided slowly and quietly upriver with the untested Massachusetts soldiers at general quarters, guns loaded. At 8:00 p.m., they churned into the navy yard's harbor, enveloped by the pitch-black night. They were challenged by the nervous crews of the *Cumberland* and the *Pennsylvania* but then were greeted with cheers.[20]

But the reinforcements were too late. McCauley had already scuttled his ships.

Alone and relying only on his own atrophied judgment, McCauley panicked that morning and ordered his fleet destroyed. He was "stupefied, bewildered, and wholly unable to act," Commander Alden reported to Welles later.[21]

"I commenced scuttling the *Germantown, Plymouth, Dolphin,* and *Merrimack,* destroying engine and machinery of the latter, cutting away the large shears [giant cranes extending over docked ships], spiking all the guns in the yard and on board ships in ordinary, including the *Pennsylvania*," McCauley wrote in a report to Welles on the twenty-fifth. "By this time, it was quite dark. My officers, with a few exceptions, had all deserted me; even the watchmen had taken part with the secessionists, so I determined on retiring to the *Cumberland* and in the morning act as circumstances might require."

Shortly after the *Pawnee* arrived, McCauley came aboard. Paulding was now in overall command. His initial intention had been to move the ships into the channel to prevent the ongoing work of obstructing it and then move them to Fort Monroe. But McCauley had finished sinking the ships by 4:00 p.m., so Paulding's plan A was impossible. His only choices now were to retreat, leaving the yard as is, or to destroy it to the greatest extent possible. That's what he ordered.

Large shore parties of Massachusetts soldiers and *Pawnee* marines and sailors were sent out into various parts of the yard, some to set up a defensive perimeter and others to destroy the property. One party tried to knock the guns off their mounts, but a hundred men with sledgehammers couldn't do it. Instead the guns were spiked—a nail or spike hammered into the holes at the back the guns through which the fuses were lit. Then they were dumped in the river.

Another group went to inspect the scuttled ships to see if they could stop them from sinking further. All but the *Dolphin* were too far gone. Com. James Alden, sent to the yard by Welles on the eleventh, was ordered to prepare for the destruction of the storehouses, shops, and other buildings. Com. B. F. Sands was assigned to prepare the ship houses for destruction. Others were responsible for setting the ships themselves on fire. Army captain Wright and Navy commander John Rodgers would destroy the dry dock. Forty soldiers from the Third Massachusetts hauled powder and tools to the dock.[22]

The dry dock was the most important asset in the yard. Without the dry dock, the Confederates would have had a much more difficult task in building their own navy. Shipbuilding, salvage, maintenance, and repair capability would be impeded. "If the government are not sure of holding the Gosport navy yard, for God's sake totally destroy the drydock there," the Buffalo, New York, lawyer A. Buist wrote to Welles.[23]

Wright and Rodgers, assisted by their party of navy bluejackets and Massachusetts militia, fumbled through the dry dock in the darkness. They found a pumping gallery along the back of one of the side walls, in two feet of water. They used whatever materials they could get their hands on to build a platform above the surface of the water and loaded two thousand pounds of gunpowder on the platform. They connected it via a long gunpowder train to four separate match points.[24]

Now they had to race back to their boats before the signal to detonate went off and the navy yard exploded in flames.

FIG. 1. President Lincoln with his secretaries, John Nicolay, left, and John Hay. Their jobs encompassed parts of the modern roles of body man and confidant, communications director and chief of staff, in addition to secretary. Library of Congress, Prints and Photographs Division, Washington DC, LC-USZ61-216.

FIG. 2. William Stoddard, Lincoln's third secretary, wrote extensively about Lincoln's White House. Courtesy of the Indiana State Museum

FIG. 3. The White House during the war. Lincoln's office is on the second floor,
the second and third windows from the right. National Archives.

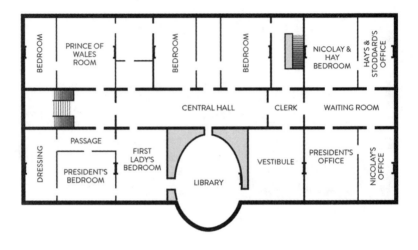

FIG. 4. The White House second-floor layout in 1861, showing Lincoln's office along with Nicolay's, Hays's, and other features. Created by Erin Greb.

FIG. 5. The State Department on Executive Square. The Treasury Department building, still under construction, is seen in the background. Note the sandy cobblestones on Pennsylvania Avenue, lower left. Library of Congress, Prints and Photographs Division, Washington DC, LC-B8184-10017.

FIG. 6. The Willard Hotel, around the corner from the White House, was a
social center of the city. Library of Congress, Prints and Photographs Division,
Washington DC, LC-USZ62-35231.

FIG. 7. Gen. Winfield Scott, Lincoln's top military commander, was widely viewed as a soldier well past his prime. Library of Congress, Prints and Photographs Division, Washington DC, LC-USZ61-7.

FIG. 8. Newly elected governor John A. Andrew was the man behind
Massachusetts's ability to put five fully equipped regiments into the field within a
week. Courtesy of the Massachusetts Historical Society

FIG. 9. Col. Edward Jones led the Sixth Massachusetts Regiment through the Baltimore Riots. His was the first armed and equipped federal unit to make it to Washington. Courtesy of the U.S. Army Heritage and Education Center, Carlisle PA.

FIG. 10. The bombastic Massachusetts brigadier general Benjamin Butler is credited with forcing troops through to Washington, but in reality he hesitated at every step. National Archives.

FIG. 11. Samuel Felton, president of the strategically vital Philadelphia, Wilmington, and Baltimore Railroad, played a pivotal role in getting Northern troops to Washington. Wikimedia Commons, D. Hamilton Hurd, *History of Essex County, Massachusetts.*

FIG. 12. The world-famous journalist William Howard Russell's reporting in this period is a rich lode of first-person contemporary scenes—by turns comical, colorful, insightful, and searing. Library of Congress, Prints and Photographs Division, Washington DC, LC-USZCN4-361.

FIG. 13. Charles Stone, inspector general of the Washington militia, weeded out disloyal members and acted quickly in a variety of ways to secure the capital. Library of Congress, Prints and Photographs Division, Washington DC, LC-DIG-cwpb-04847.

FIG. 14. Col. Marshall Lefferts led the elite Seventh New York Regiment, whose triumphant arrival ended a week of helplessness and isolation in the nation's capital. National Portrait Gallery.

FIG. 15. Nick Biddle, a sixty-five-year-old escaped enslaved man who marched with a Pennsylvania militia company, was badly wounded by a racist, insurrectionist mob in Baltimore. Library of Congress, Prints and Photographs Division, Washington DC, LC-DIG-ppmsca-78201.

PASSENGER AND FREIGHT STATIONS, PRESIDENT STREET, BALTIMORE.

FIG. 16. President Street Station, Baltimore. The terminal, now a museum, still stands. Library of Congress, Prints and Photographs Division, Washington DC, HAER MD,4-BALT,25.

FIG. 17. Maryland governor Thomas Hicks vacillated between Southern sympathy and loyalty to the Union. Collection of the Maryland State Archives.

FIG. 18. Baltimore mayor George Brown lost control of his city as insurrection raged. Collection of the Maryland State Archives.

FIG. 19. Baltimore police chief George Kane was a fiery secessionist. Many eyewitnesses said he encouraged the mob during the Baltimore Riots. Courtesy of the Maryland Center for History and Culture.

FIG. 20. Sixth Massachusetts Regiment Company captain Albert Follansbee marched more than two hundred soldiers more than a mile through a violent, murderous mob of thousands. Courtesy of the U.S. Army Heritage and Education Center, Carlisle PA.

FIG. 21. The B&O's Camden Station, Baltimore. The terminal is now a museum at the site of a commuter rail hub. DeGolyer Library, Southern Methodist University.

FIG. 22. After the surrender of Fort Sumter, Confederate general Pierre
Beauregard failed to comprehend the big picture. National Archives.

FIG. 23. Robert E. Lee had black hair and lacked his familiar gray beard when he resigned from the U.S. Army to take command of Virginia forces. Library of Congress, Prints and Photographs Division, Washington DC, LC-USZ62-11705.

FIG. 24. Jacob Dodson, a Senate employee and participant in some of the great journeys of exploration in the nineteenth century, offered to provide three hundred Black men in defense of Washington. He was curtly turned down by Secretary of War Simon Cameron, whose racist response was "This department has no intention at present to call into the service of the Government any colored soldiers." (Not drawn from life.) *Los Angeles Times*.

FIG. 25. Secretary of War Simon Cameron raced to keep up with the events required to secure the capital and mobilize an unprecedentedly large army of state militia troops. Library of Congress, the Photographic Album.

FIG. 26. Treasury Register Lucius Chittenden filled his personal journal with vivid contemporaneous accounts of Washington during the first two weeks of the war. National Archives.

FIG. 27. Lt. Col. Edward Hincks of the Eighth Massachusetts Regiment served as the unit's de facto commander and took the initiative in freeing the grounded USS *Constitution* and capturing the railroad station at Annapolis and then pushing his men toward Annapolis Junction. National Archives.

FIG. 28. The elite New York Seventh Regiment, comprised of the rich and connected young men of New York City, was perhaps the most famous military unit in the world. Library of Congress, Prints and Photographs Division, Washington DC, LC-DIG-ppmsca-34435.

17
- - -

Confederate Troops Move North

The South

I t was mild and seasonable in Washington this Sunday and
had been one week since Lincoln wrote the call for troops.
Southern scheming to capture Washington continued. The
racist and secessionist former U.S. senator from Virginia, James
Murray Mason, wrote Confederate president Jefferson Davis saying he hoped the city would soon be occupied by Confederate
forces. "I trust in god that Lincoln's Congress called for July 4th
will find the capitol under your guns," he wrote to Davis.[1]

In Charleston, the first official steps were made to move Confederate troops north. "To-day Brigadier-General Bonham, with
two regiments of South Carolina volunteers [Col. Maxcy Gregg's
First South Carolina and Col. Joseph B. Kershaw's Second South
Carolina] are to leave for Norfolk," General Beauregard wrote to
the Confederate secretary of war, Leroy Walker.

The troops didn't leave this day—they and four companies of
Georgia volunteers from Macon and Columbus were delayed until
the following day. Some were heading to Richmond, and others
were assigned to Norfolk and Portsmouth. At least one Georgia
unit reached Portsmouth by Tuesday the twenty-third. Elements
of Gregg's First South Carolina, led by Brig. Gen. Milledge Bonham, ultimately began arriving in Richmond on April 26, with
advance units of Kershaw's Second South Carolina arriving on

the twenty-eighth and others in early May. Once in Virginia, Bonham's command was formally organized into a brigade consisting of the First, Second, Third, and Eighth South Carolina regiments.[2]

Virginia was moving fast too. Troops were pouring into Richmond. The state took its first steps toward a formal military arrangement with Maryland. Gov. John Letcher had established a three-man advisory council to help manage the transition from the United States to the Confederacy.[3] On this Sunday, the council recommended the appointment of Mason to go to Maryland and learn all he could about the condition of affairs there and report back to Letcher.[4]

Mason—who'd been a U.S. senator for fourteen years—assured Davis that Virginia was irrevocably out of the Union. "I take for granted, you all fully understand the true position of our state," he wrote. "The submission of the ordinance to the People, [is] a question of form only. In truth there is almost no unionist left."[5] Mason told Davis that with the capture of Harpers Ferry, much of the arms-manufacturing equipment was saved and being moved to Richmond.

Direct military cooperation between Maryland and Virginia was ramping up. Kenton Harper, commanding the Virginia militia at Harpers Ferry, reported to the state's adjutant general, William Richardson, that he had about two thousand troops on hand, and an understanding with Maryland forces on the northern shore of the Potomac to report any hostile approach. Maryland authorities also allowed him to occupy the Maryland heights above the town. "I expect an additional force tomorrow of five hundred men. If needed, I could have thousands," Harper reported.[6]

Interestingly, General Beauregard himself appeared disinterested in a move to Virginia. His focus remained on the defense of Charleston.[7]

Norfolk Navy Yard

Sailors and Massachusetts soldiers had worked overnight to prepare to burn the facility, finishing the work the yard's commander, Charles McCauley, started when the ships were scuttled the prior day. Working in the dark, they set charges and filled the shops, storage buildings, the barracks, the dry dock, and the ships themselves with flammable materials.

"For four hours we continued the work of destruction, some rolling several thousands of heavy shells into the sea, while others laid powder trains, and still others stood guard," remembered Edward L. Pierce, a private in the Third Massachusetts. "We were very weary when we went on board the 'Pawnee.'"[8]

At 1:45 a.m., Navy commanders Rodgers, Alden, and Sands signaled that all was ready. "All the men that could be spared should be sent on board their ships immediately, retaining only those necessary to ignite the material," wrote Capt. Charles Wilkes, who had been assigned to take command of the *Merrimack* before it was scuttled. "The signal would be a rocket from the *Pawnee*."[9]

Two small boats from the *Cumberland* were brought alongside the *Pawnee*, and a handful of crewmen disembarked, tasked with setting charges. Now on this murky, predawn Sunday morning, deep in secessionist territory, the problem was McCauley. He was having a nervous breakdown. His young son boarded the *Pawnee* crying uncontrollably. He told Com. Hiram Paulding, in overall command, that McCauley was refusing to leave his post. Alden was sent to bring him to the *Cumberland* and found him "lying, in a stupefied state, on a sofa. Lt. Alden took him on board—otherwise he would have been burned alive," Wilkes remembered in his autobiography.[10]

At 2:00 a.m., the marine barracks were set ablaze. At 2:25 a.m., the *Pawnee* left the dock. Heavy ropes—hawsers—were passed to the *Cumberland*, which would be towed downriver. The steam tug *Yankee* came alongside to assist.

At 4:20 a.m., the signal was given, the rocket went up, and the Norfolk Navy Yard exploded. The ship houses, the workshops, the storage buildings, the barracks, the ships themselves—the whole yard was one giant inferno. Wilkes's small boat was waiting dockside near the half-sunk *Germantown*, but the conflagration moved rapidly, with vast sheets of flame and dense smoke.

Soon, Lt. Henry A. Wise, in a second small boat, emerged from the smoke. It was apparent that Rodgers and Wright, the navy commander and army captain sent to destroy the dry dock, would not be able to make it through. "The mast and the spars of the *Germantown* were on fire and portions of her hull enveloped in flame," Wilkes wrote the next day. The flames reached sixty feet. The heat scorched the faces of the men in the boat. "I directed the boats to pull out, the large flakes of fire falling around us." The landscape and towns were illuminated in an orange glow for miles around, lit up by the flames of the burning navy yard.[11]

Wilkes thought the *Pawnee* would wait for his boats. But the ships were already gone, steaming down the river. "We took to our oars, followed by the other cutter under the charge of Lt. Wise," Wilkes remembered. The small boats pursued the three ships for nearly ten miles and didn't reach the flotilla until they got to the mouth of the river.[12]

"On our return, we passed under the batteries of the secessionists, the officers of the '*Cumberland*' expected that they would now open upon us in revenge for this destruction," the Massachusetts soldier Edward Pierce wrote. "The batteries did not, however, open."[13]

By 8:00 a.m. the three ships were anchored safely off Fort Monroe. "We received the congratulations of the regular soldiers and of our comrades of the Fourth, both of whom had expected to see us with thinned ranks," Pierce wrote. "We were safe; we had penetrated farther South than any other regiment has yet gone."[14]

Wright, Rodgers, and O. S. John Reynolds, who had stayed to help destroy the dry dock, were left on their own to escape the inferno. They got out through the yard's main gate and found a boat. Eventually, they surrendered to the Virginia militia.

Virginia general Taliaferro received them warmly. They were put up in a local hotel and sent to Richmond the next day. Virginia governor Letcher personally met them and made them his guests until Wednesday, when they were paroled and sent to Washington.

In the end, for some reason, the dry dock—the most valuable asset in the yard and therefore the most important feature to destroy—was not demolished.[15] The value of the dry dock was borne out over the coming eleven months, when the Confederates raised the sunken *Merrimack* and refitted it as an ironclad vessel, the CSS *Virginia*. Ironically, the *Merrimack*-turned-*Virginia* rammed and sank the USS *Cumberland* less than a year later, on the first day of the Battle of Hampton Roads, March 8, 1862.

18

A Northern Convoy Departs

Annapolis

The steam ferry *Maryland*, with the Eighth Massachusetts aboard, arrived at Annapolis soon after midnight early Sunday morning, the twenty-first, following a six-hour voyage down the Chesapeake Bay. The most excitement that evening turned out to be the growling of sleepy men when Gen. Benjamin F. Butler accidentally stepped on them.

Annapolis was an old city, founded by Puritan exiles from Virginia in 1649. It became the Maryland colonial capital in 1695, and its statehouse, built in 1792, is the oldest capitol in the United States in continuous legislative use.

Once intended as a port of entry for Washington DC, Annapolis eventually lost the shipping trade to Baltimore, and now, in 1861, it was a quiet city of about 4,529 people, including 826 free Black people and 475 enslaved people.[1]

Annapolis was about a mile up the Severn River from the bay. The Naval Academy, founded as the "Naval School" on a former army installation in 1845, was on the river, with the city beyond its walls. Butler expected the town to be asleep on this balmy evening. Instead, he found alarm. Drummers on the academy grounds were beating the "assembly," calling men to rendezvous points. Lights were moving around rapidly on shore. The buildings were lit up.

The *Maryland* was anchored and waited. It was a dark night, and Butler's plan was to go ashore in the morning. But he decided to send someone out to see what was happening and deliver a note to the naval school's superintendent. Butler's brother, Andrew, in civilian clothes, volunteered. His boat slipped off into the black night.[2]

After about an hour, the men on the *Maryland* heard oars lapping in the water and then saw a boat approaching with five people, none of whom were Andrew Butler.

"What boat is that?" Butler cried out.

"What steamer is that?" came the reply.

Butler feared the naval academy had fallen to the insurrectionists. "None of your business. Come alongside, or I will fire into you."

A young officer in a U.S. Navy uniform climbed aboard. He was sent by the academy's superintendent, Capt. George S. Blake. He asked again who was on the steamer. Butler explained that he was from Massachusetts, with a militia regiment on its way to Washington.

The officer, Lt. Cdr. Edmond O. Matthews, an assistant to the commandant of midshipmen, was relieved. He told Butler that Blake feared the *Maryland* had been commandeered by Baltimore "roughs" and was coming to seize the academy.[3]

At daybreak the contours of the city and the academy began to emerge. On the southern (or left) bank was the academy, dominated by Fort Severn, a circular masonry structure enclosed by a fourteen-foot stone wall. Beyond the fort were barracks and academic buildings. In 1861 the most prominent feature of the academy, other than the fort, was a line of buildings called Stribling Row, which ran parallel to the river and consisted of red brick buildings with slate roofs. Beyond the academy, the state capitol rose on a hill above the town.[4]

Just as the sun was coming up, a boat arrived at the *Maryland* carrying the superintendent, Captain Blake. Blake had just turned fifty-nine, but to the forty-two-year-old Benjamin Butler, he must have seemed elderly. Butler told the naval commander who he was and why he was there. "The old man burst into tears, and shed them like rain for a moment, and then broke out: 'Thank God! Thank God! Won't you save the *Constitution*?'"

Butler thought Blake meant the U.S. Constitution. Blake actually meant the USS *Constitution*, the famous old ship—Old Ironsides—now a training vessel for midshipmen, currently aground in the mud alongside the wharf and vulnerable to sabotage by the secessionists, or worse, being captured and repurposed as a Confederate privateer.

Blake asked Butler what his orders were. With typical bravado, Butler replied, "I have no orders. I cut loose from my orders when I left Philadelphia. I am making war on my own hook." In fact, he wasn't. Maj. Gen. Robert Patterson, commander of the Pennsylvania militia and head of the federal Department of Pennsylvania, had met Butler in person in Philadelphia just the day before, instructing him that both the Massachusetts Eighth and the New York Seventh should proceed to Washington via Annapolis. Butler was to hold one regiment in Annapolis and one at the Annapolis Junction and report to Scott for further orders. Patterson said he couldn't find Lefferts but gave the orders to Butler and asked him to pass them along to Lefferts.[5]

At some point that morning, Massachusetts captain Peter Haggerty—who'd also been sent ashore by Butler—returned and delivered two notes to Butler. One was from a quartermaster sent by General Scott. The other was from Maryland governor Thomas Hicks, warning Butler not to disembark.

"To the Commander of the Volunteer Troops on Board the Steamer," Hicks wrote, already reneging on his deal with Lincoln. "I would most earnestly advise that you do not land your men at Annapolis. The excitement here is very great, and I think it prudent that you should take your men elsewhere. I have telegraphed the Secretary of War against your landing your men here."[6]

Butler's reply was conciliatory: "I am sorry that your excellency should advise against my landing here. I am not provisioned for a long voyage. Finding the ordinary means of communication cut off by the burning of the railroad bridges by a mob, I have been obliged to make this detour. There is no cause of excitement in the mind of any good citizen. I should at once obey, however, an order from the Secretary of War."[7]

And so began three days of excruciating negotiations and inept decisions. The bombastic Massachusetts brigadier-lawyer faced off first against a Maryland governor who may or may not have been pro-Union and then against Marshall Lefferts, the blue-blooded telegraph executive and citizen soldier leading the New York Seventh Regiment.

Butler didn't land the Eighth Massachusetts Regiment, but the truth was he needed no permission to disembark. The Naval Academy was U.S. government property. Landing the troops was precisely the domestic policy established by Lincoln—the government would hold and possess U.S. forts and facilities. No state authority had the power to overrule this policy.

Instead, Butler kept most of his men on the *Maryland* and sent some to the USS *Constitution*, setting them to work on freeing the sixty-three-year-old warship from the mud. His men offloaded the heavy guns and carriages. They pulled the ship's anchors out of several feet of muck. Finally, the vessel itself was hauled off the bottom by the *Maryland*. It was towed to deep water and anchored safely away from the town. "All seemed to be going well," Butler's biographer, James Parton, wrote. "The general dozed in his chair. He woke to find the *Maryland* fast in the mud."[8]

So now the *Maryland*, with more than seven hundred Massachusetts soldiers aboard, was helpless, run aground in Annapolis Harbor, a calamity that occurred while the general in charge was literally sleeping on the job. The men's already meager provisions were nearly consumed, the water casks dry, and the afternoon sun was bearing down hard. Food and water had to be brought out to the stranded ferry from the academy.

At Sea aboard the Transport *Boston*

The New York Seventh Regiment, meanwhile, was making its own voyage south from Philadelphia. "April 21 was Sunday—a glorious, cloudless day," the private Fitz James O'Brien reported. "At five o'clock P.M. we passed a light-ship, and hailed her, our object being to discover whether any United States vessels were in the neighborhood, waiting to convoy us up the Potomac River. We heard that the forts at Alexandria were ready to open fire upon us if we attempted to pass up. We kept on."[9]

New York City

All over New York people knew from nonstop newspaper coverage that several regiments were preparing to depart from the city this Sunday morning. It was a warm, sunny, cloudless day in Manhattan, a soft breeze blowing in from the ocean.

This was the fourth troop departure from New York City in four days. If New Yorkers were getting jaded or bored, they weren't showing it yet. Each departure had been different. First there was the Sixth Massachusetts on Thursday—special because it was the first regiment to come through the city. The next day the Massachusetts Eighth came through, and New York's own Seventh Regiment departed.

Saturday was a one-day pause. That day a pro-Union rally—the largest public meeting up to that time in U.S. history, with an estimated half-million people—was held in Union Square. Today, a force of more than 4,300 men was massing. This was different for its sheer scale.

The troops consisted of the New York Seventy-First, Sixth, and Twelfth regiments, half of the First Rhode Island militia, plus the Fifth Massachusetts. The New York and Rhode Island regiments would steam together in a five-ship flotilla, with the Massachusetts soldiers leaving later that night.

The Rhode Island regiment arrived in New York Harbor aboard the leased transport steamer *Empire State* at 7:00 a.m. It anchored off Jay Street, near the tip of Manhattan in the North River, as the Hudson was then called.

Col. Ambrose Burnside's troops were impressed with the city—and vice versa. "The great city had reached the climax of enthusiasm," the Rhode Island regimental chaplain and historian Augustus Woodbury wrote in an extended account of the campaign. "The flag of the United States was floating from every prominent point."[10]

The *New York Tribune* sized up the Rhode Islanders: "The men are from 20 to 30 years of age, in robust health and finest spirits.

The regiment was enrolled, uniformed, drilled and ready for service in three days. Each man carries a large red blanket strapped diagonally across his back, which has a striking effect."[11]

By 9:00 a.m., the streets were filling up. Flags that celebrated yesterday's giant rally in Union Square were still flying. New York was once again beside itself. Around the state armories especially, in Greenwich Village and the Lower East Side, masses of friends, family and supporters swarmed. Shortly after 10:00 a.m., the Seventy-First New York began to form up on Bond Street near the intersection with Broadway, two blocks southeast of Washington Square Park.

The new recruits of the Seventy-First numbered between six and seven hundred men. The regiment was leaving with about a thousand men, up from just 380 men days earlier. Some of the recruits were in uniform, and the majority had arms, but many wore a hodgepodge of civilian clothes. Some wore slouch hats. Some had "plug" hats. Some wore short, tightfitting jackets called roundabouts, and others had peacoats. Some had their best Sunday clothes and some looked like they recently left the workshop. Boxes of muskets, supplies, and some uniforms would be provided on the transport.[12]

The New York militia's Sixth Regiment, including its own new recruits, began to muster at 7:00 a.m. near the Centre Market, at the corner of Centre Street and Grand Street, in today's Little Italy.[13] The regiment was markedly German and was led by Col. Joseph C. Pinckney, thirty-nine. It had turned out in unexpected force, the *Herald* noted, numbering 812 men, with each company having close to 80 soldiers. Only a small number of the Sixth had uniforms, but every man had a musket and other supplies.

The Twelfth Regiment formed up on the west side of Union Square. Its leader was twenty-nine-year-old Col. Daniel Butterfield, who had been the lieutenant colonel of the Seventy-First until December 1859. Butterfield, born in Utica, New York, was the son of one of the founders of American Express and worked at that company both before and after the war. He rose up quickly to the top ranks of the Union Army and won the Medal of Honor for gallantry in action during the battles of the Seven Days in 1862.

The Twelfth Regiment had numbered barely four hundred members just a few weeks earlier. But like the Seventy-First and the Sixth, it had filled its ranks over the last four days, more than doubling in size. Now it had over one thousand men. For the moment only half the departing troops were uniformed but all had muskets, blankets, and knapsacks.[14] New uniforms were being manufactured and would be forwarded when the troops arrived in Washington. The money came from a ten-thousand-dollar fund raised by friends of the regiment.[15]

The three regiments waited till about noon in the hot April sun. Finally the march began. The Sixth Regiment moved first, with the Twelfth and Seventy-First Regiments following. Along the route, crowds were joined by twenty-five fire engines and hook-and-ladder companies posted at each corner stretching down Broadway, bells clanging when the troops moved past. This, the *Tribune* noted, was appropriate, because hundreds of the departing soldiers served in the fire departments—or in the parlance of the day, they were men who had once "run with the machine."

At Broadway and Grand, a block above Canal Street, the crowd extended as far as the eye could see in all directions. Women strained in vain to catch a glimpse of husbands, fathers, brothers, or beaux.

"These are dreadful times," they'd say.

"Our poor country."

"How few of these will return."

The motley appearance of the recruits would produce a laugh but was always followed by a cheer and an exclamation along the lines of, "They'll know the use of a musket before they come back."[16]

The Sixth marched down Canal Street to the North River and boarded the *Baltic*, a 2,700-ton side-wheeled steamer, which had an official capacity of 280 passengers. But soon, between the cheers on the dock and the boarding of the vessel, came the distant sounds of more drums and cheering, heading toward the pier on Canal Street. It was the Twelfth Regiment, led by Colonel Butterfield on a black charger, also marching to embark on the *Baltic*. Someone had fouled up.

The *Baltic*, though luxurious for the era, couldn't possibly accommodate two regiments, nearly two thousand men. The Twelfth halted short of the pier.

Transportation assignments for the two regiments had gotten confused. The Twelfth was assigned to the *Baltic*, upon which its baggage was already stowed. But the Sixth Regiment also received orders to march to the *Baltic* and boarded first. While all this was being sorted out, the recruits smoked pipes and cigars and waited. Ultimately, the Sixth had to disembark and march downtown to the steamer *Columbia*. This delayed the departure for hours.[17]

The Seventy-First—and eventually the Sixth—marched to Lower Manhattan. The Seventy-First went to the foot of Albany Street on the North River. "The regiment never looked better as it glanced in and out of the light and shade that the open streets and tall houses caused to alternate," the *Herald* reported.[18]

An immense crowd gathered along the piers on West Street, which ran (and still runs) south to north along the river. As the Seventy-First boarded its transport, the *R. R. Cuyler*, onlookers burst out with a continuous yell.

The men on the *Cuyler* exchanged cheers with the Rhode Islanders on the nearby *Empire State*, the Rhode Islanders' brilliant red blankets observable from the city.[19]

One *Tribune* reporter speculated that this scene along the New York piers wouldn't occur again in a century. "At least a dozen large ocean steamers, blowing and smoking, had been quietly freighted, and were now waking up their gigantic powers to depart in concert on a most important mission." Here's the *Tribune*'s vivid description:

The *Ariel* was at Pier Three, with steam up and "making much noise. She had been taking on provisions and stores for some days. In the afternoon a squad of Metropolitan Policemen was sent to the spot to keep order on the arrival of troops from Massachusetts."

The *Columbia* was at the next pier. It had steam up at 4:00 p.m.

At the same pier, the *Marion* was also ready for departure and had steam up at 4:00 p.m.

The *James Adger* was at the stern of the *Marion*, also with steam up, some people already aboard, ready for departure.

The *Cuyler* was at Pier Twelve. It laid in steam after 3:00 p.m.

The *Coatzacoalcos* was at the foot of Warren Street with steam up. It went out to the *Empire State* at 6:00 p.m. and embarked the Rhode Island troops.

The *DeSoto*, at the next pier south of the *Coatzacoalcos*, was steaming up with a lot of noise, as if about to sail, at 4:00 p.m.

The propeller steamship *Monticello* had steam up and was freighted with large quantities of war material, such as muskets, brass, field pieces, grape shot for very large guns, and large stacks of boxes and bundles.[20]

All these steamers and others—including the *Baltic* up at Canal Street—would be transporting troops to Annapolis over the next few days.

With the Seventy-First on the *Cuyler* was George W. Wilkes, an author, journalist, entrepreneur, and the owner of the New York weekly newspaper *Spirit of the Times*, which focused on sports with a mix of theater and humor for an upper-class audience. Wilkes, forty-four in 1861, embedded with the Seventy-First New York and wrote an extended history of the campaign.

"No one who accompanied the military expedition from New York on that bright Sunday will ever forget the impressiveness of the departure," Wilkes began. "No one can fail to recollect how the dense swarms, which choked the streets along the line of march, flowed upward until they welled over the roofs, screaming for half a mile around."

The *Cuyler* slipped from its moorings about 3:00 p.m., followed by the *Columbia*, the *Baltic*, and the *Coatzacoalcos*, now carrying the Rhode Island troops. This convoy would be led by the *Harriet Lane*, a six-gun, side-paddled revenue cutter. (The *Lane*'s usage alternated between the Treasury Department and the Navy, and it was used to collect port fees.) At 5:30 p.m., a gun from the *Harriet Lane* ordered the ships to move. With the *Lane* in the lead, the task force steamed toward the narrows.

"That was the signal for a burst of voices such as never before awoke the echoes of the bay, even of our mighty city," Wilkes wrote. "It rolled for miles. As we passed the junction of the East River with the Hudson, it was like looking through a vast tunnel of star-spangled flags. Brooklyn Heights, with its dense audience of human life, repeated the performance of the New York and New Jersey shores."

Anyone looking on must have felt "the heart of a great people and had sworn that our country and its constitution should not pass away without a desperate and bloody struggle," Wilkes wrote.[21]

Southern New England

As the New York and Rhode Island regiments—four in all—departed to a thunderous torrent of applause, the Fifth Massachusetts was slowly making its way by rail through southern New England. It had left Boston at 6:50 that morning with 805 men on the train. In Springfield, Massachusetts, it seemed more like a Fourth of July celebration, wrote the Fifth Regiment biographer Alfred Roe: "Even a passing funeral could not resist the temptation to applaud."[22]

The Fifth Massachusetts arrived in New York at about 8:00 p.m. After a stop for dinner, it marched to Pier Four, where it embarked on the steamers *Ariel* and *DeSoto*. Accompanying the Fifth Regiment was the Boston Flying Artillery, with about ninety horses and six guns. "Massachusetts has within six days responded with five full regiments of infantry, a battalion of rifles, and a splendid corps of artillery," the *Tribune* noted.[23]

19

Brinksmanship in Washington

The City

Pres`dent Lincoln and his assistant secretary, John Hay, climbed to the roof of the White House early this morning for a look down the Potomac River. For the last two days, Washington was severed from the North and surrounded by hostile secessionists. The federal civilian workforce and the military officer corps were disintegrating. Lincoln would often gaze downriver, looking for steamers carrying Northern troops. On this day they would not come.

The climb to the roof, Hay wrote in his diary, was a "water haul"— a fruitless task. "Tant pis," he said. Everything's for the worse.[1] For two days now, the capital had virtually no communication from the North.

The railway depot was closed. In ordinary times four B&O trains arrived and departed daily between Washington and Baltimore, along with at least one freight train.[2] Rail and telegraph service from Virginia had terminated on the nineteenth.[3]

But this was no ordinary time. No trains arrived or departed this Sunday morning. Waterfront piers were deserted. People clustered on street corners and in hotel lobbies, anxious for whatever information they could find. The city was practically defenseless. Wild rumors predicted attacks from the south and from the north. The newspapers had no ability to refute any of them.

Sunday, April 21, was another moderately warm day in Washington DC. At 8:00 a.m. the temperature was around fifty degrees. It reached seventy-two degrees later that day, with a mix of clear and cloudy skies and nearly no wind.[4]

"This has been a pleasant but anxious day," Horatio Nelson Taft wrote in his diary. "We seem to be surrounded by enimies, and enimies [*sic*] in our midst. No troops have yet arrived since the Mass. Regt. How anxiously have we looked for the 7th Regt of NY today. I left the National tonight at 11 o'clock but could get no reliable information. We may be in the midst of blood-shed any hour, and I am looking for an outbreak or attack all the time. Famine stares us in the face unless the routes are kept open. Where are the expected troops?"[5]

The journalist Henry Villard arrived in Washington this Sunday after just five days away. He'd been called to New York by *New York Herald* publisher James Gordon Bennett, who wanted Villard to hand deliver a message to President Lincoln. Arriving back in Washington, Villard was shocked at the change.

The president's call for troops was a declaration that war existed. Washington would likely become the main point of hostilities. That, plus the clash in Baltimore and the interruption of railroad and mail service, made Washington a different place. The telegraph was sporadic and available only to the government. "A panic had ensued," Villard wrote.[6]

Thousands of people left the city, heading north or south by any transportation available. People were streaming out "not leisurely, but in haste; not singly, but in groups; not by scores, but in crowds," remembered the Rev. George Williamson Smith, a twenty-four-year-old assistant pastor at St. John's Episcopal Church on Lafayette Square.

"Every kind of vehicle was pressed into service. Even baby wagons were employed. Wheelbarrows carried trunks and boxes for people who started for Rockville [fifteen miles away] on foot."

Smith also remembered a long procession moving up Seventeenth Street in disorder. "In carriages, wagons, drays, trucks and push-carts loaded with babies and kitchen utensils, and on foot, they fled, carrying what they could on their persons," he wrote fifty-six years later for a presentation to the Columbia Historical Society in 1917.

"Property could be had 'for a song,' even badly sung," Smith continued. "No one wanted to buy a house in a city that might be on the eve of destruction."

And then the city was dead. Houses were left with open blinds and some with open windows, Smith remembered. "Day after day I went to the foot of the Treasury Building and saw not so much as a dog on the long stretch of Pennsylvania Avenue to the foot of the Capitol."[7]

Walking on Pennsylvania Avenue, Villard could count on his fingers how many people strolled by. A month earlier, Willard's was crammed with a thousand guests. Now at dinner time, not forty people occupied the hotel. "I was surprised to find the halls and sitting rooms almost empty," Villard wrote. A clerk told him, "It will be news to you that we are going to shut this hotel tomorrow, and this meal will be the last served here."[8]

"Everybody who could get away has already left town," the *New York Times* reported. "And if the usual railroad routes were open, thousands more would follow."[9]

Early that morning in Baltimore, around 3:00 a.m., Mayor Brown had heard back from Lincoln, who'd summoned Hicks and Brown to Washington. Hicks was in Annapolis. Lincoln ordered Brown to come to Washington immediately, even without the governor.[10]

After a series of railroad delays, the mayor, with two members of yesterday's delegation—John C. Brune and George W. Dobbin—plus the secessionist lawyer Severn Teackle Wallis, left Baltimore around 7:30 a.m. They got to Washington at 10:00 a.m. and drove to the White House. It was the third group of Maryland officials to visit Lincoln in less than twenty-four hours.[11]

They came up the broad, sandy, semicircular path to the White House's North Portico, passing a statue of Thomas Jefferson on the right. The stones of the pavement were foot-worn into furrows.[12]

Lincoln's meeting with this latest delegation lasted the rest of the morning. General Scott and the cabinet were summoned to the president's office. Lincoln acknowledged the state of affairs in Baltimore. He said his duty was to avoid an armed clash. At the same time, the president emphasized the absolute necessity of getting troops to the capital. The protection of Washington, he insisted, was the sole purpose. With the Potomac River off limits and the Baltimore rail hub unavailable, they had to come some other way—and that had to be through Maryland.

Lincoln asked Scott for his opinion. Scott reiterated what he said the day before—the troops should be rerouted around Baltimore using one of two options. The first was to bring the troops by train from Harrisburg and then march fourteen miles from the junction at Lake Roland on the Northern Central Railway (seven miles north of the city) to the junction on the B&O Railroad (eight miles southwest of the city). The second was to take the train from Philadelphia to the Susquehanna River, and then by ferry to Annapolis, and from there by train to Washington.[13]

As Lincoln was meeting with the Baltimore officials, Maj. Benjamin Watson of the Sixth Massachusetts came to the White House. Watson had bravely led a company of soldiers through the swirling mob in Baltimore two days ago. Now Watson wanted to ask the president or General Scott to improve his men's rations, which Watson said were "absolutely offensive."

The regiment had not had a square meal since it left Philadelphia, more than forty-eight hours earlier. Since their arrival, the men of the Sixth Massachusetts had received rotten meat and hardtack crackers. Watson found Scott upstairs with Lincoln and the Maryland authorities. "I thus accidentally became a participant in a meeting which has become historic and of which, so far as I know, I am now the only survivor," said Watson.

Scott, hearing the request for better food, announced, "The Sixth Regiment of Massachusetts, sir, shall have anything it wants; we depend upon the Sixth Regiment of Massachusetts to save the Capital, sir."

Lincoln introduced Watson to Baltimore mayor Brown. The president asked Watson to confirm Brown's statement that Brown personally protected the Sixth in Baltimore and marched much of the way through the city at the front of the regiment. The senior leadership of the U.S. government clustered around Watson.

"I fear my manner was not complimentary toward the Mayor," Watson remembered. "I am sure my speech was not. So recent had been my 'baptism of fire,' I doubtless bore my testimony with indiscreet zeal. . . . I said, in effect, that under the circumstances it was unfortunate for the Mayor of Baltimore to appeal to me for a certificate of character." Watson went on,

> We, as citizen soldiers, had endeavored to pass through Balti-more, not only in a peaceable and proper manner, but strictly in obedience to superior order, that insult and assault should be submitted to, and that wounds with firearms alone should jus-tify retaliation; that at the beginning of our passage the police had threatened me that not a man of us would be allowed to go through the city alive, and that our graves had already been dug; that neither the police, nor other officials, in any instance to my knowledge, had attempted any protection; that prior to that moment I had never seen the Mayor; that I had been informed by one of the captains of one of the detachments that the Mayor did march about one hundred yards beside him, when he left saying that the position was too hot for him. So far as I was con-cerned, the interview was then ended by my withdrawing, the President having said that the rations should be made satisfactory.

"Many times since I have recalled the scene," Watson contin-ued. "The Mayor's look of intense disgust, the astonishing dig-nity of the Commanding General, and the expression, half sad, half quizzical, on the face of the President at the evident infelic-ity of his introduction. If I did not leave that distinguished pres-ence with my reputation for integrity unimpaired, the pressure of Abraham Lincoln's honest hand as we parted deceived me. My mission, at all events, was successful and the rations improved."[14]

Eventually, on this Sunday in Washington, Lincoln and the Bal-timore committee reached an understanding—with basically the same terms as the day before. Advancing troops would avoid Bal-timore, but they had to get to Washington through Maryland. It wasn't negotiable. For his part, Brown was satisfied, too, just as he was after Lincoln met his emissaries the previous day. He promised the federal authorities that he'd use all lawful means to prevent city residents from going out of Baltimore to attack Northern troops.

At one point, an indignant Simon Cameron, the secretary of war, asked Brown what authority he had to disable the bridge at Lake Roland, which belonged to the city of Baltimore. Brown addressed his response to Lincoln, not Cameron. It was a measure of protection, he said, intended to prevent bloodshed. War fever was sweeping the city. The call for Northern troops struck many Marylanders as an aggressive threat—an act of war, explicitly seeking to suppress the Southern insurrection.

Lincoln became angry. He sprung out of his chair. He began to pace rapidly back and forth through the room. His proclamation had been misunderstood, he said. It wasn't intended as an invasion force; it was for the protection of the capital. "Mr. Brown, I am not a learned man! I am not a learned man!" Lincoln exclaimed.[15]

But Lincoln had committed an unforced error. His proclamation had called for troops to "suppress combinations" of insurgents, to maintain the existence of the Union, and to retake property seized from the federal government. The rebels were ordered to disperse. Protecting the capital was not mentioned in the proclamation. And now Lincoln was saying that Washington was the objective and that no invasion of the South would occur. Obviously circumstances had changed. It's possible that Lincoln was frustrated with the deliberately obtuse Marylanders. Perhaps he thought playing an undereducated frontiersman would cause the Marylanders to make concessions that he could then publicize in the newspapers.

The Baltimore committee departed for the train station. Lincoln moved on to other business. The weather was lovely now—not really hot, but still a perfect midspring day. It seemed quiet around the White House, almost languid. But then, as the train was about to leave Washington around 2:00 p.m., the Baltimore delegation, already on board, received an incendiary dispatch from B&O Railroad president John Garrett.

"Three thousand Northern troops are reported to be at Cockeysville [fifteen miles north of Baltimore]," Garrett reported. "Intense excitement prevails. Churches have been dismissed, and the people are arming in mass. To prevent terrific bloodshed, the result of your interview and arrangement is awaited."[16]

Garrett wasn't exaggerating. Pennsylvania troops had left Harrisburg around 1:00 a.m. Sunday morning and arrived at Cockeysville around 8:00 a.m. The burned-out bridges were the only thing stopping them. So they set up camp and waited.

Baltimore

Just after 10:00 a.m., the prominent Baltimore County resident and local judge Gist Cockey reached Baltimore and raced to the office of Police Marshal Kane with word that invaders were headed directly for Baltimore. The news spread like wildfire. The police commissioners issued orders to assemble and arm the city's militia companies.

Church services were interrupted, their bells ringing loud and wildly. Rumors mounted—the advancing army grew from two thousand to eight thousand to ten thousand with each repetition. Armed men formed into squads, which then coalesced into companies. Terrified women ran to their homes, while throngs of men surged to the center of Baltimore.[17] Just at that time in Washington, Lincoln was in the meeting with Mayor Brown and his group.

The advancing Northern troops, about 2,210 men in all, composed companies of the First, Second, and Third Pennsylvania three-month volunteer regiments, all under the command of Brig. Gen. George C. Wynkoop, who'd been commissioned by Pennsylvania governor Andrew G. Curtin just two days earlier. They were ill-equipped for camp life. Only a third of them had uniforms or arms. They weren't even soldiers, really, having mustered in just days ago.[18] But Garrett and Brown knew nothing about this.

Brown telegraphed back to Garrett, "Your telegram received on our return from an interview with the President, cabinet, and General Scott. Be calm, and do nothing until you hear from me again. I return to see the President at once. Wallis, Brune and Dobbin are with me."[19]

The Baltimore committee went back to the White House, arriving before 3:00 p.m. They were more frantic than angry. Brown knew he couldn't return to Baltimore and report he'd been hoodwinked. They had an agreement—there must have been a misunderstanding. The delegation went back upstairs.

Lincoln was stunned. He reconvened the cabinet and General Scott, who once again labored up the Grand Staircase to Lincoln's office. Scott and Secretary of War Cameron pointed out that the Cockeysville troops were only doing what had just been agreed—advancing south to the Northern Central junction and then marching around Baltimore to the B&O Railroad junction, thereby skirting the city.

Lincoln saw it differently. He shocked his national security team by urging that the troops return to Harrisburg. He'd made a deal with the committee. He wanted no suspicion of bad faith. Cameron and apparently Scott and Seward opposed Lincoln.[20] Gideon Welles was especially incensed. He jumped up, shoved his hat under his arm, and stormed out, saying he refused to share responsibility for such a decision.[21]

But Lincoln insisted. The troops were going back to Harrisburg. Mayor Brown later claimed Scott supported Lincoln: "When the President gave his deliberate decision, General Scott, stern soldier as he sometimes was, said with emotion, 'Mr. President, I thank you for this, and God will bless you for it.'"[22]

Lincoln certainly felt the intense pushback from his team. It would be the last time that he'd interfere in military matters, he told Brown and others.[23]

Both Cameron and Scott issued orders to turn the Cockeysville troops around. Cameron didn't even know who was in charge at Cockeysville, addressing himself "to the Officer in command." He hinted at disagreement: "The president, with a desire to gratify the mayor of Baltimore, who fears that bloodshed would unnecessarily result from the passage through that city of troops from Pennsylvania at this moment on the way, directs that they shall return to York."

In his own dispatch, Scott corrected Cameron and added more detail. The troops should return not to York but to Harrisburg.

From there they would keep moving, turning east by railroad to Perryville and then by steamer down the Chesapeake Bay to Annapolis. This was the same Perryville-to-Annapolis route taken by the Eighth Massachusetts the previous day. So they weren't retreating at all—they were only taking a different route to Washington. In addition, instructions would be left at Harrisburg for additional troops not to come near Baltimore.[24]

Assistant Secretary of the Treasury George Harrington arrived late to the meeting with Brown and his delegation. He was looking for Salmon Chase at the White House to report on his unsuccessful overnight attempts to get telegrams through to St. Louis. The Civil War was a far-flung event. As crisis erupted in Washington and Baltimore, similar flashpoints were emerging all along the frontier between Northern and Southern states. Missouri—a slave state between two free states, Illinois and Kansas—was especially polarized in 1861.

It was before noon when Harrington arrived at Lincoln's office. Chase and Cameron turned toward him in unison. "'Well?' 'I still have them here,'" Harrington said of the telegrams, touching his pocket. "I've tried in vain to get them off."

But General Scott was sending messengers on various missions and took over Harrington's efforts. This time the messengers succeeded in eluding arrest.[25]

Harrington wrote a riveting first-person account of these Sunday meetings with the Baltimore committee, providing specific details of Lincoln's behavior that make it worth describing. When Harrington arrived, Lincoln and the cabinet were talking about the telegrams to Missouri.

While this discussion was occurring in one room, Harrington wrote, Mayor Brown's committee was in an adjoining room. Lincoln moved repeatedly from room to room, but he never brought everyone together. He would listen to the mayor and his associates and reply to them and then join the cabinet to update them on what had been discussed. "He invited no expression of opinion," Harrington said. "It was a case in which he wanted no opinions, no advice, for he would lean on no judgement except his own."

Finally the Baltimore committee left. When Lincoln reappeared, silence pervaded. Harrington, who had been standing near General Scott, turned to the door. Chase leapt from his chair, grabbed Harrington by the arm, and blurted out a single word: "Go!"

Harrington understood. He was to accompany the mayor's delegation to Baltimore, if possible, and learn the character and extent of the insurrectionist threat. Harrington rushed out to Pennsylvania Avenue, found a taxi, offered the driver a double fare to drive him to the station at top speed, and found the Baltimoreans seated in their train car and ready to start. He knew several of them and in cheerful tones said, "Gentlemen, I am a man of peace, and I have some business with Gov. Hicks. Will you take me to Baltimore with you?"

Brown never mentioned this dual-room arrangement, nor do Nicolay and Hay in their account. It seems cumbersome, but George Harrington was there, as were other officials below cabinet level, whose portfolios would not have required them to participate directly in the conversation, and therefore they might well have waited in an adjoining room.[26]

Later this same day, Lincoln convened an even more important cabinet meeting. This was held secretly, at the Navy Department, away from prying eyes at the White House. The walk to the Navy Department was about a block and a half across the White House grounds along a gravel walkway in front of the Conservatory.[27]

The cabinet met in Welles's offices. Lincoln's confidence in his own ability and his war-making powers had grown dramatically. He'd risen to the crisis in the days since Sumter. He'd issued a call for seventy-five thousand troops on the fifteenth. He'd declared a blockade on Southern ports on the nineteenth. Now on the twenty-first, he took his most astonishing steps so far, issuing a series of orders—some of which went far beyond his constitutional authority. Lincoln

directed an armed revenue cutter to guard vessels bringing shipments of gold from California;

ordered the commandants of the navy yards in Boston, New York, and Philadelphia to charter or purchase merchant steamers—fifteen in all—and convert them for military use;

ordered John Gillis, commander of the uss *Pocahontas*, to similarly acquire and outfit two ships and for Capt. Samuel F. Du Pont
to do the same, with an eye toward keeping the Chesapeake Bay
and Potomac River open and protecting Northern troops arriving at Annapolis; and

directed that two million dollars (about fifty-eight million in
2020 dollars) be advanced from the U.S. Treasury to three private citizens—former treasury secretary John A. Dix, George
Opdyke, and Richard M. Blatchford, all New Yorkers—to be used
at their discretion for the defense and support of the government.

They were to work with the War and Navy Departments and with
New York governor Edwin D. Morgan and several other prominent New Yorkers, public and private, designated by Lincoln. Virtually all the New Yorkers were members of New York's Union
Defense Committee, the group of rich and influential citizens
working with the state government to raise money for the war
effort. The committee had been formed the prior day. All of the
money was intended to purchase munitions and supplies and
to forward troops. They were to continue their work until regular communication with the North was reestablished, and they
were to report on their efforts regularly. None of the men were to
be compensated.

Dix was president of the Union Defense Committee. Later that
year, George Opdyke would be elected mayor of New York.

In his memoirs, Dix wrote that the committee's work was pro-
digious. "It raised money for the prosecution of the war, provided
supplies of all kinds for the army, and equipped and sent off ten
regiments," he said. "It was for the time being the executive arm
of the State and National governments."[28]

Lincoln himself explained the situation the next year, in May
1862, in response to a House committee investigating allegations
of inflated contracts engineered by Simon Cameron and Alexander Cummings, an emergency purchasing agent for the War
Department. After Sumter, Lincoln wrote, the routes to Washington
were obstructed and the capital was in a state of siege. "It became

necessary for me to choose whether I should let the government fall at once into ruin, or whether, availing myself of the broader powers conferred by the Constitution in cases of insurrection, I would make an effort to save it with all its blessings for the present age and for posterity," he wrote. "I believe that by these and other similar measures taken in that crisis, some of which were without any authority of law, the government was saved from overthrow."[29]

At this extraordinary Navy Department cabinet meeting, Lincoln did not seek to debate. He asked for, and received, "unanimous concurrence."[30]

Navy secretary Gideon Welles later described this meeting as the single most exciting incident of the entire Lincoln administration. And according to Welles, Secretary of State William Seward agreed. On March 30, 1864, the artist Francis B. Carpenter was painting the cabinet members in commemoration of their signing of the Emancipation Proclamation.

"Mr. C. thinks this act the great feature of the administration," Welles wrote in his diary. "But Seward said it was wholly subordinate to other and much greater events. When C. asked what, Seward told him to go back to the firing on Sumter, or to a much more exciting one than even that—the Sunday following the Baltimore massacre, when the Cabinet assembled in the Navy Department and, with the vast responsibility that was thrown on them, issued papers and did acts that might have brought them all to the scaffold."[31]

It's probable that these steps, and the people assigned to carry them out, had been determined in advance. It's probable that Lincoln collaborated with Chase, Seward, and others in advance of the meeting—especially Seward.

As a former New York governor and senator, Seward knew the people in New York intimately. He also viewed himself as the premier, first among cabinet members. He employed intrigue, he enjoyed secrecy, and he favored audacious plans. More than that, Seward connected with Lincoln on a personal level. The two would spend significant parts of every day together, sometimes on walks, other times on carriage rides, and frequently Lincoln visited Seward at his house on Fifteenth Street, on the east side of

Lafayette Square, to discuss all manner of things. Seward treated the cabinet as a nonentity. His style, well documented by Welles and others, was to arrive at meetings early and stay behind after meetings for private consultations with Lincoln.[32]

As this Sunday afternoon faded to evening in Washington, fears of extended isolation—and even famine—began to set in. The last buses of the day plodded slowly through the dusty cobblestone streets, and the hotels and restaurants served meals to diminished crowds.

The district's military leader, Col. Charles P. Stone, tasked with overseeing the defenses of the city, was having dinner with a friend at about 3:15 p.m. For weeks, Stone had militia companies posted at the public buildings and the bridges crossing to Virginia. When it became clear the city might be cut off for some time, he'd begun asking about where the city's food supply came from and how long supplies would last. "I knew that a beleaguered town of sixty thousand people might be kept in order if the population were well provided with food," he wrote later. If the city couldn't be supplied with at least bread, it would be in trouble.

The city was, indeed, in trouble. There was rarely more than a three-day supply of bread in Washington because bakers and grocers could order it from mills in Georgetown, just three miles away. Those mills currently had about ten thousand barrels of flour—enough to supply the city for as long as three weeks. But the supplies generally shipped out of the region as soon as they were produced.

During his dinner this afternoon, Stone learned from his sources that nearly all the flour at the Georgetown mills was being loaded onto schooners for shipment the next morning. "I left the table immediately and went to the War Department, where I met the Secretary of War just leaving his office," Stone recalled. "I recommended the seizure of all of the flour at Georgetown and its conveyance to safe magazines in the public buildings in Washington."

Cameron had two questions: Did Stone have a military force capable of seizing the flour, and could it be safely stored? Stone

replied yes to the first question and said the basements of the Capitol, the Post Office, and the Treasury Department had enough
storage space. "You, Colonel Stone, see to the soldier part—seize
the flour and guard it, and I will see to the transportation," Cameron replied.

Cameron—a tall, lanky man of sixty-two years who still had
a full head of gray hair—set off at a full run. He reached the
nearby quartermaster's office—in the five-story Winder's Building at Seventeenth Street and F Street, a block south of the War
Department—and ordered transportation. Washington militia
troops boarded the schooner *Hamilton* at the pier along Georgetown's Water Street just before it left for New York with two thousand barrels of flour. "Within an hour," Stone wrote, "a long line
of drays, express wagons and wheeled vehicles" loaded with flour
were rolling from the pier and adjacent red brick warehouses, clattering slowly into Washington.

"Late into the night that rumbling continued," Stone wrote.
"Many of the present residents in the capital can doubtless remember the rumbling of the flour carts that Sunday afternoon and
night, and can also remember the great bakery on Capitol Hill."[33]

Stone's effort was well timed. The price of flour skyrocketed the
next day, and housekeepers throughout the city began to fear famine. "The dinner table is lorn of *cartes*, and the tea table reduced to
the severe simplicity of pound-cake," John Hay wrote in his diary.[34]

Stone next turned his attention to the river craft, which transported people and mail from point to point, including the railroad
terminal at Aquia Landing, fifty-five miles downriver on the Virginia side. Stone had heard that these vessels would be detained
in Alexandria. One, the *George Page*, had been seized by Virginia
on Saturday. Five others were commandeered by federal militia
around 4:00 p.m. on Sunday and put under guard, first sitting at
a wharf at the foot of Sixth Street and then moved to the Anacos-
tia channel, across from the Navy Yard.

At about 7:00 p.m. that evening, Stone learned that still another
steamer, the *St. Nicholas*, was preparing to get underway, bound for
Baltimore with flour and molasses. So Stone went to see Cameron

again. It was now 10:30 p.m. Cameron was back in his office, look-ing weary from his long day, Stone noticed. "Well, Colonel, you can seize her as you have the other steamers; but this violent action on the part of the government is sure to create excitement through-out the country."[35]

Not only did Stone seize the *St. Nicholas* this evening, but he also suggested the seizure of the Washington telegraph office. "Mr. Secretary, nothing should, from this time out, go over the wires unless approved by the War Department," Stone told Cam-eron. "We are in a state of war, and should act accordingly." "Do it," Cameron responded.

Stone and a squad of soldiers ran into several newspaper report-ers at the telegraph office that evening. They were sending reports to their home offices. Told that that wasn't going to happen, the outraged journalists protested that they'd take their case to Cam-eron. But Cameron backed Stone. This particular act of censor-ship lasted only about a day, but it was the first act in a prolonged campaign of telegraph censorship throughout the war.[36]

That evening, at any rate, after two days of intermittent tele-graph service available only to the government, the isolation of Washington became complete. A government-sanctioned mob in Baltimore seized that city's telegraph office. "The authorities have possession of office," the Baltimore operator wrote to the Wash-ington telegraph superintendent, Alfred B. Talcott. "Of course this stops all," Talcott noted drily.[37]

20

A Torrent of Federal Resignations

The City

T he weather was warming up fast. Just the prior Wednesday, five days ago, the diarist Horatio Nelson Taft reported
that it was cold and windy, with a "fire in the office and
as much in the house as on a winters day."

But Monday was spectacular. The temperature was sixty-six
degrees at 9:00 a.m. and crossed eighty degrees for the first time all
year—hitting eighty-three degrees at precisely 3:05 p.m. "Another
delightful day, but no troops yet," Horatio Nelson Taft wrote. "We
are in a beleaguered City with enimies on every side and and [*sic*]
at our doors. The ratling of musquetry and the booming of cannon may startle us any moment."

There were fewer than five hundred partially equipped Pennsylvania soldiers in the city and seven hundred-plus troops from
the battered Sixth Massachusetts. Plus the local militia. It wasn't
enough. Confederate general Beauregard was reported to have
arrived in Richmond this morning and reconnoitered Washington by the same evening.[1]

Many people had already left the city, and now communication
with the North was fully cut off. Taft and his and family decided
to see things through. That morning Taft took what he called the

"strong oath" that had been introduced at the department the previous Thursday: "I will defend the Treasury, under the orders of
the officer in charge of it, against all its enemies, to the best of my
ability."[2]

Military and civilian employees had been resigning in
droves. The newspapers were filled with lists. The *Baltimore Sun*
reported the April 18 resignations of three army officers, including Capt. Henry Heth, who would figure prominently at Gettysburg two years later, and thirteen naval officers, including Catesby
Jones, who would assume command of the css *Virginia* during
the Battle of Hampton Roads in March 1862.

This Monday, the outflow of workers became a stampede.[3] There
were twenty-nine resignations in the Interior Department and
eleven in the Treasury. Three resignations were reported in the Post
Office. Throughout the government fifty or sixty clerks had quit,
the *Washington Evening Star* reported. A report the next day was
striking. Names, titles, job functions, and salaries all testified to
the loss of manpower and experience. The government—civilian
and military—was coming apart.

Resignations were reported in the Census Bureau, the Patent
Office, the Land Office, the Pension Bureau, the Treasury Department, and the War Department. Sixteen Army officers resigned,
the *Star* reported, and the same day, the *Baltimore Daily Exchange*
reported forty-six resignations in the Navy Department over the
prior few days. Even the Washington police chief, W. C. Dunning-
ton, resigned and returned to Virginia.

Obscure names appeared side by side with those that still rever-
berate 161 years later. The *Star's* April 23 list included Gen. Joseph
Johnston, quartermaster general; Col. Robert. E. Lee, First Cavalry;
Lt. John B. Hood, Second Cavalry; Bvt. Lt. Col. John B. Magruder,
First Artillery; and Lt. L. L. Lomax, First Cavalry.[4]

Lunsford Lindsay Lomax, a U.S. Army officer and son of the
Washington diarist Elizabeth Lomax, wrote to his West Point class-
mate Lt. George Bayard explaining his decision to resign.

Washington, D.C.

April 21st, 1861

Dear Bayard:

I cannot stand it any longer and feel it is my duty to resign. My State is out of the Union and when she calls for my services I feel that I must go. I regret it very much, realizing that the whole thing is suicidal.

As long as I could believe in a war on the Union and the flag I was willing to stay, but it is a war between sections—the North and the South—and I must go with my own people. I beg of you not to let my decision alter the friendship between us.

They say that Baltimore will be the field of action. I hope to God there are conservatives yet in the North. I find that the Southern officers are all going.

God bless you Bayard.

L.L. Lomax[5]

George Bayard, twenty-five in 1861, from Seneca Falls, New York, remained in the U.S. Army and was killed at Fredericksburg the following year. Lunsford Lomax, also twenty-five, fought in the Confederate Army during the 1864 Overland Campaign and survived the war. He died in 1913.

Franklin Buchanan, sixty, the commander of the Washington Navy Yard, resigned this day, assuming that his home state of Maryland would secede. He'd spent forty-five years in the U.S. Navy. Lincoln had attended Buchanan's daughter's wedding only three weeks earlier, on April 3.

John Dahlgren, who succeeded Buchanan as commander of the Washington Navy Yard, recalled seeing Lincoln at the wedding. "Met the president at the marriage of Captain Buchanan's daughter," Dahlgren wrote. "He took my hand in both of his, spoke freely, conversed for half an hour."[6] The next year Buchanan commanded the ironclad css *Virginia* during the first part of the Battle of Hampton Roads.

The situation overwhelmed a few officers. "Some, torn by conflicting interests, took a more summary way of deciding the question," the Washington pastor George Williamson Smith wrote. "One officer, a valued friend, met me, chatted gaily for a few minutes, shook me warmly by the hand, went home and shot himself. While one was telling me of this shocking tragedy, ten minutes afterwards, another friend, just around the corner, had done the same thing."[7]

No resignation affected Lincoln as much as that of Capt. John Bankhead Magruder. "Only three days ago, Magruder came to me voluntarily in this room," Lincoln told John Hay. "And with his own lips and in my presence repeated over and over again his protestations of loyalty and fidelity."[8]

In the days after Sumter, the fifty-four-year-old Magruder had played a critical role in the defense of Washington, commanding a battery under Colonel Stone, first at the Executive Square and later at the Long Bridge, which crossed to Arlington. After Virginia seceded, Magruder was drawn to his home state.

At six feet tall, Magruder had bushy sideburns, a mustache, and jet-black hair. He was considered handsome and witty but was also known as a hard drinker, and he spoke with a lisp. He was a favorite of General Scott's. Magruder had served with distinction in the Mexican War and was well regarded in the army for his development of artillery tactics.[9]

In an 1870 letter, Magruder remembered the conversation with Lincoln differently. He claimed he'd told Lincoln that if Virginia seceded, he'd resign. "Mr. President, I will be perfectly true and faithful to the obligations of my commission as long as I hold it, and you and your family will sleep in safety whenever I am on guard," Magruder said he told Lincoln.

In the same letter, Magruder left a vivid account of leaving Washington shortly after Virginia's secession.

I found myself at the Long Bridge, in a hack [a taxi], just three minutes after 9 P.M., too late, the orders being not to lower the draw-bridge after 9. I found my own battery guarding the bridge. I asked the Lieutenant in charge if he would be kind enough to lower the draw-bridge for me, as I was only three minutes behind the time. He touched his hat and answered courteously, "Colonel, I will lower the draw-bridge, but I would do it with far greater pleasure if you were coming from Virginia instead of going to Virginia. I departed, taking off my hat to my old comrades, some of whom I had commanded for thirty years."[10]

The impact of the resignations on the military was significant and may have played a role in the string of defeats suffered by the Union during the first two years of the war. "This canker of secession has wonderfully demoralized the army," John Hay wrote in his diary.[11]

In December 1860 the U.S. Army had 16,367 officers and men on its rolls. Of these, 1,108 were commissioned officers. Eventually close to 25 percent of the U.S. Army officer corps, as many as 270 men, resigned in 1861 to join the Confederates, including 168 West Point graduates.[12]

The navy suffered a smaller exodus. In the month of April 1861, of a total of 887 officers and 267 midshipmen, 76 officers either resigned or were dismissed. In addition, 38 Naval Academy midshipmen headed South. In all, this represented just 5.6 percent of the officers and midshipmen. In the Marine Corps, there were 63 officers in early 1861, and 19 of them left to join the Confederacy.[13]

Enlisted men did not have the legal option to resign. They had to wait until their terms of enlistment ended—or desert.

As the federal government reeled from the departures this Monday, the Massachusetts troops that had arrived on Friday were drilling. The Sixth Regiment marched every day and practiced street-firing drills. They had orders to surround the White House at the first alarm.[14]

Colonel Stone's 2,146-man militia was deployed all over the city, guarding the public buildings, the bridges, and the main roads coming in from Maryland. Stone's habit was to visit the guards every night at all of their posts, making a full circuit of the district on a wide arc from west to north to east.

"The only sleep I could snatch was taken in a carriage while driving from one picket to another," he wrote. "I usually arrived back at the Executive Square an hour or more before daybreak."[15]

Lincoln had called a cabinet meeting for later that afternoon, at 3:00, but this Monday morning he had—incredibly—his fifth meeting in three days with Baltimore dignitaries. Their demands had evolved from insisting the troops avoid Baltimore, and Maryland altogether, to acquiescing to Southern secession in the name of peace.

This time, a religious group led by the Baptist minister Richard Fuller, pastor of the Seventh Baptist Church in Baltimore, met the president.

Fuller had a national reputation. He was a founder of the Southern Baptist Convention, which in 1845 had split with the Northern Baptists over slavery. The Southern Baptist Convention argued that slavery had its roots in the Scripture and was therefore sanctioned in the teachings of God. In a famous series of letters in 1844 and 1845, Fuller and Francis Wayland, the president of Brown University and pastor of the First Baptist Church of Providence, had debated the topic. "In the Gospels and Epistles, the institution is, to say the least, tolerated," Fuller wrote. "You pronounce slaveholding itself a sin, therefore, always, and everywhere. I, for my part, find my Bible condemning the abuses of slavery, but permitting the system itself, in cases where its abrogation would be a greater calamity than its existence."[16]

Fuller on this day—his fifty-seventh birthday—was serving as chairman of a delegation of thirty members of Baltimore's Young Men's Christian Associations. The group handed a short note to the White House doorman, who in turn brought the note to Nicolay, who showed it to Lincoln: "We have left our homes and businesses at much inconvenience, but are ready to make any sacrifice for our beloved country, and for peace." The meeting lasted an hour and was conducted mainly between Lincoln and Fuller.

Lincoln was ready. He knew who Fuller was. He knew the pastor owned 150 enslaved people on a plantation in South Carolina. Fuller sensed it. "From President Lincoln nothing is to be hoped—except as you can influence him," Fuller wrote the next day to Treasury Secretary Salmon Chase. "I marked the President closely. Constitutionally genial & jovial, he is wholly inaccessible to Christian appeals—& his egotism will forever prevent him from comprehending what patriotism means."[17]

Fuller told Lincoln he should avert bloodshed and recognize the Confederacy. The president should allow no further troops to come through Maryland. If Lincoln didn't allow peace to the seceded states, the result would be a terrible war.

"But what am I to do?" Lincoln replied.

"Why, sir, let the country know that you are disposed to recognize the independence of the Southern States," Fuller told Lincoln. "Recognize the fact that they have formed a government of their own, that they will never again be united with the North."

"And what is to become of the revenue?" Lincoln asked. "I shall have no government—no resources. Why, sir, those Carolinians are now crossing Virginia to come here and hang me. What can I do?"

Nicolay and Hay released a verbatim account of Lincoln's response. It diverges in several ways from a separate one that appeared in the *Baltimore Sun*, which was drawn from an informant who was there.

> You, gentlemen, come here to me and ask for peace on any terms, and yet have no word of condemnation for those who are making war on us. You express great horror of bloodshed, and yet would not lay a straw in the way of those who are organizing in Virginia and elsewhere to capture this city. The rebels attack Fort Sumter, and your citizens attack troops sent to the defense of this government, and the lives and property in Washington, and yet you would have me break my oath and surrender the government without a blow. There is no Washington in that—no Jackson in that—there is no manhood or honor in that. [The *Sun*'s account says Lincoln used the phrase "there is no spunk in that," not "no manhood or honor in that."]
>
> I have no desire to invade the South; but I must have troops to defend this capital. Geographically, it lies surrounded by the soil of Maryland; and mathematically the necessity exists that they should come over her territory. Our men are not moles, and can't dig under the earth; they are not birds, and can't fly through

the air. There is no way but to march across, and that they must do. But in doing this, there is no need of collision. Keep your rowdies in Baltimore, and there will be no bloodshed. Go home and tell your people that if they will not attack us, we will not attack them; but if they do attack us, we will return it, and that severely. [The *Sun*'s account uses a less dramatic construction of this last sentence: "Now, sir, if you won't hit me, I won't hit you."]

The response was predictable. The delegation conferred after the meeting and agreed on the hopelessness of their mission: "God have mercy on us, when the government is placed in the hands of a man like this!"[18]

Across the street from the War Department, at General Scott's headquarters, Colonel Stone arrived for his daily 9:00 a.m. meeting with the general-in-chief. "I found him busily engaged in writing," Stone remembered years later. "As I approached and saluted, the general looked up over his spectacles, and on seeing who had entered, said, a little sharply: 'Colonel Stone, you will please come and dine with me this afternoon at half-past four o'clock. Good morning, sir!'"

Stone had been dismissed. He wasn't astonished by this reception from the sometimes-irascible general and returned at 4:30, as directed. Stone found Scott's valet, a man named Clark, placing soup on the table. Scott was preoccupied. The soup was served and consumed in silence.

A large roasted chicken came next. "Colonel Stone, will you do me the favor to carve that chicken," Scott asked. "Very little of the breast with the wing, please!" Scott's idiosyncratic eating habits remained intact.

A decanter of wine had been untouched.

"Colonel Stone, you will find that sherry very good." I took the decanter and filled first his glass, then my own. He raised his glass slightly, and looking over at me very intently, he said, "Gosport Navy Yard has been burned!"

I replied, quietly: "Yes, General!"

He continued: "Harpers Ferry bridge has been burned!"

Again I replied: "Yes, General."

He continued: "The bridges over Gunpowder Creek beyond Baltimore have been burned!"

I still replied: "Yes, General."

He added: "They are closing their coils around us, sir!"

Still I replied, in the same tone: "Yes, General."

"Well, sir!" said the general: "I invited you to come and dine with me to-day, because I hoped that you could listen calmly to that style of conversation! Your very good health, sir!"

And he drained his glass, while I bowed and followed his example.

How long, Scott asked Stone, could the city hold out? "Ten days, General, and in that time the North will come down to us."

How will they come? Scott continued. The route through Baltimore is cut off. How many men do you have? How many miles of picket line between your outposts? Stone outlined his plan of defense, explaining that he anticipated a serious attack at only a single point, to which reinforcements could be sent as his command slowly fell back to three centers—the Capitol, city hall, and the Executive Square.

Scott generally approved but told Stone he had too many centers. The plan should be consolidated to a single center, the Executive Square. And if needed, only the Treasury Department building. "And should it come to the defense of the Treasury building as a citadel, then the President and all the members of his cabinet must take up their quarters within that building!" Scott said, emphatically. "They shall not be permitted to desert the capital!"

Scott, subordinate to both Cameron and Lincoln, was probably passionately expressing his belief that the nation's capital should never be abandoned. But taken another way, the comment implied that the senior civilian officers of the government, including the commander-in-chief, would be kept in Washington by force, if necessary.[19]

And so it went in Washington. Even as Scott vented about Washington's vulnerability, messages from the states, both North and South, continued to pour in.

"In answer to your requisition for troops from Arkansas to subjugate the Southern States, I have to say that none will be furnished," Arkansas governor H. M. Rector wrote. "The people of this Commonwealth are freemen, not slaves, and will defend to the last extremity their honor, lives, and property against Northern mendacity and usurpation."[20]

"New Hampshire tenders one or more additional regiments to the General Government. Will they be accepted?" asked state adjutant general Joseph C. Abbott.[21]

In Ohio, Gov. William Dennison reported that he already had more men in camp than Cameron had sought: "Indeed, without seriously repressing the ardor of the people, I can hardly stop short of twenty regiments."[22]

In Annapolis, Maryland governor Thomas Hicks continued his pressure campaign to keep troops out of the state. He telegraphed Lincoln: "SIR: I feel it my duty most respectfully to advise you that no more troops be allowed to pass through Maryland, and that the troops now off Annapolis be sent elsewhere." Now Hicks offered another twist. He suggested that the senior British diplomat in the United States, Lord Richard Lyons, serve as an intermediary.[23]

Lincoln told Seward to reply to Hicks. Seward was unyielding.

The route through Maryland, Seward reminded Hicks, was chosen by General Scott in consultation with prominent Maryland officials. Coming through Maryland was an absolute necessity.

Then Seward scolded Hicks. "There has been a time in the history of our country when a General of the American Union was not unwelcome anywhere in the State of Maryland," he wrote. "If eighty years could have obliterated all other sentiments of that age, the President would be hopeful, nevertheless, that one would forever remain. That no domestic contention that may arise among the parties of this Republic, ought in any case to be referred to any foreign arbitrament, least of all to the arbitrament of a European monarchy."[24]

The exchanges with Fuller and the other Baltimore delegations, and the one with Seward and Hicks, were all released to the newspapers. They were part of Lincoln's communications strategy. They dovetailed with his proclamation calling for seventy-five thousand troops, in which he vowed to "redress wrongs already long enough endured."[25]

Secessionist Maryland

Governor Hicks was trying to keep a handle on the politics of his volatile state. After delaying for months, he announced this Monday that he was calling the Maryland legislature into session in Annapolis on the twenty-sixth.

This dramatically dialed up the pressure on the Lincoln administration. Assembling the Maryland legislature increased the likelihood that it would vote to secede and that a vote would come before the Lincoln administration had the military power to stop it. Such an action would further seal Washington off from the North. It would eliminate the Annapolis route for Northern troops.

It was, by any measure, a real emergency. Hicks later claimed he felt forced to summon the legislature after an "unlawful" proclamation by the Baltimore state senator Coleman Yellott—a radical supporter of the Confederacy and open secessionist—urging legislators to meet in Baltimore, where the secessionist element was strongest. "I knew it was time for me to act," Hicks said in a message to the state legislature.[26]

Yellott's request was made on the twentieth and appeared in the April 22 edition of the *Baltimore Sun*. Hicks's own call was published the next day.[27]

It got worse. Ten Baltimore legislative seats in the prior year's election had been vacated due to corruption. Yellott was the only sitting Baltimore legislator. Now a legally questionable special election was called for the twenty-fourth. Only one slate was presented, made up of states-rights supporters.[28] This election might swing the balance of the Maryland legislature in favor of secession. Lincoln was faced with a choice. Arrest the legislature? Disperse it by force?[29]

The president expected Maryland to secede. It was probable, he told General Scott, that the legislature "will take action to arm the people of that State against the United States."[30]

Maryland's major newspapers were crying out for action. The *Daily Exchange*, noting Virginia's secession, wrote that "the Union, then, is dissolved. Nothing now is left for Maryland but to follow the path in which Virginia has preceded her."[31]

The *Baltimore Sun*, a staunch supporter of Southern rights, urged Hicks to assemble the legislature or risk a spontaneous usurpation of his authority—a move precisely represented by Senator Yellott's call to assemble the legislature. But the *Sun* stopped short of calling for secession, instead urging the legislature to appoint a convention to consider the question.[32]

Lincoln's cabinet was fed up. Attorney General Edward Bates issued a memorandum: "The people of Maryland and Virginia are in a ferment, a furor, regardless of law and common sense. They block our communications, we are careful to preserve theirs—they assail and obstruct our troops while we have done nothing to resist or retort the outrage."[33]

Treasury Secretary Salmon Chase weighed in two days later. "It has been a darling object with the disunionists to secure the passage of a secession ordinance by Maryland," Chase told Lincoln. "Do not, I pray you, let this new success of treason be inaugurated in the presence of American troops. Save us from this new humiliation. You alone can give the word."[34]

If Chase thought Lincoln was weak, he badly misread the president. For the moment, however, Lincoln exercised caution. Arresting or dispersing the legislature wasn't justifiable, he told General Scott on April 25. It had a legal right to assemble. If it was dispersed, it would reassemble elsewhere and take its vote. If its delegates were arrested, they would reassemble once released. "I therefore conclude that it is only left to the commanding general to watch and await their action," Lincoln wrote.

Then Lincoln revealed his resolve with chilling clarity. If the Maryland legislature took up arms against the United States, Scott was authorized to literally attack Maryland. Scott would counteract a secession vote, Lincoln said, "even if necessary to the bombardment of their cities, and in the extremest necessity, the suspension of the writ of habeas corpus."[35]

Cockeysville, Maryland

Seventeen miles north of Baltimore this Monday, the Pennsylvania troops that had generated such a frenzy yesterday were stranded at Cockeysville. They haplessly camped in the area, awaiting the finalization of arrangements for them to return home—as Lincoln had ordered.

A train was ready to reboard the men and take them back to Harrisburg. The telegraph from that point back into Pennsylvania was still operating.[36]

Newspaper accounts indicated that the troops were completely unprepared, not just in terms of equipment, but in basic military discipline. "They were prowling through the countryside in search of something to eat," the *Exchange* reported.[37]

Within a couple of hours of the troops' arrival at Cockeysville, a hodgepodge of volunteers formed in Baltimore to go out and engage the invaders. "Hundreds left the city in wagons, carriages, buggies and other vehicles, determined to wage a guerilla warfare against the advancing force," the *Evening Star* reported. "Not less than 500 men left Baltimore for this purpose, armed with shot guns and rifles."

But there wasn't a fight to be had. The Pennsylvanians weren't interested. The camp was visited by scores of Baltimoreans. The visits went unchallenged. In fact, the *Star* reported, the visitors, hostile and otherwise, were "cordially received and entertained." One of the companies of Pennsylvania volunteers, from Lancaster, inquired about the Baltimore City Guard company, with whom it had enjoyed fraternal ties and social connections. It "transmitted evidences of continuing good-will."[38]

Another volunteer said he had a family in Frostburg, Maryland, and had gone to Philadelphia looking for work. He joined the local militia hoping to earn a subsistence living. "He didn't volunteer for the purpose of fighting Marylanders, and didn't intend to do it."

The troops slept on their guns overnight into Monday. Fatigue and disappointment spread, and morale sank. It became so pathetic that Marshal Kane—their supposed secessionist enemy—ordered several wagonloads of bread and meat to be delivered to the encampment. "The act was a humane one, and deserves to be recorded," the *Sun* reported. These troops had been on the road barely more than a day. At any rate, by four o'clock Monday afternoon, the Pennsylvania volunteers were back in Pennsylvania, camped at York.[39]

The South

Jefferson Davis, in Montgomery this Monday, dialed up his rhetoric about moving the war north of the Potomac. With Maryland on the brink of a secession vote, he told Virginia governor John Letcher that requisitions had been made for thirteen Confederate regiments to report to Virginia. "Sustain Baltimore, if practicable," Davis urged Letcher. "We re-enforce you."[40]

Davis recognized the immense strategic potential of the Baltimore uprising. This incendiary remark was the closest he would come to directly endorsing an incursion north of the Potomac.

In Washington General Scott was picking up various rumors that aligned with Davis's message to Letcher. "Extra cars went up yesterday to bring from Harpers Ferry about two thousand troops to join in a general attack on this capital—that is, on many of its fronts at once," Scott reported to Lincoln.[41]

In South Carolina General Beauregard continued to focus on his forces in and around Charleston. But South Carolina governor Francis Pickens reported to Jefferson Davis that Gen. Milledge Bonham was on his way to Richmond with troops. "More will start every day now," Pickens said. "They are subject to your orders in all things."[42]

In Richmond Letcher's advisory council received a request that arms be sent to Maryland troops in Baltimore. The council authorized Gen. Kenton Harper, the Virginia commander at Harpers Ferry, to ship one thousand rifles to Maryland general George H. Steuart. The council also authorized a loan to Maryland of five thousand additional rifles.[43]

These guns were delivered in a daring overnight trip from Harpers Ferry to Baltimore. Leading the mission was Edward H.

McDonald, an aide to General Harper. The order from Richmond for the shipment arrived in Harpers Ferry late on the night of the twenty-second. McDonald brought it to headquarters. "I proposed to deliver them in Baltimore before morning if [General Harper] would give me a regiment and transportation," McDonald said.

By 2:00 a.m. McDonald was on his way. In Baltimore, McDonald noted, the whole city was with the South. The Marylanders urged him to move Virginian forces from Harpers Ferry to Baltimore. McDonald also met with John W. Garrett, president of the B&O Railroad, whose line was vital to both sides. "He told me to go at once to Richmond and tell the authorities there to move their men to Baltimore and make the fight there," McDonald recalled. "Everything was favorable for such a move."[44]

21

General Butler, the Belligerent Brigadier

The Advance

In Annapolis, Maryland governor Thomas Hicks was busy. In addition to pleading with Lincoln to keep troops out of Maryland and summoning the legislature into session, he was dealing with a high-maintenance Massachusetts brigadier general—Benjamin F. Butler.

For the second straight day, Butler and Hicks wrangled over the terms on which the Massachusetts Eighth Regiment—about 725 men—could come ashore at the U.S. Naval Academy.

The day before Hicks had advised Butler not to land, saying the excitement level was too high. Now Butler followed up: "I desire an immediate reply as to whether I have the permission of the state authorities to land the men under my command and pass quickly through the state on my way to Washington."[1]

Butler went ashore for an in-person meeting with Hicks and Annapolis mayor John R. Magruder. Both officials warned him not to land the troops. The rail line connecting Annapolis to the B&O Railroad and Washington had been torn up, and now it was guarded by insurrectionists. All of Maryland was ready to fight.

"I must land," Butler replied. "My men are hungry. I could not even leave without getting a supply of provisions." Nobody around Annapolis was likely to sell Yankee troops anything anyway, Hicks and Magruder told Butler.[2] "If the people will not sell those provisions, a thousand hungry, armed men have other means of getting what they want to eat without buying it," Butler responded.[3]

The meeting was inconclusive. Later Butler would write of these exchanges in his typically acerbic way: "Within thirty days, the mayor of Annapolis was an applicant for the place of post sutler. He did not get it from me, however."[4]

In the end Hicks relented. "I content myself with protesting against this movement, which, in view of the excited condition of the people of this State, I cannot but consider an unwise step," he wrote to Butler.[5]

What Butler didn't know was that Hicks apparently wanted merely to appear to be objecting to the passage of troops—for public consumption. Both Hicks and Magruder had made private assurances to the federal government that they would not impede the march. Those assurances may have come in a private meeting two Hicks emissaries had with Lincoln this same day. The Maryland secretary of state James Partridge and the pro-Union former congressman Henry Winter Davis met the president in Washington. The outcome was not publicized, but the prosecession *Baltimore Sun* was suspicious: "It is not safe to trust [Hicks] with unofficial familiar intercourse with the Lincoln government."[6]

The Maryland land commissioner, twenty-seven-year-old William L. W. Seabrook, a staunch Unionist and Hicks confidant, described the governor's strategy. In Annapolis that morning, Hicks asked if Seabrook had heard about him objecting to Butler coming ashore: "I sent him a written protest yesterday morning." First Seabrook thought Hicks was joking. Then he got angry. Butler had every right to disembark in Maryland, and Hicks knew it. What's more, the Northern troops guaranteed protection to local Unionists in Annapolis. Seabrook told Hicks he wanted the Union troops ashore.

Hicks leaned in close and said, "'And I want it as much as you do.' 'Then why in heaven's name did you protest against it?' 'I did it to keep hold as long as possible upon the other side. I don't want them to be fully aware of my attitude yet.'"[7]

The New York Seventh Arrives in Annapolis

Butler had now been in Annapolis for thirty-six hours. Fortu-
nately for him, the Seventh Regiment, on the *Boston*, had arrived
off Annapolis in the predawn hours of Monday. It waited till daylight to enter the harbor, creeping toward the city through an early
morning fog.

Hours earlier, at the mouth of the Potomac, Colonel Lefferts
had heard from the crew of a passing light ship that secessionist
batteries were positioned near Alexandria and that the Norfolk
Navy Yard was now in the hands of the Virginia militia. Rather
than risk a run up the Potomac, Annapolis became the destination.

From the decks of the *Boston*, the men of the Seventh could see
the soldiers of the Eighth trying to rock the grounded *Maryland*
free. The Massachusetts troops ran forward and aft in groups, then
port to starboard. They rolled carts and equipment off the deck.
They threw out the coal. Nothing worked. "As the tide rose, we
gave our grounded friends a lift with a hawser," Seventh Regiment
private Theodore Winthrop wrote. "No go! We got near enough to
see the whites of the Massachusetts eyes, and their unlucky faces
and uniforms all grimy with their lodgings in the coal-dust. They
could not have been blacker if they had been breathing battle-
smoke and dust all day."[8] This went on for most of Monday.

Lefferts and a delegation of New Yorkers went ashore to meet
with academy officers and local municipal officials. The word was
similar to what Butler had heard—the city and countryside were
up in arms, the railroad was torn up, and bushwhackers and guer-
rillas were roving through the region. Baltimore secessionists had
seized bridges and were said to be massing at Annapolis Junction,
twenty miles away, or marching toward Annapolis.[9]

Mayor Magruder repeated the same warnings he'd given Butler. To bring the regiment into the town would be an outrage. It
would be impossible to buy provisions or wagons. No one would
help the Yankees.

Lefferts called his officers together. They'd already been detained
longer than they anticipated. They needed to get to Washington as

fast as possible. They decided that the Seventh would round up all the wagons and provisions—including ammunition—they could, either buying them or seizing them, and move out for Washington in the morning via the wagon road, which was a more direct route to the capital than the railroad.[10]

For both regiments the long hours on the steamers were finally ending. At 5:00 p.m. the *Boston* tied up at the wharf and the Seventh disembarked, marching up the green sloping Naval Academy fields.[11]

After the *Boston* was offloaded, Lefferts sent it out to the *Maryland*, where over a succession of trips the Eighth Regiment was brought ashore and the *Maryland* eventually refloated. It was now about forty-three hours since Butler and the Eighth Massachusetts had arrived at Annapolis.

"Poor fellows!" Winthrop said. "What a figure they cut when we found them bivouacked on the Academy grounds next morning! They had come in hot patriotic haste, half-uniformed and half-outfitted. They were out of grub. They were parched dry for want of water on the ferry-boat. But, hungry, thirsty, grimy, these fellows were GRIT."[12] Lefferts met with Butler this late afternoon—or, as Butler jibed, "Colonel Lefferts reported to me at my headquarters on the grounds of the academy."[13]

The officers of the Seventh had been feeling a slow burn about Butler for days. The Massachusetts brigadier presumed the Seventh was part of his command. He issued a series of "brigade orders" at Annapolis that covered drill requirements and general behavior for both regiments, sometimes issuing these orders from the headquarters of the "Brigade of United States Militia," a reference to a nonexistent command structure that made the New Yorkers bristle.[14]

In the meeting with Lefferts, Butler sought to advance along the line of the railroad to Annapolis Junction in cooperation with the Seventh, repairing the tracks as he went. Lefferts stuck to his own plan to move along the turnpike. He would depart the next morning, Tuesday, after wagons and other supplies were procured. Butler dismissed Lefferts's plan. He claimed Lefferts really just wanted to wait in Annapolis for more Northern troops to arrive.

He derided Lefferts's concerns about a secessionist threat at the junction. He thought Lefferts was scared. In his 1892 autobiography, he needled the New Yorkers, saying he never saw a secessionist force that "could not have been overcome with a large yellow dog."[15]

Butler's biographer, James Parton, also mocked Lefferts. The New York colonel had been convinced by the locals that large bodies of troops were waiting outside the gates of the academy, Parton wrote. Lefferts posted guards at the gates. "Nor were his apprehensions allayed when a *Tribune* reporter, accompanied by two friends, strolled all over town unmolested, brought back word that no enemy was in sight, and that the storekeepers of Annapolis were willing to sell their goods to Union soldiers," Parton wrote.[16]

Butler worked on Lefferts: "I impressed upon him as strongly as I could the necessity to march at once."[17] But contemporary evidence indicates Butler actually had little inclination to march at once. "General Butler, of Massachusetts, who commands all the forces at Annapolis, did not deem it prudent to move forward until they had been reinforced," the *New York Times* reported.[18]

The Maryland land commissioner, William Seabrook, also thought Butler was hesitant. "He makes much of the wild rumors that met him in Philadelphia, and on his passage to Perryville, of the supposed hostile attitude of the people of the State," Seabrook wrote. "Yet he saw no signs of such hostility along the line of the railroad, nor at Perryville, where he seized the ferryboat *Maryland*."[19]

In the end, there was no way Butler and Lefferts could definitively know what was true. They operated in a fog of uncertainty that's hard to comprehend now, in an age of instant handheld communications. As fledgling commanders, they also bore the burden of the always-present possibility of a disastrous mistake.

Butler pressed the case for his plan this late afternoon—the elite lawyer memorably addressed the officers of the Seventh. Butler flattered the regiment for its fame and patriotism. He described his "plain Massachusetts boys." He alluded to the historical past and talked of both regiments and how the country was now dependent on their success.

The scene was extraordinary, Second Company captain Emmons Clark remembered. It was late afternoon on a strikingly beautiful day, and it struck Clark as fit for a historical painting: "In the center, a group of handsome and intelligent officers listening to General Butler, who commands, by his brilliant oratory, their respectful and undivided attention. In front, the broad bay of Annapolis, with the *Boston* at the wharf, the *Maryland* hard aground, and the *Constitution* in the distance. To the right, members of the Seventh Regiment at rest in picturesque groups and all conceivable attitudes, and the imposing buildings of the Naval School, with its officers and students in neat uniforms."[20]

Butler succeeded in winning over the officers of the Seventh. "It is safe to say that, in all his oratorical efforts, he was never more successful," Clark wrote. Butler had "established in the minds of the men before him the strength, character and energy that all of the American people would come to know about Butler, despite his faults and imperfections."[21]

Butler was pleased. "I thought I got their assent; for as I made my points they turned their eyes very steadfastly on Lefferts."[22]

But Lefferts still declined to march along the rail line. Butler was enraged. The trouble with Lefferts, he spat out, "appeared to be that he had picked up somewhere a man who had once been at West Point to cosset him in his command. Lefferts never called upon me without him, and he at times was somewhat officious, and not always too courteous. But I pardoned that on account of the color of his nose, and because I was not seeking difficulties."[23]

Lefferts brushed off the insults and put his decision on the record. He addressed a note to "General B. F. Butler, Commanding Massachusetts Volunteers," a pointed reference to the limits of Butler's authority: "Sir:—Upon consultation with my officers, I deem it not proper, under the circumstances, to co-operate in the proposed march by railroad, laying track as we go along—particularly in view of a large force hourly expected, and with so little ammunition as we possess."[24]

Lefferts mostly declined to acknowledge Butler's "fulminations." This just infuriated Butler more.[25] In a report two days later, Butler claimed that he was ready to march to Washington at daybreak the next morning, Tuesday the twenty-third, but that he was foiled because Lefferts refused to seize the railroad depot on Monday evening.[26]

This isn't credible. The events of Monday afternoon and Tuesday morning precluded it. The Massachusetts men were in no shape for a march. They'd sweltered on the *Maryland* all day Monday, exhausted and hungry. Butler also told Hicks that he desperately needed provisions for his men.

In a dispatch to the federal commander, Butler acknowledged that didn't even get his men off the grounded *Maryland* until the "middle of the night" and landed at the wharf the next morning. These two factors alone—lack of provisions for hungry, exhausted men and a regiment stranded on a ferry until the middle of the night—would have prohibited an immediate march early Tuesday morning.

But there was more. Also on Monday, Butler issued a four-page "Brigade Order Number 37," which called, among other things, for daily company drills from 5:00 a.m. to 7:00 a.m. No one anticipating an immediate march at daybreak would have issued that order. Then the next day, Tuesday the twenty-third, he volunteered to put the Eighth Massachusetts at the service of the Maryland state government to quell a rumored insurrection among enslaved people.[27]

These things were not the activities of a commander urgently focused on advancing to Washington. "General Butler, however apt he might be for the profession of arms, had considerable yet to learn," the journalist William Swinton wrote.[28]

An Ocean Convoy Steams South

More Northern reinforcements were on the way. The five-ship convoy of New York and Rhode Island troops was churning down the Eastern Seaboard on its first day at sea. A two-ship squadron carrying the Fifth Massachusetts and its accompanying artillery battalion was just hours behind.

The first tranquil hours of the voyage, during which some recruits enjoyed a liquid celebration late into the night, had turned into a stormy Monday. The wind was up; the sea was running white and rough. "I found, when I went forth, that some of the most jocund revelers of the night before were among those prostrated with sea-sickness," wrote the New York journalist George Wilkes, embedded with the Seventy-First Regiment. "What made matters worse was the day was wet and raw, and the entire thousand men who compose our force were obliged to huddle in stifling proximity below the decks." Some of the tougher recruits, Wilkes noticed, were impervious. They "sat hooded in their blankets on the outer deck, and were heard frequently indulging in the luxury of a cheer."[29]

A hundred miles back was the Fifth Massachusetts, moving south on the *DeSoto* and the *Ariel*. Third Lt. Charles Bowers and many of his fellow soldiers were also having a rough time. "About 2 o clock I roused myself and prepared to go on deck—I felt a sort of dissiness and an unpleasant action of my stomach," Bowers wrote home. "I saw dozens of men holding on upon the sides of the boat, and another party appearing to take peculiar delight at their expense. I soon found myself united to the former party and the way bitter yellow bile flowed from my mouth was unprecedented in my experience."

After a while Bowers went below decks again only to rush back topside, still sick. The interior air "had become very close and offensive, dozens lying on their backs being unable to stand upon their feet, and vomiting. I found it impossible to remain and went again on deck, and there remained until morning."[30]

Augustus Woodbury, the Rhode Island chaplain, didn't report on the foul weather or bouts of seasickness. But he filled in some gaps. "During the afternoon of Monday, a little tug came dancing over the billows, bearing the flag of the Union," Woodbury wrote. "She came up under our quarter and communicated the destruction of our navy yard at Norfolk, then steamed away again for New York." It was the steam tug *Yankee*, which had been at Sumter and was just one day removed from helping tow the *Cumberland* away from the conflagration at the navy yard.

Before the close of the day, the convoy came in sight of the entrance to the Chesapeake Bay. The *Coatzacoalcos* anchored just inside the bay, in Lynn Haven Roads (a crescent-shaped cove near present-day Virginia Beach), and spent what Woodbury described as a spooky overnight. "As the shadows deepened, we looked in vain for the beacon lights by which the skillful sailor lays his course," Woodbury wrote. "They had been extinguished or misplaced, and at any time we might be among the breakers or exposed to capture by the forces of an enemy."

These Rhode Island novices were anxious. They were just a few miles off a hostile shoreline. The Confederate government had issued letters of marque, meaning that enemy privateers might even now be roaming through the nighttime seas. Ammunition was distributed to the troops, and guards were posted around the ship. If an attack came, the troops would be as ready as they could.[31]

Albany, New York

Far to the north, another New York State militia regiment was deploying this Monday, April 22. The Twenty-Fifth Regiment, organized in the state capital of Albany, was ordered into immediate service and directed to Washington on the nineteenth. Its colonel was Michael K. Bryan, forty, a restauranteur and a native of County Cork in Ireland whose family had emigrated to upstate New York in 1827.[32]

When the regiment departed for New York on the Hudson River Railroad, it had 575 men. The Twenty-Fifth embarked on the steamer *Parkersburgh* in New York on Wednesday morning, the twenty-fourth, and sailed for Annapolis, arriving on the morning of April 26.[33] The North's slow-building military wave was inexorable.

22

Stalled in Annapolis

The City

Some three-day-old newspapers came through from the North this Tuesday morning. "It seemed like a glimpse of a better world to contrast the warm open enthusiasm of the Empire City with the cold distrust of the dwellers in Washington," John Hay wrote.[1]

The newspapers told of a storm of Northern fury. There were rallies in every Northern city. Recruiting was outpacing demand. There were reports of the departure of the New York Seventh. The First Rhode Island Volunteers led by Col. Ambrose Burnside and the thirty-year-old governor, William Sprague, was on its way. Maj. Robert Anderson and his Fort Sumter command had made it to New York and were received with acclaim.

On Saturday, a giant pro-Union rally had been held in Union Square in Manhattan. The Union Defense Committee in New York and similar groups elsewhere were raising money for the troops. So were city and state governments. So were the banks. But in Washington this was all just on paper, literally.

In the real world, the capital city of a powerful nation had somehow become marooned, isolated from the rest of the country. Massive sandbag walls surrounded the public buildings, and troops guarded them. Companies of soldiers patrolled the streets, and armed small vessels patrolled the Potomac. Checkpoints were established at the approaches to the city.

Secession fever raged. At any moment, thousands of hostile troops from Virginia and Maryland might swarm into the city. Every hour that went by, the tension increased. Even General Scott, always confident the capital could be defended, lost his patience. Asked by a visitor what Scott expected the New York Seventh to do, Scott said, "March to Washington."

"March!" the visitor responded. "Why, general, its tracks will be marked with blood; it will have to fight its way through hordes of rebels!"

"Fight, sir, fight!" Scott replied. "That is what the regiment came for! This is not a time to play soldier on parade!"[2]

This Tuesday, the troops didn't march or fight. "A large and dispirited throng gathered at the Depot this morning hoping to get deliverance," Hay wrote in his diary. "But the hope was futile."[3]

This was the second very warm day in a row—eighty-three degrees in the shade, recorded Horatio Nelson Taft in his diary. It reached a high of eighty-nine degrees by midafternoon, a sweltering heat that seemed to cause everyone to move a little slower.[4]

"The city seems quiet this beautiful spring morning," wrote Elizabeth Lindsay Lomax. It was just a day since her son, ex-U.S. Army captain Lindsay Lunsford Lomax, had joined the Confederate army.[5]

President Lincoln perked up at the few hopeful signs of military activity. Around noon, the president had gathered the cabinet for its regular Tuesday meeting. Just then, messengers announced the arrival of two steamers at the Washington Navy Yard. Had the troops finally arrived? Lincoln sent a message to Navy Secretary Gideon Welles, who wasn't at the meeting.

> Dear Sir: I think I saw three vessels go up to the Navy Yard just now. Will you please send down and learn what they are?
>
> Yours truly A. Lincoln[6]

Lincoln's hope was short-lived. It turned out that the ships were the USS *Pawnee* and a transport, the *Keystone State*, returning from the expedition to Norfolk. Word had reached the government on Sunday that the worst outcome there had been realized. The yard was lost, and the ships had been scuttled, but much of the equipment survived the fire. A lot of it subsequently was salvaged by the Confederates.

John Hay was there when Lincoln heard about the vessels. Douglas Wallach, owner of the *Washington Star*, had rushed to the White House with what he considered important news—the two ships were the *Pawnee* and the *Keystone State*. Hay's diary entry states, "The premier [Seward] cursed quietly because the *Baltic* [carrying Northern troops] had not come, told Wallach not to contradict the report that the *Baltic* had come—said treason by Governor Hicks would not surprise him—that the Seventh could cut their way through three thousand rioters—that Baltimore delenda est [a Latin phrase meaning "it must be destroyed"]—and other things, and strode back into the audience chamber."[7]

Despite the lack of troops in Washington, warlike talk from the Northern states continued, but it was also combined with contradictory acknowledgments of unpreparedness. It was both heartening and frustrating to Washington officials, still vulnerable and cut off from the North for the third day in a row. "Minnesota regiment ready in ten days. Where will they obtain their uniforms?" Minnesota lieutenant governor Ignatius Donnelly asked Cameron.

"We desire to be informed whether the Government will furnish rifled muskets to the New Hampshire troops," wrote New Hampshire adjutant general Joseph C. Abbott. "We should want 2,000 immediately. New Hampshire will respond promptly to any call for troops, even to the number of 20,000 men."[8]

In Washington help was offered from unexpected sources. Secretary of War Simon Cameron got a note this day from an employee of the senate, Jacob Dodson. Dodson, about thirty-six in 1861, was a free Black man who'd already made an extraordinary life for himself. He had accompanied John C. Fremont on three of the famous "Pathfinder's" trips of exploration to the western parts of North America during the 1840s, gaining status on these expeditions as a full equal—and one of the most capable and important members of the group. Later, he helped Fremont edit his memoirs.[9]

April 23rd, 1861

Sir: I desire to inform you that I know of some 300 reliable colored free citizens of this city who desire to enter the service for the defense of the city. I have been three times across the Rocky Mountains in the service of the country with Fremont and others. I can be found about the Senate Chamber, as I have been employed about the premises for some years.

Yours, respectfully,

Jacob Dodson (Colored)[10]

Cameron's reply came six days later. It was deflating. The endangered city desperately needed able-bodied men. Just not Black men, apparently. There was a hint of embarrassment in the naked racism of Cameron's response.

Sir: In reply to your letter of the 23rd instant, I have to say that this department has no intention at present to call into the service of the Government any colored soldiers.

With respect, etc.,

Simon Cameron,
Secretary of War.[11]

The Northern militia advance had slowed to a crawl, but one person who was not moving slowly was Colonel Stone. Just yesterday, he'd commandeered four small Potomac mail steamers and taken control of the telegraph office. Now early this morning, Secretary Cameron and General Scott ordered him to seize the railroad depot, the rolling stock, and the B&O line as far as the Annapolis junction.[12]

In typical circumstances, the B&O terminal in Washington delivered close to one hundred thousand passengers per year to the capital from Baltimore, points west, and the local towns along the line.[13]

But for several days now, the usual Baltimore-Washington schedule had been interrupted. There were no regular trains, though from time to time a locomotive with one or two cars would chug into the station. Colonel Stone ordered a battalion of DC militia to meet him at the depot. He posted soldiers at key points, where they wouldn't be seen from inbound trains. If a train did come in, Stone told his men to form up on the tracks behind it to prevent it from leaving. The depot had been stripped of most of its essential equipment, but the station master lingered.

Soon enough, a whistle pierced the air and a pillar of black smoke could be seen moving south along Delaware Avenue. It was an inbound train. A powerful locomotive, with two passenger cars and one baggage car, rolled slowly into the station, bell clanging loudly. It carried only three people, and they quickly leaped from the first car and walked rapidly through the terminal into the street without noticing the troops. The crew unloaded luggage and freight. "The engineer was about to back off with his train when I stepped near him and ordered him to shunt his train in the yard," Stone said. "He looked astonished and informed me that he had orders to go directly back to Baltimore, and go he must."

That wasn't going to happen. Stone was in charge of the line now. The engineer glanced back, saw the line of troops, and sullenly complied.

Stone decided to combine the best engine and cars, load them with troops, and proceed to Annapolis Junction, twenty-three miles to the northeast, through potentially hostile sections of rural Maryland. He sent a message to General Scott asking for regular army captain William B. Franklin, then overseeing construction of the new Treasury Department building, to lead the endeavor.

Then Stone learned that the locomotives had been tampered with—probably by someone on the crew. It occurred to Stone that some of the Sixth Massachusetts men might be mechanics—and Stone knew they were at the Capitol, just a block away.

"So I sent a mounted officer at speed to the Capitol, with my compliments to the commanding officer of that regiment, requesting

him to send a half dozen locomotive builders with their tools."
Within minutes several delighted mechanics in Massachusetts
uniforms came running into the station. "Where is she? Let us
get at her!" In another few minutes, both engines were working.

The engineer wanted no part of this assignment. He was convinced he'd be fired. If that happened, Stone promised, he'd find
the engineer a better job. But Stone posted two armed soldiers
on the locomotive. "If you wreck this train, you will then be
justly shot on the spot," he told the engineer and fireman. Off the
train went.

Captain Franklin's orders were to try to reach Annapolis Junction and, if possible, link up with Butler's troops. He also was
ordered to assess the condition of the tracks on the Annapolis
branch and make a list of sidings on the line where rails could be
taken up to replace the destruction that might have been done on
the Annapolis line.[14]

Franklin returned a few hours later. He'd made it to Annapolis
Junction but found no Northern troops. The rails toward Annapolis had been torn up and carried off as far as Franklin could see.
He compiled a list of sidings and a rough estimate of the rails and
ties found along the line.

Stone sent the train back out, the new assignment being to move
from Washington to the junction and back repeatedly, to keep
communications open. "From that time we held control of the
railroad, ready to bring in such troops as General Butler might
succeed in sending there," Stone reported.

General Scott was pleased. Stone continued: "Turning to Colonel Townsend, he said: 'Anticipated again! Oh, these rascally
regulars!' The expression, 'rascally regulars,' was a pet one of the
lieutenant-general, and he would often add: 'I call them rascals
because I love them.'"[15]

Since Sunday, General Scott and Colonel Stone had made
repeated attempts to get scouts to Butler at Annapolis. The government needed to know Butler's plans and, especially, when he
would get to Washington. Butler needed to understand the urgency
of the situation.

But day after day, the messengers failed. Scott couldn't risk sending a larger force out of Washington. Too much was at stake, and the city's defenses were too weak. Plus, most of the DC militia had signed up on the promise that they would not be deployed outside the district. But now Stone believed he'd found someone who could get through. He recommended William Abert, an aide-de-camp on his staff, for the mission.

Abert started immediately. He wore civilian clothes, except for his army vest, whose buttons would serve as proof to the knowledgeable observer that he was a U.S. soldier. At Annapolis Junction, he turned east down the Annapolis and Elk Ridge line. He soon ran into a train, moving toward Annapolis, with a party of men tearing up the tracks and loading rails and ties onto flatbed cars.

Abert reacted quickly. He took off his coat, laid it on a car, and started working with the party destroying the track. Soon someone recognized that he wasn't part of the original team and asked his name, while also praising his strength and skill.

He replied, frankly, "My name is Abert."
"Where do you live?"
"Born in Washington. I have lately lived in Virginia."
"All right."

And so it went until the work was done and the train got to Annapolis. Near the city, Abert slipped off, followed directions that General Scott had given him, and within minutes had gotten his dispatches through to General Butler at the Naval Academy. Abert's successful mission would have a direct impact in the hours ahead.[16]

The South

In the Southern states, demands to overthrow Washington raged out of control. Confederate president Jefferson Davis was urged to advance as fast as possible. Several prominent Richmond citizens assured him that "his army will grow like a snow-ball as it progresses," the Confederate clerk and diarist John Beauchamp Jones recorded this Tuesday. "It would swell to 50,000 before reaching Washington, and the people on the route would supply the quartermaster's stores," Jones wrote. "I believe he could drive the Abolitionists out of Washington even yet, if he would make a bold dash."[17]

The *Richmond Examiner* argued the same point. "The capture of Washington City is perfectly within the power of Virginia and Maryland, if Virginia will only make the effort by her constituted authorities. Nor is there a single moment to lose," an *Examiner* editorial said. "There is one wild shout of fierce resolve to capture Washington City. The filthy cage of unclean birds must and will assuredly be purified by fire. The people are clamorous for a leader to conduct them to the onslaught."

"It is not to be endured that this flight of Abolition harpies shall come down from the black North for their roosts in the heart of the South, to defile and brutalize the land," the fevered ranting continued. "Our people can take it—will take it—and Scott the arch-traitor, and Lincoln the Beast, combined, cannot prevent it."[18]

The Confederates had powerful allies north of the Potomac—treacherous people in high federal positions. The U.S. Supreme Court justice John A. Campbell was serving as an intelligence source and counselor to Confederate president Jefferson Davis even while retaining his seat on the court. He told Davis about the insurrection in Baltimore, and the Lincoln administration's response.

"Since the 15th this city [Washington] has been in the most excited condition," Campbell wrote. "Maryland is the object of chief anxiety with the North & the administration." Campbell suggested that the North was prepared to forego military efforts below the Potomac but would hold Maryland. "Maryland is weak," Campbell said. "She has no military men of talents. Lee is in Virginia—think of the condition of Baltimore & provide for it for there is the place of danger. The events at Baltimore have placed a new aspect upon everything. There is a perfect storm there."[19]

The most significant move for Virginia and the Confederacy this Tuesday was the official appointment of Robert E. Lee as a major general and commander of Virginia military and naval forces.

Lee's presence at the head of the Virginia forces would change the course of the war in these last days of April.[20]

Lee's strategy for Virginia would be expressed in five simple words to a hyperaggressive senior officer who had just resigned from the U.S. Army and was now traveling to Richmond. That officer was John Bankhead Magruder, and Magruder had a plan for following through on the *Richmond Examiner's* tirade. "Give me five thousand men and if I don't take Washington, you may take not only my sword, but my life," Magruder told Governor Letcher's military council.[21]

One Magruder supporter was the Richmond lawyer and politician James Lyons. Lyons met both Lee and Magruder on April 23. Lyons believed the Confederacy ought to have invaded the North in those early days of the Civil War.

In a letter years later, Lyons described the meeting. "When Genl Lee took command in Virginia [on the twenty-third] I called on him, and having been for many years on the most friendly and familiar terms with him, I ventured to urge him to 'carry the war into Africa' and plant his standard on the North bank of the Potomac," Lyons recalled.[22] "A slave-holding nation was the strongest for an invasive war, and the weakest for a defensive, because the colored laborers could stay at home and make food without being affected by the enemy's proclamations, and Maryland would spring to our feet an armed border state," Lyons continued.

Lee would immediately rally an army of half a million men for such an incursion, Lyons believed. "Washington City would fall and the enemy compelled to fly to Havre-de-Grace and ultimately to Pennsylvania, upon whose soil, and not ours, the battle would be fought," Lyons wrote. Peace would follow, and in any event the South would possess the U.S. Capitol. Lee's reply was "we have not the men."

Later that day Lyons took Magruder to meet with Lee and Governor Letcher's military council. "Genl. Magruder made the same statement and I made a speech in support of it. The President of the council called for the opinion of Genl. Lee, and he gave the same answer which he had given to me," Lyons recalled.[23]

Meanwhile, in an early morning telegram to Gen. Kenton Harper in Harpers Ferry, Maryland general George Steuart wrote that "unexpected movements of the troops at Annapolis have altered the plans I was preparing to carry out. Our eyes are now turned to another point, where your cooperation could not be easily availed of. All honor to Old Virginia and everlasting union between her and Maryland."[24] Steuart was referring to the belated landing at the naval academy of both the Seventh New York and the Eighth Massachusetts, the latter having been stranded on the grounded ferry *Maryland* for nearly two days.

His bland mention of "unexpected movements of the troops at Annapolis" was one of the first Confederate references to the Northern advance, and it was more portentous than perhaps even Steuart knew. The prize, the possible key to the whole war, was going to be contested.

The Advance

It was now more than two days since the *Maryland* steamed into Annapolis harbor. It was more than twenty-four hours since the Seventh New York arrived on Monday morning. It was bright and warm in Annapolis, about seventy degrees at 10:00 a.m., on its way to the high eighties.[25]

Beleaguered Washington was just forty miles away. But the city was filled with despair and depression. Where were the Northern regiments? Why weren't they advancing? Did the soldiers have no legs?[26]

In Annapolis 1,700 Northern troops were enjoying breakfast at the Naval Academy, courtesy of the school's kitchens. The young midshipmen were generous. Later the soldiers paraded across the wide-open green fields of the academy, reviewed by Captain Blake as a band blasted martial tunes.

Tuesday would be yet another day of delay. There was too much of a perceived threat from insurrectionists. Ammunition was limited. Colonel Lefferts had sent his quartermaster into the countryside to forage for supplies. But as Annapolis mayor Magruder and others had predicted, there was very little to be had: no horses, no wagons, no provisions, not available at any price. Whatever was available, the sellers demanded cash on the spot.[27]

The antagonism between Butler and Lefferts didn't help. They met again this morning, and again it was with Congressman Curtis / "Red Nose." Butler was incensed that Lefferts refused a command the night before to seize the railroad depot. Lefferts and his officers reasoned that they'd been ordered to Washington and that by occupying the depot or repairing the railroad, they would be delaying. Worse, they feared they'd be left behind by Butler, relegated to guard duty, and ultimately fail to carry out their mission.[28]

Butler finally ordered Lt. Col. Edward W. Hincks, the Eighth Regiment's second-in-command, to take control of the depot and the tracks, going out two miles up the line: "Colonel Lefferts with his whole regiment is afraid to go, Colonel Hincks, but you will obey orders."[29]

Hincks had a completely different recollection of these events. At noon on Tuesday, after a nap on the now-empty *Maryland*, Hincks went to see Butler. He found Butler "not a little disturbed," by Lefferts's refusal to go along with his plan.

Hincks asked Butler if anything had been done to secure the railroad. "None," Butler replied. "What can I do with this refractory New York butcher boy and his town meeting refusing to aid us?"

Hincks told Butler it was very important to immediately take possession of the railroad as a show of force and to prevent further destruction: "Give me two companies and a party of skilled mechanics to work on locomotives and the track and I will take possession of the railroad and see what I can find."[30]

Soon after lunch Hincks and two companies went to the depot. It was about six-tenths of a mile away from the Naval Academy, on a hill. The men were spooked. "I marched out of the naval academy, passing squads of the seventh regiment, who with furtive glances seemed to regard us as a forlorn hope, ordered for a sacrifice," Hincks said. "When the heavy iron gate swung together behind us, with its deep and piercing clang, a sense of utter loneliness came over me. No levity pervaded our little band."[31]

Butler characteristically put himself in the middle of this action. He says he "at once mounted my horse" and accompanied Hincks and the detachment to the train station.

In Butler's account the Massachusetts troops occupied all the buildings of the depot without opposition, except for one storehouse, which was locked. He says he personally ordered a reluctant station keeper to open the locked door to a storehouse, and when the keeper refused, Butler told his men to force the door. Inside, they found a "small, rusty, dismantled locomotive." Next Butler claims he asked the soldiers, in a line in front of the depot, which of them knew how to operate the locomotive. Charles Homans, a private from Beverly in Company E, stepped forward. "That engine was made in our shop," he said. "I guess I can fit her up and run her."[32]

The problem with Butler's account, Hincks said later, is that not a single word of it is true. Butler wasn't there. Hincks said the main depot building was closed and inaccessible from the front, so the troops marched around to the back, which was enclosed by an eight-foot wooden fence. They heard workmen on the other side of the fence and demanded entry. "The key is lost," came the reply.

Hincks ordered his men to take the gate off its hinges. Faced with that threat, the key was suddenly found. The gate was opened, and Hincks found fifteen men busy dismantling two locomotives and scattering the parts.[33]

The workers were ordered out of the yard. Led by Pvt. Homans, Hincks' mechanics set to work repairing the locomotives.

Once the yard was secured, Hincks directed Sgt. B. F. Peach to make an inventory of the property that was seized and notify General Butler that the depot had been taken. Little could Hincks have known that Butler's own false version of this story would resonate for the next 160 years, becoming the default historical account.[34]

With the depot secured, Hincks took the balance of the detachment and headed out on a hand car loaded with tools for repairing the track. They proceeded about three and a half miles, repairing the track as they went. Night fell, and the troops stopped their work and camped in a field along the tracks. "The first bivouac of the war was formed," Hincks said. "It was the first instance during the rebellion when a body of men large or small rolled themselves into their blankets and in an enemy's country laid down upon the cold ground to sleep, with no shelter save the broad heavens above."[35]

Back at the academy, two scouts made it through from Washington before noon this Tuesday. One was Col. Frederick W. Lander, on a mission to Fort McHenry in Baltimore. The state of affairs in Washington was critical, Lander said. And the countryside was teeming with insurrectionists. Lander urged Lefferts to move as quickly as possible, and to anticipate heavy resistance, losing as many as two hundred to three hundred men.[36]

A bit later another scout—not named, but presumably William Abert—made it through with a message from General Scott that he wanted the advance to come along the railroad route, with the men repairing the tracks on the way, opening the route to Washington for rail traffic.[37]

This was exactly what Butler had proposed and Lefferts had rejected. But now Lefferts got on board. A combined force was more likely to succeed. Scott preferred that the advancing troops secure the railroad. Washington was still in the hands of the federal government, but that could change literally at any moment.

The only question was when to start—before inbound reinforcements arrived or after? The evidence suggests that both Butler and Lefferts were ambivalent. That evening, the twenty-third, Lefferts wrote to Gov. Edwin Morgan of New York: "To-morrow morning at daylight I leave for Washington via Annapolis and Baltimore Railroad, and may have to march forty miles, as the people have torn the rails, bridges, etc. We shall also have fighting. I am directed to press on. I hear today of fresh troops to arrive, and, in my judgment, they are needed here to replace us as soon as we leave, so as to keep communication open."[38]

Butler agreed with this, even if he belittled Lefferts for saying it.[39]

The Ocean Convoy

Tuesday morning dawned bright and beautiful off Cape Henry, as the men of the First Rhode Island Regiment woke up in Lynn Haven Roads. The night had passed without any incidents, and the *Coatzacoalcos* took up its anchors and proceeded across Hampton Roads. Its first destination this morning was Fort Monroe, fifteen miles away.

The sloop-of-war *Cumberland* was already anchored off the fort and so was the *Baltic*, with the Twelfth New York Regiment, which had arrived before dark the previous day.[40]

About 6:00 a.m. the rest of the fleet glided into the Chesapeake. The orders were to proceed to Annapolis.

The ships got into a line, with the *Harriet Lane* in the lead followed by the *Cuyler*, the *Columbia*, the *Baltic*, and the *Coatzacoalcos*. The effects of yesterday's seasickness had now worn off. The food was still awful. Uninviting lumps of pork and bread were shoved through a hole by a greasy, bare-armed steward, George W. Wilkes, the New York newspaper owner said.

Wilkes wasn't alone in his evaluation of the food. "On the *Cuyler* the eating was perfectly disgusting—the junk was served out to the men from the hands of the cook," one member of the regiment wrote in a letter home. "I could not touch it for two days; the third day I became reconciled to it, and now I believe myself capable of eating anything. The water was of the dirtiest kind imaginable, filled with all sorts of specks—but I became accustomed to this also."[41]

All the way up the Chesapeake Bay the convoy sailed on this beautiful spring day—four large transport ships packed with soldiers, with a graceful well-armed cutter at the head of the line. The soldiers could see the vibrant green shores of Maryland. The houses, the trees—even passing vessels—loomed like some strange mirage, the First Rhode Island's Augustus Woodbury wrote. Occasionally the men would hail one another on the accompanying ships with cheers and songs.

On the *Cuyler*, Wilkes described the reactions of people on passing vessels: "Their astonished crews grouped close together, wondering at those fast black hulls thumping and thundering through the quiet water like so many monsters, unknown to them before."

Finally, between 8:00 and 9:00 p.m., the fleet reached the mouth of the Severn, and an hour or two later it approached Annapolis. The Seventh New York and the Eight Massachusetts were still in town but likely to depart for Washington early the next morning. "It was decided that we should not debark before that time," Wilkes recorded. "We, therefore, had nothing else to do than go to bed and get as much rest as possible for the exigencies of tomorrow."[42]

The arrival of the fleet was stirring for the soldiers ashore. On the grounds of the naval academy that evening, the weather was perfect—clear, calm, warm. It was the latest in a string of unseasonably beautiful days and nights. Most of the men of the Seventh New York and the Eighth Massachusetts were sleeping. Some quietly walked the grounds; others smoked their pipes.

Around 11:00 p.m. the calm disappeared. Three flares shot up into the sky from out in the river. The "long roll" started beating—the signal to form up for battle: danger was imminent. In an instant the scene became one of urgency, men grabbing their weapons and running to take their places in the ranks. "From the stroke of the drum until the time that every man, fully equipped and in fighting order, was in the ranks, was exactly, by watch, seven minutes," Fitz James O'Brien noted. "Such celerity speaks for itself."[43]

The men all peered through the darkness in the direction of the city, where they expected an attack to come from. But this was not an insurrectionist attack; it was the arrival of four transports packed with New York and Rhode Island troops. Now whatever ambivalence Lefferts or Butler felt was swept away. The North's military potential had catalyzed into actual kinetic force.

Arriving at Annapolis were the *R. R. Cuyler, Columbia, Baltic,* and *Coatzacoalcos,* accompanied by the *Harriet Lane,* carrying 3,300 men in all. Combined with the 1,700 men of the Seventh and Eighth, there were—for a brief few hours this late Tuesday evening, April 23—some 5,000 Northern troops at Annapolis bound for Washington.

Eighteen hours behind the *Harriet Lane* convoy, the Fifth Massachusetts, with another 1,000 men, was on the way. Two days behind that regiment, departing this day from New York, were three more regiments—two from Manhattan, one from Brooklyn—another 2,700 men. And right behind that group was the Albany regiment, the New York Twenty-Fifth. The Northern wave was both strengthening and advancing.

For the Seventh New York and the Eighth Massachusetts, stalled in Annapolis for three excruciating days, everything changed. "From that time forward, there was no hanging back," Parton wrote. "Both regiments worked vigorously in concert."[44]

23

New York's Irish Join the Fight

When Albert Edward, the eighteen-year-old Prince of Wales and son of Queen Victoria, came to the United States in October 1860, he was the first member of the British royal family to visit the empire's former colony. It was a big deal. The young prince was greeted by huge American crowds in Detroit, Chicago, St. Louis, Mount Vernon, Philadelphia, Boston, and Albany.

The prince arrived in New York the morning of October 11. America's largest city was overtaken with "feverishness," the prominent Irish republican and lecturer Thomas Francis Meagher remembered a few years later. "Merchants, artizans [sic], bill brokers and bill posters, high and low, rich and poor, went crazy with excitement."[1]

Meagher certainly intended to exclude his present audience—he was addressing the Irish nationalist Fenian Brotherhood at Cooper Institute.[2] Among the Irish there was deep antipathy for the British, whose queen and parliament ruled their country.

On that chilly autumn day in 1860, the prince rode up Broadway to city hall, where he mounted a viewing platform and reviewed a parade of seventeen New York State Militia regiments—about six thousand men—marching past in his honor. But one regiment was missing. The Sixty-Ninth New York had refused to participate.

They were Irish New Yorkers, and young Albert was a hated symbol of British oppression.

The Sixty-Ninth was led by Col. Michael Corcoran, thirty-three years old in April 1861, born in County Sligo, Ireland. Corcoran was a committed Irish nationalist. He served simultaneously with the Sixty-Ninth Regiment and as a military commander of the U.S.-based Fenian Brotherhood, sworn to overthrow British rule in Ireland.[3]

When it came to honoring the prince, Corcoran was adamant. "Whatever the consequences, however rude the act might seem, he would not lift his bayonets or dip his colors to the prince," Meagher recalled. "To parade his regiment in honor of this prince would be to cancel the protests made by the Irish on the battle-field, in captivity, at the stake, on the scaffold, in exile, in hunger, against the subjugation of Ireland to a foreign yoke."

Corcoran was court-martialed in November 1860 for disobeying orders. The trial opened in January and had not concluded by early April.[4]

But the attack on Fort Sumter changed the equation for Irish Americans, just as it did for all Northerners. The Irish, who were often-despised newcomers, rallied around the flag and democratic values of their new country. Just five days after Sumter was evacuated, on April 19, Corcoran read a letter to his officers: "I earnestly entreat my very warm friends, who have been in favor of deferring action until after the decision of the Court Martial in my case, to drop such an idea under the present circumstances, obliterating all other considerations but duty and patriotism."

"It is quite unnecessary to remind you that a great responsibility rests in your hands," Corcoran continued. "For my own part, you know my sentiments. I stand ready to throw myself into the ranks for the maintenance, support, and protection of the Stars and Stripes, as soon as the decision in my case may be announced, no matter what that may result in."[5] After Corcoran read his letter, the officers of the Sixty-Ninth voted unanimously to offer the services of the regiment to the federal government.

The next day, New York governor Edwin Morgan ordered the charges against Corcoran dropped, and the Sixty-Ninth began recruiting to bring the regiment up to strength. Irish Americans flocked to sign up. The authorized strength of the Sixty-Ninth Regiment was 1,000 men. It needed an additional five hundred soldiers to reach its full complement. Within two days, 6,500 men had applied.[6]

But Corcoran, Meagher, and many other Irish republican activists still harbored a certain ambivalence. On April 21, two days before the Sixty-Ninth departed, Corcoran urged members of the Fenian Brotherhood—some of whom were not members of the regiment—not to enlist in the service of the Union and instead stand ready for a more important fight by Ireland against England. If Fenians must enlist, they should join an Irish regiment, Corcoran counseled. This war, Meagher, Corcoran, and others believed, was an opportunity to establish a battle-hardened corps of Irish warriors for the coming fight against England.[7]

This, then, was the complicated story of the Sixty-Ninth New York, the founding unit of what would become the Union Army's famed Irish Brigade, and one of the three New York regiments leaving this Tuesday.

The Eighth and Sixty-Ninth were leaving from Manhattan, and the Thirteenth New York was leaving from Brooklyn. The next day, the Twenty-Fifth Regiment from Albany, already in Manhattan, would depart. War excitement was raging. The troops began assembling early in the day. There were long delays caused by the lateness in deliveries of blankets, muskets, knapsacks, ammunition, and other essential equipment.

The Sixty-Ninth met at Corcoran's headquarters on Spring Street and then formed into a regimental line for six blocks north. There were about 1,200 men making the journey, winnowed from the thousands who sought to join.

The regiment, "composed almost exclusively of the sons of Erin, departed with great éclat, setting the entire population in the lower wards in a state of excitement almost bordering on madness," the *Herald* reported. Irish Americans came not only from Brooklyn, Jersey City, and Williamsburg but even as far off as Hartford to watch Hibernia's sons depart.[8]

Corcoran appeared on Great Jones Street between 1:00 and 2:00 p.m. He'd just recovered from a severe illness and looked worn and emaciated, but he was still an imposing figure. He was tall—6 feet, 2 inches. He was very thin, with deep sunken cheeks. He held himself in a notably erect posture, even when sitting. He wore his hair short, slicked back on top and combed forward on the sides. He had a small beard on his chin and a droopy mustache.

But when Corcoran reviewed his regiment this hot afternoon, he moved along the line "with an elastic step, and issued orders with vigor and cheerfulness." Shortly before 3:00 p.m. the regiment began to march, a squad of policemen in the lead followed by a wagon drawn by four horses and decorated with American and Irish flags. Fire engines on the sidewalks blew their steam whistles and rang their bells, with the firefighters cheering the regiment as it marched by.

If there was a symbol of Northern war fervor, this was it. To the last person, the Northern states were all in. Like the German Americans two days earlier, a New York regiment comprised of Irish Americans was ready to fight for its adopted country. The regiment that refused to salute the Prince of Wales was going to war for the Union.[9]

The Eighth Regiment, meanwhile, began assembling at the state armory above the Centre Street Market at 6:00 a.m. Unlike the Seventh, Twelfth, and Seventy-First regiments, which had left days earlier and were drawn from well-to-do levels of New York society, the Eighth was made up mostly of mechanics—"hardworking fellows with no money to spare and families to provide for," the *Herald* reported. This regiment was headed by Col. George Lyons, fifty.

The scene at the armory was much more ordered than other troop departures. The police had crowd control down to a science by now. Today's departures brought to ten the number of regimental deployments from—or through—New York in just six days.

Most of the regiment, over one thousand men, was in uniform, including many of the new recruits. They were well-equipped with blankets, plates, straps, knapsacks, and cups. "They all went to work like regulars," the *Herald* reported.[10]

Table 2. In-service militia pay

Title	Per Month
Colonel	$218.00 (about $6,400 in 2020)
Lieutenant colonel	$194.00
Major	$175.00
Captain	$118.50
First lieutenant	$108.50
Second lieutenant	$103.50
Brevet second lieutenant	$103.50
First, or orderly sergeant	$29.00
Other sergeant	$27.00
Corporal	$22.00
Private	$20.00 (about $588 in 2020)
Musician	$21.00

Note: "Rates of Pay of the Militia While in Service," *Frank Leslie's Illustrated Newspaper*, May 4, 1861, 387.

Before departing, the regiment was issued new muskets and bayonets. The rifles had arrived just the day before, the plan being to ship ammunition and luggage to the waiting transport, the steamer *Alabama*. Clearly the Northern military logistics supply chain was getting itself ramped up.

The men of the Eighth, perhaps more than the men of the wealthier regiments, were interested in their pay. At the beginning of the war, the pay schedule shown in table 2, above, existed for incoming militia.

The lawyer and diarist George Templeton Strong, like all New Yorkers, was getting used to these departures. "Broadway packed full as I walked downtown and up again," he wrote this evening. "The Sixty-ninth and Eighth Regiments marched down at about four. The former is the Irish Regiment, Colonel Corcoran's, and there was a large infusion of Biddies in the crowd 'sobbing and sighing,'" Strong added—using a pejorative nineteenth-century slang word that at the time referred to young Irish housemaids.

A third New York State militia unit departed this April 23—the Thirteenth Regiment, based in Brooklyn. Eight companies, about

486 men in all, under Col. Abel Smith, forty-eight, departed at 4:30, marching from their arsenal at Henry and Cranberry Streets in Brooklyn Heights a half mile down the hill to the Fulton Street ferry terminal.[11] They boarded the ferry *Atlantic* and sailed around the bottom of Manhattan to the Hudson River, serenaded with the sounds and salutes of steamboat whistles, bells, and cheers. At Pier 4, they embarked on the transport *Marion* and were underway by early evening—bound, under sealed orders, for Annapolis.[12]

24

The March of the Seventh and Eighth Regiments

The Advance

The Seventh New York and Eighth Massachusetts regiments began their march to save Washington well before dawn on Wednesday morning. It was the fourth day at Annapolis for the Eighth and the third day for the Seventh. After the posturing, blunders, distractions, recriminations, and uncertainty over the secessionist threat, they were finally on the move.

Under Butler's "Special Brigade Orders, No. 48," two New York companies would march in the lead. They'd link up with Hincks's companies, already several miles up the line. From there, the advance companies would board the repaired train and proceed as far as the tracks were undamaged. At that point, the New York troops would leave the train and throw out skirmishers to protect Hincks's Massachusetts men, who would form working parties to rebuild the tracks. The Eighth's main body would march at 6:00 a.m. The Seventh would follow as soon as possible.[1]

The Seventh New York's advance companies made their way through the silent predawn streets, some curving and others jutting in all directions and past the statehouse, where George Washington had resigned his commission in the Continental Army. They encountered no opposition.

At the depot, the Massachusetts men were on alert. Private Homans had his machine ready, exuding power even for a small locomotive. He'd already been out on the tracks, where Hincks and his men had worked through the afternoon yesterday repairing the first few miles.

The train had four cars plus the locomotive.[2] In front of the engine were two platform cars. One of the Seventh's howitzers was mounted on the front car, with its ammunition wagon on the second. Eight troopers guarded the cannon on both sides. Behind the locomotive were two passenger cars, where the 250-man battalion crowded aboard.[3] It was daylight when the men started out from the depot amid applause from the men of the Eighth who guarded the station.[4]

Two miles out, they met Hincks and his 150-man Massachusetts detachment. These men had been on duty for a full day repairing tracks, searching for rails, and guarding the line, all without eating any food. The New Yorkers immediately shared their rations with their Massachusetts comrades. "Words could not express their gratitude," Emmons Clark, captain of one of the New York companies, remembered. "Henceforth, the two regiments were firm friends."[5]

"These brave boys were starving while they were doing all this good work," recalled Fitz James O'Brien. "What their Colonel was doing I could not say. There was not a haversack in our regiment that was not emptied into the hands of these ill-treated heroes."[6] Hincks—who was later the colonel of the Nineteenth Massachusetts Regiment, promoted to brigadier general, and severely wounded at Antietam in 1862—described this generous fraternal meetup as the most pleasing and memorable incident of his eventful army career.[7]

At three miles out, a band of secessionists was busy tearing up the tracks. A squad was sent forward to disperse them, and they escaped into the woods. Because there was clear evidence of hostile elements nearby, the companies disembarked from the passenger cars and instead marched alongside the tracks. They left their gear, but not their rifles, on the train.[8]

Now the advance units were in rural country. A thick forest narrowed the road. From time to time it opened into fields. The land was sparsely inhabited. Farther west, the landscape became arider, the soil sandy. It was tobacco country. Theodore Winthrop saw pine trees on the right, green fields on the left. The rich smells and light-green leaves of spring were everywhere. "Cattle are feeding quietly about. The air sings with birds. Frogs whistle in the warm spring morning," he wrote.[9]

Back at the academy, the main bodies of both regiments rose around dawn. They packed their knapsacks, rolled up their overcoats, filled their canteens, and loaded their guns. Annapolis residents watched in silence as the two regiments trudged through the streets, guided by a hand-drawn map created by Naval Academy superintendent Blake.[10]

The departing soldiers left behind nearly four thousand newly arrived reinforcements from five Northern militia regiments. "We do not go on without having our rear protected and our communications open," Winthrop reflected. "It is strange to be compelled to think of these things in peaceful America."[11] And yet this was the dawning of the most violent cataclysm in American history.

Butler's orders for the lead elements were to advance six miles and then wait for the main bodies. It was now 9:00 a.m. The air was clear. There was no wind. It was getting very hot. Sixth Company captain Benjamin M. Nevers, in overall command of the Seventh's detachment, ordered his scouts to stack arms. The men clustered in groups, ate a modest breakfast, smoked their pipes, and splayed out on the ground for a few minutes of sleep.[12]

In the Maryland countryside, the Seventh's Second Company captain Emmons Clark noticed, people seemed to want to keep on good terms with the advancing Northern troops and with the secessionists. They mostly stayed away from the railroad, taking their horses and their enslaved workers with them. When pressed by the troops on political issues, they feigned ignorance.[13]

At 10:00 a.m. the main body of the Seventh, walking on the tracks, caught up with the advance guard. The Eighth was still coming up, now behind the Seventh, opposite from the sequence Butler laid out in his brigade order.[14]

The fields were freshly plowed. Zigzagging split-rail "worm" fences were all around, some worn out, others stacked ten rails high. Winthrop took some time to chat with a new friend from the Eighth, Stephen Morris of Marblehead, Massachusetts. "I shared breakfast yesterday with Stephe," he wrote. "So we fraternize. His business is,—'I make shoes in winter and fishin' in summer.'"[15]

The men pushed on. They moved through rock-ridged railroad cuts thirty feet high. The midday sun was brutal, passing ninety degrees. Scouting parties and skirmishers, a half mile ahead and a half mile out on either side, crashed through brambles and sloshed through wetlands. On the tracks, the men hauled the platform cars with ropes and let their exhausted and dehydrated comrades rest on the flatbeds. The Seventh, because it was in front, had taken on a lot of the work of foraging for torn-up rails and reinstalling them on the track, though the Massachusetts men were working with them too.

"New York dandies, sir—but they built bridges, laid rails, and headed the regiment through that terrible march," Fitz James O'Brien wrote.[16]

Delays were constant. They'd come about eleven miles, with almost as many more to get to the junction. In midafternoon a massive, fast-moving thunderstorm came through. The men huddled in the woods and used their blankets as tents, but they got drenched anyway.[17]

By 3:00 p.m., the troop came to Millersville, a railroad water station a little more than halfway between Annapolis and the junction. Just beyond, a bridge had been destroyed. It was twenty feet high and sixteen feet long, and though some of the burned timbers could be used, the repair would take several hours. The men got to work. Trees were selected and cut down. They were hewn and shaped as well as possible, even without the right tools for the job. The timbers were laid in place.

It took three hours. Rather than stop for the night, the march continued. The weary men of the Seventh passed the main body of the Eighth, which had leapfrogged into the lead at Millersville. So began the night march of the Seventh Regiment, a march that extended the expedition to nearly twenty-four hours of nonstop walking and pushed the young men to the limits of their endurance.

Track repairs caused frequent delays. Teams were sent out in the dark to find missing rails. "Scouting parties scoured fields and fords," William Swinton wrote. "Sometimes a rail was sunk in the gloom of the woods, sometimes it was but a few rods distant in a neighboring field. Far or near, it was ferreted out."[18]

Now it was the middle of the night. Tree frogs chirped, larger frogs croaked, and owls hooted in the forbidding woods. The soil was soft and heavy, making the walking that much harder.[19]

At Sea Nearing Annapolis

Two ocean steamers carrying the Fifth Massachusetts Regiment reached the mouth of the Severn River on the morning of the twenty-fourth. The men surged topside as the ships neared the dock. They stared wide-eyed at the scene before them—the quaint city, the magnificent academy, and the presence of a growling, bristling fleet of transports packed with troops. "Every soldier noted the presence of many great steamers," Fifth Regiment historian Alfred Roe wrote. "It was a warlike showing never seen by them before."[20]

At 10:00 a.m. the Seventy-First New York was ordered to disembark, followed by the First Rhode Island in the early afternoon. These two regiments would advance along the railroad line early the next morning, followed later that day by the Fifth Massachusetts. The Sixth and Twelfth New York regiments would remain on their vessels for the moment.

The journalist George W. Wilkes, traveling with the Seventy-First, continued his narrative. "We were very kindly treated by the commander of the yard," Wilkes wrote. "The only drawback was the annoyance at seeing our regiments trampling down the lawn. He endeavored to protest against this desecration of the grounds, but General Butler told him ordinary considerations must yield to the necessities of the war. So the Northern buffaloes were turned upon it, and the green mantle already begins to evince a threadbare look."

In Wilkes's view, Butler was doing all he could to conciliate the locals. But there was little or no communication between the townspeople and the troops. "They glower at us all with deep suspicion and have nothing they are willing to sell us, even at a most liberal price," Wilkes wrote. "Everything of value is kept out of sight."[21]

The Massachusetts Fifth disembarked late that afternoon during the same torrential storm that was drenching the men of the New York Seventh and Massachusetts Eighth, twelve miles up the tracks. At this moment, five regiments occupied the academy grounds and the ships in the harbor. And three more steamers were at sea off the southern coast of New Jersey carrying the Eighth, Thirteenth, and Sixty-Ninth New York regiments.

Washington didn't know it yet. The South didn't know it yet. But the pace of Northern troop arrivals would soon be unrelenting.

The South

Southern newspapers continued their drumbeat for a march on Washington.

"We understand that [the North Carolina politician and editor] Duncan K. McRae, Esq., who came here last night, bears a special order for one regiment of North Carolina troops to march to the city of Washington," the *Goldsboro Tribune* reported this Wednesday. "This is by order of Gov. Ellis. To have gained Maryland is to have gained a host. It insures Washington City. It transfers the lines of battle from the Potomac to the Pennsylvania border."[22]

The *Raleigh Standard* on the same day added, "Washington City will soon be too hot to hold Abraham Lincoln and his Government. North Carolina has said it, and she will do all she can to make good her declaration."[23]

The Louisiana politician John Slidell, who had resigned from the U.S. Senate when Louisiana seceded, wrote to Jefferson Davis this day saying he was delighted to see Davis planned to carry the war "into Africa." "I think take & hold Washington & if we do so, can soon dictate our own conditions of peace," Slidell wrote to Davis.[24] "Would it not be well to let it be known at once that the troops you have called for are destined to Washington? If the war is to be prolonged our great difficulty will be the financial one, if we are in possession of Washington we can negotiate our loans in Europe. But if reduced to the defensive, we cannot look there for pecuniary aid & I do not feel very confident of our ability to raise large sums at home."

The Virginia Secession Convention debated a military alliance with the Confederacy this Wednesday. It called for the state's military to be put under the command of the Confederate president. The alliance was approved the next day, on the twenty-fifth, by an eighty-to-sixteen vote.[25]

Also this Wednesday, Virginia governor John Letcher urged the creation of a military policy for the state. "It now becomes indispensable that you shall declare the policy which is to be adopted," he wrote in a message to the state convention.[26]

But many members of the convention argued it was too soon to declare a military policy. They urged that the newly appointed commander, Robert E. Lee, be given a chance to prepare.[27]

Lee, in his second day on the job as commander of Virginia's military and naval forces, was indeed learning the lay of the land. He had a specific policy in mind, and it was defensive. John Bankhead Magruder's plan to take five thousand men and move on Washington had been rejected. In Harpers Ferry it was clear Gen. Kenton Harper, who had several thousand men, was not planning an advance to Baltimore or Washington.[28]

The Confederate situation on the banks of the Potomac River precluded any chance of an advance from that point—at least not without reinforcements. "I stand here to-day in sight of the enemy's position," Brig. Gen. Philip St. George Cocke wrote to Lee on this Wednesday. "[They have] an army now numbering from ten to twelve thousand men, under arms, and rapidly increasing by re-enforcements from the North, while I have today but three hundred men fit for duty."

Virginia forces along the river were "disorganized and feeble," Cocke said. Rather than an aggressive push to Washington, Cocke—without a staff, without artillery, without ammunition—was thinking about an ignominious retreat. "It will be my part to mask your designs and operations, to act for the present absolutely on the defensive, to watch the enemy, to organize, and await re-enforcements from every possible quarter," he told Lee.[29]

This made General Lee exceedingly happy. "I rejoice that you so fully recognize the proper policy to be pursued, and initiated it on your arrival at the scene of your operations," he told Cocke this same day. "Continue it till compelled to change." For the moment, Lee counseled Cocke, he should establish training camps. "Let it be known that you intend no attack, but invasion of our soil will be considered an act of war," Lee continued.[30]

Lee was even more direct to Virginia Militia general Daniel Ruggles, who commanded in the Fredericksburg area. "You will act on the defensive," he instructed. "You will endeavor to allay the popular excitement as far as possible."[31]

The die was cast—a defensive posture was Lee's objective. "Virginia could not undertake an offensive or even an offensive-defensive, and [Lee] reasoned that if limited operations were temporarily successful, they would quickly bring upon Virginia attacks that would complicate if they did not defeat his preparation," his biographer wrote.[32]

Meanwhile, Edward H. McDonald, the aide to Virginia general Kenton Harper who had delivered rifles from Harper's Ferry to Baltimore, met with Lee this day. He was not impressed. Lee seemed to be single-handedly squandering an opportunity to assist Maryland and change the direction of the war. Instead of an audacious strike, Virginia's leading general was cautious. "He did not approve of moving our forces to Baltimore," McDonald wrote. "If the command of the troops had not been turned over to him the armies of Virginia would have marched to join the Marylanders in the defense of Baltimore and the first battle of the war would have been fought there."[33]

Charleston

The war correspondent William Howard Russell was spending his next-to-last day in Charleston this Wednesday. He met again with General Beauregard, whom Russell said was "very lively and in good spirits." Beauregard told Russell he was surprised at the intensity of the Northern response to the attack on Fort Sumter and the start of the war.

"A good deal of it is got up, however," Beauregard told Russell. "It belongs to the washy sort of enthusiasm which is promoted by their lecturing and spouting."[34]

Beauregard still wasn't focused on Washington. Rather, he told Russell, he was apprehensive of an attack by the Northern "fanatics" before the South was fully prepared. In particular, he worried about an attack along the Mississippi River, where federal forces might cut the levees, flooding the plantations.[35]

The City

Morning dawned warm in Washington for the third day in a row. It reached sixty-eight degrees by 9:00 a.m. and rose to eighty-six at 2:00 p.m. But it was windy and cloudy and rained in the afternoon. With each day that passed with no arrival of troops, the anxiety and frustration built.[36] "This has been a day of gloom and doubt," John Hay wrote in his diary. "Everybody seems filled with a vague distrust and recklessness."[37]

Doors remained shuttered. Hotels remained empty. Servants and enslaved workers quietly made their way around town on their assigned tasks. Troops guarded the Capitol, the Treasury, the Executive Square, and the bridges. Every few hours, a locomotive arrived at the B&O depot, part of the militia's regular runs to Annapolis Junction and back.

"No troops from the North. No mails since Friday, and in fact no news at all from the North," Horatio Nelson Taft noted in his diary. "Large bodies of Virginians have gathered near Alexandria and also north of us, and a descent may be made upon us anytime, but we are getting used to strange things. I am alone at the office now and have to do all the writing."[38]

That morning, a group of wounded officers and men from the Sixth Massachusetts visited Lincoln at the White House. They came in intimidated and flushed, John Hay noticed. But they went out proud and happy. "A few kind words are very powerful if they go down. Coming up, they have less weight," Hay wrote.[39]

Lincoln, who usually maintained a calm, undemonstrative demeanor, let down his guard for the second straight day. The pressure was intense.

Lincoln was a giant in physical and intellectual stature, Hay and Nicolay wrote. That a U.S. president would find himself partially in the hands of his enemies was personally humiliating. That the nation should be at such risk, and its symbols of authority in such jeopardy, was worse. Usually, no one saw this in Lincoln. But the stress was taking its toll. Yesterday, the president had cried out, "Why don't they come!"

Today, the demoralized president bitterly told the Massachusetts soldiers, "I don't believe there is any North. The Seventh Regiment is a myth. Rhode Island is not known in our geography. You are the only Northern realities."[40]

The New York journalist Henry Villard witnessed the exchange with the Massachusetts troops. "The impatience, gloom, and depression were increasing," Villard wrote. "No one felt it more than the President. I saw him repeatedly, and he fairly groaned at the inexplicable delay in the help from the loyal States."[41]

Lincoln didn't know it—no one in Washington knew it—but this morning the Seventh New York and the Eighth Massachusetts were on the march. Thousands more troops were queued up behind them in Annapolis. Help was very close.

Lincoln had yet again another high-profile rhetorical exchange this morning, this time with Reverdy Johnson, the well-known former Maryland senator and U.S. attorney general. Johnson, like the Baltimore YMCA committee days earlier, sought assurances from Lincoln that he intended no offensive action—no invasion of the South. And once again, Lincoln made his position clear and blunt.

Confidential.

Hon. Reverdy Johnson Executive Mansion, April 24th 1861.

My dear Sir: Your note of this morning is just received. I forebore to answer yours of the 22d because of my aversion (which I thought you understood,) to getting on paper, and furnishing new grounds for misunderstanding. I do say the sole purpose of bringing troops here is to defend this capital. I do say I have no purpose to invade Virginia, as I understand the word invasion. But suppose Virginia sends her troops, or admits others through her borders, to assail this capital, am I not to repel them, even to the crossing of the Potomac if I can? Suppose Virginia erects, or permits to be erected, batteries on the opposite shore, to bombard the city, are we to stand still and see it done? In a word, if Virginia strikes us, are we not to strike back, and as effectively as we can?

Again, are we not to hold Fort Monroe (for instance) if we can? I have no objection to declare a thousand times that I have no purpose to invade Virginia or any other State, but I do not mean to let them invade us without striking back.[42]

Even though Lincoln marked the exchange with Johnson confidential, within four days it had found its way to Jefferson Davis via Supreme Court justice John A. Campbell.[43]

25

Washington Is Saved

The Advance

The men of the Massachusetts Eighth and New York Seventh regiments were closing in on Annapolis Junction as they moved along the Annapolis and Elk Ridge Railroad. But they were fatigued beyond endurance from an overnight march that still wasn't over. "As the night advanced our march was almost a stagger," Pvt. Fitz James O'Brien remembered.[1] One of Colonel Lefferts's officers begged him to stop for the night, saying it was "inhuman" to continue. Lefferts refused.[2]

As it was, no one knew what they'd encounter at the junction. The worst of the rumors suggested a large Maryland militia force would fight them there. Evidence was everywhere that insurrectionists were close. There were recent foot and horse tracks. There were torn-up rails, obviously dismantled recently. At one point, one of the Northern soldiers accidentally discharged a rifle and nearly touched off a friendly fire incident.[3]

Between 3:00 and 4:00 a.m., just before dawn, the regiment got to within a mile of the junction. Skirmishers went ahead to scout the area. Most of the men moved off the rail tracks and into an adjacent wheat field.

Nearly overcome with sleepiness, shivering from the early dawn cold, and "grumbling in a quite a mutinous way," according to

Pvt. Robert Gould Shaw, the soldiers built bonfires. "The night air had gone through us. We stood about the fires cogitating on the gloomy prospect before us," Shaw said. "Provisions all gone—a good chance of having to march to Washington, twenty miles further, as we heard no train had come up to the Junction for us—and the expectation of being attacked in a little while. Our officers told us we should have to fight then, if ever."[4]

The company sent to the junction found it deserted except for a few people sleeping in a half dozen structures. Second Company captain Clark allowed his men to visit nearby houses, and eventually the locals began to provide whatever food they had to the hungry soldiers. Clark learned that a train had been sent from Washington the day before and would be returning this morning. So the men of both regiments, at their fires about a mile away, got a few hours of sleep waiting for the Washington train. One New York man, Sixth Company private George S. Comstock, found a handcar and got permission to advance toward Washington and see what he could find.[5]

Reinforcements on the Move

Dawn was still glimmering in Annapolis as the Seventy-First New York got ready to march. The men were formed up on the Naval Academy's grounds, armed, issued ammunition, and eager to move. Colonel Burnside's First Rhode Island was right behind them.

It had been less than twenty-four hours since the New York Seventh and the Massachusetts Eighth began an identical march from the academy to Annapolis Junction. Those regiments were out there now, somewhere up ahead. Unlike yesterday's march, there was no days-long hesitation. It had been barely thirty hours since their transports had arrived at Annapolis.

All manner of rumors made their way through the Seventy-First, ensuring that the march would be tense. Yes, there were friendly troops up ahead, probably near the junction, but so too might there be a large secessionist force.

The morning was mild, clear, and crisp, the journalist George W. Wilkes wrote. As the Seventy-First passed through the Naval Academy gate, Colonel Burnside was there, cautioning the New Yorkers not to get too far ahead—his troops would be close behind, but they wouldn't be ready to go for another hour.[6]

The regiment moved through Annapolis silently. The only sound was the tramping of one thousand men on cobblestone streets. "Nevertheless, almost every upper window contained its knot of half-dressed people," Wilkes noted. "And groups of awestruck negroes appeared at frequent intervals along the streets. Our troops kept a complete and respectful silence as we passed along, and scarcely any conversation was indulged in till we were quite beyond the town."

By 9:00 a.m., the regiment reached the seven-mile station, at which the Seventh had halted on the previous day. The Seventy-First halted here too, taking breakfast and stretching out for a quick nap as it waited for the Rhode Islanders. At eleven, the First Rhode Island's advance guard caught up. When Rhode Island governor Sprague rode up, "our boys gave him a hearty cheer, followed with a universal clapping of hands."

The two regiments remained here for an hour and then resumed. "At a distance of about eleven or twelve miles out, we came to a two- or three-mile stretch of straggling roadside dwellings," Wilkes reported. "And there we met the first signs of life and loyalty we had seen. People came to their doors and cheered us on, and in two or three instances showed American flags. Our boys responded lustily to those salutes, and twice the Colonel addressed our line with, 'Three cheers for the ladies of Maryland!'"[7]

Much farther up the railroad line, the New York Seventh and Eighth Massachusetts regiments were still at the junction. It was midmorning. Some of the men of the Seventh ventured off looking for food. They found breakfast at a nearby farmhouse. "A real pretty, nice woman," frightened at first, then reassured, offered these foragers hoecakes, pork, bread and butter, coffee, tea, and milk, all in abundance. "This worked a wonderful change in us, and we took an entirely new view of life," Private Shaw wrote. "I was ready to start for Washington at a minute's notice."

After their fortuitous breakfast, Shaw's group went back to the camp and learned that a train was waiting for them at the junction. Private Comstock, the New York soldier who'd taken the handcar down toward Washington, made it six miles before meeting the inbound train on its way to the junction. The long-sought connection had finally been made.[8]

But the men of the Seventh were still lying around the field and in the road, sleeping where they dropped. "The air was filled with snorings in every key and of every variety," Shaw reported.

Eventually, the exhausted but jubilant men marched the last mile. At 10:00 a.m. the men of the New York Seventh Regiment boarded the Washington train. It was crowded almost to suffocation. "The nodding and snoring went briskly on for an hour in the cars," Private Shaw remembered. "And then we all turned out for a parade just as we were, covered with dust, and with our blankets slung over our shoulders. Our knapsacks came after us in another train."[9] The Eighth Massachusetts Regiment, coming up behind the Seventh under Col. Timothy Munroe, stayed at the junction, keeping the railroad line open until it was relieved the next day by the Seventy-First New York and the Rhode Island troops.[10]

General Butler remained in Annapolis. General Scott assigned him the task of managing the landings of incoming regiments and deploying them to secure the city and railroad, with the rest pushed to Washington.[11]

Also still in Annapolis were the Fifth Massachusetts, which arrived Wednesday afternoon, and the Twelfth and Sixth New York Regiments, which had arrived late Tuesday evening. Nine more Northern regiments were on their way. New York's Sixty-Ninth, Thirteenth, Eighth, and Twenty-Fifth were days away. The Fifth, Eleventh, and Twenty-Eighth New York Regiments were just behind them, as were the Fourth and Fifth Pennsylvania Regiments.

The South

Time was running out on the Confederates' chances to seize Washington. In Richmond, Robert E. Lee again underscored his defensive strategy this Thursday in a letter to his cousin, Cassius Lee. "No earthly act could give me so much pleasure as to restore peace to my country," he wrote. "But I fear it is now out of the power of man. I think our policy should be purely on the defensive—to resist aggression and allow time to allay the passions and permit Reason to resume her sway. Virginia has to-day, I understand, joined the Confederate States. Her policy will doubtless, therefore, be shaped by united counsels."[12]

The City

The capital had been cut off, with no troops and no communication, for six excruciating days. With each passing day, the likelihood of a Confederate move on Washington increased. Lincoln had the local militia, plus some Massachusetts troops and the unorganized companies of Pennsylvanians on hand, but no intelligence from the field. The entire command structure of the United States was essentially powerless. Everything depended on Northern mobilization.

On the morning of April 25, William Aiken, an emissary from Connecticut governor William A. Buckingham, visited Lincoln. Aiken's mission was to assure the president of Connecticut's support for the Union and to find out why there were no replies to the telegrams Buckingham had been sending. Aiken had arrived in Washington the night before. He'd been struck by the state of the city—silent hotels, desolate streets, a sense of foreboding. "Half a dozen persons crowded around me to ask questions about the North, and then I realized the complete isolation of the city," Aiken remembered.

On arriving the night before, Aiken had gone immediately to General Scott's headquarters, at close to 11:00 p.m. He found the general still working, assisted by two members of his staff. "Sir, you are the first man I have seen with a written dispatch for three days," Scott told Aiken. "I've sent out men every day to get intelligence of the Northern troops. Not one of them has returned. Where are the troops?"[13]

Next, Aiken went to Secretary of War Cameron's chambers and heard the same questions. "The situation was indeed alarming," Aiken remembered. "The district was surrounded by hostile territory. The spirit of rebellion as rampant in Maryland as in Virginia or South Carolina."

On Thursday morning Aiken met Lincoln. It was the first time he'd met Lincoln, and it was a conversation he'd never forget. He recalled, "Mr. Lincoln was alone, seated in his business room, upstairs, looking towards Arlington Heights through a wide-open window. Against the casement was a long telescope, which he had obviously just been using. He seemed depressed beyond measure. 'What is the North about?'" Lincoln asked slowly, with sharp emphasis. "'Do they know our condition?'"

"'No,' I answered," wrote Aiken. "'They certainly did not when I left.'"

Lincoln described the nonarrival of the troops under General Butler. Aiken saw the opportunity the insurrectionists had. Enemies were all around.[14]

Washington's pulse was unchanged that morning. Activity was minimal and the mood was tense. The president engaged in the same wishful activities that he had for days. "At the request of the Tycoon [Lincoln], who imagined he had seen something significant steaming up the river, I went down to the Navy Yard," John Hay wrote in his diary. "The boat was the *Mt. Vernon*, who reported everything right in the River."[15]

Suddenly everything changed. George Williamson Smith, the young assistant pastor at St. John's Episcopal Church on Lafayette Square, who'd described the panicked exodus from the city a few days earlier, was walking near the Treasury Department on Pennsylvania Avenue, two blocks from his church.

Almost before he became conscious of it, he got the feeling that something was happening. People were moving faster. They were heading in the same direction. Then Smith looked down

Pennsylvania Avenue. He thought he saw people gathering at the Capitol, nearly two miles away. Here and there, people ran into the street. "I hastened down the avenue at a fast walk," he remembered. "And soon, I heard the sound of distant martial music." Was it possible that troops were finally here? Soon all doubt was gone.[16]

William Aiken had heard that a white flag raised on the Capitol would be the signal the troops had arrived. Suddenly, the flag appeared. "Such a stampede of humanity as was witnessed at that hour towards the depot can only be appreciated by one who took part in it," Aiken wrote. "One glance at the gray jackets of the New-York 7th restored hope and confidence."[17]

The Seventh, led by their band and hauling two cannons, approached along Pennsylvania Avenue. The massive regiment, nine-hundred-plus men, moved down the broad boulevard in perfect unison. It was an overwhelming sight—magnificent pageantry, overpowering force, determination and reassurance, all in equal measure. "Communications with the North were opened," Pastor Smith wrote. "Washington was relieved. Virginia had lost her prize. I thought then, and I think now, that it had been held through those days by pure bluff. Washington narrowly escaped capture several times during the war but never so narrowly as at its very outbreak."[18]

The march was triumphant, but it wasn't easy for the exhausted soldiers. "It required no little spirit to march that hot, dusty two miles, over heated pavements," wrote the *New York Herald*. "One of the most stalwart men in the regiment, a leader in gymnastics and boating, told me that his feet felt at every step as though knives were running through them. A sergeant's feet were a mass of blisters, and many others were in a bad plight."[19]

The regiment marched to the White House and up the sandy driveway. "'Old Abe' and family stood at the doors and saw us go by," Pvt. Robert Gould Shaw reported.[20]

President Lincoln was "the happiest-looking man in town," an Illinois man remarked. "He smiled all over." Mrs. Lincoln presented the regiment with a magnificent bouquet from the conservatory at the White House.[21]

Relief and exultation pervaded. "I cannot express the revival of hope and confidence that I felt and that filled all loyal hearts as that crack body of New York Volunteers, nearly a thousand strong, marched up Pennsylvania Avenue," the journalist Henry Villard wrote.

The arrival of the Seventh was a defining moment in the life of anyone who was in Washington that day. "The 7th Regt is at last here, came at 12 o'clock and created much enthusiasm—we breathe a little free now," Horatio Nelson Taft recorded in his diary.[22]

The presence of this single regiment seemed to tip the scales of fate, Nicolay and Hay wrote: "As the Seventh passed up the magnificent street, they seemed to sweep all thought of danger and all taint of treason out of that great national thoroughfare and every human heart in the Federal city. . . . Cheer upon cheer greeted them, windows were thrown up, houses opened, the population came forth as for a holiday. For the first time, the combined spirit and power of Liberty entered the nation's capital."[23]

The Seventh was followed the next day by the Eighth Massachusetts and the First Rhode Island Regiments. After that, reinforcements arrived daily.[24]

Col. Marshall Lefferts, who'd led the Seventh Regiment to Washington, spent this afternoon and evening in consultation with Lincoln and his commanders. Lincoln probed for intelligence on the state of the Maryland uprising. Lefferts noted that he'd gotten through a twenty-mile march without the loss of a single man, repairing the railroad as he advanced. To Scott, Lefferts apologized for the delay at Annapolis. Scott objected: "You have made a fine march, sir; you have done all that could be done."[25]

With the arrival of the Seventh Regiment, one of the most dangerous moments in Washington DC's history had passed. The triumphant march was the happy conclusion of two weeks of terror: the call for troops, the secession of Virginia, the loss of Harpers Ferry, the harrowing passage of the First Defenders, the bloody assault in Baltimore, the burning of the bridges, the torn-up tracks and the cut telegraph wires, the loss of the navy yard, the wave of resignations, the delays in Annapolis. It all came against a very real backdrop that the federal capital would be overrun, that Maryland would secede, and that the British might be tipped into recognizing the Confederacy. It all was finally over.

There were twelve days between the evacuation of Fort Sumter and the arrival of the Seventh Regiment. "It was," Nicolay and Hay wrote, "an epoch in American history."[26]

26
- - -

The Aftermath

The City

Accolades poured in for the Seventh Regiment. "What a thrill of delight pervaded our loyal population," U.S. Army adjutant general Lorenzo Thomas wrote. "In every direction you could hear, 'The Seventh has come!' The anxious week had passed, and we felt secure." "I have commanded some of the best in our army, but I confess I never saw the peer of the Seventh Regiment," wrote Maj. Gen. Samuel R. Curtis, who'd accompanied the regiment to Washington.[1]

The other incoming regiments were also feted in their first days in Washington. Lincoln visited the troops frequently. The soldiers reported charming stories.

The Fifth Massachusetts's Charles Bowers, a Company G third lieutenant, wrote home describing a reception. "I wish you could have been with me last night at Mr. Seward's," he told his son. "I should like to have had you shake the strong, honest hand of the President. I did, and never did I have a heartier shake. He is all and more than I expected. Instead of being so homely, he is one of the finest looking men I have met in Washington."[2]

James A. Scrymser, an enlisted man in the engineering company of the New York Twelfth Regiment, wrote an article about how his regiment's colonel, Daniel Butterfield, became "chummy" with First Lady Mary Lincoln. From that relationship came an anecdote. "Mrs. Lincoln told Colonel 'Dan' that the White House cook was in trouble—the 'waterback' of the range was out of order and the range could not be used," Scrymser wrote.[3]

Mrs. Lincoln asked Butterfield, Did the regiment have some plumbers? "Of course it had—the Twelfth was full of 'em. He would have offered to furnish aeronauts or lion-tamers if she had wanted any," Scrymser continued.

Butterfield asked for help, and Scrymser suggested that there probably were some plumbers in other companies. "And so I was detailed to get them. I did—four—and I went along to 'boss the job.'"

"It certainly was a sight—five uniformed militiamen, with arms and accoutrements, marching into the White House kitchen. In a few minutes the range was yanked out, and set in the middle of the kitchen, and four able-bodied New York plumbers were wrestling with its waterback," Scrymser said.

"The details of the job have escaped my memory—but not so our first sight of Mr. Lincoln. He came down to the kitchen, and half-sitting, half-leaning on the kitchen table, and holding one knee in his hands—the Commander-in-Chief of the Army and Navy said, 'Well, boys, I certainly am glad to see you—I hope you can fix that thing right off; for if you can't, the cook can't use the range, and I don't suppose I'll get any "grub" to-day!'"[4]

The President's Sermon

Another Twelfth New York Regiment soldier, George Stewart, told how he and four comrades went to the White House. They asked the doorkeeper if the president would meet a group of New York troopers. "How impossible such a thing would have been in any European capital!" Stewart marveled years later. "But we were young—and Abraham Lincoln no doubt 'sized us up' at a glance; there could be no presumption where none was meant, and just then soldiers were a novelty to him, and a welcome one too."

The troops found Lincoln in his office, sitting at the window. He greeted them kindly and asked where they were quartered. The soldiers said many of them were at a church not far away. "Well, on Sunday (this was Friday) I'll come over and talk to you."

"We told the boys the President was coming on Sunday," Stewart wrote, but no one believed it. It wasn't until Sunday morning that the place was cleaned up. "As Mr. Lincoln entered all rose, and the tall, gaunt figure that was to become so familiar to Washington in the next four years passed up the aisle and mounted the platform," Stewart continued. "So few of us had before seen him that I doubt the church had ever held so large a crowd; and I am sure he never before or after had a more attentive audience."

The soldiers recognized Lincoln from portraits and campaign badges. But seeing him in person was different altogether. "I felt, as doubtless did many others, that I was in the presence of no ordinary man," Stewart wrote.

The president told the troops that he would not preach—he'd just give them a "talk." It lasted about fifteen minutes and was delivered in a natural, winning manner, Stewart remembered, "much as a father might address grown-up sons." Lincoln described the feeling of safety the arrival of the Twelfth gave him, and his conviction that the men would do themselves credit as soldiers. "He hoped the war would be short, and that possibly the rebels might not proceed to any further hostilities, now that the uprising of the North was certain," Stewart said. "Yet, if this was to be a real war, the loyal states were ready for it."

"Few are left of my comrades of that day and probably fewer yet who remember the event," Stewart continued. "The spring-like April Sunday, the dignified church full of young soldiers, arms stacked in the corners and knapsacks piled in the aisles and pews; on the platform the homely figure in the conventional black frock-coat suit, the kindly, rugged face of the great President and the helpful, appreciative words of what I call his sermon; it was an occasion never to be forgotten, and it is one of my valued memories that I once heard Abraham Lincoln speak from the pulpit."[5]

The Advance

The pace of advancing Northern troops ratcheted up dramatically. Twelve hours after the First Rhode Island and the Seventy-First New York had begun their march (and eight hours after the Seventh arrived in Washington), the Fifth Massachusetts started out from the Naval Academy the evening of April 25 along the same railroad route.[6]

The First Rhode Island and the Seventy-First New York were already at the junction, guarding the vital rail hub and preparing to move forward to Washington. On April 26, the Fifth Pennsylvania began marching to Washington via the junction. This poorly equipped regiment was joined by the Twelfth New York. This was the third consecutive day that paired Northern regiments advanced along the railroad. Seven regiments, representing four states and more than 5,500 troops, had marched from Annapolis in three days.

Four more Northern regiments arrived in Annapolis by steamer on the twenty-sixth—a second convoy from New York. They were the Eighth New York, the Thirteenth New York (from Brooklyn), the Twenty-Fifth New York (from Albany), and the Irish regiment, the Sixty-Ninth New York. Together they comprised another 2,850 men.

Also on the twenty-sixth, the First Rhode Island Regiment and the Eighth Massachusetts—plus elements of the Fifth Massachusetts—arrived in Washington.

The South

The most accurate assessment of the military conditions in the North and South in late April 1861 was brief—just ten words. It came on April 27 from D. G. Duncan, an informal advisor to Confederate secretary of war Leroy P. Walker: "Troops pouring into Washington without hindrance now in great numbers."[7]

Similar messages worked their way to General Lee and Virginia governor John Letcher. "The Federal troops now have possession of the entire railroad from Washington to Annapolis," Maryland general George Steuart told Letcher on the twenty-fifth. "Cars are constantly bringing troops," read another message.[8]

Whatever opportunity the South might have had to seize Washington and wrest Maryland into the Confederacy had passed. But the South still didn't fully understand—there was a lag in comprehension. Some Southern leaders clung to the hope of attacking Washington. Confederate vice president Alexander Stephens, in a speech on April 30 in Atlanta, summed up the view. "A feeling prevails that

Washington city is soon to be attacked," Stephens claimed. "If Maryland secedes, the district will fall to her by revolutionary right. When we have the right, we will demand the surrender of Washington, and we will enforce our demands at every hazard."

In fact, the Maryland House of Delegates had voted decisively, fifty-three to thirteen, against secession just the prior day, affirming a declaration from the state senate on the twenty-seventh. Maryland was not joining the Confederacy. Maryland was about to become an occupied province.[9]

The Aftermath

In the end, the North simply moved too fast. Confederate designs on Washington—as well as military support for Maryland—were foiled by the fast pace of Northern mobilization. A Maryland secession, with or without the capture of Washington, was similarly foiled. The speed of Northern troops came almost exclusively from New York and Massachusetts in the first days, with assists from Rhode Island and Pennsylvania.

Five days after President Lincoln's call for troops, a Massachusetts regiment—the Sixth—arrived in Washington. Six days after the call, four more Massachusetts regiments—about 2,600 men—were in the field. Four New York regiments, about 3,500 men, had left their state by the seventh day. Half of the First Rhode Island Regiment, about 600 men, had joined them. Nearly 500 Pennsylvania troops had made it to Washington, though another 4,000 had been turned back. By the end of April, a mere fifteen days after Lincoln's call, there were 10,415 Northern troops in the capital, including the 2,900 district militia volunteers.[10]

An equal number of state troops were guarding the approaches to Washington; two Pennsylvania regiments and four other New York regiments were posted at Annapolis and along the line of the railroad by the end of the month. Two additional New York regiments were in transit. In two weeks New York State alone had mustered, equipped, and transported ten regiments and more than 7,600 troops to Washington and other points.[11]

By contrast, troop deployments from South Carolina and Georgia came sluggishly, too late, and in numbers far too small to match the North. The first Confederate companies left Georgia and South Carolina on the twenty-second. At the end of April, there were perhaps just more than one thousand out-of-state Confederate troops in Virginia.[12]

Paradoxically the South had many advantages in these first weeks. The Confederate gulf states, all claiming to be independent republics after secession, had their military machinery up and running. As many as seven thousand troops were organized in Charleston alone, under the command of a Confederate States general—Beauregard. It was a unified force the North could not come close to matching. Thousands of Virginians were in Harpers Ferry, and Maryland had mobilized about fifteen thousand men, many of them secessionists.

Jefferson Davis—a West Point graduate, a regimental commander in the Mexican War, and a secretary of war under Franklin Pierce—was well versed in all things military. Abraham Lincoln had no executive experience at all, let alone relevant military experience.[13]

But the Confederacy couldn't seize the moment. Many senior government leaders were advocating an assault on Washington. The secretary of war urged it. The governors of North Carolina and South Carolina urged it. Some Confederate military commanders urged it, as did many influential Southern politicians, at least one Virginia railroad executive, and a then-justice of the U.S. Supreme Court from Alabama. The newspapers clamored for an assault on Washington. Northern leaders expected it.

The Confederates ordered troops to Virginia and offered that state material support even before it formed a military alliance with the Confederacy on April 24. Jefferson Davis urged Virginia to cooperate with Maryland and promised to reinforce Virginia as it supported Maryland's secession movement. But an assault on Washington never happened and Maryland never seceded.

The reasons have been debated ever since. "I did not understand then, nor could I ever understand, why the rebel hands were not stretched out to seize so easy a prey," Henry Villard wrote in his memoirs.[14]

Several things stand out. For one, Virginia's secession came too late. North Carolina's came much later. Had both states been part of the Confederacy during the two weeks after the assault on

Fort Sumter, then Davis and the Confederate governors would have been more willing to move troops across their borders on an offensive military campaign. Such a campaign might have run into opposition from some Confederate officials or potential allies overseas. Even then, there was no framework to support military coordination among Virginia, North Carolina, and Maryland on the one hand and the Confederacy in Montgomery on the other. "The states were barely adjusted to their new relations," noted the Confederate historian Clement Evans. "It was not possible for the Confederate States to do more than to rapidly gather together their men to defend their soil. No hostile movement against Washington was feasible."

Beyond that, it's clear that Davis may have wanted the prize—Maryland's secession and Washington—but wouldn't take the risk. He expected Maryland and Virginia to collaborate and perhaps strike on an opportunistic basis. That way, if things went wrong, the Confederacy could retain deniability.[15]

Even if an attempt had been considered to move troops from Charleston to the Potomac before Virginia seceded, the obstinate and difficult General Beauregard wasn't contemplating such an initiative. He was intensely focused on defending Charleston. And when his thinking shifted from Charleston, it was to the vulnerability of the lower Mississippi River.[16]

Had the Charleston troops been organized and ready for campaigning and deployed as soon as Virginia seceded, they might have reached northern Virginia by April 20 or 21, leaving little time to plan an assault or move troops into position. Within two days Robert E. Lee took command of the Virginia forces and strongly tamped down consideration of offensive operations. The opportunity was lost. The South forfeited any chance it might have had to change the course of the war before it really began.

Ultimately 91,816 Northern men responded to Lincoln's initial call for 75,000 troops. The final count easily exceeded the number sought, even though Maryland, North Carolina, Kentucky, Tennessee, Arkansas, Delaware, and Virginia did not contribute. And this was merely the first wave of a giant Union tsunami.

Table 3. The call for 75,000 troops:
the requisition and the numbers supplied

State	Regiments	Called	Ultimately Supplied
Maine	1	780	771
New Hampshire	1	780	779
Vermont	1	780	782
Massachusetts	2	1,560	3,736
Rhode Island	1	780	3,147
Connecticut	1	780	2,402
New York	17	13,280	13,906
Pennsylvania*	16	12,500	20,175
New Jersey	4	3,123	3,123
Delaware	1	780	775
Maryland	4	3,123	0
Virginia	3	2,340	900 (from western Virginia)
North Carolina	2	1,560	0
Tennessee	2	1,560	0
Arkansas	1	780	0
Kentucky	4	3,123	0
Missouri	4	3,123	10,591[†]
Illinois	6	4,683	4,820
Indiana	6	4,683	4,686
Ohio	13	10,153	12,357
Michigan	1	780	781
Wisconsin	1	780	817
Iowa	1	780	968
Minnesota	1	780	930
Washington DC	0	0	4,720
Kansas	0	0	650
Total	**94**	**73,391**	**91,816**

*Pennsylvania reduced on April 16 to 14 regiments. †Missouri's forces were raised on the basis of operating only within the state.[17]

By late April Secretary of War Cameron was declining additional regiments committed to serving only three months and pivoting to three-years-or-the-war enlistments. On May 6 he formally issued a call to stop sending three-month troops.[18]

Still, the initial response from was far from consistent. The moribund militia system meant that most states couldn't respond rapidly. New York and Massachusetts saved Washington, nearly alone.

Only four of twenty loyal states succeeded in deploying troops beyond their borders by the end of April 1861.[19] Ohio sent off two unprepared regiments on April 19 in an embarrassing campaign that made it only as far as Pennsylvania.[20]

The Maryland Uprising

The Maryland insurrectionists were dealt with decisively. On April 27 Lincoln followed up on his prior message to General Scott that suspension of the writ of habeas corpus might be necessary. This time, he gave the official go-ahead. "If at any point on any military line between the City of Philadelphia and the City of Washington, you find resistance which renders it necessary to suspend the writ of Habeas Corpus for the public safety, you, personally or through the officer in command where the resistance occurs, are authorized to suspend that writ," Lincoln wrote to Scott.[21]

Dozens of secessionist plotters were arrested and hauled off to jail, where they stayed, spending months in limbo. Most were never charged. They were arrested for disloyalty and for fomenting insurrection.

The secessionist Baltimore police chief, George Proctor Kane, was arrested on June 27. The four members of the Baltimore Police Commission—Charles Howard, William H. Gatchell, John W. Davis, and Charles D. Hinks—were arrested on July 1. None of these officials was formally charged. The Baltimore police department was disbanded. The city was placed under military control.[22]

The Baltimore mayor, George William Brown, was arrested on September 13. Twenty-six members of the Maryland legislature were arrested in mid-September, including the speaker of the House of

Delegates. They were accused of "disloyalty." Some were released later that year or early in 1862, after swearing oaths of allegiance to the United States. The clerk of the legislature was also arrested, as were several secessionist newspaper editors.[23]

That month, September 1861, and into October, an extended grand jury investigation by the U.S. Circuit Court in Maryland produced testimony from dozens of eyewitnesses to the Baltimore riots, the burning of the railroad bridges, and the theft of weapons caches by the secessionists. Many additional arrests and indictments emerged from this investigation. There were more than sixty treason cases brought against the Baltimore insurrectionists. Few were tried and convicted. In 1863, the U.S. attorney in Baltimore dismissed forty-five of them. Others were dismissed later in the war, or postwar, under President Andrew Johnson. One infamous Baltimore political brawler, George Konig Sr., was convicted in the Baltimore City Court of rioting and sentenced to a year in prison.[24]

Many participants in the Maryland insurrection scattered before they could be brought to justice. Among the most prominent was Bradley T. Johnson, the Frederick militia leader who joined the Confederate army, rising to the rank of brigadier general. Isaac R. Trimble, a leader of the railroad bridge destruction, also became a Confederate general, gaining notoriety for his role in Pickett's Charge at Gettysburg. Maryland militia general George H. Steuart, who was present at the riots, rose to the rank of general in the Confederate Army. He was indicted for treason after the war, but the charges were dropped.[25] John G. Johannes, the leader of the bridge destruction on the Northern Central Railway, ended up, enigmatically, in the Union army, an officer in the Eighth Maryland Infantry.[26]

Some of the most prominent political prisoners refused to take loyalty oaths and were denied release. In the end, Baltimore police chief Kane, Baltimore mayor Brown, police commissioners Charles Howard and William Gatchell, editors Frank Howard and Thomas Hall, and the remaining detainees were released from Fort Warren, in Boston Harbor, on November 26, 1862.[27]

One question that's difficult to answer is whether Maryland would ultimately have seceded, with or without an assault on

Washington. It's clear that Abraham Lincoln believed it would. It's equally clear that between the fall of Fort Sumter and the arrival of Northern troops in Annapolis a week and a half later, secession fever raced violently and unchecked throughout Maryland's most populous areas.

Everyone watched Hicks, who'd seemed to shift to the pro-Southern faction since his resounding speech on the nineteenth. He called the legislature on the twenty-second, and his message to the opening session on April 26 would be pivotal. "If Hicks should in vehement language denounce the policy of Lincoln, and urge cooperation with the seceded states, little doubt was felt by many that in the excitement of the moment the state would be swept into secession," wrote Hicks's biographer, George Radcliffe.[28]

But Hicks did the opposite. "I cannot counsel Maryland to take sides against the general government until it shall commit outrages upon us which would justify us in resisting its authority," he wrote. "I can give no other counsel than that we shall array ourselves for Union and peace."[29]

After that, things moved quickly. On the second day of the legislative session, April 27, the Maryland Senate unanimously passed a resolution introduced by the prosecession senator, Coleman Yellott. "The citizens of Maryland have been induced to believe that there is a probability that our deliberations may result in the passage of some measure committing this state to secession," the resolution read. "We know that we have no constitutional authority to take such action. If believed by us to be desired by you, we may, by legislation to that effect, give you the opportunity of deciding for yourselves, your own future destiny. We may go thus far, but certainly will not go farther."[30]

This was a remarkable turn of events. "It was believed that the advocates of immediate secession would show greater strength," Radcliffe wrote. Whether this was due to a clearer realization of the costs of war, or to a rise in Union sentiment, or—most likely—to the intimidating nearby presence of Northern troops, is hard to say.[31]

What's clear is that Maryland, "aided by the governor's revived Unionism, economic ties with the North and West, and the appearance of federal troops," chose the Union. The high tide of secession sentiment receded.[32]

England and the Confederacy

Great Britain was ambivalent about the disintegration of the American union. There was a deep antipathy toward slavery in England. Yet there was also a recognition that Southern cotton was vital to its economy. There was a conviction that the American split was permanent, as well as fear that an interruption in trade resulting from a naval blockade would draw Britain into the conflict. "If [Lincoln] blockades the Southern ports we shall be in a difficulty," the foreign secretary, Lord John Russell, wrote to Lord Richard Lyons, the minister to the United States in Washington, in March.[33]

The limits of technology made it unlikely that any major British decision would occur during the twelve days after the surrender of Fort Sumter—April 14 through April 25—the period when Washington was most vulnerable. It took ten days or more for news to make it to newspapers in London. Important diplomatic messages moved slightly faster but still did not arrive in less than seven days; they were sent by telegraph to Halifax, Nova Scotia, then by steamer to Liverpool, and then by telegraph to London.[34]

For example, news of Fort Sumter reached England on April 27, and the conclusion that war was certain on the twenty-ninth. News that Virginia had seceded and that a bloody confrontation occurred in Baltimore reached England on May 2.[35]

In the end, the British government quickly coalesced around a policy of neutrality. "We have not been involved in any way in that contest by any act or giving any advice in the matter, and, for god's sake, let us if possible keep out of it," Lord Russell said in the House of Commons on May 2. England formally issued a proclamation of neutrality on May 13, referring to the South as "states styling themselves the Confederate States of America."[36]

But neutrality was a double-edged sword—it conferred "belligerent" status on the South, placing it on quasi-equal footing with the United States. One thing's certain: England retained the flexibility to adjust its foreign policy as events dictated based on its own interests, not on sentiment. If the U.S. government abandoned Washington, or if Maryland seceded, all bets would be off.[37]

The President

Abraham Lincoln saved Washington along with the fast-moving Northern troops. He saved it through dozens of decisions in this twelve-day stretch, large and small.

In his call for troops on April 15, he emphasized that the troops were to be used to enforce the laws, to retake federal installations seized by the Confederates, and to suppress the insurrection. Though he later insisted the troops were solely for the defense of the capital, that objective was not in the initial call. Still, Lincoln's message was strategically brilliant. It held the enemy in place. It caused his most organized adversary, Gen. P. G. T. Beauregard, to stay on the defensive far to the south of Washington.

Lincoln delayed calling Congress into session until July 4, giving himself wide latitude to act unilaterally as circumstances required, trusting that Congress would later endorse his actions. He adroitly publicized his April 14 meeting with Stephen Douglas, his best-known Democratic rival, ensuring that the war would be viewed as a national effort and not as a dubious partisan adventure.

In more than a half dozen widely publicized meetings with informal Southern emissaries urging him to recognize the Confederacy and send the Northern troops home, Lincoln refused. He communicated a consistent message to friend and foe alike: the troops weren't intended to invade the South, but they must come to Washington through Maryland. They would avoid insurrectionist Baltimore. Lincoln repeatedly promised he would repel force with force. His message was clear and frequent.

The president took a series of extraconstitutional actions, including turning over $2 million (the equivalent of $58.2 million in 2020 dollars) to three private citizens on the Union Defense Committee in New York. He authorized Gen. Winfield Scott to attack Maryland if needed—"even if necessary to the bombardment of their cities."[38]

He was willing to risk losing the Norfolk Navy Yard rather than antagonize Virginia into secession. This gamble failed, but it likely bought some time and temporarily lulled the Virginia fire-eaters.

All these actions and more stabilized the federal government in a time of unprecedented crisis. They reassured and inspired the Northern population. They compelled headstrong members of Lincoln's cabinet to subordinate themselves to his policies. They diverted Southern attention and bluffed the Confederates into believing an offensive on Washington was too risky. And they neutralized the insurrectionist wildfire in Maryland.

"The President's call for seventy-five thousand volunteers had been rapidly answered," wrote the Maryland historian Thomas Scharf. "Any attempt to offer armed resistance would have not only resulted in failure, but in the certain destruction of Baltimore."[39]

The conclusion of this "epoch in American history," as Nicolay and Hay described it—the period when Washington was entirely cut off from the North—did not mean Abraham Lincoln could breathe easier. The threat was too multifaceted. He needed to defend Washington and ensure that the arriving troops would be quickly molded into an army. He had to implement the blockade of Southern ports. The wave of patriotism and support in the North had to continue. Maryland urgently had to be secured. "It was bedlam compared to the dignified and deliberate pigeon-hole methods of quiet times," Nicolay and Hay wrote.[40] President Lincoln, with his sharp intellect, his gift for strategy, his media savvy, and his basic humanity, held the country together in these first weeks of the war—just as he would for the next four years.

Gen. Benjamin F. Butler: A Reassessment

If Fort Sumter made Robert Anderson the first military hero in the North, then Benjamin Butler was the second. Brilliant, bombastic, vain, persuasive, and a master of PR, it's not hard to understand the effect Butler had on people. He had a penchant for dramatic anecdotes but was also willing to stretch the truth to his benefit. As a military commander, he possessed the contradictory characteristics of rash impulsivity and hesitation in equal measure.

Butler's exploits were published in newspapers around the country in April, May, and June 1861. Butler released a series of telegraphic exchanges that cleverly skewered one rival after another.

Butler was universally credited with forging the route to Washington via Annapolis. He was feted with a cover story in *Harper's Weekly* and a similar article in *Frank Leslie's Illustrated Newspaper*.

"Major-General Benjamin Butler has thus far been the most prominent volunteer officer since the President's proclamation of April 15," *Harper's Weekly* wrote. "His energy and perseverance in opening a way of communication with Washington, at a time when the capital seemed cut off, have been well known."[41]

William Howard Russell, visiting Annapolis, noted "the decision with which Butler acted when he came down here to open communications with Washington."[42] Butler didn't deserve the credit for opening the Annapolis route, but he never bothered to correct the record. On the contrary, he explicitly claimed it as his own accomplishment.[43]

This story has proven remarkably persistent. The Pulitzer Prize–winning author David Herbert Donald, in the 1995 book *Lincoln*, wrote that "General Benjamin F. Butler had discovered an ingenious way of circumventing Baltimore by ferrying men down the Chesapeake Bay to Annapolis where they could be entrained for Washington."[44]

Col. Marshall Lefferts, commander of the New York Seventh Regiment, has a stronger claim. Lefferts arrived in Philadelphia from New York about ten hours after Butler, in the early morning hours of April 20. By 8:15 a.m., perhaps five hours after his arrival, Lefferts sent a dispatch to New York indicating he was going to Annapolis. Sometime later that day, the War Department telegraphed to Philadelphia, concurring with Lefferts plan.[45] Lefferts would prove at each juncture that he was more decisive than Butler. He had better instincts and was consistently more competent.

And yet history all but ignores Lefferts. When it doesn't, the references are unflattering. "On the morning of the 25th, upon reaching Annapolis Junction, the New Yorkers pressed on for Washington, leaving Butler and his men to hold the position," the

author George B. Herbert wrote in 1885, implying the New Yorkers were glory hogs and ignoring the fact that Butler was not at
the junction at all.[46]

In a note on April 24, Secretary of War Simon Cameron wrote,
"I have only a moment to say the troops have not got round from
Annapolis. Butler says he will be here to-day. The New York Sev-
enth decline coming on some punctilio [a petty point of pro-
cedure], as I am informed."[47] In other words, whatever disputes
Lefferts and Butler might have had, it was the New Yorker's fault.

Actually, neither Butler nor Lefferts deserves credit for establishing the Annapolis route. That goes to Samuel Felton, president
of the PWB Railroad. He'd come up with the plan months earlier,
in anticipation of President-elect Lincoln's inaugural journey to
Washington and the possibility of trouble in Baltimore. It was a
geographically simple concept. The water route to Annapolis side-
stepped secessionist Baltimore, offered a landing at a protected
site—the Naval Academy—and had a railroad that connected to
Washington. And it was only forty miles from the capital.[48]

Benjamin Butler was a masterful lawyer and political performer
transferred to a new milieu, and he had a keen sense for the the-
atrical possibilities of his new role. But his actual military performance in these first days of the Civil War didn't measure up. He
hesitated at critical points. At Annapolis Butler lost sight of his
mission, choosing to extricate the USS *Constitution* rather than
land his men and proceed immediately to the endangered capital.
He negotiated deferentially for permission to land at the academy
for two days, even though he had every right to land immediately
on U.S. government property—a move that was exactly consistent
with Lincoln's policy.

Butler was apparently asleep on the *Maryland* when it ran
aground in Annapolis Harbor with more than seven hundred
Massachusetts troops on board, even though he knew the harbor was treacherous and shallow and that the harbor pilot's loyalty
was suspect. Butler lingered for three-and-a-half days at Annapolis during the most vulnerable period for Washington since it was
burned by the British in 1814.

Butler told an embellished story about the seizure of the Annapolis railroad depot, claiming credit and placing himself on the scene, when he was not there. He treated the U.S. congressman Samuel R. Curtis, later a successful Union general, with remarkable disrespect.

Butler's incessant wrangling and attempts to pull rank on Lefferts and the officers of the Seventh Regiment were unproductive and contributed to the delays at Annapolis. Indeed, it was unreasonable to assume that a militia commander from one state, with his own distinct chain of command, would submit to the authority of a militia commander from another state before being sworn into federal service.

Virtually everyone associated with Benjamin Butler during the first two weeks of the Civil War disputed Butler's claims, or objected to his behavior, or questioned his decisions. Massachusetts governor John Andrew did. Massachusetts adjutant general William Schouler did. Eighth Massachusetts Regiment lieutenant colonel Edward Hincks did. The men of the New York Seventh Regiment did. The Maryland land commissioner William Seabrook did.[49]

Butler proposed marching from Annapolis to Baltimore before going on to Washington, even though Washington urgently needed his troops. Under the same circumstances, he offered to put his regiment at the service of the Maryland authorities to quell a rumored uprising among enslaved people. He wrote a misleading and inaccurate account of his stay at Annapolis to Pennsylvania Militia general David Patterson on April 24. In that dispatch he claimed he was ready to proceed the morning of the twenty-third, except that Lefferts had neglected to seize the Annapolis depot. He was not. He also claimed the reason the *Maryland* ran aground was because it was picking up a crewman from the USS *Constitution* who'd fallen overboard. No mention of this was ever made again by Butler. Nor was it reported by others, including Hincks, the Butler biographer James Parton, or a member of the Eighth Massachusetts, Cpl. John P. Reynolds Jr., who was on the *Constitution* at the time. In that same dispatch to Patterson, Butler neglected to say that it was Lefferts who finally acted to land the Eighth Massachusetts Regiment at the naval academy.[50]

In the end, it's clear that Butler won the PR battle, and consequently, his account became the historical default. It just wasn't true.

Summing Up the War's Meaning

Abraham Lincoln during these first two weeks never lost sight of his most important role. He struggled day and night to get his mind around the meaning of this new war. He knew he had to forcefully and clearly articulate that meaning to Americans. Even in early May, he was deeply engaged in writing a comprehensive message to Congress that would be dated July 4.

"I consider the central idea pervading this struggle is the necessity that is upon us, of proving that popular government is not an absurdity," Lincoln told John Nicolay and John Hay on May 7. "We must settle this question now, whether, in a free government, the minority have the right to break up the government whenever they choose. If we fail, it will go far to prove the incapability of people to govern themselves."[51]

NOTES

Acknowledgments

1. Nicolay and Hay, *Abraham Lincoln*, 4:157.

1. Why Don't They Come?

1. Author's note: Through the course of this book, the reader will find many real-time descriptions, comments, conversations, anecdotes, events, data points, weather reports, and indeed, facts. The "fly-on-wall" approach to writing adds immediacy and drama but is sometimes cause for skepticism. One may ask, "How could the author know?" However, I decided at the start of this project that in each instance, my material would be sourced. I've relied overwhelmingly on primary sources, and frequently multiple independent sources were available. Doing that, and telling a compelling story at the same time, was the goal.

2. Brooks, *Washington in Lincoln's Time*, 57–58; Burlingame, *Oral History of Abraham Lincoln*, 78.

3. NOAA, *Meteorological Observations*; Krick, *Civil War Weather*, 23.

4. John J. Miller, "With Death on His Mind," *Wall Street Journal*, February 11, 2012; Knox, "Lincoln's Favorite Poem."

5. "Jeff Davis en Route for Montgomery," *Charleston Mercury*, February 15, 1861, 1; McPherson, *Embattled Rebel*, 5; "Jefferson Davis's Journey to Montgomery in 1861," *New York Times*, March 19, 1886, citing the *Atlanta Constitution*; Cooper, *Jefferson Davis, American*, 379.

6. Nicolay and Hay, *Abraham Lincoln*, 4:148–49.

7. Stoddard, *Lincoln's Third Secretary*, 67; Nicolay and Hay, *Abraham Lincoln*, 4:142–43.

8. Nicolay and Hay, *Abraham Lincoln*, 4:149; Villard, *Memoirs of Henry Villard*, 1:166; G. W. Smith, "Critical Moment for Washington," 103–6.

9. Nicolay and Hay, *Abraham Lincoln*, 4:143–44.

10. Nicolay and Hay, *Abraham Lincoln*, 4:151–52.

11. Nicolay and Hay, *Abraham Lincoln*, 4:152.

2. The Evacuation of Sumter

1. Nicolay and Hay, *Abraham Lincoln*, 4:48–50.
2. Nicolay and Hay, *Abraham Lincoln*, 4:34, 44.
3. OR, series 1, 1:303–4.
4. Crawford, *Genesis of the Civil War*, 443.
5. Crawford, *Genesis of the Civil War*, 446.
6. Crawford, *Genesis of the Civil War*, 446; Lee, "First Step," 1:81.
7. Crawford, *Genesis of the Civil War*, 447–48; Doubleday, *Reminiscences*, 171–73; Doubleday, "From Moultrie to Sumter," 1:48; OR, series 1, 1:28.
8. Doubleday, "From Moultrie to Sumter," 1:48.
9. Williams, *Mary Boykin Chesnut*, 38–39.

3. Washington, the Secessionist City

1. Chittenden, *Recollections of President Lincoln*, 106–7.
2. Burlingame, *Inside the White House*, 23, White House sketch 1, 145.
3. Keller, "Lincoln in His Shop"; Allman, "Lincoln Bedroom."
4. Stoddard, *Inside the White House*, 24.
5. Stoddard, *Abraham Lincoln*, 245.
6. Nicolay and Hay, *Abraham Lincoln*, 4:73.
7. Nicolay and Hay, *Abraham Lincoln*, 4:62 (for date of Sumter relief expedition); Seward, *Seward at Washington*, 544–45.
8. Basler, Pratt, and Dunlap, *Collected Works*, 4:332.
9. "Died," *Washington Times*, September 27, 1901; Burlingame, *Inside the White House*, xvii–xviii, White House sketch 2, 151; Donald, *We Are Lincoln Men*, 181.
10. W. H. Russell, *My Diary*, 44.
11. Young, *John Russell Young*, 1:59, 65, 69.
12. H. Nicolay, *Lincoln's Secretary*, 87.
13. Stoddard, *Lincoln's Third Secretary*, 193.
14. Stoddard, *Inside the White House*, 165–66.
15. "Special Despatches to the 'Press.' Rumors and Excitement," *Philadelphia Press*, April 15, 1861.
16. Taft, *Diary*, vol. 1, January 1, 1861–April 11, 1862.
17. Haley, *Philp's Washington Described*, 207–8; Poore, *Perley's Reminiscences*, 2:174–75; Northup, *Twelve Years a Slave*, 33.
18. Foreman, *World on Fire*, 5.
19. Hawthorne, "Chiefly about War Matters"; Sandburg, *War Years*, 174.
20. Kennedy, *Eighth Census 1860*, 588, appendix, 131; Davis, "Slavery and Emancipation."
21. "Black Republican" was a common insult used by Democrats and prosecession Southerners to describe members of the Republican Party who sought to limit slavery. It combined a notion of "black-hearted" evil with a racist allusion to Republican support for the rights of Black Americans.
22. Bayne, *Tad Lincoln's Father*, 15–16.

23. Bayne, *Tad Lincoln's Father*, 20.

24. Ellis, *Sights and Secrets*, 49–51.

25. Crofutt, *American Procession*, 55.

26. Seward, *Statesman and Diplomat*, 144; Stoddard, *Lincoln's Third Secretary*, 67.

27. Stoddard, *Inside the White House*, 17–18; Helm, *Wife of Lincoln*, 174.

28. Young, *John Russell Young*, 1:56.

29. Young, *John Russell Young*, 1:54.

30. H. Adams, *Education*, 107.

31. W. H. Russell, *My Diary*, 37–38.

32. W. H. Russell, *My Diary*, 41.

33. D. H. Bates, *Telegraph Office*, 26.

34. Nicolay and Hay, *Abraham Lincoln*, 4:151; W. H. Russell, *My Diary*, 37; Helm, *Wife of Lincoln*, 166.

35. W. H. Russell, *My Diary*, 43.

36. Young, *John Russell Young*, 1:55.

37. Burlingame, *With Lincoln*, 30; H. Adams, *Education*, 108–9.

38. Stoddard, *Inside the White House*, 4–5.

39. W. H. Russell, *My Diary*, 33, 51.

40. Burlingame, *With Lincoln*, 32; Stoddard, *Inside the White House*, 12–13.

41. Lincoln eviscerated this principle in his Cooper Union speech the prior year.

42. In an April 22 speech in Bellair, Ohio, Douglas said, "The proposition now is to separate these United States into petty little confederacies. First, divide them into two, and then, when either party gets beaten at the next election, subdivide again. Then, whenever one gets beaten again, another subdivision, and so it will go on." Nicolay and Hay, *Abraham Lincoln*, 4:82.

43. Nicolay and Hay, *Abraham Lincoln*, 4:81–84; Seward, *Seward at Washington*, 549.

4. "If I Were Beauregard I Would Take Washington"

1. Seward, *Seward at Washington*, 545.

2. Wood, *Elizabeth Lindsay Lomax*, 148.

3. Taft, *Diary*.

4. Stoddard, *Lincoln's Third Secretary*, 81.

5. Vladeck, "Emergency Power," 163.

6. *OR*, series 3, 1:69; for Missouri, *OR*, series 3, 5:607–8.

7. McClure, *Men of War-Times*, 57–61.

8. Upton, *Military Policy*, 226; C. P. Stone, "Eve of the War," 1:11–17; Scott, *Memoirs*, 2:625–28.

9. Nicolay and Hay, *Abraham Lincoln*, 3:394–95; Goodheart, *Civil War Awakening*, 152–53.

10. Croffut and Morris, *History of Connecticut*, 840–41.

11. Kreidberg and Henry, *Military Mobilization*, 88.

12. Townsend, *Anecdotes*, 24–27; G. W. Smith, "Critical Moment for Washington," 98.

13. Townsend, *Anecdotes*, 42–44.

14. OR, series 3, 1:70–73.

15. Dix, *Memoirs*, 2:9. Dix had been in the army during the War of 1812 through 1828, served as the New York secretary of state and a U.S. senator from New York before the Civil War and was governor after the war. At the outbreak of the war, he sent a telegram to the treasury agents in New Orleans ordering that "if any one attempts to haul down the American flag, shoot him on the spot." Although the telegram was intercepted by the Confederates and never delivered, the text found its way to the press, and Dix became one of the first heroes of the North. The saying is found on many Civil War tokens minted during the war, although the wording is slightly modified. Fort Dix in New Jersey is named for him, as is a mountain range in the Adirondacks.

16. Seward, *Seward at Washington*, 545–46.

17. Butler, *Butler's Book*, 139–40.

18. Butler, *Butler's Book*, 220–21.

19. OR, series 3, 5:690–92; Fry, "McDowell's Advance," 1:168–69.

20. OR, series 1, 53:144–45; OR, series 3, 5:689–90.

21. Pollard, *Southern History*, 46.

22. Dickert, *Kershaw's Brigade*, 29–30.

23. Moore, *Rebellion Record*, 1:188.

24. Moore, *Rebellion Record*, 1:188.

5. Northern Militia in Tatters

1. Newell, *Regular Army*, 50; OR, series 3, 1:22; Kreidberg and Henry, *Military Mobilization*, 88; Hamilton and Madison, *Federalist Papers*.

2. Kreidberg and Henry, *Military Mobilization*, 89–90.

3. OR, series 3, 1:75.

4. Terrell, *Adjutant General*, 1:3–4.

5. Gates, *Ulster Guard*, 28.

6. Reid, *Ohio in the War*, 1:19.

7. Hicks, "Volunteer Army," 325 for Illinois, 329 for Minnesota statistics; *Journal of the Senate*, 26 for governor's speech, 644–45 for disposition of the militia bill; "Message of the Governor of Illinois to the Twenty-Second General Assembly," *Chicago Tribune*, January 8, 1861, 254.

8. Bilby and Goble, *Jerseymen!*, 3–5.

9. OR, series 3, 1:77.

10. Cox, *Military Reminiscences*, 1:7–8.

11. Cox, *Military Reminiscences*, 1:9–10.

12. Hicks, "Volunteer Army," 324–68.

13. Terrell, *Adjutant General*, 1:5.

14. Bilby and Goble, *Jerseymen!*, 3–5.

15. Phisterer, *New York*, 6.

16. *Annual Report*, 1861, 8; *Annual Report*, 1860, 6–8; *Annual Report*, 1858, 4–29.

17. *Annual Report*, 1861, 11.

18. Phisterer, *New York*, 6.

19. OR, series 3, 1:165.

20. Pearson, *John A. Andrew*, 1:135–36.

21. Pearson, *John A. Andrew*, 1:136, 142.

22. Schouler, *History of Massachusetts*, 19.

23. Schouler, *History of Massachusetts*, 47; Butler, *Butler's Book*, 163, 165–66.

24. Schouler, *History of Massachusetts*, 28–33.

25. Butler, *Butler's Book*, 170.

26. Pearson, *John A. Andrew*, 1:183–84; Butler, *Butler's Book*, 140, 211 (The vote count for Davis was 140, and it was 211 for the Breckenridge candidate for Massachusetts governor.); Schouler, *History of Massachusetts*, 3 (for gubernatorial election results).

27. Pearson, *John A. Andrew*, 1:183–84.

28. Masonic Jurisdiction, *Supreme Council*, 269.

29. Hanson, *Historical Sketch*, 16–17.

30. Watson, *Old "Sixth,"* 17–18.

31. Roe, *Fifth Regiment Massachusetts*, 17–19.

32. Poore, *Ambrose E. Burnside*, 86–87.

33. Poore, *Ambrose E. Burnside*, 93; Roe, *Fifth Regiment Massachusetts*, 9.

34. Kennedy, *Eighth Census 1860*, 279; "Moving of the Masses," *New York Times*, April 22, 1861; "Report of Colonel A. E. Burnside," 84–88; Dyer, *Annual Report*, 1:1; Poore, *Ambrose E. Burnside*, 95, 100–101.

35. OR, series 3, 1:77; Kennedy, *Eighth Census 1860*, 279.

36. Taylor, *Philadelphia*, 28–29.

37. A. L. Russell, *Adjutant General of Pennsylvania*, 3.

38. S. Bates, *Pennsylvania Volunteers*, 1:3–32; Schaadt, "Company I," 545; Condit, *History of Easton*, 235.

39. S. Bates, *Pennsylvania Volunteers*, 1:4–5.

40. Hiester, "Ringgold Light," 5.

41. Taylor, *Philadelphia*, 28.

42. W. H. Russell, *My Diary*, 92–93.

6. "Take Washington City Immediately"

1. Wood, *Elizabeth Lindsay Lomax*, 149.

2. Taft, *Diary*.

3. Webb and Woolridge, *Centennial History*, 248.

4. OR, series 3, 1:74–75.

5. OR, series 3, 1:74–76.

6. OR, series 3, 1:75.

7. Crist and Dix, *Papers of Jefferson Davis*, 7:105–6.

8. Rowland, *Jefferson Davis*, 5:63.

9. OR, series 1, 53:147.

10. Butler, *Butler's Book*, 171.

11. Butler, *Butler's Book*, 171.

12. Butler, *Butler's Book*, 171–73.

13. Pearson, *John A. Andrew*, 1:184.

14. Roe, *Fifth Regiment Massachusetts*, 7, 11.

15. "The Words of the Old Soldiers Have a Patriotic Ring," *Boston Globe*, April 17, 1911.

16. Roe, *Fifth Regiment Massachusetts*, 17–18.

17. E. Clark, *Seventh Regiment*, 1:470.

18. Derby and White, *National Cyclopaedia*, 10:243.

19. The Astor Place riots were triggered by a rivalry between two Shakespearean actors, one American and one British. The actors were proxies for the raging ethnic and class conflicts of the time. The Anglophile New York upper class preferred the British thespian. The lower class, mostly Irish, had a profound antipathy toward England generally and preferred the American actor. Eventually the grievances spilled over into street violence.

20. Swinton, *Seventh Regiment*, 16; Ranney, *Terrific and Fatal Riot*, 22–23, 28–30.

21. Swinton, *Seventh Regiment*, 16–17.

22. Swinton, *Seventh Regiment*, 16–17.

23. Swinton, *Seventh Regiment*, 22.

24. Aaron, "Greatest Diarist."

25. Nevins, *George Templeton Strong*, 123–24.

26. E. Clark, *Seventh Regiment*, 1:471; Swinton, *Seventh Regiment*, 27.

27. Lowen, *American Guard*, 10, 92–94.

28. "Seventy-First's New Home," *New York Times*, April 1, 1894, 13; Lowen, *American Guard*, 1, ab initio.

29. Lowen, *American Guard*, 36.

30. Savage, "Response," 28.

31. Doty, *Third Annual Report*, 286.

32. "Meeting of Colored Citizens," *Boston Liberator*, May 3, 1861; "Blacks Volunteering," *Baltimore Daily Exchange*, April 23, 1861; "Free Colored Volunteers in Louisiana," *Baltimore Sun*, April 24, 1861; OR, series 3, 1:107; OR, series 3, 1:133.

33. Doty, *Third Annual Report*, 286.

34. Phisterer, "War of the Rebellion," 539.

7. Virginia's Decision

1. Reese, *Virginia Secession Convention*, introduction.

2. Reese, *Virginia Secession Convention*, introduction, preface by Randolph W. Church.

3. Kennedy, *Eighth Census 1860*, 131.

4. Freehling and Simpson, *Showdown in Virginia*, x.

5. Dunaway, *Kanawha Company*, 165; Dabney, *Richmond*, 63; Virtual Tour, "1825 to 1860."

6. National Register, "Tredegar Iron Works," 10.

7. Reese, *Virginia Secession Convention*, 1:62–75.

8. For the inaugural address, see Avalon, "First Inaugural Address"; and for the proposed deal with Virginia, see Nicolay and Hay, *Abraham Lincoln*, 3:423–26.

9. Reese, *Virginia Secession Convention*, 3:736, 757.

10. Reese, *Virginia Secession Convention*, 4:119.

11. Changes in votes and absentee votes raised the final count to 103 (for) to 46 (against). Reese, *Virginia Secession Convention*, preface by Randolph W. Church.

12. Reese, *Virginia Secession Convention*, 3:163; Freehling and Simpson, *Showdown in Virginia*, introduction, xiii.

13. J. L. Smith, *Autobiography*, 33–34.

14. Hadden, *Slave Patrols*, 83, 108, citing Boney, Zafar, and Hume, *God Made Man*, 175–76.

15. Hadden, *Slave Patrols*, 83.

16. Gottlieb, "George Teamoh."

17. J. D. Richardson, *Papers of the Confederacy*, 1:61.

18. OR, series 1, vol. 51, pt. 2, 14.

19. W. H. Russell, *My Diary*, 98.

20. Fuscus was a Roman general who served as the leader of the Praetorian Guard.

21. W. H. Russell, *My Diary*, 110.

22. Chittenden, *Recollections of President Lincoln*, 109–10.

23. Wallace, *American Slaveholder's Rebellion*, 13–14.

24. Thompson, *First Defenders*, 10.

25. Pearson, *John A. Andrew*, 1:182–83.

26. Frost, *Rebellion*, 149.

27. OR, series 3, 1:79.

28. Pearson, *John A. Andrew*, 1:185.

29. "The Gallant Sixth," *Lowell Weekly Journal*, April 18, 1861; Hanson, *Historical Sketch*, 18.

8. The First Defenders

1. "The Massachusetts Troops en Route for Washington," *Frank Leslie's Illustrated Newspaper*, April 30, 1861, 375.

2. Dix, *Memoirs*, 2:10–11.

3. Hanson, *Historical Sketch*, 19.

4. Watson, *Old "Sixth,"* 29.

5. OR, series 1, 2:577.

6. OR, series 2, 1:564.

7. Brown, *Baltimore*, 35.

8. Scharf, *Chronicles of Baltimore*, 588.

9. Reports differ on the size of this detachment. It was either one or two companies, and if it was two companies, it would have been over one hundred men. The *Baltimore Daily Exchange* reported two companies of regulars and "a fraction over

600 men" combined between the regulars and the militia. The U.S. regulars were commanded by Lt. and Bvt. Maj. John C. Pemberton, a native Pennsylvanian who two years later, as a Confederate general, would surrender the Confederate forces at Vicksburg to General Grant.

10. S. Bates, *Pennsylvania Volunteers*, 1:5; Thompson, *First Defenders*, 10–15.

11. Various histories of the First Defenders say the troops marched to the Camden Depot, but both the *Baltimore Daily Exchange* article "The Passage—Scenes on the Route" and the *Baltimore Sun* article "Passage of Northern Troops" of April 19, 1861, say the troops went to the nearby Mount Clare station. The newspaper accounts are the most contemporaneous accounts available, written by people with the most knowledge of the city's geography (unlike Pennsylvanians who had no familiarity with Baltimore and were writing years later), and therefore are the most credible accounts. Mount Clare is now the home of today's B&O Railroad Museum.

12. "The War Excitement," *Baltimore Sun*, April 19, 1861.

13. "The Passage—Scenes on the Route," *Baltimore Daily Exchange*, April 19, 1861.

14. Thompson, *First Defenders*, 138.

15. "War Excitement."

16. "Passage—Scenes on the Route."

17. Thompson, *First Defenders*, 51, 139.

18. Fernald, *First Defenders*, 21.

19. Thompson, *First Defenders*, 14, 151–52; Lossing, *Pictorial History*, 1:406. Lossing credits Francis B. Wallace, editor of the Pottsville *Miners' Journal*, for facts in his book about the First Defenders. Wallace compiled the 1865 book *Memorial of the Patriotism of Schuylkill County in the American Slaveholder's Rebellion*; Wallace, *American Slaveholder's Rebellion*, 77–78; Ronald S. Coddington, "Disunion," *New York Times*, April 18, 2011; Zwierzyna, "Nick Biddle." (PACW 150 was a statewide partnership of major history organizations convened by the Pennsylvania Historical and Museum Commission and the Pennsylvania Heritage Foundation to develop programming and content for the commemoration.)

20. Thompson, *First Defenders*, 139.

21. Thompson, *First Defenders*, 151; Fernald, *First Defenders*, 21–22; Hoptak, "Nick Biddle."

22. Thompson, *First Defenders*, 151.

23. Scharf, *History of Maryland*, 3:402–3.

24. Herbert, *Popular History*, 71.

25. Scharf, *History of Maryland*, 3:401; Brown, *Baltimore*, 37–38.

9. Washington Prepares for the Worst

1. NOAA, *Meteorological Observations*; Taft, *Diary*.

2. Later in the war, Francis E. Spinner would play a pioneering role in gender equality by appointing some of the first female employees in the history of the federal government. "Counted Money 49 Years," *New York Times*, June 9, 1913.

3. Chittenden, *Recollections of President Lincoln*, 111–15.

4. *OR*, series 3, 1:84–87. Only half that many Rhode Island troops departed, and that was on Saturday the twentieth, not Friday the nineteenth. The other half of the regiment was held back for a few days until it was fully equipped.

5. Virginia seceded on Wednesday, April 17.

6. Dahlgren, *Memoir*, 330.

7. C. P. Stone, "Eve of the War," 1:11; Evans, "Militia," 28:99.

8. C. P. Stone, "Eve of the War," 1:12–13.

9. C. P. Stone, "Eve of the War," 1:16–17.

10. Webb and Woolridge, *Centennial History*, 248–49.

11. C. P. Stone, "Washington in March and April," 6; Townsend, *Anecdotes*, 11–12.

12. Villard, *Memoirs of Henry Villard*, 1:168; W. H. Russell, *My Diary*, 61–62.

13. C. P. Stone, "Washington in March and April," 6–7.

14. For Lee's appearance, see J. B. Jones, *Life and Letters*, 137.

15. Freeman, *R. E. Lee*, 1:432; Nicolay and Hay, *Abraham Lincoln*, 4:99.

16. Freeman, *R. E. Lee*, 1:434.

17. *OR*, series 4, vol. 1, sec. 1, 165–66.

18. Freeman, *R. E. Lee*, 1:437; J. B. Jones, *Life and Letters*, 131–32.

19. Long and Wright, *Memoirs*, 93.

20. Townsend, *Anecdotes*, 29–32.

21. This is a quibble, a debatable point of semantics. Lee was awaiting orders to report to his next command.

22. Freeman, *R. E. Lee*, 1:438; J. B. Jones, *Life and Letters*, 131–32; Long and Wright, *Memoirs*, 93.

23. Goldfield, "Robert E. Lee."

24. Freeman, *R. E. Lee*, 1:440.

25. Freeman, *R. E. Lee*, 1:441–42.

26. Reese, *Virginia Secession Convention*, 4:370–71.

27. Nicolay and Hay, *Abraham Lincoln*, 4:101–3.

28. Townsend, *Anecdotes*, 5; Eisenhower, *Agent of Destiny*, 372.

29. Moore, *Rebellion Record*, 1:188–89.

30. Mason, *Public Life*, 192–93.

31. W. H. Russell, *My Diary*, 116–17.

32. W. H. Russell, *My Diary*, 97, 117.

33. W. H. Russell, *My Diary*, 119.

10. Indecision at the Navy Yard and Harpers Ferry Is Lost

1. W. H. Russell, *My Diary*, 81.

2. *ORN*, series 1, 4:291; Welles, *Diary of Gideon Welles*, 2:49.

3. W. H. Russell, *My Diary*, 42.

4. *ORN*, series 1, 4:274.

5. *ORN*, series 1, 4:275–76; Welles, *Diary of Gideon Welles*, 16.

6. *ORN*, series 1, 4:277.

7. *ORN*, series 1, 4:275–79.

8. *ORN*, series 1, 4:277–78.

9. *ORN*, series 1, 4:281.

10. *OR*, series 1, 2:771; Sibley, "William Booth Taliaferro," 33.

11. Reese, *Virginia Secession Convention*, 4:124; Wise, *Henry A. Wise*, 274–80.

12. *ORN*, series 1, 4:280, 282.

13. *ORN*, series 1, 4:281.

14. *OR*, series 1, 4:2:4.

15. Hale, "Surrender and Destruction," 236–38.

16. Hale, "Surrender and Destruction," 243.

17. Reese, *Virginia Secession Convention*, 4:124.

18. Hale, "Surrender and Destruction," 239.

19. Hale, "Surrender and Destruction," 241, 244.

20. Hale, "Surrender and Destruction," 239.

21. Hale, "Surrender and Destruction," 241.

22. Hale, "Surrender and Destruction," 239.

23. Hale, "Surrender and Destruction," 241.

24. *OR*, series 1, 2:5.

25. *OR*, series 1, 2:6.

11. The New York Seventh Departs

1. O'Brien, "March of the Seventh," 1:228–34; Moore, *Rebellion Record*, 1:148–54.

2. E. Clark, *Seventh Regiment*, 1:472.

3. Swinton, *Seventh Regiment*, 34.

4. E. Clark, *Seventh Regiment*, 1:473; Swinton, *Seventh Regiment*, 35; Winthrop, "New York Seventh Regiment," 744–56; O'Brien, "March of the Seventh," 1:228–30.

5. Winthrop, "New York Seventh Regiment"; E. Clark, *Seventh Regiment*, 1:473–74.

6. Nevins, *George Templeton Strong*, 126.

7. Moore, *Rebellion Record*, 1:80–81; E. Clark, *Seventh Regiment*, 1:473–75; Swinton, *Seventh Regiment*, 36–40; Winthrop, "New York Seventh Regiment"; O'Brien, "March of the Seventh," 1:228–30; Nevins, *George Templeton Strong*, 126.

8. Winthrop, "New York Seventh Regiment"; O'Brien, "March of the Seventh," 1:228–30.

9. Hall, *Baltimore*, 165–66; Kennedy, *Eighth Census 1860*, 214–15; DeBow, *Seventh Census*, xc–xci; Catton, "Baltimore Business Community."

10. Trist, sixty, had been racing up and down the Northeast Corridor for the last few months, communicating on-the-ground intelligence from the secession hotbeds to the government authorities and presenting ideas and alternatives to the senior military commanders. On April 13, he'd gone to Washington from Philadelphia to share intelligence with General Scott regarding the potential destruction of the PWB's bridges, particularly at the Back, Gunpowder, and Bush Rivers. It was by coincidence that the PWB's Felton relied on Trist at the dawn of the Civil War. Nicholas Trist was one of the significant Americans of the nineteenth century, but he's now virtually lost to history. As the U.S. negotiator of the Treaty of Guadalupe Hidalgo, he forged

an agreement that led to the acquisition of more new territory for the United States than any others except President Jefferson's Louisiana Purchase and Seward's 1867 purchase of Alaska. Trist was a West Point graduate and a lawyer. Partly because of communications challenges in the 1840s, he negotiated the treaty with Mexico virtually on his own authority. He'd then been relieved of his duties by President Polk. Because of all this, Trist was a persona non grata in Washington and had fallen into destitution. He took a job as a railroad clerk in 1855 and worked his way up to paymaster under Felton. Ketchum, "Thankless Task."

11. Watson, *Addresses, Reviews, and Episodes*, 49; Taylor, *Philadelphia*, 27–29; "General Small's Brigade at Baltimore," *Philadelphia Inquirer*, April 23, 1861.

12. Hanson, *Historical Sketch*, 22; Watson, *Addresses, Reviews, and Episodes*, 49.

13. "The Return of the Washington Brigade," *Philadelphia Public Ledger*, April 20, 1861; "Disgraceful Riot," *Philadelphia Inquirer*, April 20, 1861; "General Small's Brigade"; Johnson, "Maryland's First Patriotic Movement," 2:20.

14. Dare, *Rail Road Guide*, 59; "General Small's Brigade."

15. It's similar to taking the Amtrak or New Jersey Transit to New York's Penn Station and then walking eleven blocks to pick up the Metro-North in Grand Central Station today.

16. *OR*, series 1, 2:7.

17. Nicolay and Hay, *Abraham Lincoln*, 4:111.

18. Dare, *Rail Road Guide*, 25; National Register of Historic Places, "President Street Station," sec. 8, 5–7. The terminal was built in a Greek Revival style in 1851, using brick painted a sandy brown, and had an arched truss roof. There was a 240-foot-long train shed with four tracks—two for passengers and one for freight inside, and one for freight outside, along Canton Avenue. An adjoining freight shed and headhouse of a similar design was built four years after the main depot. An engine house was added in the late 1850s. By 1861, there were seven tracks. Today, the President Street Station building is dwarfed by a huge Marriott hotel, and the 200-plus-foot train shed and tracks are long gone. It's a curiosity, a relic in the trendy, touristy modern Inner Harbor neighborhood, adjacent to the equally trendy Fells Point and Little Italy sections. The Camden Station opened in 1857. Today, the building is a sports museum. A modern commuter line still operates at the site, making it one of the longest continuously operated railroad stations in the United States.

19. Watson, *Addresses, Reviews, and Episodes*, 48–49.

20. Tyson's version was "Everybody has a plan until they get punched in the mouth." Berardino, "Mike Tyson."

12. The Baltimore Riots

1. Krick, *Civil War Weather*, 23. Krick is citing the recordings of the Presbyterian preacher C. B. Mackee in Georgetown at 7:00 a.m., 2:00 p.m., and 9:00 p.m. each day. Mackee's ledgers were preserved through the efforts of the Weather Bureau in the 1950s.

2. Dare, *Rail Road Guide*, 28–29.

3. Watson, *Addresses, Reviews, and Episodes*, 28.

4. Library of Congress, "City of Baltimore."

5. "Another Account," *Philadelphia Inquirer*, April 20, 1861.

6. Watson, *Addresses, Reviews, and Episodes*, 28.

7. OR, series 1, 2:7; Watson, *Addresses, Reviews, and Episodes*, 49.

8. Library of Congress, "City of Baltimore."

9. White, "Forty-Seven Eyewitness Accounts," 80–82.

10. Watson, *Addresses, Reviews, and Episodes*, 49.

11. Watson, *Addresses, Reviews, and Episodes*, 28–29.

12. "The Riot," *Baltimore Sun*, April 20, 1861; Brown, *Baltimore*, 45; Nicolay and Hay, *Abraham Lincoln*, 4:113.

13. White, "Forty-Seven Eyewitness Accounts," 78.

14. Wardwell, "Military Waif," 429.

15. "Captain Sampson's Statement," *Boston Herald*, April 19, 1886; Watson, *Addresses, Reviews, and Episodes*, 52.

16. Hanson, *Historical Sketch*, 26.

17. Watson, *Addresses, Reviews, and Episodes*, 51.

18. Watson, *Addresses, Reviews, and Episodes*, 49.

19. Hanson erroneously refers to Garrett as "the Hon. Thomas Garrett."

20. Hanson, *Historical Sketch*, 27.

21. Scharf, *History of Maryland*, 3:404; Brown, *Baltimore*, 46; "The Revolution," *Baltimore Daily Exchange*, April 20, 1861. The turning back of the car is referred to in several accounts, but none of the Massachusetts men—Company C captain Albert Follansbee, Major Watson, Captain Sampson, regimental chaplain and historian John Wesley Hanson, or Colonel Jones—mention it in their accounts.

22. Scharf, *Chronicles of Baltimore*, 589; "Revolution."

23. Booth, *Personal Reminiscences*, 7.

24. Hanson, *Historical Sketch*, 27.

25. Watson, *Addresses, Reviews, and Episodes*, 33; Scharf, *History of Maryland*, 3:405.

26. Hedrick, *Incidents*, 48; Hanson, *Historical Sketch*, 49.

27. E. W. Stone, *Compend of Military Instructions*, 25, 27, 65; Hanson, *Historical Sketch*, 29.

28. Watson, *Addresses, Reviews, and Episodes*, 34.

29. Scharf, *Chronicles of Baltimore*, 591.

30. Hanson, *Historical Sketch*, 42–43.

31. John Goodspeed, "The Civil War's First Dead," *Baltimore Sun: The Sunday Magazine*, April 16, 1961, 13; "War," 279.

32. "The Fight at Baltimore," *Liberator*, Boston, May 3, 1861; J. F. Stevens, *Massachusetts Soldiers*, 1:380.

33. Watson, *Addresses, Reviews, and Episodes*, 34.

34. Wardwell, "Military Waif," 430.

35. Goodspeed, "First Dead," 13.

36. Watson, *Addresses, Reviews, and Episodes*, 36.

37. Hanson, *Historical Sketch*, 44.

38. *OR*, series 1, 2:7; Watson, *Addresses, Reviews, and Episodes*, 35.

39. Andrews, "History of Baltimore," 1:175; "Riot."

40. Hanson, *Historical Sketch*, 40–41; Watson, *Addresses, Reviews, and Episodes*, 35, 81.

41. Stockett, *Baltimore*, 85–86; Gunts, "Baltimore Subway Stop."

42. Hanson, *Historical Sketch*, 41.

43. Hanson, *Historical Sketch*, 28.

44. Andrew, *Dedicating the Monument*, 19; Headley, *Massachusetts*, 136.

45. Brown, *Baltimore*, 46.

46. Wardwell, "Military Waif," 434.

47. Hanson, *Historical Sketch*, 41; Brown, *Baltimore*, 51; Watson, *Addresses, Reviews, and Episodes*, 59, 81. Follansbee's statements come from Hanson's history and Watson's collection of letters and speeches and vary in each. The actual quote is from Watson's account.

48. "The Excitement at Baltimore," *Washington National Intelligencer*, April 22, 1861, quoting the *Baltimore American*.

49. "Riot."

50. "Riot"; Scharf, *Chronicles of Baltimore*, 592; J. F. Stevens, *Massachusetts Soldiers*, 1:397.

51. Andrew, *Dedicating the Monument*, 16–19; Watson, *Addresses, Reviews, and Episodes*, 42.

52. Hanson, *Historical Sketch*, 47–48; Andrew, *Dedicating the Monument*, 16–19.

53. Later on the day of the riots, Police Marshal Kane wrote to Bradley T. Johnson, a lawyer and militia leader in Frederick, Maryland: "Bring your men in by the first train, and we will arrange with the railroad afterward. Streets red with Maryland blood. Send expresses over the mountains and valleys of Maryland and Virginia for riflemen to come without delay. Fresh hordes will be down on us tomorrow. We will fight them and whip them or die." The police chief of the largest city in a Union state was referring to loyal soldiers as "hordes" and threatening to "whip them or die." In a May 3 report, Kane admitted to writing the note but blamed it on the excitement of the moment. Moore, *Rebellion Record*, 1:184; *OR*, series 2, 1:630. See also Brown, *Baltimore*, 51; Watson, *Addresses, Reviews, and Episodes*, 63–64.

54. "The Troops Reach the Camden Railroad Station," *Baltimore Sun*, April 20, 1861.

55. Hanson, *Historical Sketch*, 41.

56. Hanson, *Historical Sketch*, 36, 41.

57. "Troops."

58. *OR*, series 1, 2:16.

59. Watson, *Addresses, Reviews, and Episodes*, 48.

60. Watson, *Addresses, Reviews, and Episodes*, 88.

61. Watson, *Addresses, Reviews, and Episodes*, 48–49.

62. White, "Forty-Seven Eyewitness Accounts," 83.

63. "Troops."

64. Hanson, *Historical Sketch*, 31–32.

65. Scharf, *Chronicles of Baltimore*, 593.

66. OR, series 1, 2:9.

67. Hanson, *Historical Sketch*, 32.

68. "The Philadelphia Military," *Philadelphia Public Ledger*, April 20, 1861.

69. "General Small's Brigade at Baltimore," *Philadelphia Inquirer*, April 23, 1861.

70. "The Return of the Washington Brigade," *Philadelphia Public Ledger*, April 20, 1861.

71. "General Small's Brigade."

72. Scharf, *Chronicles of Baltimore*, 593; Moore, *Rebellion Record*, 1:38; White, "Forty-Seven Eyewitness Accounts," 83–84.

73. "General Small's Brigade."

74. Hanson, *Historical Sketch*, 42.

75. Hanson, *Historical Sketch*, 42.

76. Melton, "Lost Lives," 336–49; Moore, *Rebellion Record*, 1:38–39.

77. Moore, *Rebellion Record*, 1:38–39.

78. Taylor, *Philadelphia*, 27–29; "The Washington Brigade," *Philadelphia Inquirer*, April 24, 1861; "Return"; "Fishtown Remembers a Civil War Casualty," *Philadelphia Inquirer*, April 24, 2011.

79. White, "Forty-Seven Eyewitness Accounts," 80.

80. National Archives, "Grand Jury"; White, "Forty-Seven Eyewitness Accounts," 73–93.

81. Taylor, *Philadelphia*, 27–29; "Washington Brigade"; "Return"; "Fishtown."

82. Andrew, *Dedicating the Monument*, 16–19; "Riot"; "Death of a Soldier," *Daily Exchange*, April 29, 1861.

83. Watson, *Addresses, Reviews, and Episodes*, 40.

84. "Riot"; "Revolution."

85. "Will Have Monument," *Baltimore Sun*, June 20, 1910; "Search for Soldier Vain," *Baltimore Sun*, June 22, 1910.

13. Insurrection in Maryland

1. Brown, *Baltimore*, 56; "The Military," *Baltimore Sun*, April 20, 1861.

2. Plum, *Military Telegraph*, 1:65.

3. "Meeting in Monument Square," *Baltimore Sun*, April 20, 1861; "The Mass Meeting," *Baltimore Daily Exchange*, April 20, 1861.

4. "Mass Meeting"; "Meeting in Monument Square."

5. "Meeting in Monument Square"; "Mass Meeting."

6. Nicolay and Hay, *Abraham Lincoln*, 4:123.

7. Garrett was under severe pressure from Southern authorities. His railroad ran westward through Maryland and Virginia, with most of the line beyond Harpers Ferry within Virginia's borders. On April 18, Ohio governor William Dennison wrote to U.S. Secretary of War Simon Cameron, saying, "We had made arrangements with the Baltimore and Ohio Road to transport troops, and Mr. Garrett was anxious to

take them until last night, when he declined, on the alleged ground that the Washington branch will employ all his empty cars in transportation of troops. This looks ominous. We hope Harpers Ferry is safe" (OR, series 1, 2:578). The next day, the 20, Virginia governor John Letcher issued this threat to Garrett: "In the event that you allow Federal troops to be passed over your road, I will take possession of so much of said road as lies within the limits of this State. It is due to the South that your road, located within slave territory, shall not be used to the prejudice of the slave-holding States, especially the State of Virginia" (OR, series 1, pt. 2, 51:21).

8. Moore, *Rebellion Record*, 1:79; "Correspondence, Etc.," *Baltimore Sun*, April 20, 1861.

9. OR, series 1, 2:578; Nicolay and Hay, *Abraham Lincoln*, 4:123.

10. OR, series 1, 2:12; OR, series 2, 1:564; Burlingame, *With Lincoln*, 34.

11. "Seizure of Arms," *Baltimore Sun*, April 22, 1861; "Affairs in Baltimore," *Philadelphia Inquirer*, April 23, 1861; "Arms Received for Protection," *Baltimore Daily Exchange*, April 23, 1861.

12. OR, series 2, 1:570, 630. Both of these reports, though exaggerated, were essentially correct, although Brown and Kane couldn't have known that at the moment.

13. Brown, *Baltimore*, 58.

14. The name comes from the party's 1849 founding as a secret society. When members were asked about the organization, they were supposed to say, "I know nothing."

15. Radcliffe, "Governor Thomas H. Hicks," 19:21–42; Brown, *Baltimore*, 34.

16. Brown, *Baltimore*, 58; "Town Meeting," *National Intelligencer*, April 22, 1861; Seabrook, *Maryland's Great Part*, 19–20.

17. OR, series 1, 2:13; OR, series 2, 1:570.

18. OR, series 1, 2:14–15.

19. Hafner et al., "Straddling Secession."

20. OR, series 1, pt. 2, 51:17.

21. W. H. Russell, *My Diary*, 121.

22. J. B. Jones, *Rebel War Clerk's Diary*, 24–25.

23. Watson, *Addresses, Reviews, and Episodes*, 48–49; Nicolay and Hay, *Abraham Lincoln*, 4:123.

24. Burlingame, *With Lincoln*, 35.

25. Wood, *Elizabeth Lindsay Lomax*, 149.

26. Taft, *Diary*.

27. A. D. Richardson, *Secret Service*, 117–18.

28. Chittenden, *Recollections of President Lincoln*, 115–16.

29. Basler, Pratt, and Dunlap, *Collected Works*, 4:338–40.

30. Newton, *Lord Lyons*, 1:31–32; E. D. Adams, *Great Britain*, 1:66.

31. E. D. Adams, *Great Britain*, 1:68–69, 88.

32. The *Pawnee*, like many steam-powered warships of this era, retained the architecture of sailing ships. It had three masts and full rigging, in addition to its single smokestack, and no superstructure. Its guns were mounted below the main deck. It was one of the navy's newest ships, built in Philadelphia and commissioned less

than a year earlier, in June 1860. It carried ten guns and had a crew of 181 men. Its maximum speed was ten knots.

33. Meade, *Hiram Paulding*, 239; ORN, series 1, 4:284–85.

14. Washington Cut Off and Insurrection Rages in Maryland

1. Moore, *Rebellion Record*, 2:183–84; Library of Congress, "Baltimore County Union"; Library of Congress, "About the American."; Scharf, *Chronicles of Baltimore*, 603–4.

2. Cannon, *Investigation*, 1:1–280.

3. The railroad tracks are now part of a commuter line that extends to present-day Hunt Valley, north of Cockeysville.

4. National Archives, "Grand Jury."

5. "Destruction of the Bridges and Telegraphs," *Baltimore Daily Exchange*, April 22, 1861.

6. The term *relay house* described a shed, or workstation, for railroad employees responsible for managing train traffic at junctions. Switching and signaling were done manually in the years before electricity.

7. "Burning of the Bridges," *Baltimore American*, April 22, 1861; "Destruction."

8. Northern Central Railway. "Seventh Annual Report," 55.

9. "Destruction."

10. The next week, Baltimore County Militia captain John Merryman and others continued the destruction on the Northern Central Railway north of Cockeysville. Merryman was arrested on May 25, 1861, at his home near Cockeysville by a federal force at 2:00 a.m. and accused of possession of U.S. government arms. He was held at Fort McHenry without being charged. (In July 1861 Merryman was finally formally indicted for treason in connection with bridge burnings on April 23.) Merryman's lawyers petitioned Supreme Court Chief Justice Roger Taney for a writ of habeas corpus, which triggered a chain of events that led to one of the most famous legal cases in American history, *Ex Parte Merryman*. Taney declared that Merryman was being detained improperly. President Abraham Lincoln responded in July with one of his most famous rhetorical passages: "Are all the laws, but one, to go unexecuted, and the government itself to go to pieces, lest that one be violated?" Lincoln disputed that the Constitution allows only Congress to suspend the writ of habeas corpus, which by that point in July he'd already done all along the rail corridors to Washington. "It cannot be believed the framers of the instrument intended, that in every case, the danger should run its course, until Congress could be called together; the very assembling of which might be prevented, as was intended in this case, by the rebellion." Basler, Pratt, and Dunlap, *Collected Works*, 4:430–31; OR, series 2, 1:574–85; "The Baltimore Treason," *New York Times*, July 12, 1861 (for text of the indictment); Ragsdale, *Debates on Civil Liberties*.

11. Wilson, *Pennsylvania Railroad*, 1:319; Library of Congress, "City of Baltimore"; *Journal of Proceedings*, 415; Dare, *Rail Road Guide*, 25–26.

12. Schouler, *History of Massachusetts*, 65.

13. Wilson, *Pennsylvania Railroad*, 1:319.

14. National Archives, "Grand Jury."

15. Frost, *Rebellion*, 174–77; Trist, "Statement," 37–39; Wilson, *Pennsylvania Railroad*, 1:318–20.

16. Wilson, *Pennsylvania Railroad*, 1:319.

17. In two alternate accounts, including another one attributed to Felton, it was a conductor named Goodwin, on a southbound freight train, who told Trimble that Northern troops were nearby. All the accounts correspond in the major details. Plum, *Military Telegraph*, 1:66; Wilson, *Pennsylvania Railroad*, 1:319; Schouler, *History of Massachusetts*, 102–3.

18. Schouler, *History of Massachusetts*, 102–3.

19. OR, series 1, 2:739–40.

20. National Archives, "Grand Jury."

21. Wilson, *Pennsylvania Railroad*, 1:319–20.

22. National Archives, "Grand Jury."

23. National Archives, "Grand Jury."

24. Wilson, *Pennsylvania Railroad*, 1:318–20.

25. Isaac Trimble Papers, "Statement."

26. National Archives, "Grand Jury."

27. "War Movements," *Washington Evening Star*, April 22, 1861; "Things in Baltimore," *Washington Evening Star*, April 22, 1861.

28. Scharf, *Chronicles of Baltimore*, 603–4.

29. National Archives, "Grand Jury."

30. Isaac Trimble Papers, "Statement."

31. C. M. Howard, "Crisis of 1861," 259.

32. Moore, *Rebellion Record*, 2:182–83.

33. OR, series 1, 2:10–11.

15. A New Route to Washington

1. Butler, *Butler's Book*, 175; Parton, *Butler in New Orleans*, 70. The depot was at the corner of Broad Street and Prime Street (now Washington Avenue), about a mile south of the modern-day city hall in Philadelphia's Center City. It was then the outskirts of the city. Broad Street, then and now, is Philadelphia's main north-south thoroughfare. The depot, built in 1852, was the largest and most luxurious train facility in the city.

2. OR, series 1, 2:579.

3. Butler, *Butler's Book*, 183; "Dispatches from General Butler," *New York Times*, April 21, 1861; Swinton, *Seventh Regiment*, 56; Schouler, *History of Massachusetts*, 102.

4. Parton, *Butler in New Orleans*, 71–72; Butler, *Butler's Book*, 182–84.

5. Parton, *Butler in New Orleans*, 71.

6. Butler, *Butler's Book*, 183.

7. Parton, *Butler in New Orleans*, 71–72.

8. E. Clark, *Seventh Regiment*, 1:477.

9. Swinton, *Seventh Regiment*, 52.

10. Swinton, *Seventh Regiment* 56.

11. *OR*, series 1, 2:582.

12. *OR*, series 1, 2:583.

13. Swinton, *Seventh Regiment*, 57.

14. Swinton, *Seventh Regiment*, 58.

15. Winthrop, "New York Seventh Regiment."

16. "Scene at the Depot," *New York Tribune*, April 22, 1861.

17. Duncan, *Blue-Eyed Child*, 77.

18. Moore, *Rebellion Record*, 1:150.

19. E. Clark, *Seventh Regiment*, 1:486; Swinton, *Seventh Regiment*, 59; Duncan, *Blue-Eyed Child*, 77.

20. Swinton, *Seventh Regiment*, 58; Parton, *Butler in New Orleans*, 72; Butler, *Butler's Book*, 184; Marshall, *Private and Official Correspondence*, 1:20.

21. Swinton, *Seventh Regiment*, 71.

22. Swinton, *Seventh Regiment*, 61.

23. E. Clark, *Second Company*, 1:295.

24. E. Clark, *Seventh Regiment*, 1:295.

25. Parton, *Butler in New Orleans*, 72–73. James Parton was a prominent biographer in the mid-nineteenth century, having published the lives of Andrew Jackson, Aaron Burr, Horace Greeley, Thomas Jefferson, Benjamin Franklin, and others.

26. "Departure of the Massachusetts Regiment," *New York Tribune*, April 22, 1861.

27. Butler, in his typically self-aggrandizing way, wrote that he "went through the cars, saw every man, examined his rifle, found it in good order, stood over him while he loaded it, and saw that it was all right." Had Butler really inspected each of the more than seven hundred men in the regiment in that manner, allowing a minute for each man, it would have taken about twelve hours. William L. W. Seabrook, then commissioner of the Maryland Land Office, wrote that "it may be uncharitable to suppose this description overdrawn, but it may not be unreasonable to consider some other statements of his, which I shall quote, 'cum grano sails'"—to be taken with a grain of salt. Butler, *Butler's Book*, 188; Seabrook, *Maryland's Great Part*, 24.

28. Wilson, *Pennsylvania Railroad*, 1:301–2.

29. Butler, *Butler's Book*, 190–91; Parton, *Butler in New Orleans*, 75.

30. Winthrop, "New York Seventh Regiment."

31. Delmonicos was an exclusive Downtown Manhattan restaurant; O'Brien, "March of the Seventh," 1:230.

32. Woodbury, *Narrative of the Campaign*, 10–11.

33. Roe, *Fifth Regiment Massachusetts*, 7, 10.

34. Charles Bowers Letters, Charles Bowers to Lydia Bowers.

35. Lowen, *American Guard*, 94.

36. Evans, *Confederate Military History*, 2:23; Brown, *Baltimore*, 63.

37. *OR*, series 1, 2:771.

38. *OR*, series 1, 2:772.

39. *OR*, series 1, pt. 2, 51:21.

16. The Fortified Capital

1. Taft, *Diary*.

2. Wood, *Elizabeth Lindsay Lomax*, 149.

3. Burlingame and Ettlinger, *Inside Lincoln's White House*, 5.

4. Leo, "Glimpses of War, Our Washington Correspondence," *New York Times*, April 24, 1861.

5. Chittenden, *Recollections of President Lincoln*, 117, 120.

6. *OR*, series 3, 1:93.

7. Nicolay and Hay, *Abraham Lincoln*, 4:126.

8. Nicolay and Hay, *Abraham Lincoln*, 4:126.

9. Basler, Pratt, and Dunlap, *Collected Works*, 4:341.

10. *OR*, series 1, 2:581.

11. Nicolay and Hay, *Abraham Lincoln*, 4:126.

12. *OR*, series 1, 2:581.

13. "'Old Abe' Frightened," *Baltimore Daily Exchange*, April 23, 1861.

14. *OR*, series 2, 1:565; "The Position of Maryland, Correspondence with the Authorities at Washington," *New York Times*, May 4, 1861.

15. Burlingame, *With Lincoln*, 37.

16. This telegram was actually from the prior day, Friday, April 19. The telegraph line was temporarily repaired and sporadically reliable for government use into Sunday, April 21. Plum, *Military Telegraph*, 1:65.

17. The orders were for the prosecession commander of the Department of the West, Gen. William Harney, to be relieved of his command and replaced by Capt. Nathaniel Lyon, commander of the St. Louis Arsenal. Lyon was ordered to arm the loyal local militia. An additional order was to the assistant treasurer in the state to employ the necessary force to protect the treasury and, if necessary, to transfer federal funds in Missouri to the loyal state of Illinois.

18. Harrington, "Inside Glimpses," 24–27 typewritten, 34–39 handwritten.

19. Morgan et al., *Rear Admiral Charles Wilkes*, 762.

20. *ORN*, series 1, 4:292.

21. Welles, *Diary of Gideon Welles*, 2:44.

22. *ORN*, series 1, 4:288–98.

23. *ORN*, series 1, 4:287.

24. *ORN*, series 1, 4:297; A. W. Stevens, *Edward L. Pierce*, 8–10.

17. Confederate Troops Move North

1. Crist and Dix, *Papers of Jefferson Davis*, 7:113.

2. *OR*, series 1, 53:152; Roman, *Military Operations*, 1:50–51; Dickert, *Kershaw's Brigade*, 33, 35–37; "Arrival of Troops from South Carolina," *Charleston Mercury*, April 27, 1861, 2; "South Carolina Volunteers," *Richmond Enquirer*, April 27, 1861; "Prompt Response," *Richmond Enquirer*, April 27, 1861; "Troops in Motion," *Richmond Dispatch*, April 24, 1861; "Special Correspondence of the Dispatch," *Richmond Dispatch*, April 25, 1861; "From Petersburg," *Richmond Dispatch*, April 26 and 29, 1861; "South

Carolina Volunteers," *Richmond Dispatch*, April 27, 1861; "From Petersburg," *Richmond Dispatch*, April 26 and 29, 1861; "War Intelligence," *Boston Liberator*, May 3, 1861.

3. The council consisted of John J. Allen, president of the Virginia Supreme Court of Appeals, Francis Smith, superintendent of the Virginia Military Institute, and Matthew Fontaine Maury, the famous military oceanographer.

4. OR, series 1, 2:772.

5. Crist and Dix, *Papers of Jefferson Davis*, 7:113.

6. OR, series 1, 2:773.

7. OR, series 1, 53:151–52.

8. A. W. Stevens, *Edward L. Pierce*, 10.

9. Wilkes was an impulsive risk taker, a headstrong and sometimes insubordinate officer. He was not liked. Later that year he would touch off an international incident that nearly escalated into war between the United States and England. As commander of the USS *San Jacinto*, operating in the Caribbean, he intercepted and went aboard the British mail ship RMS *Trent* without orders and took two Confederate envoys bound for England and France into custody. The British demanded an apology and the release of the envoys, James M. Mason and John Slidell. England deployed 11,000 troops to Canada in preparation for war but also offered an out—it would stand down if the United States indicated that Wilkes acted on his own and not under orders. After more than a month of tension, that's what Lincoln chose to do. The crisis was averted, but Wilkes had solidified his reputation as a braggart and bully. "He will give us trouble," predicted Assistant Treasury Secretary George Harrington. "He has a super-abundance of self-esteem and a deficiency of judgment." Foreman, *World on Fire*, 177; Nevins, *War for the Union*, 1:388; George Harrington Papers, Memo.

10. Morgan et al., *Rear Admiral Charles Wilkes*, 762.

11. ORN, 4:293; Morgan et al., *Rear Admiral Charles Wilkes*, 763–64.

12. ORN, 4:295–96; Morgan et al., *Rear Admiral Charles Wilkes*, 763–64.

13. A. W. Stevens, *Edward L. Pierce*, 10.

14. A. W. Stevens, *Edward L. Pierce*, 10.

15. ORN, 297.

18. A Northern Convoy Departs

1. Kennedy, *Eighth Census 1860*, 242.

2. Parton, *Butler in New Orleans*, 76.

3. Butler, *Butler's Book*, 192; McKean, *National Almanac*, 106.

4. Sachse, "Bird's Eye View."

5. This was an odd admission from Patterson. The commander of the Department of Pennsylvania couldn't "find" Lefferts, one of the commanders of two advancing militia regiments. Lefferts had been in Philadelphia since a couple of hours past midnight on the twentieth and by all accounts spent most of his time at the Philadelphia train station; Butler, *Butler's Book*, 192; OR, series 1, 2:583, 585–86.

6. OR, series 1, 2:586–87.

7. Parton, *Butler in New Orleans*, 80; Butler, *Butler's Book*, 194.

8. Parton, *Butler in New Orleans*, 81.

9. Moore, *Rebellion Record*, 1:151.

10. Woodbury, *Narrative of the Campaign*, 11–12.

11. "Arrival and Departure."

12. "Departure of Sixth, Twelfth, and Seventy-First Regiments," *New York Tribune*, April 22, 1861; "Departure of the Seventy-First," *New York Herald*, April 22, 1861.

13. "Departure of the Sixth Regiment," *New York Herald*, April 22, 1861.

14. "Departure of Sixth, Twelfth, and Seventy-First."

15. "Departure of the Twelfth Regiment," *New York Herald*, April 22, 1861; Butterfield, *Biographical Memorial*, 21.

16. "For Our Country and Glory!"*New York Herald*, April 22, 1861.

17. "Departure of Sixth, Twelfth, and Seventy-First"; "Moving of the Masses," *New York Times*, April 22, 1861.

18. "March to the Boat," *New York Herald*, April 22, 1861.

19. "Departure of Sixth, Twelfth, and Seventy-First."

20. "West-Street and the Harbor," *New York Tribune*, April 22, 1861.

21. Lowen, *American Guard*, 97.

22. Roe, *Fifth Regiment Massachusetts*, 26.

23. "More Troops from Massachusetts," *New York Tribune*, April 22, 1861.

19. Brinksmanship in Washington

1. Burlingame and Ettlinger, *Inside Lincoln's White House*, 5.

2. At the outset of the war, there was no rail connection across the Potomac River. Passengers and freight were hauled on buses and wagons from the northern side of the Long Bridge to the southern side in Virginia, where they'd board trains belonging to the Alexandria and Washington Railroad, or they'd take a ferry to Aquia Landing, about 55 miles downriver, and pick up the Richmond, Fredericksburg, and Potomac Railroad.

3. OR, series 1, 2:615; Plum, *Military Telegraph*, 1:64–65; C. P. Stone, "Washington in March and April," 14–16; Kielbowicz, "Telegraph, Censorship, and Politics," 95–118; A. D. Richardson, *Secret Service*, 117.

4. NOAA, *Meteorological Observations*.

5. Taft, *Diary*.

6. Villard, *Memoirs of Henry Villard*, 1:166.

7. G. W. Smith, "Critical Moment for Washington," 103–6.

8. Villard, *Memoirs of Henry Villard*, 1:166.

9. "Narrative of Our Special Correspondent," *New York Times*, April 25, 1861.

10. Burlingame, *With Lincoln*, 37.

11. Nicolay and Hay, *Abraham Lincoln*, 4:131; Moore, *Rebellion Record*, 1:123–24; Brown, *Baltimore*, 71; Burlingame, *With Lincoln*, 37.

12. Burlingame, *Inside the White House*, 4.

13. Brown, *Baltimore*, 71–73.

14. Watson, *Addresses, Reviews, and Episodes*, 116–17.

15. Brown, *Baltimore*, 74.

16. Scharf, *History of Maryland*, 416.

17. "Movements of Troops," *Washington Evening Star*, April 23, 1861.

18. "Arrival of Pennsylvania Troops at Cockeysville," *Baltimore Daily Exchange*, April 22, 1861; S. Bates, *Pennsylvania Volunteers*, 1:13, 23, 32.

19. Scharf, *History of Maryland*, 417; Brown, *Baltimore*, 75.

20. The *New York Times*, picking up from an editorial on April 3 titled "Wanted—a Policy!"—which closely reflected Seward's early scathing criticisms of Lincoln—reprised the theme in a blistering follow-up on April 25, titled "Wanted—a Leader!"
"The life and death struggle for our national existence has begun," the editorial stated. "The withdrawal by the president of the soldiers at Cockeysville, merely from a scruple that there was an appearance of bad faith, is a delicate straining of a point of honor which is almost incredible in such an emergency as this." Lincoln felt the sting of the *Times's* editorial. He clipped and filed it and some others with a handwritten label that said, "Villainous articles." "Wanted—a Leader!" *New York Times*, April 25, 1861; Basler, Pratt, and Dunlap, *Collected Works*, 8:471; Holzer, *Power of the Press*, 305.

21. Burlingame, *With Lincoln*, 37, 201; Mark Howard Papers, William Faxon to Mark Howard.

22. Brown, *Baltimore*, 75.

23. Hay, *Letters*, 1:16; Burlingame and Ettlinger, *Inside Lincoln's White House*, 5.

24. Less than a week later, on Saturday, April 27, Cameron made his opposition to Lincoln's decision much more explicit. In a message to the president of the Pennsylvania Railroad, J. Edgar Thompson, he said, "One of the most painful acts I have witnessed was the order for the return of our troops from Cockeysville; but that is past and now we will amend the error." *OR*, series 1, 2:584, 604.

25. Harrington, "Inside Glimpses," 34–39.

26. Harrington, "Inside Glimpses," 39–50.

27. Walking across the park-like Executive Square was a frequent excursion for Lincoln during the Civil War. He would go to the War Department to catch the latest news from the front and engage in conversation with the telegraph operators.

28. Dix, *Memoirs*, 2:13.

29. Basler, Pratt, and Dunlap, *Collected Works*, 5:242–43; Rives, "Debates and Proceedings," pt. 4, 131.

30. Basler, Pratt, and Dunlap, *Collected Works*, 5:242–43.

31. Welles, *Diary of Gideon Welles*, 1:549.

32. Nicolay and Hay, *Abraham Lincoln*, 4:137–38; Seward, *Seward at Washington*, 551–52; Hendrick, *Lincoln's War Cabinet*, 226–28.

33. C. P. Stone, "Washington in March and April," 9–11.

34. Burlingame and Ettlinger, *Inside Lincoln's White House*, 8.

35. C. P. Stone, "Washington in March and April," 12, 14; "Interesting from Washington," *Baltimore Sun*, April 23, 1861.

36. C. P. Stone, "Washington in March and April," 16–17; Kielbowicz, "Telegraph, Censorship, and Politics," 97; Plum, *Military Telegraph*, 1:64.

37. OR, series 1, 2:586.

20. A Torrent of Federal Resignations

1. "Gen. Beauregard Reconnoitering," *New York Times*, April 25, 1861.

2. NOAA, *Meteorological Observations*; Taft, *Diary*.

3. J. G. Nicolay, *Outbreak of Rebellion*, 102.

4. "Department News," *Washington Star*, April 23, 1861; "Resignations," *Baltimore Daily Exchange*, April 23, 1861. For the Patent Office, see Usher, "Executive Documents," 2–8.

5. Wood, *Elizabeth Lindsay Lomax*, 149–50; "Lunsford L. Lomax."

6. Dahlgren, *Memoir*, 329; "Resignations."

7. G. W. Smith, "Critical Moment for Washington," 103–4; "Suicide of a Naval Officer," *Baltimore Sun*, April 29, 1861.

8. This conversation happened on either April 16, the day Virginia governor John Letcher rejected Lincoln's call for troops, or on the seventeenth, according to Magruder. Nicolay and Hay, *Abraham Lincoln*, 4:144; John B. Magruder, "Statements by Magruder," *New York Times*, May 23, 1870.

9. Williams, *Mary Boykin Chesnut*, 230; Settles, *John Bankhead Magruder*, 50–51, 53; Gallagher, *Lee and His Generals*, 119.

10. Magruder, "Statements."

11. Burlingame and Ettlinger, *Inside Lincoln's White House*, 5.

12. Newell, *Regular Army*, 50–52; OR, series 3, 1:22; Kreidberg and Henry, *Military Mobilization*, 88.

13. Dudley, *Going South*, 14–20.

14. Watson, *Addresses, Reviews, and Episodes*, 118.

15. C. P. Stone, "Washington in March and April," 12.

16. Fuller and Wayland, *Domestic Slavery*, 3–4.

17. Library of Congress, Salmon P. Chase Papers; Barbee, "Lincoln, Chase," 109, 118; Cuthbert, *Life of Richard Fuller*, 106.

18. Basler, Pratt, and Dunlap, *Collected Works*, 4:341–42; Nicolay and Hay, *Abraham Lincoln*, 4:139–40; "Interview with the President," *Baltimore Sun*, April 23, 1861.

19. C. P. Stone, "Dinner with General Scott," 528–32.

20. OR, series 3, 1:99.

21. OR, series 3, 1:100.

22. OR, series 3, 1:101–2.

23. OR, series 1, 2:588–89.

24. Moore, *Rebellion Record*, 1:133.

25. Basler, Pratt, and Dunlap, *Collected Works*, 4:332.

26. Radcliffe, "Governor Thomas H. Hicks," 19:39, 62–63, 73; Steiner et al., *Men of Mark*, 4:145–47.

27. "Call to the Legislature," *Baltimore Sun*, April 22, 1861; "Extra Section of the Legislature-Special Election in Baltimore To-Morrow," *Baltimore Sun*, April 23, 1861.

28. "The Election Yesterday," *Baltimore Sun*, April 25, 1861.

29. Radcliffe, "Governor Thomas H. Hicks," 19:63–64.

30. Basler, Pratt, and Dunlap, *Collected Works*, 4:344.

31. "Baltimore," *Baltimore Daily Exchange*, April 22, 1861, 2.

32. "A Pause for Reflection," *Baltimore Sun*, April 22, 1861, 2, "The Meeting of the Legislature," *Baltimore Sun*, April 26, 1861.

33. Beale, *Diary of Edward Bates*, 185.

34. Shuckers, *Salmon Portland Chase*, 424.

35. Nicolay and Hay, *Abraham Lincoln*, 4:167–68; Basler, Pratt, and Dunlap, *Collected Works*, 4:344.

36. "The Pennsylvania Troops in Maryland-Return to Harrisburg," *Baltimore Sun*, April 23, 1861, 1; "Arrival of Pennsylvania Troops at Cockeysville," *Baltimore Daily Exchange*, April 22, 1861.

37. "The Camp at Cockeysville," *Baltimore Daily Exchange*, April 22, 1861, 1.

38. "Movements of Troops," *Washington Evening Star*, April 23, 1861.

39. "Pennsylvania Troops in Maryland"; "The Pennsylvania Troops," *Baltimore Daily Exchange*, April 23, 1861; Wallace, *American Slaveholder's Rebellion*, 504–5.

40. *OR*, series 1, 2:773; Rowland, *Jefferson Davis*, 5:65; Crist and Dix, *Papers of Jefferson Davis*, 7:115.

41. Nicolay and Hay, *Abraham Lincoln*, 4:143–44.

42. *OR*, series 4, 1:233; *OR*, series 1, 53:152–54, 156–57, 159; Roman, *Military Operations*, 1:50–51; Dickert, *Kershaw's Brigade*, 33, 35–37.

43. *OR*, series 1, 2:773–74.

44. "Some War History," *Baltimore Sun*, December 7, 1901.

21. General Butler, the Belligerent Brigadier

1. Scharf, *History of Maryland*, 419; "Correspondence with Brigadier-Gen. B. F. Butler," *New York Times*, May 4, 1861. Hicks irked Butler by referring to Butler's militia soldiers as "Northern troops" in a telegram to Cameron on April 20. Butler chastised the governor: "They are not Northern troops; they are part of the whole militia of the United States, obeying the call of the President." *OR*, series 1, 2:589–90.

2. Parton, *Butler in New Orleans*, 82; Butler, *Butler's Book*, 195; "Correspondence with Brigadier-Gen." Hicks released almost all of his correspondence from those days, apparently in an attempt to set the record straight.

3. Butler, *Butler's Book*, 195.

4. Butler, *Butler's Book*, 196.

5. *OR*, series 1, 2:591.

6. Nicolay and Hay, *Abraham Lincoln*, 4:154; "Our Position," *Baltimore Sun*, April 24, 1861.

7. Seabrook, *Maryland's Great Part*, 36–37.

8. Winthrop, "New York Seventh Regiment."

9. Swinton, *Seventh Regiment*, 70, 72, 81; E. Clark, *Seventh Regiment*, 1:484.

10. Swinton, *Seventh Regiment*, 72–74, E. Clark, *Seventh Regiment*, 1:484–87.

11. E. Clark, *Seventh Regiment*, 1:484.

12. Winthrop, "New York Seventh Regiment."

13. Butler, *Butler's Book*, 198.

14. "Correspondence with Brig.-General B. F. Butler," *Baltimore Sun*, April 29, 1861; Swinton, *Seventh Regiment*, 86.

15. Butler, *Butler's Book*, 203.

16. Parton, *Butler in New Orleans*, 85.

17. Butler, *Butler's Book*, 199.

18. "The Route to Washington Menaced," *New York Times*, April 25, 1861.

19. Seabrook, *Maryland's Great Part*, 45.

20. E. Clark, *Seventh Regiment*, 1:486.

21. E. Clark, *Seventh Regiment*, 1:485–86.

22. Butler, *Butler's Book*, 199.

23. In his book Butler never identifies the Lefferts aide he repeatedly refers to as "Red Nose," but it was Col. Samuel Ryan Curtis, a West Point graduate and current member of Congress from Iowa who accompanied the Seventh Regiment from Philadelphia to Washington. Curtis later served as a successful brigadier general and commanded the victorious Union forces at the Battle of Pea Ridge in 1862. The Seventh's biographer William Swinton also cites a note on April 22 from Butler that seeks assistance and advice from Lefferts, Curtis, and another officer and that refers to Curtis by name. Emmons Clark, who also wrote a history of the regiment, says Curtis accompanied the Seventh from New York, not Philadelphia. Swinton, *Seventh Regiment*, 65, 86; E. Clark, *Seventh Regiment*, 2:5; Butler, *Butler's Book*, 198–99.

24. Parton, *Butler in New Orleans*, 85–86.

25. E. Clark, *Seventh Regiment*, 1:488.

26. OR, series 1, pt. 2, 51:1274; Butler, *Butler's Book*, 195.

27. OR, series 1, pt. 2, 51:1273–74; Parton, *Butler in New Orleans*, 83–84; Swinton, *Seventh Regiment*, 86–87; OR, series 1, 2:593; "Gov. Hicks and Gen. Butler," *Baltimore Sun*, April 29, 1861.

28. Swinton, *Seventh Regiment*, 92.

29. Wilkes, "71st Regiment," 98–100.

30. Charles Bowers Letters, Charles Bowers to Lydia Bowers.

31. Woodbury, *Narrative of the Campaign*, 12–14.

32. Bryan was killed in action at Port Hudson, Louisiana, June 14th, 1863; R. W. Clark, *Heroes of Albany*, 195.

33. Doty, *Third Annual Report*, 301–2; "Arrival of Troops in New York–the Albany Soldiers," *New York Herald*, April 24, 1861.

22. Stalled in Annapolis

1. Burlingame and Ettlinger, *Inside Lincoln's White House*, 9.

2. Townsend, *Anecdotes*, 20.

3. Burlingame and Ettlinger, *Inside Lincoln's White House*, 9.

4. Taft, *Diary*; NOAA, *Meteorological Observations*; Krick, *Civil War Weather*, 23.

5. Wood, *Elizabeth Lindsay Lomax*, 151.

6. Basler, Pratt, and Dunlap, *Collected Works*, 4:343.

7. Burlingame and Ettlinger, *Inside Lincoln's White House*, 8.

8. OR, series 3, 1:103.

9. Reasons and Patrick, "Jacob Dodson Rose to Meet West's Challenge," *Sacramento Bee*, November 10, 1968; Mars, "Jacob Dodson."

10. OR, series 3, 1:107.

11. OR, series 3, 1:133.

12. C. P. Stone, "Washington in March and April," 17.

13. *Thirty-First Annual Report*, 58; Library of Congress, "View of Washington"; "The Washington Railroad Depot," *Baltimore Sun*, August 1, 1851. The traffic numbers are from 1857, the closest year to 1861 where the annual report broke out passenger figures. The depot had opened just a decade earlier, in 1851. It was a light-red brick, stucco, and brownstone structure, built in the Italianate style and dominated by a 100-foot, four-sided clock tower. It was close to the Capitol, at the intersection of C Street and New Jersey Avenue, a location now within the Capitol grounds. The building faced New Jersey Avenue, with a 330-foot train shed extending diagonally from the back of the main hall toward the intersection of North Capital Street and D Street.

14. Sidings were sidetracks, usually at depots, where trains could be parked off the main lines for repairs, or to wait for a crew, or while express trains or priority trains from the opposite direction proceeded through.

15. C. P. Stone, "Washington in March and April," 17–21.

16. C. P. Stone, "Washington in March and April," 21–22; Townsend, *Anecdotes*, 19–21.

17. J. B. Jones, *Rebel War Clerk's Diary*, 26–27.

18. "The Capture of Washington," *Richmond Examiner*, April 23, 1861; Victor, *Southern Rebellion*, 2:90; Moore, *Rebellion Record*, 1:189.

19. Crist and Dix, *Papers of Jefferson Davis*, 7:117–18; Nicolay and Hay, *Abraham Lincoln*, 4:148–49.

20. OR, series 1, 1:775.

21. Settles, *John Bankhead Magruder*, 120.

22. To "carry the war into Africa" meant to take the fight into enemy territory.

23. Rowland, *Jefferson Davis*, 8:216.

24. OR, series 1, pt. 2, 51:35.

25. NOAA, *Meteorological Observations*.

26. Nicolay and Hay, *Abraham Lincoln*, 4:150.

27. Land Commissioner William Seabrook disputed that provisions were unavailable to the troops, citing several anecdotes where both food and transportation were provided to Butler's men. Seabrook, *Maryland's Great Part*, 29–30; E. Clark, *Seventh Regiment*, 1:487.

28. E. Clark, *Seventh Regiment*, 1:488.

29. Butler, *Butler's Book*, 200.

30. Hincks, *"Forty-Fifth Regiment,"* 13-14.

31. Hincks, *"Forty-Fifth Regiment,"* 15.

32. Butler, *Butler's Book*, 201-2.

33. Hincks, *"Forty-Fifth Regiment,"* 15.

34. Hincks believed Butler embellished his Civil War exploits for a campaign biography in preparation for an 1884 presidential run. He resented being omitted from the history of the rescue of the USS *Constitution*, which he led, and the occupation of the depot and the railroad, which he also led. He makes it glaringly direct that Butler wasn't even at the depot. Describing Parton's 1864 account, Hincks said in 1883 that General Butler "did not march to the depot with these companies. General Butler was at the naval academy a mile or two away. But why should I worry you with the details? Not one word in the page is correct" (Hincks, *"Forty-Fifth Regiment,"* 15, 16, 22). Nine years after Hincks published his report in 1883, Butler in 1892 recycled Parton's account in his own book, repeating practically verbatim this apparent fabrication intended to enhance his own role. "There are scores of witnesses now living who can testify to the truth or falsity of the statement I have made," Hincks added (Hincks, *"Forty-Fifth Regiment,"* 23). The claim that Butler wasn't at the depot is supported elsewhere, including a 1910 history of the "Minute Men of '61" and an extended contemporaneous dispatch from Butler himself, in which he tells Pennsylvania Militia and Federal Department of Pennsylvania general David Patterson on April 24, 1861, that he detailed two companies to take possession of the depot. *OR*, series 1, pt. 2, 51:1274; Nason, *Minute Men of '61*, 233; Hincks, *"Forty-Fifth Regiment,"* 15, 16, 22-23; Butler, *Butler's Book*, 202.

35. Hincks, *"Forty-Fifth Regiment,"* 16.

36. Ecelbarger, *Frederick W. Lander*, 91-92; Swinton, *Seventh Regiment*, 77, 80-81; E. Clark, *Seventh Regiment* 1:490.

37. Swinton, *Seventh Regiment*, 77-78.

38. Swinton, *Seventh Regiment*, 79.

39. Swinton, *Seventh Regiment*, 79-80; "The Route to Washington Menaced," *New York Times*, April 25, 1861.

40. Woodbury, *Narrative of the Campaign*, 14-15.

41. Wilkes, "71st Regiment," 100-104; Moore, *Rebellion Record*, 1:156.

42. Woodbury, *Narrative of the Campaign*, 14-15; Wilkes, "71st Regiment," 100-104.

43. O'Brien, "March of the Seventh," 1:152.

44. Parton, *Butler in New Orleans*, 87.

23. New York's Irish Join the Fight

1. Cavanagh, *Thomas Francis Meagher*, 352.

2. During the Civil War, Meagher raised troops for the Irish Brigade and rose to the rank of Union brigadier general, seeing combat during the battles of the Seven Days, Antietam, and Fredericksburg.

3. Cavanagh, *Thomas Francis Meagher*, 352; "Welcome to the Prince," *New York Times*, October 12, 1860.

4. Cavanagh, *Thomas Francis Meagher*, 353–54; "Welcome to the Prince."

5. "The Gallant Sixty-Ninth—Letter from Col. Corcoran," *Boston Pilot*, May 4, 1861.

6. Doty, *Third Annual Report*, 305.

7. Cavanagh, *Thomas Francis Meagher*, 369–70; Bruce, *Harp and the Eagle*, 58.

8. "Immense Turnout of Our Irish Citizens," *New York Herald*, April 24, 1861.

9. "The Sixty-Ninth Regiment," *New York Herald*, April 24, 1861, 6; "Off for the War—Departure of Two New-York City Regiments," *New York Times*, April 24, 1861.

10. "Departure of the Eighth Regiment," *New York Herald*, April 24, 1861.

11. Abel Smith was killed on October 18, 1861, in a railroad accident on his way to Whitehall, New York, to muster in recruits for his regiment. De Mandeville, *History of the 13th*, 31.

12. Doty, *Third Annual Report*, 297; "Departure of the Thirteenth Regiment of Brooklyn," *New York Herald*, April 25, 1861, 8.

24. The March of the Seventh and Eighth Regiments

1. OR, series 1, pt. 2, 51:1272–73; Hincks, *"Forty-Fifth Regiment,"* 17–18; Parton, *Butler in New Orleans*, 91. Hincks and Parton only offer partial quotes from the verbatim transcript. In the full order, the plan was for the main body of the Eighth to go first, followed by the Seventh. Butler also called for the two regiments to consolidate "as rapidly as possible."

2. Throughout the two-day march, the engine would shuttle up and down the tracks as needed. When the men of the Seventh Regiment advance companies disembarked, it returned to get men from the Eight Regiment's advance guard who were still at the depot. Then it returned to Annapolis for baggage. When the locomotive was gone, the men would haul the flat-bed cars themselves using dragropes. OR, series 1, pt. 2, 51:1272–73; Swinton, *Seventh Regiment*, 97.

3. Swinton, *Seventh Regiment*, 94–95; E. Clark, *Second Company*, 1:304–5; E. Clark, *Seventh Regiment*, 1:490–91.

4. Swinton, *Seventh Regiment*, 96.

5. E. Clark, *Second Company*, 1:304–5.

6. Moore, *Rebellion Record*, 1:152.

7. E. Clark, *Second Company*, 1:304–5.

8. E. Clark, *Second Company*, 1:305.

9. Winthrop, "New York Seventh Regiment."

10. Swinton, *Seventh Regiment*, 95.

11. Winthrop, "New York Seventh Regiment"; E. Clark, *Seventh Regiment*, 1:493–94.

12. E. Clark, *Second Company*, 1:305.

13. E. Clark, *Second Company*, 1:305.

14. Swinton, *Seventh Regiment*, 100; E. Clark, *Seventh Regiment*, 1:494; Patrick, *In Her Hour*, 34.

15. Winthrop, "New York Seventh Regiment."

16. Moore, *Rebellion Record*, 1:153.

17. Swinton, *Seventh Regiment*, 101; E. Clark, *Second Company*, 1:307.

18. Swinton, *Seventh Regiment*, 105.

19. Swinton, *Seventh Regiment*, 105; Winthrop, "New York Seventh Regiment"; Moore, *Rebellion Record*, 1:153.

20. Roe, *Fifth Regiment Massachusetts*, 30–32.

21. Wilkes, "71st Regiment," 105–6.

22. Moore, *Rebellion Record*, 1:189.

23. Moore, *Rebellion Record*, 1:189.

24. Like South Carolina governor Francis Pickens a few days earlier, Slidell hedged in his note to Davis: "It is difficult to exaggerate the importance of the prestige of early successes in a struggle like this & the converse of the proposition is equally true." Crist and Dix, *Papers of Jefferson Davis*, 7:122.

25. Reese, *Virginia Secession Convention*, 4:457–58, 493.

26. Reese, *Virginia Secession Convention*, 4:420.

27. Reese, *Virginia Secession Convention*, 4:421–25.

28. OR, series 1, 2:774–75.

29. OR, series 1, 2:776–77.

30. OR, series 1, 2:777.

31. OR, series 1, 2:777–78.

32. Freeman, *R. E. Lee*, 1:476–77.

33. "Some War History," *Baltimore Sun*, December 7, 1901.

34. W. H. Russell, *My Diary*, 136.

35. W. H. Russell, *My Diary*, 137.

36. NOAA, *Meteorological Observations*; Krick, *Civil War Weather*, 23.

37. Burlingame and Ettlinger, *Inside Lincoln's White House*, 11.

38. Taft, *Diary*.

39. Burlingame and Ettlinger, *Inside Lincoln's White House*, 11.

40. Nicolay and Hay changed this quote in their 1890 history of Lincoln. In Hay's contemporaneous diary entry, Lincoln says, "Rhode Island is not known in our geography any longer." In the later book, the line becomes "Rhode Island is another," following the sentence "The Seventh Regiment is a myth"; Nicolay and Hay, *Abraham Lincoln*, 4:153; Burlingame and Ettlinger, *Inside Lincoln's White House*, 11.

41. Villard, *Memoirs of Henry Villard*, 1:169–70.

42. Basler, Pratt, and Dunlap, *Collected Works*, 4:343.

43. Crist and Dix, *Papers of Jefferson Davis*, 7:137.

25. Washington Is Saved

1. O'Brien, "March of the Seventh," 1:233.

2. Swinton, *Seventh Regiment*, 108; E. Clark, *Seventh Regiment*, 1:496.

3. E. Clark, *Seventh Regiment*, 1:496.

4. Duncan, *Blue-Eyed Child*, 81.

5. E. Clark, *Second Company*, 1:309.

6. Wilkes, "71st Regiment," 110.

7. Wilkes, "71st Regiment," 113.

8. E. Clark, *Second Company*, 1:309; Swinton, *Seventh Regiment*, 150.

9. Duncan, *Blue-Eyed Child*, 81–82.

10. Munroe, commander of the Eighth Massachusetts, was nearly invisible through this entire campaign, completely overshadowed by Butler. He resigned his commission just three weeks later, on May 12. A reference in Basler, Pratt, and Dunlap's *The Collected Works of Abraham Lincoln* indicates that Munroe resigned on May 5 because of his age. "Resigned," *Philadelphia Inquirer*, May 14, 1861; Schouler, *History of Massachusetts*, 105–6; Basler, Pratt, and Dunlap, *Collected Works*, 4:346.

11. OR, series 1, pt. 2, 51:1274; OR, series 1, 2:600.

12. Long and Wright, *Memoirs*, 102; Lee Family Papers.

13. At this exact hour, the Seventh New York Regiment, followed by the Eighth Massachusetts, was eight or nine miles from Annapolis Junction, slogging through the woods, barely awake, and repairing the tracks as it advanced.

14. Croffut and Morris, *History of Connecticut*, 840–41.

15. Burlingame and Ettlinger, *Inside Lincoln's White House*, 11.

16. G. W. Smith, "Critical Moment for Washington," 113.

17. Croffut and Morris, *History of Connecticut*, 841.

18. G. W. Smith, "Critical Moment for Washington," 113.

19. "The Trip of the Seventh and Other Regiments through Maryland," *New York Herald*, April 28, 1861.

20. Duncan, *Blue-Eyed Child*, 81–82.

21. Swinton, *Seventh Regiment*, 112, 113.

22. Villard, *Memoirs of Henry Villard*, 1:170; Taft, *Diary*.

23. Nicolay and Hay, *Abraham Lincoln*, 4:156–57.

24. Villard, *Memoirs of Henry Villard*, 1:169–70.

25. Swinton, *Seventh Regiment*, 114.

26. Nicolay and Hay, *Abraham Lincoln*, 4:157.

26. The Aftermath

1. E. Clark, *Seventh Regiment*, 2:5.

2. Roe, *Fifth Regiment Massachusetts*, 36.

3. A waterback was a type of hot-water heater—a system of tubes placed in or near the firebox of an oven that connected to a water tank and was used to heat and store water.

4. Scrymser, "President Lincoln's Kitchen," 42–43.

5. Stewart, "President Lincoln's Sermon," 44–46.

6. Charles Bowers Letters, Charles Bowers to Lydia Bowers; Roe, *Fifth Regiment Massachusetts*, 32.

7. OR, series 1, pt. 2, 51:47.

8. OR, series 1, 2:779; OR, series 1, pt. 2, 51:34–35.

9. "Journal of the Proceedings," 430:21–22; Moore, *Rebellion Record*, 1:175–76; "Secession Killed in the Legislature," *New York Times*, April 30, 1861.

10. OR, series 1, pt. 1, sec. 1, 51:344.

11. Doty, *Third Annual Report*, 286.

12. "South Carolina Troops at Richmond," *Charleston Mercury*, April 25, 1861; "Arrival of Troops from South Carolina," *Charleston Mercury*, April 27, 1861; "South Carolina Volunteers," *Richmond Enquirer*, April 27, 1861; "Important from Charleston," *New York Herald*, April 27, 1861, 1; "Troops for Virginia," *Richmond Dispatch*, April 24, 1861; "Military Movements," *Richmond Dispatch*, April 25, 1861; "From Petersburg," *Richmond Dispatch*, April 26 and 29, 1861. The *Herald* reported that only part of the First South Carolina was in Richmond—only the part that agreed to fight in Virginia, about 600 men—and that 250 Georgia troops were in Norfolk.

13. Fry, "McDowell's Advance," 1:168–69.

14. Villard, *Memoirs of Henry Villard*, 1:167.

15. Evans, *Confederate Military History*, 1:394–95; Gates, *Ulster Guard*, 17; Rowland, *Jefferson Davis*, 5:65; Crist and Dix, *Papers of Jefferson Davis*, 7:116.

16. W. H. Russell, *My Diary*, 136.

17. OR, series 3, 1:69; for Missouri, see OR, series 3, 5:607–8.

18. OR, series 3, 1:161; OR, series 3, 1:117–21. The first indication of this new policy came as early as April 26, when Cameron wrote separate messages to Indiana governor Oliver P. Morton, Connecticut governor William Buckingham, Iowa governor Samuel J. Kirkwood, Michigan governor Austin Blair, and New Jersey governor Charles S. Olden, telling them that no additional three-month troops would be accepted but that three-year volunteers would be.

19. In all, twenty-four states received requisitions. Four subsequently seceded: Virginia, North Carolina, Arkansas, and Tennessee (OR, series 3, 1:69). In two other instances, Northern troops briefly moved beyond their borders, both far from Washington. On April 24, U.S. Army captain James H. Stokes carried out a daring raid that saved most of the weapons in the St. Louis Arsenal. And on April 25 and 26, Illinois governor Richard Yates ordered state militia troops then converging at Cairo, Illinois, to seize two steamers loaded with arms and munitions and headed for Tennessee. Reece, *Report of the Adjutant General*, 1:246–48; Nicolay and Hay, *Abraham Lincoln*, 4:198–200.

20. Dyer, *Compendium of the War*, pt. 3 (page references for troop departures are as follows: Connecticut, 1008; Delaware, 1016; Indiana, 1119–22; Illinois, 1046–48; Iowa, 1164; Kentucky, 1197; Maine, 1219; Maryland, 1231; Michigan, 1281; Minnesota, 1296; Missouri, 1321; New Hampshire, 1347; New Jersey, 1356–58; Vermont, 1649; Wisconsin, 1673); General Assembly, *Official Roster*, 1:1, 19; Reid, *Ohio in the War*, 2:15–80; "Report of Col. Geo. W. McCook and James M. Brown, Agents for Furnishing the First and Second Ohio Regiments with Subsistence Clothing and Equipments, to the Governor," *Cadiz Sentinel*, June 19, 1861.

21. Basler, Pratt, and Dunlap, *Collected Works*, 4:347.

22. OR, series 2, 1:620–25.

23. OR, series 2, 1:667–75, 688; F. K. Howard, *Fourteen Months*, 8–9; Anonymous, *"An Eye-Witness,"* 12–13.

24. "The United States Circuit Court," *Baltimore Sun*, November 7, 1861. White, "Forty-Seven Eyewitness Accounts," 70–93 (page 74 for White's reference to Konig, and page 76 for White's notation on the dismissals).

25. Evans, *Confederate Military History*, 2:27–28; White, "Forty-Seven Eyewitness Accounts," 79, 91; Tucker, *Isaac Ridgeway Trimble*, 92.

26. OR, series 1, 42:1118.

27. OR, series 2, 1:748.

28. Radcliffe, "Governor Thomas H. Hicks," 19:71.

29. "Special Message of the Governor of Maryland," *Baltimore Sun*, April 29, 1861.

30. "Journal of the Proceedings," 429:8–9; "Special Session of the General Assembly of Maryland," *Baltimore Sun*, April 29, 1861.

31. Radcliffe, "Governor Thomas H. Hicks," 19:74, 85–86.

32. Baker, *Politics of Continuity*, 54.

33. E. D. Adams, *Great Britain*, 1:61–62.

34. Foreman, *World on Fire*, 91; E. D. Adams, *Great Britain*, 1:90.

35. Foreman, *World on Fire*, 91; E. D. Adams, *Great Britain*, 1:83.

36. E. D. Adams, *Great Britain*, 1:94; Foreman, *World on Fire*, 92–93.

37. E. D. Adams, *Great Britain*, 1:75.

38. Basler, Pratt, and Dunlap, *Collected Works*, 4:344.

39. Scharf, *History of Maryland*, 426.

40. Nicolay and Hay, *Abraham Lincoln*, 4:255.

41. *Harper's Weekly* 5, no. 231 (June 1, 1861): 1.

42. W. H. Russell, *My Diary*, 422.

43. Parton, *Butler in New Orleans*, 71; Butler, *Butler's Book*, 182.

44. Donald, *Lincoln*, 299.

45. E. Clark, *Seventh Regiment*, 1:478; Swinton, *Seventh Regiment*, 57; OR, series 1, 2:583.

46. Herbert, *Popular History*, 93.

47. OR, series 1, 2:598.

48. Schouler, *History of Massachusetts*, 60–61; Trist, "Statement," 35, 37–38.

49. Schouler, *History of Massachusetts*, 100–101. Schouler called Butler's claim of opening the route to Annapolis "inaccurate and obscure."

50. OR, series 1, pt. 1, sec. 2, 51:1273; Patrick, *In Her Hour*, 70–71.

51. Dennett, *Diaries of John Hay*, 19–20; Hay, *Letters*, 1:31; Basler, Pratt, and Dunlap, *Collected Works*, 4:439–40.

Abbreviations

OR   Scott, Robert N., Fred C. Ainsworth, Joseph W. Kirkley, George B. Davis, and Leslie J. Perry, eds. *The War of the Rebellion: The Official Records of the Union and Confederate Armies*

ORN   *Official Records of the Union and Confederate Navies in the War of the Rebellion*

BIBLIOGRAPHY

Archives and Manuscript Collections

Abraham Lincoln Papers. Library of Congress, Manuscript Division, Washington DC. https://www.loc.gov/collections/abraham-lincoln-papers/about-this-collection/.

The Avalon Project. "First Inaugural Address of Abraham Lincoln Monday, March 4, 1861." Documents in Law, History and Diplomacy. Lillian Goldman Law Library, Yale Law School, New Haven CT. Accessed November 24, 2022. https://avalon.law.yale.edu/19th_century/lincoln1.asp.

Bowers, Charles. Letters. "Letter from Charles Bowers to Lydia Bowers, 28 April 1861." Massachusetts Historical Society, Collections Online. Accessed November 24, 2022. http://www.masshist.org/database/viewer.php?item_id=2057&pid=25.

Dyer, Elisha. *Annual Report of the Adjutant General of the State of Rhode Island and Providence Plantations for the Year 1865.* Vol. 1. Providence RI: E. L. Freeman, 1893. https://babel.hathitrust.org/cgi/pt?id=hvd.hx4u2b&view=1up&seq=5&skin=2021.

Evans, George W. "The Militia of the District of Columbia." Records of the Columbia Historical Society. Vol. 28. Washington DC: 1926.

Hale, Senator John P. "Surrender and Destruction of Navy Yards, Etc." Reports of the Committees of the Senate of the United States for the Second Session of the Thirty-Seventh Congress, 1861–62. Accessed 2020. https://books.google.com/books?id=VaUFAAAAQAAJ&pg=PA57&lpg=PA57&dq=the+committee+of+the+Senate+%22to+inquire+into+the+circumstances+attending+the+destruction+of+the+property+of+the+United+States+at+the+armory+at+Harper%27s+Ferry,%22&source=bl&ots=avCcsVq9is&sig=ACfU3U1h1ZhsJ3o8zU8dZ-hIaUze2s7WSw&hl=en&sa=X&ved=2ahUKEwjMusq7wLHpAhVEZ80KHWYPCsgQ6AEwAXoECAYQAQ#v=onepage&q&f=false.

Harrington, George R. Papers. George Harrington Memo. Huntington Library, Manuscript Collections, San Marino CA.

Harrington, George R. "President Lincoln and His Cabinet: Inside Glimpses." Unpublished handwritten manuscript. Missouri History Museum, Saint Louis Civil War Project. Accessed November 24, 2022. http://cdm16795.contentdm.oclc .org/cdm/ref/collection/CivilWar/id/799.

Hincks, Edward Winslow. *"The Forty-Fifth Regiment Massachusetts Volunteer Militia—Nine Month's Men: And the Eighth Regiment at Annapolis in 1861." Extracts from Speech at Peabody, November 5, 1883.* Cambridge MA: William M. Wessler, 1883.

Howard, Mark. Papers. Letter from William Faxon to Mark Howard, May 12, 1862. Box 5, folder 13. Connecticut Historical Society. Hartford CT.

"Journal of the Proceedings of the House of Delegates, in Extra Session, April, May, June 1861." Archives of Maryland, vol. 429–430. Frederick MD: Elihu S. Riley, 1861.

Knox, William. "President Lincoln's Favorite Poem." Library of Congress, Alfred Whital Stern Collection of Lincolniana, Stern catalog 4817, Portfolio 7, no. 11. A. W. Auner, Song Publisher, Philadelphia PA, n. d.

Lee Family Papers. Box 6, M2009.253. Archives of the Robert E. Lee Memorial Foundation. Lee Family Digital Archive. Jessie Ball duPont Library, Stratford Hall, Stratford VA. Accessed 2021. https://leefamilyarchive.org/9-family-papers/117 -robert-e-lee-to-cassius-lee-1861-april-25.

Library of Congress. "About the American. [volume] (Towsontown, Md.) 1862–1864." Chronicling America, Historic American Newspapers. Accessed 2020. https:// chroniclingamerica.loc.gov/lccn/sn83016402/.

Library of Congress. "About the Baltimore County Union. [volume] (Towsontown, Md.) 1865–1909." Chronicling America, Historic American Newspapers. Accessed 2020. https://chroniclingamerica.loc.gov/lccn/sn83016368/.

Library of Congress. "Salmon P. Chase Papers: General Correspondence, 1810–1898; 1861; Apr. 12–30." Manuscript/Mixed Material. 1861. https://www.loc.gov/item/ mss156100102/.

Library of Congress Geography and Map Division. "E. Sachse, & Co.'s Bird's Eye View of the City of Baltimore, 1869." Map. Baltimore MD, 1870. https://www.loc .gov/item/75694535/.

Library of Congress Prints and Photographs Division. "View of Washington/Drawn from Nature and on Stone by E. Sachse, Lith. and Print in Colors by E. Sachse & Comp." Photograph. Baltimore, ca. 1852. https://www.loc.gov/item/98515951.

"Lunsford L. Lomax to George B. Bayard." House Divided: The Civil War Research Engine at Dickinson College. Washington DC, April 21, 1861. https://hd .housedivided.dickinson.edu/node/42809.

Mars, Shaun Michael. "Jacob Dodson (1825–?)." Blackpast.org, January 21, 2007. https://www.blackpast.org/african-american-history/dodson-jacob-1825/.

Marshall, Jesse Ames, ed. *Private and Official Correspondence of Gen. Benjamin F. Butler during the Period of the Civil War.* Vol. 1. Norwood, Massachusetts: Plimpton (Privately Issued), 1917.

National Archives and Records Administration. "Grand Jury of the Circuit Court of the United States in Baltimore, Testimony from September 4, 1861–October 12, 1861." Philadelphia PA.

National Oceanic and Atmospheric Administration. *Meteorological Observations, April 1861,* NOAA Central Library, Silver Spring MD.

New York State Military Museum and Veterans Research Center. *Annual Reports of the Adjutant General.* Saratoga Springs NY, 1858–61.

Northern Central Railway. "Seventh Annual Report of the President and Directors of the Northern Central Railway Co. For the Year 1861." Baltimore MD, 1862. Accessed 2022. https://books.google.com/books?id=0zYAAQAAIAAJ&pg=PA28&lpg= PA28&dq=1861+Annual+Report+for+the+Northern+Central+Railroad&source =bl&ots=dh8SFlj2Io&sig=ACfU3u1ipFc97IImsbXsw3KOhArvYDvZmw&hl=en &sa=X&ved=2ahUKEwiu5v3wxfLpAhXdAZ0JHdopD8AQ6AEwC3oECAoQAQ #v=onepage&q&f=false.

"Proceedings of the First Branch City Council of Baltimore at the Session of 1900–1901." Baltimore MD City Council. First Branch. Accessed 2020. https:// catalog.hathitrust.org/Record/011483334/Cite.

Ragsdale, Bruce A. Ex parte Merryman *and Debates on Civil Liberties during the Civil War.* In "Federal Trials and Great Debates in United States History." Project, Federal Judicial Center. Federal Judicial History Office, 2007. https://www .fjc.gov/sites/default/files/trials/merryman.pdf.

"Report of Colonel A. E. Burnside, Commanding the First Rhode Island Regiment, to His Excellency Gov. Sprague, May 23, 1861." In *Acts and Resolves of the General Assembly of the State of Rhode Island and Providence Plantations Passed at the January Session 1861.* Providence RI: A. Crawford Greene, 1861.

Sachse, E. "Bird's Eye View of the City of Annapolis, MD." Miriam and Ira D. Wallach Division of Art. Prints and Photographs, Print Collection. New York Public Library Digital Collections. 1864. https://digitalcollections.nypl.org/items/ 510d47d9-7dce-a3d9-e040-e00a18064a99.

Savage, Richard Henry. "Response of Col. Richard Henry Savage." *Report of the Annual Reunion and Dinner of the Old Guard Association of the Twelfth Regiment, N.G.S.N.Y., Saturday, April 21st, 1894.* New York: Old Guard Association, 1894. https://archive.org/details/reportannualreun01newy/page/n9/mode/2up.

Supreme Council for the Northern Masonic Jurisdiction. *Proceedings of the Supreme Council in Annual Meeting Held in City of Philadelphia, 1913.* Library of the University of Michigan. https://babel.hathitrust.org/cgi/pt?id=mdp.39015068193591 &view=1up&seq=1&skin=2021. Accessed 2020 and 2021, November 2022.

Taft, Horatio Nelson. *Washington during the Civil War: The Diary of Horatio Nelson Taft, 1861–1865.* Manuscript/Mixed Material, Library of Congress, Washington DC. Accessed 2020, 2021, 2022. https://www.loc.gov/item/mtaft000001/.

Thirty-First Annual Report of the President and Directors to the Stockholders of Baltimore & Ohio Railroad Company. Baltimore: John Murphy, 1857.

Trimble, Isaac. Papers. "Statement on April 19th, 1861, Riot and Events Thereafter." H. Furlong Baldwin Library, Maryland Historical Society, Baltimore MD.

Trist, Nicholas P. "Statement of Nicholas P. Trist, Paymaster of the Philadelphia, Wilmington & Baltimore Railroad." In *Letter of the President of the Philadelphia, Wilmington & Baltimore Railroad Company to the Secretary of War*, edited by Samuel Felton, 35–40. Washington DC: Henry Polkinhorn, 1862.

U.S. Department of the Interior. "President Street Station." National Register of Historic Places Registration Form. National Park Service. August 6, 1992. https://mht.maryland.gov/secure/medusa/PDF/NR_PDFS/NR-1103.pdf.

———. "Tredegar Iron Works." National Register of Historic Places Inventory Nomination Form. National Park Service. 1969–70. https://www.dhr.virginia.gov/wp-content/uploads/2018/04/127-0186_Tredegar_Iron_Works_1976_Nomination_NHL.pdf.

Published Works

Aaron, Daniel. "The Greatest Diarist." *American Heritage* 39, no. 2 (March 1988): 94–101. https://www.americanheritage.com/greatest-diarist.

Adams, Ephraim Douglas. *Great Britain and the American Civil War*. Vol. 1. New York: Longmans, Green, 1925.

Adams, Henry. *The Education of Henry Adams*. Boston: Houghton Mifflin, 1918.

Allman, William G. "The Lincoln Bedroom: Refurbishing a Famous White House Room." *White House History*, no. 25 (Spring 2009): White House Historical Association. https://www.whitehousehistory.org/the-lincoln-bedroom-refurbishing-a-famous-white-house-room.

Andrew, John. *An Address on the Occasion of Dedicating the Monument to Ladd and Whitney*. Speech, June 17, 1865, Lowell MA. Boston: Wright & Potter, 1865.

Andrews, Matthew Page. "History of Baltimore from 1850 to the Close of the Civil War." In *Baltimore: Its History and Its People*, edited by Clayton Coleman Hall, 151–237. New York: Lewis Historical, 1912.

Annual Report of the Adjutant General. State of New York, New York State Military Museum and Veterans Research Center, Saratoga Springs, February 2, 1858. Printed by C. Van Benthuysen.

Annual Report of the Adjutant General. State of New York, New York State Military Museum and Veterans Research Center, Saratoga Springs, March 12, 1860. Printed by C. Van Benthuysen.

Annual Report of the Adjutant General. State of New York, New York State Military Museum and Veterans Research Center, Saratoga Springs, January 8, 1861. Printed by C. Van Benthuysen.

Anonymous. *"An Eye-Witness," The Bastille in America; or, Democratic Absolutism*. London: Robert Hardwicke, 1861.

Baker, Jean. *The Politics of Continuity, Maryland Political Parties from 1858 to 1870*. Baltimore: Johns Hopkins University Press, 1973.

Barbee, David Rankin. "Lincoln, Chase, and the Rev. Dr. Richard Fuller." *Maryland Historical Magazine* 46, no. 2 (June 1951): 108–23.

Basler, Roy P. ed., and Marion Dolores Pratt and Lloyd A. Dunlap, asst. eds. *The Collected Works of Abraham Lincoln.* Vols. 4, 5, and 8. New Brunswick NJ: Rutgers University Press, 1953.

Bates, David Homer. *Lincoln in the Telegraph Office 1861–1866.* New York: Century, 1907.

Bates, Samuel. *History of Pennsylvania Volunteers, 1861–5.* Vol. 1. Harrisburg PA: B. Singerly, 1869.

Bayne, Julia Taft. *Tad Lincoln's Father.* Boston: Little, Brown, 1931.

Beale, Edward K., ed. *The Diary of Edward Bates, 1859–1866.* Washington DC: United States Government Printing Office, 1933.

Berardino, Mike. "Mike Tyson Explains One of His Most Famous Quotes." *South Florida Sun-Sentinel*, November 8, 2012. https://www.sun-sentinel.com/sports/fl-xpm-2012-11-09-sfl-mike-tyson-explains-one-of-his-most-famous-quotes -20121109-story.html.

Bilby, Joseph G., and William C. Goble. *Remember You Are Jerseymen!* Hightstown NJ: Longstreet House, 1998.

Boney, Nash, Rafia Zafar, and Richard Hume, eds. *God Made Man, Man Made the Slave: The Autobiography of George Teamoh.* Macon GA: Mercer University Press, 1990.

Booth, George Wilson. *Personal Reminiscences of a Maryland Soldier in the War between the States, 1861–1865.* Baltimore: Fleet, McGinley, 1898.

Brooks, Noah. *Washington in Lincoln's Time.* New York: Century, 1896.

Brown, George William. *Baltimore and the Nineteenth of April, 1861, a Study of the War.* Baltimore: Johns Hopkins University, 1887.

Bruce, Susannah Ural. *The Harp and the Eagle: Irish-American Volunteers and the Union Army, 1861–1865.* New York: New York University Press, 2006.

Burlingame, Michael, ed. *Inside the White House in War Times: Memoirs and Reports of Lincoln's Secretary, William O. Stoddard.* Lincoln: University of Nebraska Press, 2000.

———. *An Oral History of Abraham Lincoln John G. Nicolay's Interviews and Essays.* Carbondale: Southern Illinois University Press, 1996.

———. *With Lincoln in the White House: Letters, Memoranda, and Other Writings of John G. Nicolay, 1860–1865.* Carbondale: Southern Illinois University Press, 2000.

Burlingame, Michael, and John R. Turner Ettlinger, eds. *Inside Lincoln's White House: The Complete Civil War Diary of John Hay.* Carbondale: Southern Illinois University Press, 1997.

Butler, Benjamin F. *Autobiography and Personal Reminiscences of Major-General Benj. F. Butler: Butler's Book.* Boston: A. M. Thayer, 1892.

Butterfield, Julia Lorrilard, ed. *A Biographical Memorial of General Daniel Butterfield.* New York: Grafton, 1904.

Cannon, Arthur. *Investigation into the Alleged Official Misconduct of the Late Super-intendent of the Philadelphia, Wilmington and Baltimore Railroad Co.* Vol. 1. Philadelphia: James H. Bryson, 1854.

Catton, William B. "The Baltimore Business Community and the Secession Crisis, 1860–1861." Master's thesis, University of Maryland, 1952. Digital Repository. https://drum.lib.umd.edu/handle/1903/16838?show=full.

Cavanagh, Michael. *Memoirs of Thomas Francis Meagher*. Worcester MA: Messenger, 1892.

Chittenden, L. E. *Recollections of President Lincoln and His Administration*. New York: Harper & Brothers, 1904.

Clark, Emmons. *History of the Second Company of the Seventh Regiment*. Vol. 1. New York: J. G. Gregory, 1864.

——. *History of the Seventh Regiment of New York, 1806–1889*. Vols. 1 and 2. New York: Seventh Regiment, 1890.

Clark, Rufus W. *The Heroes of Albany a Memorial of the Martyrs of the City and County of Albany Who Sacrificed Their Lives during the Late War in Defence of Our Nation, 1861–1865*. Albany NY: S. R. Gray, 1866.

Condit, Uzal W. *The History of Easton, Penn'a from the Earliest Times to the Present, 1739–1885*. Easton: George W. West, 1885.

Cooper, William J., Jr. *Jefferson Davis, American*. New York: Vintage, 2000.

Cox, Jacob D. *Military Reminiscences of the Civil War*. New York: Charles Scribner's Sons, 1900.

Crawford, Samuel Wylie. *The Genesis of the Civil War: The Story of Sumter*. New York: Charles L. Webster, 1887.

Crist, Lynda Lasswell, and Mary Seaton Dix, eds. *The Papers of Jefferson Davis*. Vol. 7. Baton Rouge: Louisiana State University Press, 1992.

Croffut, William Augustus. *An American Procession, 1855–1914, a Personal Chronicle of Famous Men*. Boston: Little, Brown, 1931.

Croffut, William Augustus, and John M. Morris. *The Military and Civil History of Connecticut during the War of 1861–1865*. New York: Ledyard Bill, 1868.

Cuthbert, J. H. *Life of Richard Fuller*. New York: D. D. Sheldon, 1878.

Dabney, Virginius. *Richmond, the Story of a City*. 1976. Reprint, Charlottesville: University Press of Virginia, 1990.

Dahlgren, Madeleine Vinton. *Memoir of John A. Dahlgren, Rear-Admiral United States Navy*. Boston: James R. Osgood, 1882.

Dare, Charles P. *Philadelphia, Wilmington and Baltimore Rail Road Guide*. Philadelphia: Fitzgibbon & Van Ness, 1856.

Davis, Damani. "Slavery and Emancipation in the Nation's Capital." *Prologue Magazine* 42, no. 1 (Spring 2010). https://www.archives.gov/publications/prologue/2010/spring/dcslavery.html.

DeBow, J. D. B. *The Seventh Census of the United States: 1850*. Washington DC: Robert Armstrong, 1853. https://www2.census.gov/library/publications/decennial/1850/1850a/1850a-06.pdf.

De Mandeville, James, ed. *History of the 13th Regiment, N.G., S.N.Y.* Brooklyn NY: James De Mandeville, 1894, 31.

Dennett, Tyler. *Lincoln and the Civil War in the Diaries of John Hay.* New York: Dodd, Mead, 1939.

Derby, George, and James Terry White. *The National Cyclopaeda of American Biography.* Vol. 10. New York: James T. White, 1900.

Dickert, D. Augustus. *History of Kershaw's Brigade, with Complete Roll of Companies, Biographical Sketches, Anecdotes, Etc.* Newberry SC: Elbert H. Aull, 1899.

Dix, Morgan, ed. *Memoirs of John Adams Dix, Compiled by His Son Morgan Dix.* Vol. 2. New York: Harper & Brothers, 1883.

Donald, David Herbert. *Lincoln.* New York: Touchstone, 1995.

———. *We Are Lincoln Men: Abraham Lincoln and His Friends.* New York: Simon & Schuster, 2003.

Doty, Lockwood. *Third Annual Report of the Bureau of Military Record State of New York.* Albany NY: C. Wendell, 1866.

Doubleday, Abner. "From Moultrie to Sumter." In *Battles and Leaders of the Civil War*, edited by Robert Underwood Johnson and Clarence Clough Buel 40–49. Vol. 1. New York: Century, 1887.

———. *Reminiscences of Forts Sumter and Moultrie in 1860–'61.* New York: Harper & Brothers, 1876.

Dudley, William S. *Going South—U.S. Navy Officer Resignations & Dismissals on the Eve of the Civil War.* Washington DC: Naval History and Heritage Command, Naval Historical Foundation, 1981.

Dunaway, Wayland Fuller. *History of the James River and Kanawha Company.* New York: Columbia University, 1922.

Duncan, Russell, ed. *Blue-Eyed Child of Fortune: The Civil War Letters of Robert Gould Shaw.* Athens: University of Georgia Press, 1992.

Dyer, Frederick H. *A Compendium of the War of the Rebellion.* Des Moines IA: Dyer, 1908.

Ecelbarger, Gary L. *Frederick W. Lander: The Great Natural American Soldier.* Baton Rouge: Louisiana State University Press, 2000.

Eisenhower, John S. D. *Agent of Destiny: The Life and Times of Winfield Scott.* Norman: University of Oklahoma Press, 1997.

Ellis, John B. *The Sights and Secrets of the National Capital: A Work Descriptive of Washington City in All Its Various Phases.* Chicago: United States Publishing, 1869.

Fernald, Granville. *The Story of the First Defenders.* Washington DC: Clarence E. Davis, 1892.

Foreman, Amanda. *A World on Fire: Britain's Crucial Role in the American Civil War.* New York: Random House, 2010.

Freehling, William W., and Craig M. Simpson, eds. *Showdown in Virginia: The 1861 Convention and the Fate of the Union.* Charlottesville: University of Virginia Press, 2010.

Freeman, Douglas Southall. *R. E. Lee: A Biography*. Vol. 1. New York: Scribner's Sons, 1934.

Frost, Mrs. J. Blakeslee, ed. *The Rebellion in the United States (or the War of 1861)*. Boston: Degen, Estes & Priest, 1862.

Fry, James B. "McDowell's Advance to Bull Run." In *Battles and Leaders of the Civil War*, edited by Robert Underwood Johnson and Clarence Clough Buel. Vol. 1, 168–69. New York: Century, 1884–87.

Fuller, Richard, and Francis Wayland. *Domestic Slavery Considered as a Scriptural Institution*. New York: Lewis Colby, 1845.

Gallagher, Gary W. *Lee and His Generals in War and Memory*. Baton Rouge: Louisiana State University Press, 1998.

Gates, Theodore B. *The Ulster Guard 20th New York State Militia and the War of the Rebellion*. New York: Benjamin Tyrrel, 1879.

General Assembly. *Official Roster of the Soldiers of the State of Ohio in the War of the Rebellion, 1861–1866*. Vol. 1. Akron OH: Werner, 1893.

Goldfield, David. Review of *Robert E. Lee, A Life*, by Allen C. Guelzo. "The True Story of Robert E. Lee." *New York Times*, September 28, 2021.

Goodheart, Adam. *1861: The Civil War Awakening*. New York: Alfred A. Knopf, 2011.

Gottlieb, Matthew S. "George Teamoh (1818–after 1887)." Dictionary of Virginia Biography, Encyclopedia Virginia, 2021. https://encyclopediavirginia.org/entries/teamoh-george-1818-after-1887.

Gunts, Edward. "New Baltimore Subway Stop Is a Ride into History," *Baltimore Sun*, June 1, 1995.

Hadden, Sally E. *Slave Patrols, Law and Violence in Virginia and the Carolinas*. Cambridge MA: Harvard University Press, 2001.

Hafner, Jennifer, Owen Lourie, Edward C. Papenfuse, Rob Schoeberlein, and Emily Oland Squires, producers. "Straddling Secession: Thomas Holliday Hicks and the Beginning of the Civil War in Maryland," Maryland State Archives, Museum Online. Accessed 2022. https://msa.maryland.gov/msa/educ/exhibits/hicks/html/toc.html.

Haley, William D., ed. *Philp's Washington Described: A Complete View of the American Capital*. New York: Rudd & Carlton, 1861.

Hall, Clayton Colman, ed. *Baltimore: Its History and Its People*. New York: Lewis Historical, 1912.

Hamilton, Alexander, and James Madison. *The Federalist Papers Numbers 8, 29, 47*. Avalon Project, Documents in Law, History and Diplomacy. New Haven CT: Yale Law School, Lillian Goldman Law Library, 1787–88. https://avalon.law.yale.edu/subject_menus/fed.asp.

Hanson, John Wesley. *Historical Sketch of the Old Sixth Regiment of Massachusetts Volunteers*. Boston: Lee & Shepard, 1866.

Hawthorne, Nathaniel. "Chiefly about War Matters." *Atlantic* 10, no. 7 (July 1862).

Hay, Clara S., ed. *Letters of John Hay, and Extracts from Diary*. Vol. 1. Unpublished manuscript, 1908.

Headley, Phineas Camp. *Massachusetts in the Rebellion.* Boston: Walker, Fuller, 1866.

Hedrick, Mary A. *Incidents of the Civil War.* Lowell MA: Vox Populi, 1888.

Helm, Katherine. *Mary, Wife of Lincoln.* New York: Harper & Brothers, 1928.

Hendrick, Burton Jesse. *Lincoln's War Cabinet.* Boston: Little, Brown and Company, 1946. Reprinted Garden City NY: Dolphin, 1961.

Herbert, George B. *The Popular History of the Civil War in America.* New York: F. M. Lupton, 1885.

Hicks, John D. "The Organization of the Volunteer Army in 1861 with Special Reference to Minnesota." *Minnesota History Bulletin* 2, no. 5, edited by Solon J. Buck (February 1918): 329–68.

Hiester, William. "The Place of the Ringgold Light Artillery of Reading among the First Five Companies from Pennsylvania Which Marched to the Defense of Washington, April, 1861." *Transactions of the Historical Society of Berks County* 1 (1904): 1–13.

Holzer, Harold. *Lincoln and the Power of the Press.* New York: Simon & Schuster, 2014.

Hoptak, David. "Nick Biddle: A Forgotten Hero of the Civil War." *Pennsylvania Heritage Magazine* 37, no. 2 (Spring 2010).

Howard, Charles McHenry, ed. "Baltimore and the Crisis of 1861." *Maryland Historical Magazine* 41, no. 4 (December 1946): 257–81.

Howard, Frank Key. *Fourteen Months in American Bastiles.* Baltimore: Kelly, Hedian & Piet, 1863.

Johnson, Bradley T. "Maryland's First Patriotic Movement in 1861." In *Confederate Military History*, edited by Clement A. Evans, 15–28. Vol. 2. Atlanta: Confederate, 1899.

Jones, John Beauchamp. *A Rebel War Clerk's Diary at the Confederate States Capital.* Philadelphia: J. B. Lippincott, 1866.

Jones, J. William. *Life and Letters of Robert Edward Lee, Soldier and Man.* New York: Neale, 1906.

Journal of Proceedings of the First Branch City Council of Baltimore at the Session of 1900–1901. Baltimore: Wm. J. C. Dulany, 1900.

Journal of the Senate of the Twenty-Second General Assembly of the State of Illinois. Springfield IL: Bailhache & Baker, 1861.

Keller, Ron J. "Lincoln in His Shop." *White House History* 37 (Spring 2015): White House Historical Association.

Kennedy, Jos. C. G. *Preliminary Report of the Eighth Census 1860*, Bureau of the Census Library, Census Bureau. Washington DC: Government Printing Office, 1862. https://www2.census.gov/library/publications/decennial/1860/population/1860a-45.pdf?#.

Ketchum, Richard M. "The Thankless Task of Nicholas Trist." *American Heritage Magazine* 21, no. 5 (August 1970).

Kielbowicz, Richard B. "The Telegraph, Censorship, and Politics at the Outset of the Civil War." *Civil War History Magazine* 40, no. 2 (June 1994): 95–118.

Kreidberg, Marvin A., and Merton G. Henry. *History of Military Mobilization in the United States Army, 1775–1945.* Washington DC: Department of the Army, 1955.

Krick, Robert K. *Civil War Weather in Virginia*. Tuscaloosa: University of Alabama Press, 2007.

Lee, Stephen D. "The First Step in the War." In *Battles and Leaders of the Civil War*, edited by Robert Underwood Johnson and Clarence Clough Buel, 74–81. Vol. 1. New York: Century, 1887.

Long, A. L., ed., and Marcus J. Wright, asst. ed. *Memoirs of Robert E. Lee: His Military and Personal History*. New York: J. M. Stoddart, 1886.

Lossing, Benson J. *Pictorial History of the Civil War in the United States of America*. Vol. 1. Philadelphia: George W. Childs, 1866.

Lowen, George Edward, ed. *History of the 71st Regiment, N.G. N.Y., American Guard*. New York: Eastman, 1919.

Mason, Virginia. *The Public Life and Diplomatic Correspondence of James M. Mason, with Some Personal History*. New York: Neale, 1906.

McClure, Alexander K. *Abraham Lincoln and Men of War-Times*. Philadelphia: Times, 1892.

McKean, William Vincent, ed. *The National Almanac and Annual Record for the Year 1863*. Philadelphia: George W. Childs, 1863.

McPherson, James M. *Embattled Rebel: Jefferson Davis as Commander in Chief*. New York: Penguin, 2014.

Meade, Rebecca Paulding. *Life of Hiram Paulding Rear Admiral, USN*. New York: Baker & Taylor, 1910.

Melton, Tracy Matthew. "The Lost Lives of George Konig Sr. & Jr.: A Father-Son Tale of Old Fell's Point." *Maryland Historical Magazine* 101, no. 3 (Fall 2006): 332–61.

Moore, Frank, ed. *The Rebellion Record*. Documents sections, Vols. 1 and 2. New York: G. P. Putnam, 1861–62.

Morgan, William James, David B. Tyler, Joye Leonhart, and Mary F. Loughlin, eds. *Autobiography of Rear Admiral Charles Wilkes, U.S. Navy 1798–1877*. Washington DC: Naval History Division, 1978.

Nason, George W. *History and Complete Roster of the Massachusetts Regiments, Minute Men of '61 Who Responded to the First Call of President Abraham Lincoln, April 15, 1861*. Boston: Smith & McCance, 1910.

Nevins, Allan, ed. *George Templeton Strong: Diary of the Civil War 1860–1865*. New York: MacMillan, 1962.

———. *War for the Union: The Improvised War 1861–1862*. Vol. 1. New York: Charles Scribner's Sons, 1959.

Newell, Clayton R. *The Regular Army before the Civil War 1845–1860*. Washington DC: Center of Military History, 2014.

Newton, Thomas Wodehouse Legh. *Lord Lyons: A Record of British Diplomacy*. Vol. 1. New York: Longmans, Green, 1913.

Nicolay, Helen. *Lincoln's Secretary: A Biography of John G. Nicolay*. New York: Longmans Green, 1949.

Nicolay, John G. *The Outbreak of Rebellion*. New York: Charles Scribner's Sons, 1914.

Nicolay, John G., and John Hay. *Abraham Lincoln: A History*. Vols. 3 and 4. New York: Century, 1890.

Northup, Solomon. *Twelve Years a Slave*. New York: Derby & Miller, 1853.

O'Brien, Fitz James. "The March of the Seventh Regiment." In *The Civil War in Song and Story 1860–1865*, vol. 1, edited by Frank Moore, 228–34. New York: Peter Fenelon Collier, 1865.

Official Records of the Union and Confederate Navies in the War of the Rebellion. Series 1, vol. 4. Washington DC: Government Printing Office, 1896.

Parton, James. *General Butler in New Orleans*. New York: Mason Brothers, 1864.

Patrick, Jeffrey L., ed. *In Her Hour of Sore Distress and Peril, the Civil War Diaries of John P. Reynolds, Eighth Massachusetts Volunteer Infantry*. Jefferson NC: McFarland, 2013.

Pearson, Henry Greenleaf. *The Life of John A. Andrew, Governor of Massachusetts, 1861–1865*. Vol. 1. Boston: Houghton, Mifflin, 1904.

"The Philadelphia Military." *Philadelphia Public Ledger*, April 20, 1861.

Phisterer, Frederick. *New York in the War of the Rebellion 1861 to 1865*. 2nd ed. Albany: Weed, Parsons, 1890.

———. "New York in the War of the Rebellion 1861 to 1865." Documents of the Assembly of the State of New York. Vol. 31, pt. 1. Albany NY: J. B. Lyon, 1912.

Plum, William R. *The Military Telegraph during the Civil War in the United States*. Vol. 1. Chicago: Jansen, McClurg, 1882.

Pollard, E. A. *Southern History of the War*. New York: Charles B. Richardson, 1866.

Poore, Benjamin Perley. *The Life and Public Services of Ambrose E. Burnside*. Providence RI: J. A. & R. A. Reid, 1882.

———. *Perley's Reminiscences of Sixty Years in the National Metropolis*. Vol. 2. Philadelphia: Hubbard Brothers, 1886.

Radcliffe, George Lovic Pierce. "Governor Thomas H. Hicks of Maryland and the Civil War." In *Johns Hopkins University Studies in Historical and Political Science*, edited by H. B. Adams. Diplomatic and Constitutional History, vol. 19. Baltimore: Johns Hopkins University Press, 1901.

Ranney, H. M. *Account of the Terrific and Fatal Riot at the New-York Astor Place Opera House*. New York: H. M. Ranney, 1849.

Reece, J. N., ed. *Report of the Adjutant General of the State of Illinois Containing Reports for the Years 1861–66*. Vol. 1. Springfield IL: Phillips Bros., 1900.

Reese, George H., ed. *Proceedings of the Virginia Secession Convention of 1861*. Centennial Edition. 4 vols. Richmond: Virginia State Library, 1965.

Reid, Whitelaw. *Ohio in the War: Her Statesmen, Her Generals, and Soldiers*. Vols. 1 and 2. Cincinnati OH: Moore, Wilstach & Baldwin, 1868.

Richardson, Albert D. *The Secret Service*. Hartford CT: American, 1865.

Richardson, James D. *A Compilation of the Messages and Papers of the Confederacy*. Vol. 1. Nashville: United States Publishing, 1906.

Rives, John C. "The Debates and Proceedings, Second Session, the Thirty-Seventh Congress." Ex. Doc. No. 43. Receipts and Disbursements of the Patent Office.

Letter from the Secretary of the Interior, J. P. Usher, January 22, 1863. *The Congressional Globe*: 1862 pt. 4.

Roe, Alfred S. *The Fifth Regiment Massachusetts Volunteer Infantry in Its Three Tours of Duty*. Boston: Fifth Regiment Veteran Association, 1911.

Roman, Alfred. *The Military Operations of General Beauregard in the War between the States, 1861 to 1865*. Vol. 1. New York: Harper & Brothers, 1884.

Rowland, Dunbar, ed. *Jefferson Davis, Constitutionalist, His Letters, Papers and Speeches*. Vols. 5 and 8. Jackson MS: Mississippi Department of Archives and History, 1923.

Russell, A. L. *Annual Report of the Adjutant General of Pennsylvania for the Year 1862*. Harrisburg PA: Singerly & Myers, 1862.

Russell, William Howard. *My Diary North and South*. Boston: T.O.H.P. Burnham, 1863.

Sandburg, Carl. *Abraham Lincoln: The War Years*. New York: Harcourt Brace, 1939.

Schaadt, James L. "Company I, First Regiment Pennsylvania Volunteers, a Memoir of Its Service for the Union in 1861." *Penn Germania* 13, no. 1 (January 1912): 538–50.

Scharf, J. Thomas. *The Chronicles of Baltimore*. Baltimore: Turnbull Brothers, 1874.

———. *History of Maryland from the Earliest Period to the Present Day*. Vol. 3. Baltimore: John B. Piet, 1879.

Schouler, William. *A History of Massachusetts in the Civil War*. Boston: E. P. Dutton, 1868.

Scott, Robert N., Fred C. Ainsworth, Joseph W. Kirkley, George B. Davis, and Leslie J. Perry, eds. *The War of the Rebellion: The Official Records of the Union and Confederate Armies*. Series 1–4. Washington DC: Government Printing Office, 1880–1901.

Scott, Winfield. *Memoirs of Lieut.-General Scott, LLD*. New York: Sheldon, 1864.

Scrymser, James A. "In President Lincoln's Kitchen." *Magazine of American History with Notes and Queries* 15, no. 1 (January–June 1912): 42–43.

Seabrook, William L. W. *Maryland's Great Part in Saving the Union*. Westminster MD: Self-published, printed by the American Sentinel Company, 1913.

Settles, Thomas M. *John Bankhead Magruder: A Military Reappraisal*. Baton Rouge: Louisiana State University Press, 2009.

Seward, Frederick. *Reminiscences of a War-Time Statesman and Diplomat, 1830–1915*. New York: G. P. Putnam's Sons, 1916.

———. *Seward at Washington as Senator and Secretary of State, 1846–1861*. New York: Derby & Miller, 1891.

Shuckers, J. W. *The Life and Public Services of Salmon Portland Chase*. New York: D. Appleton, 1874.

Sibley, Martha Arle. "William Booth Taliaferro: A Biography." Master's thesis, College of William and Mary, 1973.

Smith, George Williamson. "A Critical Moment for Washington." *Records of the Columbia Historical Society* 21 (1918): 103–6.

Smith, James L. *Autobiography of James L. Smith*. Norwich CT: Bulletin, 1881.

Steiner, Bernard Christian, Lynn Roby Meekins, David Henry Carroll, and Thomas G. Boggs. *Men of Mark in Maryland*. Vol. 4. Baltimore: B. F. Johnson, 1912.

Stevens, A. W., ed. *Edward L. Pierce: Addresses and Papers*. Boston: Roberts Brothers, 1896.

Stevens, Jesse F. *Massachusetts Soldiers, Sailors, and Marines in the Civil War*. Vol. 1. Norwood MA: Norwood, 1931.

Stewart, George. "President Lincoln's Sermon," *Magazine of American History with Notes and Queries* 15, no, 1 (January–June 1912): 44–46.

Stockett, Letitia. *Baltimore: A Not Too Serious History*. Baltimore: Grace Gore Norman, 1928.

Stoddard, William O. *Abraham Lincoln: The True Story of a Great Life*. New York: Fords, Howard & Hulbert, 1885.

———. *Inside the White House in War Times*. New York: Charles L. Webster, 1890.

Stoddard, William O., Jr., ed. *Lincoln's Third Secretary: The Memoirs of William O. Stoddard*. New York: Exposition, 1955.

Stone, Charles P. "A Dinner with General Scott in 1861." *Magazine of American History with Notes and Queries* 11, no. 1 (January–June 1884): 528–32.

———. "Washington in March and April 1861." In *Magazine of American History with Notes and Queries* 14, no. 1 (July–December 1885): 1–24.

———. "Washington on the Eve of the War." In *Battles and Leaders of the Civil War*, edited by Robert Underwood Johnson and Clarence Clough Buel, 11–17. Vol. 1. New York: Century, 1884–87.

Stone, Ebenezer W. *Compend of Military Instructions for the Massachusetts Volunteer Militia, 1857*. Boston: William White, 1857.

Swinton, William. *History of the Seventh Regiment of the State of New York during the War of the Rebellion*. New York: Fields, Osgood, 1870.

Taylor, Frank H. *Philadelphia in the Civil War 1861–1865*. Published by the City, 1913.

Terrell, W. H. H. *Report of the Adjutant General of the State of Indiana*. Vol. 1. Indianapolis IN: Alexander H. Conner, 1869.

Thompson, Heber S. *The First Defenders*. [Pottsville PA?]: First Defenders Association, 1910.

Townsend, E. D. *Anecdotes of the Civil War in the United States*. New York: D. Appleton, 1884.

Tucker, Leslie R. *Major General Isaac Ridgeway Trimble: Biography of a Baltimore Confederate*. Jefferson NC: McFarland, 2005.

Upton, Emory. *The Military Policy of the United States, Fourth Impression*. Washington DC: Government Printing Office, 1917.

Usher, J. P. "Executive Documents." Ex. Doc. No. 43. Receipts and Disbursements of the Patent Office. Letter from the Secretary of the Interior, January 22, 1863, 37th Congress, 3rd Session, House of Representatives.

Victor, Orville J. *The History, Civil, Political, & Military, of the Southern Rebellion*. Vol. 2. New York: James D. Torrey, 1861.

Villard, Henry. *Memoirs of Henry Villard, Journalist and Financier, 1835–1900*. Vol. 1. Boston: Houghton Mifflin, 1904.

Virtual Tour of the History of Virginia. "1825 to 1860, The Growth of Industry." Virginia Museum of History and Culture, Virginia Historical Society. https://virginiahistory.org/learn/story-of-virginia/chapter/growth-industry.

Vladeck, Stephen I. "Emergency Power and the Militia Acts." *Yale Law Journal* 114, no. 1 (October 2004): 149–94.

Wallace, Francis B. *Memorial of the Patriotism of Schuylkill County in the American Slaveholder's Rebellion.* Pottsville PA: Benjamin Bannan, 1865.

"The War." *Harper's Weekly,* vol. 5, no. 227 (May 4, 1861).

Wardwell, Ernest. "A Military Waif: A Memoir of the Old Sixth." *Maryland Historical Magazine* 89, no. 4 (Winter 1994): 427–46.

Watson, B. F. *Addresses, Reviews, and Episodes Chiefly concerning the Old "Sixth" Massachusetts Regiment.* New York: "Old Sixth" Association, 1901. https://archive .org/details/addressesreviews00wats/page/n5/mode/2up.

Webb, William B., and J. Woolridge. *Centennial History of the City of Washington* DC. Dayton OH: United Brethren, 1892.

Welles, Gideon. *Diary of Gideon Welles: Secretary of the Navy under Lincoln and Johnson.* Vol. 2. Boston: Houghton Mifflin, 1911.

White, Jonathan W. "Forty-Seven Eyewitness Accounts of the Pratt Street Riot and Its Aftermath." *Maryland Historical Magazine* 106, no. 1 (Spring 2011): 70–93.

Wilkes, George W. "Trip of the 71st Regiment." In *History of the 71st Regiment, N.G. N.Y., American Guard,* edited by George Edward Lowen, 95–105. New York: Eastman, 1919.

Williams, Ben Ames, ed. *Mary Boykin Chesnut: A Diary from Dixie.* Boston: Houghton Mifflin, 1949. Reprinted Cambridge MA: Harvard University Press, 1980.

Wilson, William Bender. *History of the Pennsylvania Railroad Company.* Vol. 1. Philadelphia: Henry T. Coates, 1895.

Winthrop, Theodore. "The New York Seventh Regiment—Our March to Washington." *Atlantic* 7, no. 6 (June 1861): 744–56.

Wise, Barton H. *The Life of Henry A. Wise.* New York: MacMillan, 1899.

Wood, Lindsay Lomax, ed. *Elizabeth Lindsay Lomax: Leaves from an Old Washington Diary, 1854–1863.* Mount Vernon NY: Golden Eagle, 1943.

Woodbury, Augustus. *A Narrative of the Campaign of the First Rhode Island Regiment in the Spring and Summer of 1861.* Providence RI: Sidney S. Rider, 1862.

Young, May D. Russell, ed. *John Russell Young, Men and Memories, Personal Reminiscences.* Vol. 1. New York: F. Tennyson Neely, 1901.

Zwierzyna, John. "Nick Biddle and the First Defenders." Pennsylvania Historical and Museum Commission, Pennsylvania Civil War 150 (PACW 150), July 2015. Accessed 2022. http://pacivilwar150.com/ThroughPeople/AfricanAmericans/NicholasBiddle.html.

INDEX

Page numbers in *italics* refer to tables.

Fourth Massachusetts Regiment, 47, 57, 73, 174

Fourth Pennsylvania Regiment, 268

Frank Leslie's Illustrated Newspaper, 289

Franklin, William B., 235

free Black people, 19, 81, 109, 182; denied military enlistment, 62, 233–34

Freeman, Douglas Southall, 91, 92

Fry, James B., 36

Fuller, Richard, 212–13

Galloway, Edward, 9

Garrett, John W., 118, 197–98; pressure on, 136, 167, 221, 306–7n7

Gatchell, William H., 283, 284

Georgia, 36, 67, 177, 279–80

German Americans, 62–64, 110, 187, 250

Gillis, John, 202

Goldsboro Tribune, 258

Gosport Navy Yard. *See* Norfolk Navy Yard, Norfolk, Virginia

government resignations, 208–11, 258, 272; suicide and, 210

Great Britain, 34–35, 216, 247, 286–87, 311n9; Confederacy recognition risk, xv, 3, 143, 273

Green, James, 151

Gregg, Maxcy, 177

Griffith, Patrick, 124

Guelzo, Allen C., 92

habeas corpus, 218, 283, 308n10

Haggerty, Peter, 184

Hall, Thomas, 284

Hanson, John Wesley, 48, 119, 122, 123, 125

Harlan, James, 22

Harney, William, 32, 173

Harper, Kenton, 178, 220–21, 240, 259, 260

Harpers Ferry, 2, 4, 67, 220–21, 272; attack on, 102–4; Confederate control of, xiv, 104, 166, 178, 259, 260; rumors about, 86, 87; strategic importance of, 96, 101–2, 104

Harper's Weekly, 289

Harriet Lane (cutter), 190, 244, 245

Harrington, George R., 72, 86, 172–73, 200–201

Harris, J. Morrison, 172

Harrisburg, Pennsylvania, 50

Havre de Grace, Maryland, 110, 111, 112, 115, 149, 156

Hawthorne, Nathaniel, 18

Hay, John, 3, 169, 192, 231, 233; on arrival of troops, 272; background, 15; diary of, 205, 261, 270; on military resignations, 211; personal qualities, 15, 16; on the twelve days, 273, 288

Herbert, George B., 290

Heth, Henry, 208

Hicks, Thomas H., 78, 135–39, 217–18, 285, 315nn1–2; Baltimore and, 82–83, 134; railroad sabotage and, 153–54; troop routes through MD and, 171, 216, 222–23

Hincks, Edward W., 241–43, 253, 254, 318n34

Hinks, Charles D., 283

Holt, Joseph, 102

Homans, Charles, 242

Hough, Daniel, 9

Howard, Charles, 150, 283, 284

Howard, Frank, 284

Hudson River Railroad, 230

Hunt, Henry, 102

Illinois, 29, 40, 282, 310n17

immigrants, 61–64, 109

Indiana, 29, 34, 39–40, 42, 282

Iowa, 29, 53, 54, 282

Irish Americans, 62, 230, 247–50, 251, 278, 298n19

Irish Brigade. *See* Sixty-Ninth New York Regiment

Isherwood, Benjamin Franklin, 99, 100, 101

James Adger (steamer), 190

Jepson, John, 122

Johannes, John G., 146–48, 284

Johnson, Bradley T., 284

Johnson, Reverdy, 91, 262–63

Jones, Catesby, 208

Jones, Edward F., 45, 47, 57, 108–13; Baltimore riots and, 115–16, 118, 126–28, 133; in Washington, 169

Jones, John Beauchamp, 140, 237–38

Jones, Roger, 102–4